Seal of Universidad Autonoma de Santo Domingo
Founded October 28, 1538

Universities of the Caribbean Region— Struggles to Democratize

an annotated bibliography

*Reference
Publications
in
Latin American
Studies*

William V. Jackson
Editor

Universities of the Caribbean Region— Struggles to Democratize

an annotated bibliography

BARBARA ASHTON WAGGONER
and
GEORGE R. WAGGONER

G.K.HALL *&*CO.

70 LINCOLN STREET, BOSTON, MASS.

Library of Congress Cataloging in Publication Data

Waggoner, Barbara Ashton.
  Universities of the Caribbean region— struggles to
democratize.

  (A Reference publication in Latin American studies)
  Includes index.
  1. Universities and colleges— Caribbean Area—
Bibliography.   2. Higher education and state— Caribbean
Area— Bibliography.   I. Waggoner, George R., 1916-
II. Title.   III. Series.
Z5815.C35W34   1986   016.378729   85-21864
[LA439.C27]
ISBN 0-8161-8159-4

This publication is printed on permanent/durable acid-free paper
MANUFACTURED IN THE UNITED STATES OF AMERICA

Contents

Preface

In the span of one day, some years ago, we went from a Venezuelan campus to a Trinidadian campus; the countries are only air-minutes apart but their universities are artifacts from different worlds of time and custom. The questions that arose during these visits were many, prompting a bibliographic quest to learn what similarities and differences characterize the region's universities, with their varied patterns and influences from Spain, France, England, The Netherlands, the USSR, and the United States. This task proved to be considerably longer and more complex than we had planned.

Already familiar with the traditional Latin American universities and the efforts of some since the 1940s to make major reforms, we thought it would be instructive to look at universities in the non-Spanish-speaking Caribbean as well. We chose the period since World War II as the temporal focus of the bibliography.

We defined "Caribbean" as the region reaching around the Caribbean Sea in a vast, irregular arc from the Yucatan Peninsula southeast through Central America and Panama, eastward along the coasts of Colombia and Venezuela, Guyana, and Suriname, and northwest to Cuba.

Following are the countries or territories included in this work. (French Guyana is included in the University Centers of the French departments of Guadeloupe and Martinique, under the heading of French Antilles.) Aruba and Curaçao are under the heading Netherlands Antilles.

*Antigua	Haiti
Aruba	Honduras
*Bahamas	Jamaica
Barbados	Martinique
*Belize	**Mexico
*British Virgin Islands	*Montserrat
*Cayman Islands	Nicaragua
**Colombia	Panama

Costa Rica	Puerto Rico
Cuba	*St. Kitts
Curaçao	*St. Lucia
*Dominica	*St. Vincent
Dominican Republic	Suriname
*Grenada	Trinidad and Tobago
Guadeloupe	U.S. Virgin Islands
Guatemala	**Venezuela
Guyana	

*Non-campus territories of the University of the West Indies
**Coastal universities only

There may appear to be a certain arbitrariness in the places selected for inclusion. "Caribbean" is a word stretched to fit, for our purposes, both the megalopolis of Caracas, with its international flavor, and the Creole-speaking island of Haiti, with the lives of its populace little touched by contemporary values or institutions of other cultures. Why truncate, for example, Colombia and Venezuela? Why call Caracas "Caribbean" when it seems so unlike, say, Barbados? Why not include Florida and other southern U.S. states? San Jose, Costa Rica, lies at considerable physical and cultural distance from the creole coastal city of Limon, yet virtually all the Costa Rican works cited were written and published in San Jose.

The only Mexican university included, Universidad de Yucatán, is physically close to the Caribbean Sea; it is in the region but in some ways not of it. We did not include El Salvador for its lack of Caribbean coastline, although it may be considered historically, culturally, and politically part of the region.

In Venezuela virtually all the population clusters along the coast. Here, as well, is concentrated administrative, financial, political, and educational control of the nation. We thus did not include universities in the vast and newly developing reaches to the south, or in the Andean area, with its population and special characteristics which make it more akin to Bogota.

By contrast, coastal Colombia's leaders see themselves in perpetual competition with what they consider an alien power elite in Andean Bogota, particularly with regard to policy-making and financing of higher education. They point with special pride to their Caribbean heritage and cultural flavor, to the African beat of their music, and to their commercial link with the sea.

That a given university is X number of miles from the seashore is not a wholly sufficient reason for its inclusion or exclusion. Generally, we have included universities located in countries tied to a European or North American metropolis by a plantation economy, where the labor force was comprised of unwilling indigenous or imported workers, and where the educational systems were mandated by others: by Spain into the nineteenth century, by England and the Netherlands until recently, and by the U.S. and France in the present.

No mold or pattern can be universally applied in our scheme. If there are inconsistencies in geographical coverage, it is to be hoped that they contribute to rather than detract from the pursuit of inquiry.

Working toward consistency of content in this bibliography meant imposing order on some material already at hand and later seeking other data to fill temporal and topical interstices. We had long been observers of those heady and often heated debates in Latin America over the social role of universities, over whether democratization of education leads to loss of quality, over whether justice can be served by allocating scarce resources to graduate education in societies lacking primary schools for large numbers of their children.

In the Caribbean region, the rhetoric of the 1960s resonated with the promise of "national development" as a product of bigger and better universities. By the 1970s, doubts were being expressed. Although the issues vary from place to place, they are nearly universal. A major theme, especially among the island nations of the Caribbean, was the challenge of creating educational systems that attended to the cultural uniqueness of populations rich in both African and European heritages. These nations and territories found themselves financially impoverished and under rational compulsion to collaborate on university development at the same time that politics and the vagaries of world economies worked their centrifugal forces. Hence, there is the literature of building and that of pulling apart, both from European dominance and from each other. These same forces have been at work in Central America, as is evident in the bibliography of individual country materials and in the literature by and about the regional organizations in the General section of the bibliography.

Another issue interwoven with these, particularly in Central America, is the push for and resistance to la reforma universitaria, particularly in the concept of estudios generales. U.S. and European foundations and governmental and international agencies eagerly sent monies and experts to assist in the transformation of these clusters of professional schools, comprising the Napoleonic model of a university, into institutions committed to preparing students in basic disciplines before plunging them into unproductive, and hence costly, professional courses of study.

Users of the bibliography will find a considerable number of items on the topic of changing institutional structure, into which an abundance of scholarly effort remains to be invested.

Because the new University of the West Indies (UWI) was strongly in the British tradition (with its series of academic hurdles to be gotten over, from the early grades on, to earn the right even to prepare for entry into university), the literature on the English-speaking Caribbean shows strong interest in university entrance examinations and their relation to secondary schools. There are marked contrasts in the literature on Spanish- and English-speaking universities. There is considerable evidence of student activism in the former, virtually none in the latter. In Spanish-speaking countries the clamor for universities to be agents for social change appears at times nearly to drown out the voices calling for academic accomplishment; this theme is seldom heard in the English-speaking territories.

One issue seems universal in the region, regardless of heritage, philosophy, language, or ties to a metropolis: how to cope with the unprecedented demand that burgeoned after World War II for access to universities. This shows up throughout the literature: in newspaper accounts of hunger strikes in protest against limiting entry to Venezuela's Central University Medical School; in various ministries' efforts to develop official positions; in Panamanian efforts at regionalization; in debate over creation of more faculties in Guadeloupe and Martinique versus sending students to metropolitan France; and in Cuba's total restructuring of education in its attempt to give those never before eligible, by reason of poverty and in- adequate preparation, access to its universities.

It is on such issues that we have sought to focus this bibliogra- phy. Although our time frame is the post-World War II period, it was clear that understanding universities in their historical context mandated inclusion of selected background material, which has meant in some cases reaching back into a past century when patterns were set and norms established. Similarly, a university should be seen in the context of a nation's educational system. In other words, who has access to education? We have included some material that places uni- versities in that social context.

However, we have not attempted to address one issue of great concern throughout the region: the development of postsecondary al- ternatives to universities, although that concern shows up tagentially in some entries. But a bibliography on the region's sudden-sprouting technological institutions, both public and private, would comprise a separate work. Because the Instituto Tecnológico de Santo Domingo functions as a university and is a member of several university organi- zations, such as the Caribbean Association of Universities and Research Institutes [UNICA], we have included it.) We also decided to omit normal schools and pedagogical institutions that are not a part of a university.

RESEARCH

During twenty years of working visits to Latin America, mainly concerned with some aspect of university reform, we obtained a large number of documents related to the institutions visited. Generally, they were descriptive in nature, such as catalogs and rectors' reports; memoranda used by U.S. foundations and governmental or international agencies in their assistance programs; and newspaper articles. Books and articles written or selected by colleagues in the various countries were often reflective of issues and viewpoints.

What we had was an accumulation. These materials served their then-intended purpose, but they would not have satisfied an acqui- sitions librarian. As we indicate in the section on coverage, much remains untouched; we are well aware that more time than was available to us for the purpose of collecting would be necessary to do a thorough job of, for example, finding runs of journals or determining the con- sistency of their publication.

Yet, such caveats aside, that basic accumulation was a more than adequate starting point for more systematic collecting. We added to those holdings on a 1978 return visit to Mexico, Central America, Colombia, Venezuela, Puerto Rico, and the Dominican Republic. There were further visits by one or both of us between 1979 and 1983 to various of these sites. While collecting materials there, we also set about searching for documents in libraries at home and abroad.

Because Latin American universities traditionally have been comprised of separate professional schools, with few centralized library systems and even fewer librarians, the main repositories of materials are professors' personal holdings. Holdings in sequence about an institution per se are hard to come by. Current descriptive materials, if they are available, are best sought through rectories and/or offices of secretaries general.

On each campus we asked for current descriptive material, copies of recent institutional studies, and speeches or articles by university leaders. Where student newspapers exist, we tried to find them.

For Latin American universities as a whole, the publications of the Unión de Universidades de América Latina (UDUAL) have become increasingly professional and of predictable periodicity in recent years. However, we learned little of the relatively weak coastal universities of Colombia, for example, from this source.

The headquarters of the Consejo Superior de Universidades Centroamericanas near the University of Costa Rica has remained, through regional political upheaval, war, and revolution, an open communication center among the region's public universities and a valuable source of information. The young secretary general of the Federación de Universidades Privadas de Centroamérica y Panamá (FUPAC), which serves private universities, was new to his position when we visited his office in Guatemala City in 1978. We were told that he was planning to move the operation to Panama in 1980 for safety. He was assassinated before he could depart. FUPAC publications of the past were strongly issue oriented.

All these agencies, with their efforts at promoting regional cooperation and professionalism in higher education, have created communication networks and publications only dreamed of a few decades ago. More recently, the Instituto Centro Americano de Administración y Supervisión de la Educación (ICASE) has fostered cooperation among Central American universities and ministries of education and is producing useful documents. Printings of university publications are often small in number. In the Dominican Republic, for example, the Universidad Nacional Pedro Henríquez Ureña (UNPHU) produced in 1980 the first university-wide catalog since its 1966 founding. Our copy is number 14 of 1,000, in an institution of some 9,000 students.

One great asset during our collection of materials was the help of many cultural affairs officers in U.S. embassies. They had collaborated with us on the Seminars on Higher Education in the Americas held yearly between 1963 and 1975 at the University of Kansas and at several universities in Latin America and the University of New Mexico. Their knowledge and understanding of local issues was generously shared, as was that of several United States Agency for International Development (USAID) officials with a special concern for universities. Colleagues in the Inter-American Development Bank and the Organization of American States (OAS) in Washington, D.C., shared their insights on significant issues. Scholars would do well to look to these sources of information.

Bibliographies and Libraries

Perusing bibliographies in the early stages of this compilation produced several observations: Researchers for generations have sharpened their pens--if not their wits--on micro studies of elementary schooling. As Third World countries opened up secondary education in recent decades to a larger clientele, U.S. schools of education pursued their micro studies there. Attention to the larger issues confronting and being confronted by higher education in Latin America either received scant attention or writings on them escaped the ken of bibliographers.

A starting point was the <u>Handbook of Latin American Studies (HAPI)</u> and the <u>Latin American Research Review</u>. HAPI was not a fruitful source for this work. Several specialized bibliographies consulted are included among the entries, among them <u>Higher Education in Developing Nations</u> and the very useful <u>Education in Latin America: A Bibliography</u>. These and the <u>Complete Caribbeana</u> provided several important items for this compilation. An outstanding work, available late in our compilation process, is the <u>Bibliografía selectiva sobre educación superior en América Latina y el Caribe</u>. Various national bibliographies were of limited help.

An exception was <u>Anuario bibliográfico cubano</u>, also known over a span of years as <u>Bibliografía cubana</u>. Compiler Fermin Peraza included a number of entries on universities from its inception in 1937 on. Additionally, one finds in prefaces to works published during those watershed years before and after the revolution something of the changes wrought-in this case, the relocation of a bibliographic resource, first to Medellin and then to Gainesville, and the personal expression of anguish over "the imperialist Russian invasion of Cuba." Meanwhile, back in Havana other compilers carried on with the title <u>Bibliografía cubana</u>. By the time of the 1963-64 volume there is a diminution of entries on universities, and denunciation of an "imperialist [U.S.] blockade which tries to deny access to world thought about Cuba." The records of publication of these two parallel serials are more complex than here described.

The University of the West Indies and the University of Guyana publish useful bibliographies, but without much material on their institutions <u>per se</u>.

Because U.S. writers on higher education in Latin America are not numerous, the scanning of journal indices, of dissertation abstracts, and the following up of sources cited in footnotes consumed considerable time but did not yield much.

U.S. library collections with good holdings on universities in the Spanish-speaking Caribbean are to be found at the University of Florida, the University of Kansas, and the University of Texas at Austin. The Library of Congress collection is extremely useful; the need to know the location of a university (e.g., the suburb of Havana where the pre-revolutionary Masonic university was) before finding the listing for it was an impediment, since corrected. We searched its catalogs under such headings as "universities," "university of _____," "higher education," "research," and "students."

The best of these library materials were descriptive items of the kind in our own collection and some few studies and many opinions expressed in books and articles, generally by Latin American authors. Because of the U.S. involvement in Cuba's educational development early in the twentieth century, background materials from that epoch were fairly easy to find in U.S. university libraries, and, because of the controversy following the revolution, there was considerable literature, passionate with praise or outrage, on events at the University of Havana.

In Spanish-speaking countries, we used libraries in Mexico City, San Jose, Panama, San Juan, and Caracas, often finding intriguing background material not included in the bibliography, as well as some useful entries.

However useful U.S. libraries and bibliographies were, the collecting of documents done during on-site visits was essential. Each country posed its own special challenges and opportunities.

The Spanish-Speaking Universities

In Mexico, we found a modest amount of material on the University of Yucatan in Merida. Some institutional cleavages made acquisition there difficult. Other documents, pertaining to the highly centralized Mexican university system as a whole, provide information necessary to describe the institution.

In Guatemala, the registrar of the Universidad de San Carlos had produced excellent statistical volumes yearly for twenty years before his assassination. Collecting became more difficult each year as university leaders, students, and professors were killed or went into exile. There should be an immense amount of literature and unpublished papers on the efforts toward reform at San Carlos, and on the role of contending political viewpoints in that university. Visits to the private universities were also useful.

In Honduras, we obtained information in Tegucigalpa, but lack of time prevented visits to universities outside the capital. A visit to coastal La Ceiba should yield additional material.

Nicaragua's orderly, literate university leadership has continuously produced descriptive and analytical documents on higher education, before, during, and since the revolution. After the revolution, the Consejo Nacional de Educación Superior (CNES) was created to formulate policy. A similar agency for planning and coordination is

Costa Rica's Consejo Nacional de Rectores (CONARE). These agencies facilitate collecting, as do similar centralized agencies in Colombia and Venezuela: the Instituto Colombiano para el Fomento de Educación Superior (ICFES), and the Oficina de Planificación Sector Universitario (OPSU). These are essential sources of descriptive information, but their holdings are not comprehensive. In Caracas OPSU has a small but useful library.

We began accumulating materials in Costa Rica in the early 1960s, due in large measure to the strong ties, including student and faculty exchanges, between the Universidad de Costa Rica (UCR) and the University of Kansas. With the rebirth and reform of UCR after 1948, the institution itself took on a character less weighted with tradition and less fragmented than the previous Napoleonic model. As a result there were more coherent and consistent centralized services, such as a central library and the regular publication of catalogs and rectors' reports.

There was always, as well, a great deal of dialog on major issues, well reported. In Costa Rica, as in Venezuela and Puerto Rico, researchers would do well to mine the newspapers in key periods for very good and complete coverage of the issues and the personalities that shaped events. Our lack of time to do so leaves many opportunities still open. In Costa Rica, the creation in the last decade of alternative institutions to UCR, both public and private, has enlivened and enlarged the discussion of issues in the press.

In coastal Colombia, the overburdened and underfunded public universities we visited in Monteria, Cartagena, and Barranquilla have almost nothing in print at all. The Caribbean universities' problems and attendant passions are documented at scattered sites; their few writings are not easily collected. Since Colombia's public universities are controlled in large measure by the national government, most data are best collected in Bogota.

Most of Venezuela's universities traditionally have been in Caracas, but national policy since the 1960s has been toward decentralization. There are strong, large universities in Maracaibo, Valencia, and Cumana and its núcleos, which it was helpful to visit. Some kinds of statistical information are readily available in Caracas in the increasingly professional OPSU but it is necessary to get it in person. Other information is sometimes guarded from political rivals and, hence, the public. The realities of some of the recently created "experimental" universities and the Open University have yet to fulfill the dreams of their advocates, and one garners stacks of glossy publicity pieces on "the transfer of technology" and promises of "education for national development." Who are the professors? Where are the students? It is difficult in some cases to find the details. Despite the size and scope of the Scholarship Plan Gran Mariscal de Ayacucho, it has been nearly impossible to obtain hard data, as other researchers also testify.

In the Dominican Republic, what began as the Reform Commission of the Autonomous University of Santo Domingo in the mid-1960s is now its Planning Office; despite its small size it has continued to provide institutional information, although Dominican professors have long expressed their need for better prepared statisticians. Material was also collected in private universities such as Madre y Maestra in Santiago, and the new Universidad Central del Este. As mentioned earlier, material such as the UNPHU catalog is not always abundantly produced or available.

Collecting in Cuba was made possible and pleasant by the minister of higher education and his staff during our 1979 stay there, after we had communicated with them through the Cuban Interests Section in Washington, D.C. We prepared a list of topics we were inquiring about at all the Caribbean universities, and indicated our wishes for interviews and documents regarding them. The requests were granted. The government is strongly committed to describing and explaining its policies in print, so material on events since the revolution abounds. Locating documents on universities in pre-revolutionary Cuba was more difficult. For example, the librarian in the OAS Education Department in Washington, D.C., had been told to throw away the Cuban materials after Cuba was expelled from the organization. Some university documents had been kept inadvertently; a few of these gave us needed clues for inquiry elsewhere. The library of the University of Havana did not have, or have available for us, documents on the university before the revolution, but we found several items in the library of the Universidad de Santa Clara de las Villas. Cuba is not, of course, the place to seek writings critical of current university policies or practices.

In all the Spanish-speaking countries there is much yet to be gathered by and about the universities. People in the offices of rectors, secretaries general, vice-rectors, planners, and public relations officers were invariably helpful, but rarely would a single office have on hand all the documents we sought. In all cases the process requires time and patience. Of the latter we had enough. Shortcomings in our collection may be due more to our lack of time than to an institution's lack of publications or their unavailability.

The English-Speaking Universities

The British educational system was less familiar to us than that of Latin America. We sought background material in London, where we consulted the British Library, the Library of the Institute of Education of the University of London, and official policy documents and position papers by various people who visited the West Indies in the nineteenth and twentieth centuries. The Association of Commonwealth Universities also provided materials.

It seemed important to visit some British secondary schools, particularly those with high concentrations of immigrants from the West Indies, and also to read the contemporary British press for coverage of debates over access to universities, the Open University, and post-secondary technical education. The traditions in the former British West Indies remain strongly influenced by the historical links of the classroom and the examination system; though leaders of the University of the West Indies are developing the institution in ways they deem appropriate for Caribbean realities, the structure of and many of the issues concerning the educational systems are usefully studied with an eye on developments in England and other Commonwealth universities.

In the English-speaking Caribbean, traditions in higher education produce patterns and practices different from those in Spanish-speaking countries. UWI and the University of Guyana (UG), newer than most of their Spanish-speaking counterparts, have from their beginnings kept careful records, owing in part to a strongly centralized system of administration and to the continuity that goes with a full-time professional faculty and administration. The orderliness of their planning in the post-World War II era is reflected in their day-to-day operation; even UG, which exists in a not always tranquil setting, publishes faculty research, institutional data, and administrative reports. Registrars and professional librarians are careful custodians, and vice-chancellors produce candid annual reports.

Our visits to the campuses in Port-of-Spain, Bridgetown, and Kingston were easily accomplished. Guyanese police and security forces allowed us only provisional entry to Georgetown; there, after further scrutiny by other officials, we were deemed scholars, not journalists, and permitted to move about freely. We found useful reading material in libraries at UWI and UG.

The Dutch-Speaking Universities

Our reception in Suriname and Curaçao was more than acceptable by anyone's professional standards, even though we had no command of the Dutch language. This shortcoming limited our success in finding other than official documents. The small, private University of Aruba serves a Dutch- and Papiamento-speaking populace, with courses offered in English. Its founder-president supplied the available documents to us.

The French-Speaking Universities

At the University of Haiti printed materials are few. The dean of the School of Education had one typed copy of the list of courses offered. Jurisdiction of academic programs is scattered among ministries, so basic documents are hard to find. Commentary on the academic system is not encouraged by the government.

Martinique and Guadeloupe, overseas departments of France since 1946, do not make policy or officially shape events in their university centers. Descriptive materials were given us there, but with cautionary comments that some are obsolete. Somewhere there has to be in print information on the issues being debated--some quite heatedly--on the Caribbean campuses and in the communities. We failed to find it. Efforts to elicit documents in France in person and by written request met refusal or silence. We did feel it essential, regardless of availability of local material, to include some of the avalanche of print on the debates and disputes that have accompanied French educational reform efforts since 1968. This was gleaned from libraries in the U.S. and London.

Preface

Universities in The Commonwealth of Puerto Rico and the U.S. Virgin Islands

Collecting in Puerto Rico begins with the central administration of the University of Puerto Rico, which governs the various campuses and shares responsibilities for regional public colleges. But it is essential to collect information at the individual institutions, both public and private, when possible.

The College of the Virgin Islands, St. Thomas, produces good data on itself and research on the region, well-stored and available.

Other Sources

Collecting in the region was facilitated by our participation in meetings of UNICA, which, despite its limited budget, has been a source of information for and about all the Caribbean universities. Meetings of the Caribbean Studies Association, of steadily increasing quality, and those of the Latin American Studies Association (LASA), have been helpful as well.

COVERAGE

Where materials were most available, as in Costa Rica, we selected representative issues. We looked for documents descriptive of the nature and size of each of the forty-six universities we visited, of courses offered, governance, legal status, history, faculty, and degrees; what was generally nonexistent was the compendium known in U.S. universities as the catalog.

Descriptive materials and those dealing with issues noted above were chosen, where choice was possible, for their illustrative value and for their differing viewpoints, where these were available in print. All universities in the region have grown in size and in range of offerings. These trends are reflected in documents of the early 1950s, the mid 1960s and the late 1970s. In some cases we had access to annual publications such as rectors' reports, many of which are included in the bibliography. We did not have access to many we know to have been published so it cannot be inferred that their absence from the bibliography indicates they did not merit inclusion.

There are, of course, many universities that have no annual report beyond the statistics furnished to national ministries. For no country or period of time does our coverage represent the ideal model of se- quence or comprehensiveness. There are in every country and territory books, journals, unpublished speeches, and newspaper accounts that we have not uncovered. We have been learning enough of the issues in most of the region to pick up, say, Venezuela's El Nacional during a visit there, and read with some insight the current chapters of an ongoing saga. There is a certain obvious randomness in the newspaper ci- tations, owing to our manner of collection.

Preface

Generally the coverage consists more of documents produced by universities for internal use than of books, just as would be true in studying U.S. institutions. For the issue-oriented, press coverage of policy debates may be more eloquent than annual reports. Ideally, one should have such a variety of documents. Sometimes we did.

One important element underrepresented in this bibliography is literature by and about the lending agencies that played a major role in trying to shape higher-education policies in Latin America after World War II. Large numbers of individuals and institutions benefitted, in varying degrees, from the financial and technical assistance provided by the Ford Foundation, the Latin American Scholarship Program of American Universities (LASPAU), and USAID, for example. Their activities represented a significant aspect of U.S. liberal thought of the period, and in turn generated both enthusiastic cooperation among many university colleagues in the U.S. and Latin America, and animated and highly visible antagonism from the political far Right and Left at home and abroad. Both the philosophy and the philanthropy are worthy of inquiry beyond what this work offers as sources.

Many of the most revealing documents of national and international agencies are, of course, often confidential internal reports. Some we saw cannot be cited. We did not systematically pursue foundation papers simply for lack of time and resources.

In sum, the coverage is intended to give the reader a comprehensive view of the issues, both under country headings and in the General Section, and to indicate sources of descriptive material.

ARRANGEMENT

Entries in this bibliography are presented within the following headings: First, General; then by country name in alphabetical order, including the University of the West Indies, which is alphabetized within the country headings. Entries for UDUAL and UNESCO are under General, along with regional agencies such as UNICA, CSUCA, FUPAC and ICASE.

Because UWI serves fourteen different nations and territories, the most efficient presentation is to use University of the West Indies as a category as if it were a single country. Its campuses are located in Trinidad and Tobago, Barbados, and Jamaica, but it has a common administration, budget, and policy framework. Entries pertaining to both UG and UWI are cross-referenced.

One might have grouped all Spanish-speaking countries and territories together, but the commonwealth of Puerto Rico has offered higher education in both Spanish and English at different times, even within the same institution. Puerto Rico and the U.S. Virgin Islands, patterned on the U.S. system of higher education in the Caribbean, are listed as individual territories.

Preface

Within each of the headings there is an alphabetical listing by
author (personal or corporate). For books, each entry contains name of
author, title, place of publication, publisher, date, and number of
pages. Journal references consist of author, title of article, name of
journal, volume number, date, and page numbers. Not all newspaper
citations bear page numbers, since some were obtained in the form of
clippings. Missing data were supplied from internal evidence whenever
possible. When we could not do this for dates, we used "[n.d.]".
Corporate or institutional publishers are treated as both author and
publisher. The libraries where we used monographic works or from which
they were borrowed are indicated in code following the annotation. The
code WKU indicates items in the Waggoners' personal collection. Location codes are on pp. xxxix-xlii. Locations for serials are not
given, but these may be checked through the Union List of Serials and
New Serials Titles. For periodicals from outside the United States we
indicate the place of publication on pp. 299-303. We standardized
corporate entries under their institutional names, for example, Universidad de . . . (this eliminated problems like needing to know the
location of a particular university).

Government agencies appear directly under the first word of their
names, within the appropriate country heading: not Guatemala, Ministerio de Educación but Ministerio. . . .

ANNOTATIONS

Our purpose in the annotations is to make materials as useful to
readers as possible. If a work is a source of quantitative information, such as enrollment, this is noted; to the extent that a work
deals with issues, we have tried to so indicate. Although we tried not
to make judgments, letting the works speak for themselves, occasionally
a title that promised more than its contents delivered earned a dis-
paraging word. In many entries we have identified authors by their
positions (e.g., scholar, educator, or political leader).

USING THE BIBLIOGRAPHY

Many works offer insights into issues of common concern to all of
Latin American universities. For example, the effects of the 1918
Reform of Cordoba are still subject to debate throughout the hemisphere. So, too, is the political role of students. Other issues
receive attention throughout the Caribbean basin area by virtue of some
common geographical and historical condition. The reader is invited to
look first at country headings; topics will best be discovered by
scanning the annotations. Entries are cross-referenced where appropriate. If the preponderance of content addresses a general question, the
entry and annotation are under General. If an entry also applies to a
particular country there is a cross-reference indicating its listing

there; within the country heading, the entry is cross-referenced back to the main entry, where the annotation is to be found.

ACKNOWLEDGMENTS

We are much indebted for the advice and counsel of friends and colleagues at the Organization of American States and at the Inter-American Development Bank, and for the help provided by cultural affairs officers of U.S. embassies and USAID personnel. They and their assistants have been very helpful in our ongoing relationships with our colleagues in Latin America. With few exceptions, they are knowledge-able and immensely resourceful in tracking down the mobile academicians who may be found at one time in a university, at another in the political arena or in the diplomatic service. We thank especially David Gray, CAO, Caracas and his assistant, Hildegarde Fischer. Their help spans many years.

We have already indicated that dozens of friends and colleagues in the Spanish-speaking countries provided encouragement, materials, interviews, and contact with other appropriate officials and re-searchers. But the people we were meeting for the first time in the English-, Dutch-, and French-speaking areas were equally helpful and generous with their time. Many work under the stressful political or financial constraints of the Caribbean region, yet they comprise a fraternity of able and dedicated professionals.

The University of Kansas provided support for George R. Waggoner during a sabbatical semester, and financial assistance for a part-time research assistant during another semester. Colleagues in the Center of Latin American Studies lent counsel and technical assistance. Arnold Weiss gave us his richly endowed editorial skills in the final stages of preparing the book. The personnel at the University of Kansas Libraries have been endlessly patient and persistent in aiding our searches and answering our questions. We are especially indebted to Ellen Brow and Rachel Miller, bibliographers for Spain, Portugal, and Latin America; and to Mary Kay and her staff in Inter-library Services.

Suzette McCord helped with typing in the early stages. Michelle Minnis was a resourceful detective in helping to locate materials, as was Sara Townsend, who also mastered the arts of copyediting and ordering the entries, assisted by Michelle Sommerville. Joan Moore coped with several languages in typing the original manuscript and Louise N. Dever put it in final form. Janice Meagher and Karin Kiewra made essential suggestions; and we have benefited from the help of William V. Jackson as series editor. Marjorie Schmitt has maintained the domestic infrastructure with kindness and efficiency.

We acknowledge with pleasure our indebtedness to all who contributed to our task.

B.A.W.
G.R.W.

Introduction

Images of the Caribbean vary: Tourist paradise of free ports and vivid seas; dark nest of social ills, feuding politicians, client states. Its universities are viewed as fulfilling the democratic dream of a meritocracy, as perpetuators of hierarchical societies, as agents for peaceful change, as instruments of the state, as hosts to violent revolution.

Lands once bloodied by contending European states were variously plundered, planted, and peopled. Political independence, rhetorically praised, has not always guaranteed economic or social well-being for these former or present colonies or territories of Spain, England, France, the Netherlands, and the U.S.; their institutions of government and education are deeply marked by the metropolises they served and upon which they were dependent.

Differences among these Caribbean lands and their institutions are several, but their common characteristics are many. They share the sea itself, warm climate, and past or present colonial status; all have some degree of the African presence left from slavery and the plantation economy.

All have promised—and many have made—substantial investments in education; all have dreamed—and some are awakening from the dream—that education, especially higher education, would be the key to a shining future of material goods and more egalitarian societies. Here as elsewhere after World War II, enormous hopes rested on the institutions known as universities, different as they might be from each other.

While U.S. educators and the public and private agencies called upon to fund them were engaged in debate in the 1960s and 1970s over the nature and function of their own universities, far more profound and perhaps far reaching educational policy matters were drawing the attention of leaders in Latin America and the Caribbean region.

As the nature of the American academic institution became the subject of much popular and scholarly scrutiny, it seemed only natural to some of us to seek some different perspectives, to look beyond our political and cultural boundaries, at what was happening elsewhere.

Introduction

This bibliography had its beginning, then, long before we knew it, in that remarkable mobility of scholars and ideas in the 1960s.

We lived at various times in several Latin American countries, always with some academic activity at the center, and were hosts to several hundred Latin American university rectors and deans in the Seminars on Higher Education in the Americas, sponsored by the Bureau of Education and Cultural Affairs of the U.S. State Department and the Conference Board of Associated Research Councils. These seminars, each of several weeks' duration, were held annually from 1963 through 1975, meeting not only at the University of Kansas but also in different years in Puerto Rico, Costa Rica, Colombia, Venezuela, and Peru. During part of this time the University of New Mexico also shared the U.S. portion of the seminars.

The results were an accumulation of experiences, books, letters, articles, and interview notes; an ever-widening and strengthening international network of colleagues; and an abiding interest in our own and other universities. We began a somewhat more systematic assemblage of materials in 1977. It was then that we turned our attention also to the broader Caribbean, curious about the issues and the problems confronting the non-Spanish-speaking countries and territories.

Higher education arrived in Latin America from Spain not only centuries before the English system was introduced in Britain's colonies, but also from a vastly different religious and philosophical tradition. By the middle of the twentieth century, theological concerns had long since given way to secular ones, and in the entire region political and academic leaders were being confronted with unforeseen demands on universities, difficult choices to be made, and few agreed-upon or tested guidelines.

Long-independent nations, those aspiring to independence, and those firmly locked into a metropolitan embrace were all confronted with the unsubtle need for change. Here is a microcosm of different university patterns and practices derived chiefly from Europe and variously modified by time and place, reflecting, we discovered, some universal questions. This bibliography is an effort to introduce to scholars of many disciplines these institutions in their various contexts.

Changes in technology in the post-World War II era would forever alter communication and transportation patterns in the world, affecting the Caribbean region with the ferment of new ideas, the stirrings for political and/or economic independence, and the yearnings for the substance and symbols that certified arrival into the middle-class dream.

Coupled with the aspirations for upward social mobility was the widely held belief in Universities as essential components in national development. For many, especially in the Latin American part of the Caribbean region, one developmental model was to be found in the United States, where frontiers seemed forever challenging and forever conquerable, if enough people had the right university degrees. There was the evidence: a prosperous middle class, abundant consumer goods, and—who could doubt the connection—democratic access to universities universally renowned.

If universities were to play their proper role in Latin American development, many of their leaders in the 1960s and 1970s were arguing, they must be radically restructured and their professional personnel given very different kinds of preparation, reward systems, and institutional tasks.

Residents of the English-speaking Caribbean had perhaps a steeper mountain to climb after World War II than their Latin American neighbors. Educational opportunity was still bound by the cultural shackles of slavery, and setting foot in a university meant, for the few who got there, a journey measured in thousands of miles into a sometimes hostile culture.

International agencies carried various university models abroad. The United Nations fostered the 1960s Decade of Development when the current of postwar enthusiasm for higher education was running strongly. In all of Latin America the demand for higher education swelled. In the English-speaking Caribbean, the steady movement toward independence brought the obvious need to develop leaders who could fill the void left by those sent earlier from England to administer in the private and public sectors.

Apostles of the good cause filed regularly through offices of university rectors and chancellors. Canadian, British, U.S., and Dutch agencies of international development offered loans, grants, visiting professors, scholarships, and equipment. Representatives of the USSR and some Eastern bloc countries were likewise offering support for education, for a quite different social model. Until the early 1970s the Inter-American Development Bank proudly called itself "the bank of the universities." The Ford Foundation, the Rockefeller Foundation, the Carnegie Corporation, the U.S. Agency for International Development (USAID), the Latin American Scholarship Program in American Universities (LASPAU), and other philanthropic agencies sent competent, dedicated agents to foster planning in higher education and faculty development. They, along with other agencies, encouraged entities for regional cooperation. Local initiatives created and nurtured the Unión de Universidades de America Latina (UDUAL), the Association of Caribbean Universities and Research Institutes (UNICA), Confederación Universitaria Centroamericana (CSUCA), Federacion de Universidades Privadas de Centro América y Panamá (FUPAC), and a host of other more specialized regional bodies, all of which still profoundly affect attitudes and awareness, if not always local practices, in universities in the Caribbean.

Within each country demographic pressures and social demands fostered controversy. Increasingly, assertions were heard that U.S. and European models of universities were inappropriate, that "classic" secondary-school curricula in the English-speaking Caribbean ill served the majority of their clients, who were excruciatingly prepared for a university in which they would likely never set foot. In Latin America manpower planners were heard, paid for, and little heeded by students, who rejected their importunings to attend technical schools. Law School enrollments grew exponentially; schools of agronomy went begging for students while, in all the Caribbean countries, agricultural production was failing to serve domestic needs. But throughout the region the university promised success; who would settle for less?

Many have done so. The bulge at the secondary level of enrollment passed into the universities, whose coffers and classrooms were unable to support and contain the matriculants. University structures and practices were increasingly seen as obsolete—as were some of their professional practitioners. Productivity in the universities, especially in the Spanish-speaking countries, was low.

Choices had to be made on resource allocation, and increasingly the questions loomed: Is it just, practical, or politically appealing to spend pounds or pesos on high-cost university facilities in societies still lacking in primary schools; Is spending on university education for the upper classes justified if much of the populace is doomed to illiteracy; should philosophers be schooled if the country needs pipe fitters; and, increasingly throughout the region as the population burgeoned to overload all components of the infrastructure, how was education to be paid for? Other woes threatened to becloud their future in the 1980s as national economies proved unable to employ either the minimally educated or university graduates.

As writers on education trace these currents, few could ignore Cuba's revolution in education and the questions it raised for the entire region. (Indeed, only one university in the Spanish-speaking countries comes to mind that did not have multiple images, larger than life, of Ché Guevara on its walls in the 1960s.) A system that seemed to promise justice, efficiency, and development of human and material resources through democratic access to education was revered as a model by some; it was cursed by others for its closed social system, its dependence on the USSR, its ideological rigidity, and its enthusiastic prosyletizing abroad. Ripples from Cuba moved throughout the region, touching very different shores, where faith in education may have been the only common vision.

Whatever blemishes are featured in the literature on universities in the Caribbean region, the lives of thousands of people have been transformed, in their own view for the better, by educational opportunities once unavailable. No longer are the region's leaders and educators forced to rely solely on North American or European institutions. Increasingly, with the various reform movements underway to professionalize the university teaching career, scholars join their international peers; at the same time, there has been in recent decades a strong demand that what is uniquely part of the Caribbean culture be identified, taught, and cherished. However, any large-scale movement of students or professors within the pan-Caribbean region is still hindered by a fierce chauvinism that prevails among these divided entities, fostered by the nationalistic rhetoric of the political leaders.

Introduction

What, then, of the differences among university systems beside and within this sea? We begin with the universities of Spanish-speaking America.

There was jubilation in the Dominican Republic some twenty years ago when archives in Spain yielded proof of the authenticity of the Papal Bull that established the predecessor institution of what is today the Universidad Autónoma de Santo Domingo. The Bull was dated 1538, and the flag of antiquity has proudly flown ever since. Peru and Mexico won their universities only a few years later. Guatemala's Universidad de San Carlos was founded in 1676, but, like all these early institutions it lacked continuity of function before World War II.

If they often have been short on scholars, they are all long on tradition, even such newer establishments as Venezuela's Universidad Central. The notion of universitarios as heroes goes back to wars for independence from Spain, and when regicide turned to fraticide in nineteenth-century Latin America, students resisted local tyrannies with both slogans and arms. The literature on student political behavior is not only considerable, it abounds with ideological ferment as well.

Blood was spilled and martyrs were made in the past. As recently as 1958 students and professors helped overthrow a dictatorship in Venezuela; in 1959 a revolution largely begun earlier at the Universidad de la Habana brought its law-school graduate Fidel Castro to power. In any week into the 1980s the government of Guatemala is charged with another assassination of a professor administrator, or student leader who has not yet fled into exile. Guatemala's brief period of democracy from 1945 to 1954 was strengthened by the participation of intellectuals before it was snuffed out; it was in that era that the Universidad de San Carlos won its autonomy.

The energy and rhetoric devoted to university autonomy was often more conspicuous than that devoted to academic matters, for as universities moved away from their ecclesiastical purposes and toward serving secular societies, their clientele chafed at political control by often authoritarian or repressive regimes. The 1918 manifesto of Cordoba, Argentina, is the chief icon of the movement, and its true nature is still debated. Not only was academic freedom needed, but institutional controls were sought and generally won in other university matters. There is a strong tradition of faculty and student participation in the election of university officials.

Invoking the doctrine of extraterritorialidad has occasionally provoked violence as government troops pursued miscreants or political foes into university precincts declared sanctuaries. The debate over policies determining uses of government-provided funds—and the quest for more—is part of the annual rhythm of most institutions. Efforts to empower bodies such as U.S.-style state boards of regents to make national higher-education policies have been frequently resisted as threats to institutional autonomy.

Out of these inquietudes, generally subsumed under the rubric of politicización, grew the demand for private universities. Many have been founded since the mid-forties, often by religious groups. Most are heavily oriented toward preparation for commercial and industrial careers, for students here as in the public universities are often full-time workers and part-time scholars. While tuition at public institutions is generally nonexistent or negligible, the cost of education at private universities may be considerable despite the state subsidies most receive.

If students have necessarily put paid work ahead of study (medical students are most likely to be full-time students), so too have their professors traditionally practiced their professions by day and their pedagogical duties by night, often at more than one institution. Only to U.S. scholars, steeped in a different tradition, has this system seemed strange. Although a few have modified their academic structures in recent years the Latin American university, following the Napoleonic model, continues to be a cluster of professional schools (in some cases still at scattered sites), the purpose of which is the creation of practicing professionals. The degree they offer, the licenciatura, is literally a license to practice. Who better to instruct the neophyte than the practitioner?

Another and related problem confronting Latin American universities was the high rate of failure. Familial pressures to become "my son, the doctor," often coupled with poor secondary preparation in the sciences locked many students into a curriculum for which they were unsuited. Students entered the first year of study at medical and other professional schools with a fixed program of courses. Failing a single course resulted in having to repeat the entire year. Traditionally, there was no system of academic credits as a kind of coinage transferable from one program of study to another. There were countless years of unproductive effort, at high public and personal cost.

By the mid-forties questions began to arise: Were these practitioner-professors sufficiently prepared; were the traditional "liberal" professions—law, medicine, engineering—sufficient in number and scope to meet the new and suddenly increasing social expectations of growing and upwardly mobile populations, and of nations committed to the use of new technologies?

The calls for la reforma universitaria were soon resonating within academic and parliamentary halls. How those calls were answered, and resisted, comprises much of the literature of the period. The changes were perhaps far vaster than any undertaken in the United States or Western Europe. The restructuring of institutions toward centralized services such as libraries and matriculation was accomplished in some cases with new, unified campuses.

Efforts were made to professionalize the university teaching career, in some cases generating generational conflict as the demands for graduate study and research were making the knowledge of some catedráticos obsolete. Selection and reward systems would have to change. And, above all, people would have to be prepared outside of Latin America, particularly in the sciences, in alien languages and educational systems.

Solution of one problem sowed the seeds of others. Cost became a major consideration. The appropriateness of a foreign doctoral degree to the Latin American university was questioned. The suspicion was, and in some quarters still is, that it does not transplant well. Some countries suffered from a brain drain as their scholars were attracted to better laboratories and libraries, more colleagues and money, and better educational opportunities for their children abroad. That many items in the bibliography deal with research and graduate study is indicative of these concerns.

U.S. university professors were conspicuously mobile as they climbed their professional ladders to higher salaries and greater prestige, with ratification by their scholarly peers determining their ascent into an academic firmament ruled by research and publication. Few vehicles for career advancement, such as national professional fraternities and journals, existed in Latin America. In the Dominican Republic a conference for history professors was scheduled for 1983; it was reported to be the first such gathering in over a quarter of a century

The word "relevance" was heard more than once in the campus turbulence in Western Europe and the U.S. in the late 1960s and 1970s. So, too, in Latin American universities the demand was growing for education to solve what students and political leaders saw as social and developmental problems; as well, there was a demand, often violently expressed, that universities throw their institutional weight into battle on the side of the oppressed.

Above all, no campus or national politician who questioned open access to public universities could hope to survive. Holders of the secondary school bachillerato diploma held the admission ticket, automatically in most cases, to enter the public universities. And here the word "crisis" would be featured in local headlines describing the state of higher education.

The comments to follow elaborate on these and other characteristics of universities country by country and/or in appropriate grouping (e.g., Central America and Panama). Our own personal observations are reflected, but these comments are distilled chiefly from the literature in an effort to indicate some of the major issues of the era and the region. Note that, as explained in the Preface, we have attempted to deal only with the coastal universities in our coverage of Mexico, Venezuela, and Colombia.

Mexico

The Universidad de Yucatán celebrated its centennial in 1967, evoking memories of its precursor institutions and also celebrating its own enduring sense of uniqueness within the Mexican nation. It was descendants of the Maya temple builders, not slaves from Africa, who provided most of the labor on the henequen plantations, wealth from which created the now decaying nineteenth-century mansions along the main streets of Merida. Then, as now, policies made in Mexico City governed most aspects of life, including education; the resentment and resistance of the yucatecos persists.

The university itself has suffered various intramural cleavages over its role in complying with national norms as against meeting local needs. All of Mexican higher education has been in a state of perpetual tension in the post-World War II period, much of it the result of demographic and social pressures, some efforts at reform, and strong ideological manifestations.

Venezuela

Perhaps Venezuela's university situation is, if not the most acute, the most loudly described; it is the heady stuff of headlines.

Central to understanding Venezuela's university system is an understanding of its Universidad Central. For several decades, as the only university in the country, it produced all of Venezuela's professionals and political, financial, and social leaders. The degrees it offers have never lost their prestige despite severe overcrowding and periodic episodes of violence and strikes. By the mid-sixties, in an effort to curb partisan political activity, new "experimental" institutions were being designed and founded, limiting the right of their students and faculty members to elect their own rectors and deans. But even as educational planners sought new directions, the attraction of patterns and practices at the Universidad Central could not be abolished from the national ethos.

In the U.S. educational system, patrons count on the universities' liberal arts curricula to perform several functions. Students are obliged to explore a variety of areas of knowledge, in both sciences and humanities, before choosing a major field of study or a professional school; they have in the process an opportunity for honing academic skills, acquiring self-knowledge, and encountering new fields of knowledge. In the Napoleonic model of a university, the career choice is made early, and the student plunges into his or her specialization either well prepared—academically and psychologically—or headed for failure.

Here several forces come into play in the Venezuelan situation, perhaps to a less strident degree elsewhere. Aspirants to the university and their political advocates charge that elitism is at work in any university system that requires qualifications for entry. It is, they assert, the poor and educationally disadvantaged, chiefly from the public school system, who will be penalized by tests. Efforts to limit enrollment in the medical school at the Universidad Central in Caracas, for example, have touched off invasions of the rector's office and hunger strikes by postulants perhaps lacking any hint of qualification for entry. And their cause is seized upon by politicians inside and outside who champion their constitutional "right" to study where they wish.

Those who were admitted into the system but failed their courses
in the first year often caused a kind of institutional blockage, for
any effort to remove them was also denounced as elitist, since it would
surely discriminate against less advantaged students. The repitentes
have in the past been allowed to continue repeating indefinitely, while
the throngs of new bachilleres burned buses in protest outside because
there was no room within. Similar demonstrations are part of the
annual rhythm mentioned earlier, when appeals for funds are made to the
government. Headlines are familiar: No hay cupo ("there is no
space").

In Venezuela, as elsewhere in the Spanish-speaking countries, the
rendimiento, or yield, of graduates is poor in terms of the monies
invested. Such figures, although sometimes hard to track down, are
available in several of the items in the bibliography.

Venezuela's response to these problems has been enormous. Not
only has petroleum income been poured into expansion of higher education within the country, but a massive system of scholarships—
probably never equalled anywhere else—has sent thousands of students
abroad for education designed for la transferencia de la tecnología.
The scholarships of Plan Gran Mariscal de Ayacucho have been augmented
by those of the Consejo Nacional de Ciencias y Tecnología (CONICIT) and
other government agencies, and both major political parties have
supported these efforts.

They have likewise supported what would once have been unthinka-
ble: a national system of pre-enrollment, conducive of a less chaotic
distribution of students among the many public and private universities, especially those outside Caracas, and admissions practices that
are more likely to limit failure and repetition. Other efforts officials believe will improve the efficiency of the system include
pressing students to make career choices even earlier in their secondary school years; more than a year before graduation, students must
choose a profession to which they will dedicate their academic future,
in order to acquire an "orientation" to it. Some see this, of course,
as the source of the problem, not the solution.

Metropolitan Caracas has more than filled the long valley above
the seacoast, where only a few years back cane fields flourished beside
the mountains. Its growth as the national center of industry, government, commerce, marketing, transportation, politics, and culture has
erased its agrarian past and layered it over with skyscrapers, free-
ways, and shopping centers. It long remained the nation's educational
center as well, but efforts to disperse its facilities to other regions, many of which also lie along the coast, are notable.

One such endeavor, the Universidad de Oriente, has been transforming eastern Venezuela since its creation some twenty years ago.
The once impoverished town of Cumana is now seat of its main campus; it
is one of those "experimental" dependencies of the Ministry of Education designed specifically to serve regional developmental needs and
to be a less fertile ground for contending ideologies by virtue of its
less autonomous system of governance. Its several núcleos have had a
marked and positive impact on the towns and regions in which they are

located. The Universidad Simón Bolívar near Caracas has become a prestige experimental institution. There are also significant autonomous and growing universities in Maracaibo and Valencia.

Other efforts to respond to the demand for university education in the 1970s included creation of several colegios universitarios, resembling in some ways U.S. junior colleges, under the Ministry of Education. Both public- and private-sector planners recognized the need for trained technicians, but the very name instituto tecnológico smacked of the blue collar in a land where the white collar is Everyman's dream. The bureaucracy could not adequately build, administer, or staff these agencies, and the pressure has continued on the traditional universities to expand.

The Open University began with great publicity in the late 1970s, with much research on market demand, manpower needs, course development, and appropriate technology. Initially, emphasis was to be put on teacher education and the basic sciences. Acceptance by the potential clientele has been slower than authorities had hoped.

By 1983, as our compilation was coming to a close, essays arrived in the mail from Caracas indicating what may lie ahead. A reassessment of the dreams and promises of higher education and a limitation of access to it are proposed, in response to shrinking petrodollars. Politically, that rhetoric will be hard to sell.

Colombia

The contrast between coastal Venezuela and coastal Colombia is striking. That region is part of what geographer Preston James once described as "mostly outside the effective national territory." Power resides in Colombia's Andean cities, most conspicuously in the capital, Bogota, where policy for public education is made. Nationally, demand for schooling has by far outstripped capacity in a country whose wealth is less abundant than that of neighboring Venezuela, and whose class lines are more firmly drawn.

The divisiveness of political allegiances has moderated since the years of social upheaval known as La Violencia, but the conspicuous poverty of some of the coastal regions still makes for a politically unstable populace, and for campesinos understandably eager to participate in the extralegal drug industry.

Public universities in the Caribbean area of Colombia reflect impoverishment in their pathetically overcrowded, shabby, ill-equipped facilities. Private universities are in some cases models of modern efficiency and academic aesthetics, products of local philanthropy. All of Colombian education was generously subsidized in the 1960s by international contributions, by one estimate to the extent of fifty percent of the national budget for education, and perhaps no country's system of higher education received more attention from cultural and educational agencies of the United States. The results were not always gratifying to donors or recipients.

Pressures mounted both within and without the country to allocate more resources to elementary education to serve the poorest of the poor, and universities have lost their paramountcy in the educational picture. There has been a persistent tug-of-war between the Ministry of Education and the individual universities for control of finances, administration, and programs. In the eyes of officials of the Instituto para el fomento de Educación Superior (ICFES) in Bogota, too many replications of program offerings have been allowed to develop, with each university given to building its small costly empire. University officials in the regional institutions defend their creations as necessary to local development. A law school dean in Cartagena referred to remote Bogota as "our Tibet."

As for collaboration among coastal universities themselves to solve local problems, communication is scant. Even the lure of outside grants for common projects failed to provide the requisite cohesion. They are no more eager to share power and resources than universities within a state system of higher education in the United States.

Regional Organizations and the Universities of Central America and Panama

In the General section of this bibliography, the acronym CSUCA, which stands for both the Confederación de Universidades Centroamericanas and the Consejo Superior Universitario Centroamericano, is a major author heading. It has been and continues to be a major source of information about Central American universities. It is difficult to discuss these individual institutions in the post-World War II era without noting the mutuality of their influence through the medium of communication that CSUCA became.

Some of its early adherents hoped it would provide a genuinely unified system of higher education in Central America. Others resisted any possible threats to national sovereignty. What CSUCA ultimately had was some power of persuasion and occasional political leverage in behalf of beleaguered academicians whose persons and precincts were violated by repressive governments. It has continued as an agency fostering the improvement of institutional quality and professorial competence. Its publishing company, Editorial Universitario Centroamericano (EDUCA) is located near the Secretariat, a short walk from the main campus of the Universidad de Costa Rica. Among the goals of CSUCA and its member universities in the 1960s was the promotion of Estudios Generales, in the conviction that all students needed more than the purely professional curricula. Moreover, faculty preparation in the basic disciplines was weak and the scattering of courses in, for example, physics, throughout a university's separate schools of engineering, medicine, education, and architecture was costly and unproductive. Efforts were made—and resisted—to create departments and break what many saw as the tyranny of the catedrático, or principal professor, to improve the quality of teaching and to develop research as part of the university function.

Achievement of these goals has been uneven. The strands of academic policy making and local, regional, and international politics should be recognized as being perpetually intertwined in Central

America. Nationalist sentiments were always stronger than regional
loyalties in all of Central America, making power sharing difficult.
The bright hopes of CSUCA's members and leaders for a truly regional
system of universities, with specialized institutions and mobile professors and students, dimmed in 1969 as war erupted between El Salvador
and Honduras.

Internal struggles for power were often complicated by the competition between the United States and the Soviet Union for adherents in
the region; with the U.S. conspicuously supporting repressive regimes,
campus ideological enthusiasts became increasingly suspicious of and
hostile to any idea or policy emanating from the U.S. The university
reforms embraced in Costa Rica were adopted and then abandoned in
Guatemala. General Studies was doomed in the Universidad de San
Carlos, whatever its merits, for bearing the U.S. imprint.

FUPAC has had a role in aiding communication among the private
universities, including fostering meetings of student leaders; the
students' strong sense of regional and national identity shows in their
reports, as does their dislike of an "imperialist" presence. Not all
of the Central American private universities are members. In 1980, the
FUPAC secretary general was assassinated in Guatemala, where FUPAC had
its headquarters.

The Universidad de San Carlos in Guatemala is the oldest in the
region, although its doors were often closed by political or seismic
events. Remains of its ancient seat in Antigua show a very different
world of learning from its striking modern buildings on the outskirts
of Guatemala City, where the major academic mission of the country is
carried on.

Representatives of the U.S. government and the brokers of power in
Guatemala publicly denounced "leftists" in San Carlos in the 1960s and
1970s; professors, administrators, and student leaders became acceptable targets for assassination. The sixty-year-old registrar of San
Carlos, perhaps the best and most consistently professional university
statistician in Central America, was shot as he walked his dog near his
home; it was a gesture against the university, one of many in the late
1970s and early 1980s.

The Catholic Universidad Rafaél Landívar has a handsome new campus
on the outskirts of the capital. The Evangelical Universidad Mariano
Gálvez was making plans for its own new campus before its founder-
rector left for Mexico after receiving a death threat.

El Salvador's universities are not, per se, included in this
bibliography, but its public Universidad de El Salvador was often a
concern of its fellow members of CSUCA as its officials were killed or
jailed by the government. Its medical school was especially strong in
the region. Private funds, helped by grants from international agencies, created the rapidly growing Universidad Católica José Simeón
Cañas.

Less populous Honduras has been seen by many of its own upper-
class citizens as peculiarly underdeveloped. The Universidad Nacional
Autónoma de Honduras established a division of General Studies,

although recently some of its former leaders have been promoting a
private university. Political concerns are never far below the surface
of academic matters.

The poverty, corruption, and foreign domination that has characterized Nicaragua's twentieth-century history would seem to make it
unlikely soil for any kind of intellectual endeavor, yet a stubbornly
persistent and often endangered group of professors and administrators
of the Universidad Nacional Autónoma de Nicaragua (UNAN) has not only
built new campuses in colonial Leon and in the capital, Managua, but
has rebuilt what earthquakes and its dictator's troops destroyed.
Diplomatic skills, applied inside and outside the troubled country,
made possible the raising of funds for science buildings and medical
facilities; but perhaps most important has been the vision of what a
modern, quality university should be.

Students and faculty members of UNAN and the Catholic Universidad
Centroamericana (UCA) participated in the national literacy campaign
following the revolution. UNAN's rector is president of the newly
formed National Council of Higher Education. A former rector of UNAN
is minister of education; the vice-minister is a former rector of UCA.
The national commitment to education amounts to a passion, but so does
national survival; threats to the latter jeopardize funds for the
former in a country left threadbare by its departing dictator.

A demonstration of the theory that universities reflect their
societies is provided by Costa Rica. Its beneficent accidents of
history and geography illumined its rational dream: more schoolhouses
than soldiers. This Latin American anomaly, a democracy since 1948,
promised much and delivered much until its post-1973 confrontation
between a rapidly growing population with rising expectations and the
devastating cost of imported energy.

The Universidad de Costa Rica in the 1960s and early 1970s as-
tounded visitors from other Latin American nations: its central
library was a reality that worked; students were led into a wider world
of knowledge than the narrowly professional; professors were expected
to be part of the world community of scholars.

Compelling slogans about social justice, at a time when they were
the coin of the academic realm in Western Europe and the United States,
accompanied the founding of the Universidad Nacional de Costa Rica in
Heredia in the early 1970s. It was for a time an institution with more
slogans than substance, but alternatives to Costa Rica's single alma
mater had begun to appear.

The private Universidad Autónoma de Centroamérica challenged UCR's
monopoly on the licensing function for the professions. Regional
colleges were opened to accommodate unmanageable numbers seeking entry
into UCR, and growth in the size and numbers of institutions produced a
variety of stresses, some of which the new Open University is opti-
mistically promising to alleviate. Costa Ricans and Venezuelans have
held some joint conferences on the subject of the Open University, and
consultants from England have been giving advice. The questions are
many, but the transcendent issue is whether the country can pay for the
education of which its people have been so proud.

Introduction

The Universidad de Panamá has increased its participation in CSUCA in recent years; its chief regional thrust is now through the Instituto Centro Americano de Administración y Supervisión de la Educación (ICASE), the Organization of American States (OAS) agency working with other Central American universities and ministries of education to improve secondary education. The university has grown rapidly and has established several regional centers. The constancy of the desire to win control of the Panama Canal was a kind of ideological glue that unified generations of students. Reform proposals have sparked lively debate recently, but more heat is observable in personal than ideological differences. The Catholic Universidad Santa María la Antigua is building a new campus outside the capital.

The Dominican Republic

With the 1961 demise of dictator Rafael Trujillo, the Universidad de Santo Domingo began a rapid transformation from a weak, terrorized, sycophantic enterprise into a major university. The wonder was that a remarkably apt body of people had somehow survived that epoch to emerge as professors and administrators able to carry on to the next stage of institutional transformation, including achievement of autonomy.

The following years were far from tranquil, as ideological battles and the quest for political power turned violent. The Universidad Autónoma de Santo Domingo (UASD) was to become heavily involved, a focus of rebellion and dissent to some, an agency championing democracy and freedom to others. The civil war that erupted in 1965 brought U.S. intervention to counter "another Cuba."

With United Nations troops stationed in the capital, an uneasy truce prevailed in 1966 when a USAID advisory group began meeting with leaders of the UASD to assist in their efforts to develop academic programs and prepare their professors. Campus walls were covered with posters reading "afuera la yanqui bota."

Visiting U.S. professors found the UASD Reform Commission well aware of its academic deficits. Few people were prepared to teach in the sciences. A chemistry professor, lacking a textbook in Spanish, translated a text from English and mimeographed it nightly, a few lessons ahead of his class. An engineer was pressed into service to offer a statistics course for sociologists.

The social mission of the university was constantly emphasized, to the alarm of the government of President Joaquín Balaguer. The private Universidad Pedro Henríquez Ureña (UNPHU) was founded in 1966 by former UASD professors who saw a left-leaning faculty at UASD as inimical to academic pursuits and alien to their beliefs. Public monies provided a bare subsistence for UASD, and helped to build UNPHU and the Universidad Católica Madre y Maestra (UCMM) in Santiago de los Caballeros; UASD lived with the overt hostility of the Balaguer government and a budget inadequate to maintain its buildings and serve the growing numbers of students who crowded into them.

It was an event that made newspaper headlines when the police department in Santo Domingo in 1981 donated paint to students to paint campus buildings. Police, once symbolic of the enemy state, were eating *empanadas* beside the students on university grounds during Antonio Guzmán's presidency.

UNPHU has grown from its makeshift beginning in a private home to a major campus. In 1981, UCMM expanded from Santiago into a branch in Santo Domingo, primarily to serve the business community. The Instituto Tecnológico (INTEC) set up shop on the edge of town, has plans to become yet another university in the capital fulfilling what its rector sees as the unmet need for skilled professionals. They all pledge to produce graduates with social consciences as well as skills.

It was with a sense of outrage that students at the new Universidad Central del Este (UCE) learned that the Wall Street Journal had referred to their town, San Pedro de Macorís, as a "primitive, dusty village." That the paper would take note of the place or its institutions at all is due to UCE's growing enrollment of U.S. medical students, many of whom, having failed to gain entry into medical schools in their own country, willingly pay high fees to study abroad. UCE, a family enterprise financed by private philanthropy and medical tuition monies, is rapidly building a carefully planned campus on a site, dusty indeed, in a typical Caribbean village impoverished by the abandonment of its plantations and its people and the flight of capital. UCE's rector, like his father before him, intends to transform the community by developing its infrastructure and providing jobs. A community hospital is already functioning.

UNICA

Dominican universities are among the most active participants in UNICA. Founded in 1968 and held together thereafter by a pioneer West Indian educator, the organization has linked institutions separated by geography, language, and contrasting educational systems.

Production of crops for export rather than local consumption has resulted in a costly dependence on imported food and the abandonment of domestic agriculture in nearly all the Caribbean countries and territories. A current UNICA endeavor is a pilot agricultural project to be carried out by Dominican universities in collaboration with the University of Miami, in the Dominican Republic, to stimulate research and education elsewhere in the region on this serious common problem.

Cuba and the Influence of the USSR

The other universities in the Spanish-speaking Caribbean are those in Cuba and some of those in Puerto Rico. The people of both places have enjoyed a love/hate relationship with the U.S. and its educational system; both have benefited educationally from the U.S. presence and both have resisted various aspects of it.

When the U.S. severed its ties with Cuba and set out to isolate it in the hemisphere, it did more than interrupt the marketing system that sold Cubans everything from tires to toothbrushes. It also cut off the

Introduction

flow of scholarly communication from the Western world and provided a haven for disaffected Cubans, many of whom were academicians and professional people.

Looking through scrapbooks in the library of the Universidad de Santa Clara de Las Villas, professors proudly show yellowed newspaper clippings dating from their youth in the 1940s and 1950s: our baseball team, our chess team. They are nostalgic, then bitter. Here, a man has an X drawn across his picture, in another three or four have been crossed out. "They left."

Those who stayed have a clear sense of mission, and the strongly centralized system, controlled from Havana first by the Ministry of Education and since 1978 by the Ministry of Higher Education, has given them a sense of worth.

Ideology and practice in all of education are woven into a continuous mesh, on paper a diagram to reinforce the Marxist-Leninist view of the classless state, a system that integrates education, productive needs, and rewards. Cuba may be the only Spanish-speaking country in the hemisphere that has succeeded in reducing its surplus of graduates in law, and where higher education for the sake of personal gain and enhanced social status is not deemed a goal worthy of state support. Private schools no longer exist.

The needs of the state are paramount, and since Cuba's lawmakers declared the people to be the state, they likewise declared that the university, as part of the state, had no need for autonomy. Gone are the bonches who made intrigues at the Universidad de la Habana before dictator Fulgencio Batista's fall. Student organizations are part of the Party, and attendance at universities is determined by success in academic endeavors and willingness to perform the work that is seen as an integral part of learning, from grade school on.

Decentralization of function, while keeping policymaking strongly centralized, has separated the components of the Universidad de la Habana into several institutes. The humanities are to be found in the Classic Revival buildings that were once the university's principal seat; the medical institute and technological and engineering institutes are in separate sites, the latter having an entire new campus that includes student residences, virtually nonexistent in most of Latin America. Fine arts offices are housed in what is immediately recognizable as a former country club, U.S. suburbia style, ca. 1950; studios are newly built handsome brick buildings.

But it is not the administration or dispersal of buildings as much as those whom they are intended to serve that sets Cuba's accomplishments apart. In the fine arts studios, middle-aged men and women whose regular jobs may be drafting or house painting are learning to do life drawing. The fisherman's son, now a driver for the ministry, is entering electronics school. Architecture students leave their classrooms, sent off to build a wall. Their instructor? A skilled bricklayer. The need to both learn and practice the dignity of manual labor pervades the entire system.

Introduction

Regional universities in Santiago and Las Villas are strongly oriented toward regional developmental needs, such as agriculture. Many of the professors at Santiago are young. They identify themselves as recent graduates in a kind of bootstrap operation. So do those in the various technological institutes that are a major part of higher education, all of which is intended to create a just and egalitarian society in which opportunities are no longer limited to the select few.

Cuba's independence came much later than that of other Latin American countries. Cuba shared the Spanish tradition of ecclesiastical higher education, sporadic in nature, prior to the creation of the modern Universidad de la Habana in 1902. Although the U.S. had had a strong influence on elementary and secondary education, the Latin American model of a university of professional schools was adopted. The Russian presence is now conspicuous; those who once attended U.S. graduate schools must go to Eastern bloc institutions. Soviet journals are translated into Spanish, Russian-language study is required, and Russian advisors and technicians fill several posts in the Ministry of Higher Education and universities. Rooms in the libraries once filled with material in English are largely empty, in part casualties of U.S. policy.

The 1961 Literacy Crusade taught virtually everyone to read and write. "La Batalla para el sexto grado" was the slogan on billboards in 1979. President Castro joked that if people were overeducated and engineers had to drive tractors "the tractors will probably run better." The main questions for Cuba: Can the economy provide jobs for such a labor pool? Will workers find the reward system adequate and equitable? Can the country pay for its investment in education?

The same questions confront Venezuela, which until the Nicaraguan revolution was the only Caribbean nation making such massive effort to democratize access to education at all levels and to satisfy the demands of a large proportion of its populace. Venezuela's open, consumer-oriented society, enriched by petroleum, is one model; the nations less richly endowed and whose economies are more highly structured by the state offer some opportunities for comparison in the years ahead.

The United States: Puerto Rico and the U.S. Virgin Islands

Spain had never assiduously cultivated its scholarly gardens in Puerto Rico; thus when U.S. politicians wrested the island from Spanish control in 1898 their patriotic fever was followed by considerable educational fervor. Deficits in elementary and secondary schools would be remedied, teacher training would rapidly be increased; in 1903 the Universidad de Puerto Rico (UPR) was founded. Benefits of the Land Grant legislation of the U.S. mainland helped strengthen the UPR campus in Río Piedras, and the applied sciences became the chief curriculum in Mayagüez. The forerunner of Inter American University was a result of religious visions by a Protestant missionary. The Catholic University began making its programs available in 1948. Other institutions proliferated. The presence of a prosperous middle class is very visible in San Juan and elsewhere, a product of a more democratic educational system than those of other Spanish-speaking places in the hemisphere.

That U.S. educators brought a more democratic, more orderly approach to the educational endeavor in Puerto Rico in the first half of the twentieth century is beyond question. Its universities are accredited by the Middle States Association of Colleges and Secondary Schools; UPR was the first, in 1946. By the second half of the century Puerto Rican educators themselves were being consulted in other Spanish-speaking countries.

Yet, measured by mainland standards, the achievements failed to satisfy many critics. The endemic poverty persisted; the cultural barriers between those who achieved literacy in Spanish or English (or both) and those who did not became accentuated. Agonizing over cultural identity consumed energies inordinately. In recent years it has become evident that Puerto Rico's economy promised more than it could provide in the way of employment, and university graduates there as elsewhere found themselves pursuing further education for escalating job requirements, if jobs could be found at all. Record high enrollments have been propped up by Basic Educational Opportunity Grants and on this shaky and vulnerable foundation institutional growth continues.

What were once acts of faith and optimism are now the subject of some doubt and pessimism. Puerto Rico's population grew; its income and rate of literacy surpassed those of other Spanish-speaking countries. But a profoundly divided university community was caught up in the dispute over Puerto Rico's political status: statehood, commonwealth status, or independent nation. Pride in the Hispanic tradition is extremely strong and constitutes a potent political force.

The College of the Virgin Islands, in St. Thomas, exists in an environment less committed to political cleavages of the past, in a smaller, less complex space than that of Puerto Rico, with fewer language problems, and more manageable tasks. Its officials assume a leadership role in addressing microstate problems, and express concern that their graduates find employment at home rather than in the continental U.S. The college is also accredited by the Middle States Association of Colleges and Secondary Schools.

THE DUTCH-SPEAKING TERRITORIES: SURINAME AND THE NETHERLANDS ANTILLES

Neck irons and leg chains are in the Slavery Museum on Paramaribo's waterfront, within walking distance of the Universiteit van Suriname where descendants of Africans, laborers from Indonesia and China, and Dutch settlers all attend and teach classes. The language of schooling, Dutch, has always limited access and success for the many whose creole tongues set them apart from the formal learning process. Indeed, some early writers on education in Suriname addressed the injustice and inappropriateness of preparing young people for an alien lifestyle and value system.

In Suriname and on the islands, the structure and substance of education were determined in Europe, and aspirants to higher education had to study in Holland. The Universiteit van Suriname, established in

1966, now offers several degree programs. Independence for Suriname, with some attendant political tensions, has resulted in increased leadership roles for local people, but many who attended universities in Holland had already chosen to remain there.

The Netherlands Antilles consists of the islands of Aruba, Bonaire, and Curaçao, near Venezuela, and the islands of St. Maarten, Saba, and St. Eustatius some 500 miles away. The hilltop campus of the Universiteit van de Nederlands Antillen, 10 kilometers outside of Willemstad, Curaçao, was created by combining two antecedent institutions in 1979.

The private Universidat di Aruba, in Oranjestad, offers instruction in English.

THE FRENCH-SPEAKING ISLANDS: HAITI, GUADELOUPE, AND MARTINIQUE

"To be in France—for a Haitian it is to be as a fish swimming in the sea." If France is a natural habitat for the professor who said this, it can be so only because he is one of the small fraction of Haitians who speak French rather than Creole; he thus made it into the educational system, stayed there, and completed graduate studies at the Sorbonne. (The Francophile professor has been in voluntary exile for some years, directing research in international studies at the University of the West Indies and later at a Venzuelan university.)

Most of Haiti's populace is in the impoverished rural hills, schooled, if at all, in the official language they do not comprehend, in a public school system run until recently by the Ministry of Agriculture with the smallest per capita expenditure on education in the Western Hemisphere. The slave uprising of 1804 that created the independent nation just as firmly created its own hierarchical society, which has perpetuated itself into the present untroubled by pretensions to democracy.

L'Université d'Etat d'Haiti has various professional schools at several sites in Port-au-Prince. They have been more closely tied to various government ministries than to each other. In a period of rapid university growth elsewhere in the Caribbean region, the university was serving six tenths of one percent of Haiti's population in 1960; that percentage had not changed by the late seventies.

Reform proposals have not been lacking. A UNICA/OAS study presents a tidy, rational plan for the university; its implied assumptions may be unwarranted. USAID assistance may or may not have improved matters for any given student. Critics of foreign aid cry out that it only perpetuates the power of the bourgeoisie.

The colonies of Martinique and Guadeloupe were declared to be departments of France in 1946. Henceforth their citizens received the service accorded those in the metropolis, including an educational system planned, financed, and controlled by the French Ministry of Education. The Université de Bordeaux had until recently virtually

total responsibility for policy at the two campuses of the Centre
Universitaire des Antilles et de la Guyane.

The hilltop campuses beside the cities of Pointe-à-Pitre and Fort-
de-France were designed abroad, as was the content of courses. One
learns more from listening than from reading about local concerns. As
in all colonial situations, the role of the metropolis as model cannot
be ignored. Approximations of the model are attempted and defended as
means to protect quality; at the same time local needs and sensibili-
ties are sometimes ignored.

The voluminous literature of French educational reforms of the
late 1960s and early 1970s is replete with conflicts over decentralization of policy making and efforts to democratize access to the system, but the consequences for this peripheral area are hard to measure.
Certainly the Creole-speaking population has a major hurdle to cross in
mastering the language of instruction. The worry about employment for
university graduates of both mainland and local campuses is a constant
in their lives. And, as in continental France, there is debate about
the university's role as perpetuator of class distinctions.

THE ENGLISH-SPEAKING COUNTRIES: THE UNIVERSITY OF THE WEST INDIES

Fourteen territories in the English-speaking Caribbean issued
commemorative stamps in 1951 in honor of the 1948 founding of University College of the West Indies; Princess Alice is pictured in the
chancellor's robes, symbolizing the firm ties with the mother country
for this precursor institution of UWI and the University of Guyana
(UG). Its degrees for the next several years would be awarded by the
University of London. Campuses were built to serve the fourteen contributing territories in Jamaica, Barbados, and Trinidad and Tobago.

Education of any sort for the slave-descended population of the
colonies was not enthusiastically supported in nineteenth-century
England, with what little there was carefully planned and executed by
church groups enjoined to offer learning suitable for a docile labor
force. The literature does not thunder with any democratic rhetoric
until well into the post-World War II era. As in Great Britain itself,
schooling was punctuated by a series of tests to be survived on the way
to a university only a very few would enter.

Thus the taxi driver in Port of Spain boasts/laments that his
child passed/failed the '0' level examinations because he/she worked
hard/didn't apply him/herself. The contrast with the Venezuelan response to access to higher education as a "right" is conspicuous. The
examinations themselves are both the symbol and substance of much of
the inquietude surrounding the educational enterprise.

Being as British as possible had become a survival technique for
black West Indians and their fellow citizens from East India for
generations, for it led to whatever rewards the system offered. In
schooling, the history offered was that of British derring-do; the
literature was full of pastoral poets; and with perseverance,

xl

sacrifice, and luck, a degree from an English university was within reach. But along the way was that series of examinations from Cambridge that opened university doors or slammed them forever. And before those examinations had come others, determining as early as age eleven-plus whether one might enter the college-preparatory pathway at all.

Rapid population growth and rising expectations overloaded the educational system in the post-World War II era at a time when demands for independence from Britain were mounting throughout the Commonwealth. Likewise, awareness of African heritage was finding a new clientele, and pride in being Caribbean people came very much alive in the arts, literature, politics, and finally in education.

By the 1960s both UWI and the by now separated UG had professors whose scholarly peers were to be found all over the world. By the late 1970s that formidable examination system was coming under the control of the Caribbean Examinations Council, to remain an enterprise that protects quality in education but above all tailors the education itself to the realities of the Caribbean region.

The political and economic ties of the West Indies Federation frayed and fell apart. Those of UWI are also badly frayed, but constant mending has thus far kept the bonds from failing. The distances between the St. Augustine campus in Trinidad, the Cave Hill campus in Barbados, and the Mona campus in Jamaica are forbidding. As these island nations and their leaders went their separate political ways, more and more pressures were exerted in the late 1970s and early 1980s to separate various components of the system.

To physical and political distances must be added fiscal distance, for petroleum-rich Trinidad and Tobago has little in common with impoverished Dominica, for example. None of the contributing territories to UWI are wealthy; they long ago yielded their agrarian bounty to British prosperity; some of them are simply unable to contribute their promised quotas to the university. The question then arises over whether their young people shall be allowed to attend the university.

Poverty has another dimension in these West Indian territories and in Guyana. Many argue—and convincingly—that higher education and the reward system of the marketplace push the rich and the poor farther apart, that education is conducive neither to the democratic dream nor to national development in societies left with the less benign remnants of the colonial past. For those who make it out of the cane fields—or who hope that their children will—the dream of education will be pursued.

Guyana's society has long been conspicuously polarized along ethnic lines, between those of African and those of East Indian descent. Not only their different roles in the nineteenth-century economy, but also language, custom, and religion separated them. Their politicians have sought power by emphasizing these differences. For decades education reinforced separateness, but change is evident, if by no other indicator than the list of professors at the University of Guyana: together there are the names of Asian and English/African scholars.

Introduction

The government of recent years has struggled and continues to struggle with the endemic poverty of the region, ideological rigidities, and maintenance of political power. By contrast to the antagonistic role of the university in many Latin American countries vis-à-vis the government, UG's policy generally has been to bend its efforts to contribute to the solution of national problems. There have, however, been some acute episodes of conflict with individual professors who attempted to claim more academic freedom than their government was prepared to grant.

Academicians of both UWI and UG collaborate among themselves and play leadership roles in regional agencies such as UNICA, and in international bodies such as the Association of Commonwealth Universities, headquartered in London. Some years ago an observer described the British Empire as a structure held together by the University of London. There is a grain of truth in this.

The Caribbean universities have forever marked the lives of their graduates and their societies. Further inquiry into the nature of these institutions and their various roles offers some lively prospects for research. So that this bibliography may serve as an introduction to some significant issues, we have tried to offer descriptive and contextual sources. From the affective values of the university experience on individual lives to the effective results in each country or territory, there are both universal and particular questions to be studied in this unique part of the world.

The viewpoints and values manifested since World War II may be distinguished here as elsewhere from those of, say, the late nineteenth century, when a far smaller percentage of children in the Western world had access to education. The uncautious optimism of recent decades concerning universities as agencies for national development can be further chronicled, and vast institutional growth on the basis of such optimism can be viewed in perspective. Or perhaps there are comparisons to be made among different times and places concerning the role of universities and the expectations held out for them.

It is even conceivable that in some societies at least, a swing of the philosophical pendulum might bring a consensus that university education is an end in itself, a good and necessary part of being human, and more affordable than the artifacts of power, even in developing nations. The questions did not end with Socrates.

September, 1983   Barbara Ashton Waggoner
Lawrence, Kansas   George R. Waggoner

Country Codes

COL	Colombia
CoR	Costa Rica
CUB	Cuba
DoR	Dominican Republic
FrA	French Antilles
GEN	General
GUA	Guatemala
GUY	Guyana
HAI	Haiti
HON	Honduras
MEX	Mexico
NeA	Netherlands Antilles
NIC	Nicaragua
PAN	Panama
PRi	Puerto Rico
USV	U.S. Virgin Islands
UWI	University of the West Indies
VEN	Venezuela

Library Codes

ACU   Association of Commonwealth Universities, London.
AzTeS   Arizona State University, Tempe, Arizona.
CaOTU   University of Toronto, Canada.
CuHU   University of Havana, Cuba.
CuSCUC   Univiersidad Central de Santa Clara, Cuba.
DLC   Library of Congress, Washington, D.C.
DOAS   Organization of American States, Columbus Memorial Library, Pan American Union, Washington, D.C.
DPU   Obsolete. See DOAS.
FMU   University of Miami, Coral Gables, Florida.
FTaSU   Florida State University, Tallahassee.
ICarbS   Southern Illinois University, Morris Library, Carbondale, Illinois.
ICIU   University of Illinois, Chicago Circle, Chicago, Illinois.
IU   University of Illinois, Champaign-Urbana, Illinois.
KU   University of Kansas, Lawrence, Kansas.
KWiU   Wichita State University, Wichita, Kansas.
KyU   University of Kentucky, Lexington, Kentucky.
LNHT   Obsolete. See LNT.
LNT   Tulane University, New Orleans, Louisiana.
MexCo   Colegio de México.
MnU   University of Minnesota, Minneapolis.
MoS   St. Louis Public Library, St. Louis, Missouri.
MoSW   Washington University, St. Louis, Missouri.
MoU   University of Missouri, Columbia, Missouri.
NBC   Brooklyn College, New York, New York.
NcU   University of North Carolina, Chapel Hill, North Carolina.
NIC   Cornell University, Ithaca, New York.
NiLU   National University of Nicaragua, Leon.
NmLcU   New Mexico State University, Las Cruces, New Mexico.
NmU   University of New Mexico, Albuquerque, New Mexico.
OASDC   Organization of American States, Office of Education. Washington, D.C.
OSU   Ohio State University, Columbus Ohio.
PPiU   University of Pittsburgh, Pittsburgh, Pennsylvania.
PPT   Temple University, Philadelphia, Pennsylvania.
PrU   University of Puerto Rico, Río Piedras, Puerto Rico.
TxLT   Texas Technological Institute, Lubbock, Texas.
TxU   University of Texas, Austin, Texas.

Library Codes

Uk	British Library.
UkLU-IE	University of London, Institute of Education Library, London, United Kingdom.
WKU	Waggoner Collection, University of Kansas, Lawrence, Kansas.
WMUW	University of Wisconsin, Kenwood Campus, Milwaukee, Wisconsin.
WSU	University of Wisconsin, Superior, Wisconsin.
YUS	Yale University, New Haven, Connecticut.

List of Acronyms

ACHE   Admissions Council for Higher Education. Guyana.
ACU   Association of Commonwealth Universities
ACURIL   Association of Caribbean Universities and Research Institute
           Libraries
AD   Acción Demócratica. Venezuela.
AID   See USAID.
AISFORDOVE Asociación de Instituciones de Formación Docente de
           Venezuela
ANIES   Asociación Nicaragüense de Instituciones de Educación
           Superior
ANUIES   Asociación Nacional de Universidades e Institutos de
           Educación Superior. Mexico.
APICE   Asociación Panamericana de Instituciones de Crédito
           Educativo
APPU   Asociación Puertorriqueña de Profesores Universitarios
ASCUN   Asociación Colombiana de Universidades. Bogota.
AUCA   Agrupación Universitaria Centroamericana
BID   Banco Interamericano de Desarrollo. See IDB.
CAMESA   Centro Ajijic para el Mejoramiento de la Educación Superior
           en América. Mexico.
CDI   Consorcio de Ingenierías e Investigaciones Ltda. Bogota.
CEE   Centro de Estudios Educativos. Mexico.
CEE   Common Entrance Examination
CELAM   Consejo Episcopal Latinoamericano
CENDES   Centro Estudios del Desarrollo. Universidad Central de
           Venezuela
CENIDES   Centro de Información y Documentación Superior
CEPAL   Comisión Económica para América Latina. See ECLA.
CERAG   Centre d'Etudes Régionales Antilles-Guyane
CGCE   See GCE.
CHEAR   Council on Higher Education in the American Republics
CIDOC   Centro Intercultural de Documentación. Cuernavaca, Mexico.
CINDA   Centro Interuniversitario de Desarrollo Andino
CINEP   Centro de Investigación y Educación Popular Colombiano.
           Bogota.
CINTERPLAN Not defined in text. Venezuela.
CIUN   Centro de Investigación de la Universidad del Norte.
           Barranquilla.
CLACSO   Consejo Latino Americano de Ciencias Sociales

Acronyms

CLADES	Consultores Latinoamericanos en Desarrollo y Educación Superior. Venezuela.
CNES	Consejo Nacional de la Educación Superior. Nicaragua.
CNU	Consejo Nacional de Universidades. Venezuela.
CONACYT	Consejo Nacional de Ciencia y Tecnología. Mexico.
CONARE	Consejo Nacional de Rectores. Costa Rica.
CONES	Consejo Nacional de Educación Superior. Dominican Republic.
CONICIT	Consejo Nacional de Investigación, Ciencia y Tecnología. Venezuela.
CONIES	Consejo Nacional de Instituciones de Educación Superior
COPEI	Comité Organizado por Elecciones Independientes. Venezuela.
CORDIPLAN	Oficina Central de Coordinación y Planificación. Venezuela.
COSEC	Coordinating Secretariat of National Union of Students. Leiden.
CRESALC	Centro Regional para la Educación Superior de América Latina y el Caribe. Caracas.
CRI	Caribbean Research Institute. U.S. Virgin Islands.
CRL	Center for Research Libraries
CSA	Caribbean Studies Association
CSUCA	Confederación de Universidades Centroamericanas and Consejo Superior Universitario Centroamericano
CUAG	Centre Universitaire Antilles-Guyane. Guadeloupe and Martinique.
CURLA	Centro Regional de la Costa Atlántica. Honduras.
CXC	Caribbean Examinations Council
DANE	Departamento Administrativo Nacional de Estadísticas. Bogota.
DARNDR	Département d'Agriculture, Ressources Naturelles et Dévelopment Rurale. Haiti.
DEALC	Development and Education in Latin America and the Caribbean
DIPUVEN	Not defined in text. Venezuela.
ECLA	U.N. Economic Commission for Latin America. See CEPAL.
ETS	Educational Testing Service. Princeton, N.J.
FAMV	Faculté d'Agronomie et de Médecine Vétérinaire. Haiti.
FES	Fundación para la Educación Superior. Bogota.
FEU	Federación Estudiantil Universitaria. Cuba.
FEUCA	Federación de Estudiantes Universitarios de Centro América
FUPAC	Federación de Universidades Privadas de Centroamérica y Panamá
GCE	General Certificate of Education
GMA	Gran Mariscal de Ayacucho. Venezuela.
GULERPE	Grupo Universitario Latinoamericano de Estudios para la Reforma y Perfeccionamiento de la Educación
HAPI	Hispanic American Periodical Index
HMSO	His or Her Majesty's Stationery Office
IAPA	Inter-American Press Association
IASEI	Instituto Ajijic Sobre Educación Internacional
ICASE	Instituto Centroamericano de Administración y Supervisión de la Educación
ICCE	Instituto Centroamericano de Crédito Educativo
ICETEX	Instituto Colombiano para Especialización y Estudios Técnicos en el Exterior. Bogota.
ICFES	Instituto Colombiano para el Fomento de Educación Superior. Bogota.
IDB	Inter-american Development Bank. See BID.

Acronyms

IESA	Instituto de Estudios Superiores de Administración. Venezuela.
IGC	Inter-Governmental Council. West Indies.
IIME	Instituto de Investigación y Mejoramiento Educativo. Universidad de San Carlos y Michigan State University
IMF	International Monetary Fund
INPRHU	Instituto de Promoción Humana. Nicaragua.
INTEC	Instituto Tecnológico de Santo Domingo
ISA	Instituto Superior de Agricultura. Dominican Republic.
ITCR	Instituto Tecnológico de Costa Rica
IUC	Inter-University Council for Higher Education Overseas
IVIC	Instituto Venezolano de Investigación Científica
LASA	Latin American Studies Association
LASPAU	Latin American Scholarship Program of American Universities
MAS	Movimiento al Socialismo. Venezuela.
MINEDLAC	Ministers of Education for Latin America and the Caribbean
MSR	Movimiento Socialista Revolucionario
NUFFIC	Netherlands Universities Foundation for International Cooperation.
OAS	Organization of American States. See OEA.
ODECA	Oficina de Educación Centroamericana
OEA	Organización de Estados Americanos. See OAS.
OEI	Oficina de Educación Iberoamericana. Madrid.
OIE	Oficina Internacional de Educación
OPES	Oficina de Planificación de la Educación Superior. Costa Rica.
OPIE	Oficina de Planeamiento Integral de la Educación. Guatemala.
OPLAU	Oficina de Planificación Universitaria. Universidad Autónoma de Santo Domingo, Dominican Republic.
OPSU	Oficina de Planificación Sector Universitario. Venezuela.
OREALC	UNESCO Regional Office for Education in Latin America and the Caribbean
PEP	Proyecto de Educación Profesional
PLANES	Plan Nacional de Educación Superior. Costa Rica.
PLECAT	Programa de Entrenamiento Cooperativo y Ayuda Técnica
PNUD	Programme des Nations Unies pour le Développement
PPA	Programa Nacional de Desarrollo para el Pequeño Agricultor
PREDE	Programa Regional de Desarrollo Educativo. Organización de Estados Americanos, Washington, D.C.
PROVEAS	Profesionales Venezolanos Asociados
ROCAP	Regional Organization for Central America and Panama, USAID
SICAPER	Sistema de Capacitación Permanente y Para el Personal de Supervisión y Dirección en Servicios
SIE	Sistema de Información Sobre Estudiantes
SIECA	Permanent Secretarias of the General treaty for Central American Economic Integration.
SMA	Servicio Militar Activo. Cuba.
UACA	Universidad Autónoma de Centroamérica. Costa Rica.
UAG	Universidad Autónoma de Guadalajara. Mexico.
UASD	Universidad Autónoma de Santo Domingo
UCA	Universidad Centroamericana. Nicaragua.
UCAB	Universidad Católica Andrés Bello. Venezuela.
UCE	Universidad Central del Este. Dominican Republic.
UCMM	Universidad Católica Madre y Maestra. Dominican Republic.
UCR	Universidad de Costa Rica

UCV	Universidad Central de Venezuela
UCWI	University College of West Indies
UDO	Universidad de Oriente. Venezuela.
UDUAL	Unión de Universidades de América Latina
UG	University of Guyana
UGC	University Grants Committee
UIA	Universidad Interamericana. Puerto Rico.
UIE	Unión Insurreccional Revolucionaria
UJCV	Universidad José Cecilio del Valle. Honduras.
UNA	Universidad Nacional Abierta. Venezuela.
UNAH	Universidad Nacional Autónoma de Honduras
UNAM	Universidad Nacional Autónoma de México
UNAN	Universidad Nacional Autónoma de Nicaragua
UNED	Universidad Estatal a Distancia. Costa Rica.
UNESCO	United Nations Educational, Scientific and Cultural Organization
UNET	Undefined in text. Venezuela.
UNH	Universidad Nacional de Heredia. Costa Rica.
UNICA	Association of Caribbean Universities and Research Institutes
UNITAR	United Nations Institute for Training and Research
UNPHU	Universidad Nacional Pedro Henríquez Ureña. Dominican Republic.
UP	Universidad de Panamá
UPOLI	Universidad Politécnica. Nicaragua.
UPR	Universidad de Puerto Rico
URL	Universidad Rafael Landívar. Guatemala.
USAC	Universidad de San Carlos. Guatemala.
USAID	United States Agency for International Development
USB	Universidad Simón Bolívar. Venezuela.
USC	See USAC.
USMA	Universidad Santa María La Antigua. Panama.
UWI	University of the West Indies

Universities: General

GEN
1
The Admission and Academic Placement of Students from the Carib-
bean. A Workshop Report: British Patterned Education, Cuba,
The Dominican Republic, Dutch Patterned Education, the French
West Indies, Haiti, Puerto Rico, the U.S. Virgin Islands. Edited
by Cynthia Fish. San Juan: The North-South Center, National
Association for Foreign Student Affairs, American Association of
Collegiate Registrars and Admissions Officers, 1972. 198 pp.
    Systems diagrammed; special characteristics and quality
factors, required academic credentials, placement recommendations,
bibliographies, sample credentials for each system. AzU

GEN
2
AGUIRRE BELTRAN, GONZALO. Organization and Structure of Latin
American Universities. Washington, D.C.: Pan American Union,
General Secretariat, Organization of American States, 1961. 21
pp.
    Former rector of University of Veracruz, Mexico, reports on
"academic organization within the framework of economic development"
rather than the pedagogical aspects, asserts necessity of treating
education as a component in economic development. Strongly cautions
potential international donors against demanding modifications of university structure to replicate U.S. or European models, citing need for
concomitant changes in Latin American systems and societies which they
themselves must make. History, organization, ideology, social role at
national levels; description of institutional level of patterns, curriculum, professors, administration, financing, autonomy, politics. An
important work, candid and informative. KU

GEN
3
Aid to Education: An Anglo-American Appraisal. Report of a
Ditchley Foundation Conference Held at Ditchley Park 26-29 March
1965. [Oxford?]: Overseas Development Institute in association
with the Ditchley Foundation, 1965. 52 pp.
    British and American programs and policies for aid to Africa,
Asia, the Caribbean. Most significant of the very general remarks of
the meeting: cautionary comments from recipients about their roles and
problems. Foretaste of difficulties ahead. MoU

GEN
4
ALBORNOZ, ORLANDO. "Educación superior y política estudiantil en
América Latina." In Estudiantes y política en las Américas,
edited by Orlando Albornoz, pp. 9-27. Caracas: Publicaciones
del Instituto Societas, 1968.

1

Differences between U.S. and Latin American student activism.
Since 1945 there have been strong student politics in Latin America but
there is no international student movement, beyond mere contacts. The
rigid social structure in most countries makes student movements
difficult. WKU

GEN   ------. Libertad académica y educación superior en América
5   Latina. Caracas: DIPUVEN, 1966. 61 pp.
Examines role of universities in modernization process in
Latin America, taking academic freedom as an indicator. Finds progress
impeded by lack of objectivity and devotion to tradition in academia.
WKU

GEN   ------. "Las universidades norteamericanas y América Latina."
6   La Verdad, 17 March 1970, p. B-3.
Essay describes meeting of educational leaders of hemisphere
discussing U.S. universities' efforts in Latin American university
reform movements. Controversies over role of U.S. foundations and
government, cultural penetration; resistance to change for ideological
and personal reasons. Proposes systematic study by Latin Americans of
North American culture and values.

GEN   ALCALA, V.O. A Bibliography of Education in the Caribbean.
7   Port-of-Spain, Trinidad: Caribbean Commission, 1959. 144 pp.
Over ninety entries for Puerto Rico and the U.S. Virgin
Islands and forty-plus for remainder of the English-speaking Caribbean,
under heading of "Higher Education." UkLU-IE

GEN   ALLARD, RAUL. Education, Training and Human Resources. Document
8   presented in the Meeting on Science, Human Resources and Quality
of Life, Quito, 22-26 April 1981, Aspen Institute for Humanistic
Studies. [Washington, D.C.: OAS], 1981. 34 pp. plus 3 pages
appendix and notes.
Director of Department of Educational Affairs of OAS notes
changes from faith of 1950s and 1960s in education as an investment in
development in Latin America to concept of "development centering on
man." Consequences of population increase and urbanization; some
trends in higher education, e.g., decentralization and diversification.
Efforts to relate education with work, productivity studies ("social
rate of return" over twice as great for basics as for higher education). OAS contributions given in aggregate; activities of IDB in
university modernization in 1960s, early 1970s and policy changes;
UNESCO and World Bank policies. General conclusions. WKU

GEN   ------. "La universidad y el desarrollo social." Caribbean
9   Education Bulletin 5, no. 3 (September 1978): 1-6.
In address to meeting of UNICA, director of educational
affairs describes various multinational programs: educational technology, adult education, curriculum improvement, planning, research.
Lists difficult social questions affecting universities, need for
collaboration.

GEN   ALTBACH, PHILIP G. and KELLY, DAVID H. Higher Education in De-
10   veloping Nations: A Selected Bibliography, 1969-1974. New York:
Praeger, 1975. 229 pp.

Universities: General

An excellent work, from the insights of its introduction to
the variety of sources from which the entries are drawn. Arranged by
countries. Suggestions for research in eleven significant areas. KU

GEN   AMÉRICA LATINA 11, no. 2 (April-June 1968). 150 pp.
11   Entire issue devoted to "Second Meeting of Centers and Institutes of Research on Development and Constitutive Documents of the
Latin American Council of the Social Sciences." Top social scientists
in Latin America take important steps toward regional independence and
cooperation. Some centers are within universities.

GEN   AMERICAN ASSOCIATION OF COLLEGIATE REGISTRARS AND ADMISSIONS
12   OFFICERS, Foreign Student Committee. Caribbean: A Guide to the
      Academic Placement of Students from European Affiliated Areas of
      the Caribbean in Educational Institutions in the U.S.A., 1961.
      World Education Series. [n.p.], 1961. 9 pp.
          Document to be used with U.S. Office of Education Bulletins.
Covers British, Netherlands, French affiliated areas. NcD

      THE AMERICAN UNIVERSITY OF THE CARIBBEAN. School of Medicine.
      See entry UWI 1.

GEN   ANTONINI, GUSTAVO A. "Programa de desarrollo rural integrado
13   para la región del Caribe." Caribbean Educational Bulletin 5,
      no. 3 (September 1978): 15-39.
          Coordinator describes effort by UNICA for collaboration of
universities and the public sector to implement socioeconomic changes
in small and medium sectors of agriculture. Nutritional insufficiencies and poor agricultural production and distribution major problems
of Caribbean. Pilot project: applied research with help of UWI in
English-speaking regions and UCMM in Spanish-speaking area. Notes
differences among islands in farming practices and attitudes deriving
from their different colonial pasts.

GEN   ------, and YORK, MASON A. "Integrated Rural Development and the
14   Role of the University in the Caribbean: The Case of Plan
      Sierra, Dominican Republic." Caribbean Educational Bulletin 7,
      no. 3 (September 1980): 15-33.
          Plan for focusing university attention on rural problems,
with interdisciplinary cooperation. Pilot program in Dominican Republic encouraged by UNICA.

GEN   "La Asociación de Universidades e Institutos de Investigación del
15   Caribe concretó un convenio con la Secretaría de Agricultura de
      la República Dominicana." Universidades 77 (July-September
      1979): 861-62.
          Agreement, in collaboration with some fifty area insti-
tutions, including University of Florida, to train Dominican specialists in agricultural engineering graduate work during next three years.
See entry GEN 16.

GEN   ASSOCIATION OF CARIBBEAN UNIVERSITIES AND RESEARCH INSTITUTES
16   (UNICA). Borrador del acuerdo para la implementación del "Pro-
      grama de Entrenamiento Cooperativo y Ayuda Técnica" (Programa
      PLECAT), Gobierno de la República Dominicana, Asociación de Uni-

versidades e Institutos de Investigación del Caribe, Universidad de la Florida. Gustavo A. Antonini, coordinator. San Juan:
UNICA, 1977. 9 leaves.
    Agreement among institutions for programs in rural
development to help improve conditions for poorest members of agricultural sector; components include education, applied research, technical assistance. Graduate degree plans require focus on problems,
interdisciplinary approach. Budget, model of degree program. WKU

GEN   ------. Caribbean Development and Caribbean Universities: Steps
17   for Survival. San Juan: UNICA, 1980. 6 leaves.
    Description of forty-five member institution with 350,000
students and 30,000 faculty members, its activities and finance. Creation of UNICA Foundation, with president of University of Miami as its
chief officer. WKU

GEN   ------. Desarrollo social a través de la comunicación en el
18   Caribe: Reporte de las actividades de UNICA patrocinadas por la
       Fundación Inter-Americana, marzo 1976-abril 1977. Gustavo A.
       Antonini, director. San Juan: UNICA, 1977. 12 leaves.
    Universities contributed to study of region's population
policies; most territories lack them. Seminar on new world thought,
various publishing and documentation efforts. Several workshops for
people from sixteen countries. WKU

GEN   ------. The Food Supply and The Caribbean Universities. Papers
19   presented at UNICA IV, Santo Domingo, 1975. [San Juan]: UNICA,
       1975. 51 pp.
    Sir Philip Sherlock, UNICA secretary-general, in intro-
duction, calls hunger "the greatest single threat to the stability of a
number of Caribbean countries." Causes rooted in systems based on
production for export, need to import basic goods, population growth,
other factors. Papers put problem in world and Caribbean perspectives.
Proposal to offer consultations by specialists through UNICA. WKU

GEN   ------. UNICA. [Kingston]: UNICA, 1976. 6 pp.
20   Begun in 1966 to foster contact and collaboration among all
regional universities. UNICA has forty-five member institutions.
Projects include education technology, teacher education, Caribbean
management studies, social development. WKU

GEN   ------, Educational Technology Project. Directory of Available
21   Resources. Directorio de recursos existentes. [Bogotá]: UNICA,
       Educational Technology Project, [1975]. 54 leaves.
    Directory of available resources; people with knowledge in
educational technology and the variety of equipment available. UkLACU

       THE ASSOCIATION OF COMMONWEALTH UNIVERSITIES. Universities
       Facing the Challenge of the Eighties. See entry UWI 4.

GEN   ATCON, RUDOLPH P. "La educación superior, el PREDE y la OEA."
22   La Educación: Revista Interamericana de Desarrollo Educativo 23,
       no. 81 (1979): 39-72.
    As an activity of the Regional Program for Educational
Development (PREDE) and the Organization of American States (OEA), a

procedure and philosophical framework are developed by OEA specialist in higher education. Résumé of PREDE activities since 1961. Components necessary to achieve model university organization to be spelled out in its master plan.

GEN ------. The Latin American University, La Universidad Latino
23 Americana. Bogotá: ECO, Revista de la Cultura de Occidente, 1966. 160 pp.

Interleaved, English and Spanish. Specific plans for coordination—economic, social and educational—for the Latin American university. Advocates general studies for all, integration, consultants' services, completely consolidated autonomy, political neutrality. Atcon would eliminate the power of the cátedra, adopt the semester system, eliminate "repeat" examinations; advocates centralization in university administration and a British style of budgeting. WKU

GEN ------. A UNICA/OAS Management Survey of Twenty-three Caribbean
24 Universities. [Washington, D.C.]: OAS, 1978. 190 pp.

Categories studied: decision-making, institutional orientation, academic control, research management, student assistance, university extension, service coordination-management. Areas: Caribbean South America, Dominican Republic, Puerto Rico, French-, Dutch-, English-speaking universities. Although study "avoids personal opinions or valuations" its author notes, in observing theory and practice at Venezuela's Universidad de Oriente, "...human nature itself transforms [ideal systems] with a certain rapidity into something less than efficient, into something much more complex, slow and costly than was expected." Study carried out in 1975. WKU

BACCHUS, M. KASSIM. Education for Development or Under-development? Guyana's Educational System and Its Implications for the Third World. See entry GUY 4.

BANCO INTERAMERICANO DE DESARROLLO. See INTER-AMERICAN DEVELOPMENT BANK.

GEN BARAHONA RIERA, FRANCISCO. "The University for Peace." Paper
25 presented at the VI Triennial Meeting of the International Association of University Presidents, San José, 28 June-3 July 1981. Mimeographed. San José: International Commission on the University for Peace (UN) and Presidential Commission on the University for Peace (Costa Rica), [1981]. 6 pp.

Costa Rica donated land and President Rodrigo Carazo presented proposal for University for Peace to the United Nations in 1978. In 1980 UN General Assembly resolved to create a postgraduate agency, to be financed by voluntary contributions, which will concentrate initially on seven academic areas of study and research. Agreement will be signed by university and Costa Rican government, giving university its status as an international organization. WKU

GEN BATISTA DEL VILLAR, BOLIVAR. Papel de las universidades latino-
26 americanas en la integración regional; ponencia presentada en el VI Congreso Interamericano de Planificación celebrado en Caracas del 6 al 12 de noviembre de 1966. [Santo Domingo: Universidad Autónoma de Santo Domingo, 1966]. 9 pp.

Typical paper concerning the need for regional and Latin American integration; proposes that in each university there be at least one course in integration in the faculties of economics, politics, and law; that some specialists be created in Latin America; and creation of some interdisciplinary institutes. TxU

GEN   BENITEZ, JAIME. Crisis en el mundo y en la educación, and
27   SHERLOCK, PHILIP. La Asociación de Universidades del Caribe.
      [Río Piedras]: Presidencia de la Universidad de Puerto Rico,
      [1969]. 31 pp. Includes English translation.
          Opening address by president of University of Puerto Rico at
Second Conference of the Universities of the Caribbean, November 1968.
Twenty-nine institutions from fourteen countries attended. Sir Philip
Sherlock, University of the West Indies, sets forth needs, goals,
structure of the Association of Caribbean Universities. FMU

GEN   BENJAMIN, HAROLD R. W. Higher Education in the American Re-
28   publics. New York: McGraw-Hill, 1965. 224 pp.
          Introductory work includes sections on Caribbean and Central
American universities. KU

GEN   Bibliografía Selectiva sobre Educación Superior en América Latina
29   y el Caribe. Selective Bibliography on Higher Education in Latin
      America and the Caribbean region. Bibliographie Selective de
      l'Education Supérieure dans l'Amerique Latine et les Caraibes.
      Caracas: CRESALC-UNESCO. 1981. 155 pp.
          CRESALC director Enrique Oteiza, supervised compilations,
which reflects concerns, chiefly about universities, related to growth,
change in 1960s and 1970s. Selections, mostly by well known Latin
American writers; books, periodicals, newspapers focus on structure,
policies, organization, research and evaluation, the social context of
higher education. CRESALC and OPSU in Caracas, ICFES in Bogota, and
the Colegio de Mexico have most of the works listed. OSU

GEN   BRANA-SHUTE, GARY. "Social Development Through Communications:
30   A Progress Report on UNICA-Related Activities in the Caribbean."
      Boletín de Estudios Latinoamericanos y del Caribe, no. 22 (June
      1977): 127-30.
          Brief discussion of the purposes and goals of UNICA (Associ-
ation of Caribbean Universities and Research Institutions). Stresses
that universities should serve the needs of their own societies, and
the best means is by cooperation and communication among Caribbean
universities.

GEN   BREUER, SENTA ESSENFELD DE. "Reflexiones doctrinarias en torno a
31   los asuntos estudiantiles." Universitas 2000 4, nos. 2-3 (1980):
      33-52.
          Physical, social, emotional development of student has not
been seen as proper goal of education, hence the sorry state of student
services. Educators give lip service to humane values but concentrate
on purely intellectual and technical tasks. Exaltation of specialization and technological tyranny have failed to produce people who are
creative, flexible, sensitive and socially responsible. Sharp comments
on views of humanist-behaviorist polemic, the myth of neutrality in
counseling. Raises some key philosophical issues.

GEN   BRODERSOHN, MARIO, and SANJURJO, MARIA ESTER, Comps. <u>Financia-</u>
32   <u>miento de la educación en América Latina</u>. México: Fondo de Cul-
      tura Económica, Banco Interamericano de Desarrollo, 1978. 654
      pp.
            Papers from Seminar on Financing Higher Education in Latin
America, November 15-19, 1976, at the Inter-American Development Bank in
Washington. Useful data in introductory chapter by compilers, and
analysis of topic by economist Victor Urquidi in second chapter.
Papers and comment on various aspects of financing higher education in
Latin America include charts comparing expenditures and other indi-
cators for Central America and the Caribbean with other regions. WKU

GEN   BUCHANAN, KEITH. <u>Reflections on Education in the Third World</u>.
33   Nottingham: The Bertrand Russell Peace Foundation, for Spokesman
      Books, 1975. 80 pp.
            "We have compared the educational model presented by the
white north to the nations of the Third World to the proverbial white
elephant, the gift of which ruined the recipient..." Attacks transplanted schooling system as self-serving and exploitative, widening
"the gap between elites and masses and between the affluent and prole-
tarian nations." Supporting data. Alternative: non-school education.
UkLU-IE

GEN   BYL'SKAIA, M. I. "Students in the Liberation Struggle of the
34   Peoples of Latin America." In <u>Contemporary Latin America: A</u>
      <u>Documented History, 1960-1968</u>, compiled and translated by J.
      Gregory Oswald, pp. 64-67. Austin: University of Texas Press,
      1970.
            Emphasis on "special position in socio-political life" of
Latin American public universities, not only in education but in intellectual and political leadership. Students seen in vanguard, with
workers, of university reform as part of class struggle. Reform movement of Cordoba, Argentina, in 1918 affected all Latin American universities, including those in Caribbean, and author contends autonomy
gave right to "voice social demands." Examples of political activism,
especially in Venezuela's Central University. Advocates Marxist-
Leninist revolutionary activity. WKU

GEN   "Calendario de reuniones que auspiciará el CSUCA en 1964." <u>Uni-</u>
35   <u>versidades</u>, no. 14-15 (November 1963-March 1964): 64.
            Typical of the active role of CSUCA in promoting communi-
cation and increased professionalization in Central American universities is this list of meetings: the Central American Institute of
Comparative Law; the Central American commission on General Studies (in
the University of Kansas); professors of public administration, social
sciences, philosophy, chemistry, pharmacy; university librarians.

GEN   CARDONA, MARIA ELENA ARGÜELLO DE. "Asociación de Bibliotecas
36   Universitarias y de Investigación del Caribe, ACURIL: Extracto
      del informe de la presidenta presentado a la VII Conferencia de
      ACURIL." <u>Caribbean Educational Bulletin</u> 3, no. 2 (May 1976):
      43-51.
            Meeting of university librarians in Curaçao, September 1975,
reported by president, shows efforts to develop regional professional
training with Canadian help; six years of organization have produced
working committees and communication in spite of difficulties.

GEN   "Caribbean Education Needs." <u>Development Newsletter</u> 3, no. 6
37   (June 1980): 4.
         Vice-dean of University of the West Indies reports to Organ-
ization of American States meeting in Panama, urging "an enlightened
policy toward Creole languages," and increased emphasis on teaching
Spanish, Portuguese, French and Dutch in English-speaking nations.
Implications for higher education in broadening potential student pool
for those now eliminated from system by their speech patterns, and
increased needs for UWI graduates in humanities, social sciences, and
education.

GEN   CARNOY, MARTIN; LOBO, JOSE; TOLEDO, ALEJANDRO; and VELLOSO,
38   JACQUES. <u>Can Educational Policy Equalise Income Distribution in
       Latin America</u>? Westmead, England: Saxon House for the Inter-
       national Labour Office, 1979. 110 pp.
         Empirical studies in Brazil, Peru, Mexico as part of World
Employment Program of the ILO examine role of schooling as it relates
to equity of income distribution, a goal of the developmental thrust of
the sixties. Recent evidence indicates doubt that increased level of
schooling of the population will automatically lead to increased economic growth, more equal income distribution, and greater social mobility. Schooling may perform a "screening function" which is
partially independent of any actual contributions to workers'
productivity. KU

GEN   <u>Carreras universitarias: Títulos que otorgan las instituciones
39   latinoamericanas de enseñanza superior</u>. Vol. 1: <u>México,
       Guatemala, El Salvador, Honduras, Nicaragua, Costa Rica, Panamá,
       Haití , República Dominicana</u>. Washington, D.C.: Unión
       Panamericana, 1962. 67 pp.
         Data on university careers available in these countries.
Includes lists of institutions, data on their academic years, and on
all programs by discipline. LU

GEN   <u>Carreras universitarias: Títulos que otorgan las instituciones
40   latinoamericanas de enseñanza superior</u>. Vol. 2: <u>Bolivia,
       Colombia, Ecuador, Perú, Venezuela</u>. Washington, D.C.: Unión
       Panamericana, 1962. 81 pp.
         Data on university centers in the Andean region and Colombia
and Venezuela in the Caribbean. Aspects of higher education: lists of
institutions, data on academic years, and on all programs by
discipline. LU

GEN   CARRINGTON, LAURENCE D. <u>Education and Development in the
41   English-Speaking Caribbean: a Contemporary Survey</u>. Introduction
       by Germán W. Rama. DEALC, no. 16. Buenos Aires: Economic
       Commission for Latin America, 1978. 127 pp.
         Part of ECLA project on Development and Education in Latin
America and the Caribbean. Available data show lack of coherence
between societal goals and educational structure, with continued social
stratification and inadequate or inappropriate educative output. Short
section on UWI and the University of Guyana shows problems derived from
historical roots, contemporary regional politics, and economic woes.
Both educational and developmental planning have been carried out in
the region without an adequate philosophical base. Progress is

measureable "by reference to a past rather than to a future." Useful
charts, good bibliography. FMU

CASAS ARMENGOL, MIGUEL. "La UNA, experiencia a considerar en la
planificación de un sistema de educación abierta y a distancia
para el Caribe." See entry VEN 33.

GEN CASTILLO MONTALVO, ROLANDO. "Políticas de población de América
42 Latina." Universidades, no. 76 (April-June 1979): 367-78.
Dean of Faculty of Medical Science at University of San
Carlos, Guatemala, speaks on birth control policies at UDUAL's XI
Conference of Faculties and Schools of Medicine of Latin America.
Outlines developed, capitalist states' Malthusian point of view and
their efforts to impose limiting births in less developed nations.
Describes socialist view on better availability of resources with
restructured societies. Opts for national sovereignty in policy making
and resistance to U.S. pressure; overpopulation not cause of underdevelopment but "social relations of production."

GEN CATHOLIC CHURCH, Consejo Episcopal Latinoamericano (CELAM), De-
43 partamento de Educación. Universidad católica hoy: seminario de
expertos sobre la misión de la universidad católica en América
Latina, 12 al 18 de febrero de 1967. Bogotá: Departamento de
Educación, CELAM, 1967. 278 pp.
Important seminars were held in the sixties to address
mission of Catholic universities. Among proposed reforms: improve
planning and evaluation; seek more full-time professors; strengthen
research; improve social sciences, mathematics and education; improve
university governance with broader participation; make access possible
for less favored students; coordinate functions with other
universities. KU

GEN CENTER FOR RESEARCH LIBRARIES (CRL). Latin American and Carib-
44 bean Research Materials Available from the Center for Research
Libraries. Chicago: CRL, 1978. 18 pp.
Titles in microform and hard copy collections. Especially
valuable for newspaper collections. TxArU

GEN "Certamen sobre la mejor tesis de grado centroamericana."
45 Noticias del CSUCA 3, no. 7 (June 1966): 2-3.
The CSUCA prize is established, rules given for competition
in several academic areas and method of jury selection. Prize: a gold
medal and a five-day visit to all the Central American universities.

GEN COMITAS, LAMBROS. The Complete Caribbeana 1900-1975: A Bibli-
46 ographic Guide to the Scholarly Literature. Vol. 2: Institutions. Millwood, N.Y.: KTO Press, 1977.
Majority of 627 items in Chapter 32, "Education," pertain to
non-university education in Surinam, French Guiana, Guyana, Belize, the
Bahamas, Bermuda, and the scores of inhabited islands of the Antillean
archipelago except Haiti, Cuba, Puerto Rico, and the Dominican Republic. KU

GEN "Comunicado del Dr. Eustaquio Remedios de los Cuetos." Gaceta
47 UDUAL, no. 41 (February 1981): 4.

Rector of University of Havana writes secretary general of
UDUAL to protest denial of visa by government of Dominican Republic to
Cuban dean to attend a UDUAL-sponsored meeting of faculties of eco-
nomics and social sciences of Latin America. Dean of Autonomous Uni-
versity of Santo Domingo faculty had issued invitation during visit to
Havana to UDUAL member institution. Secretary general hopes govern-
ments will not interfere with freedom of expression basic to Latin
American cultural integration.

CONFEDERACION UNIVERSITARIA CENTROAMERICANA (CSUCA). See CONSEJO
SUPERIOR UNIVERSITARIO CENTROAMERICANO (CSUCA).

GEN   "La Confederación Universitaria Centroamericana (CSUCA) prepara
48   sistema de cooperación universitaria para la reconstrucción de
      Nicaragua." Universidades, no. 77 (July-September 1979): 804-5.
      Central American Confederation of Universities approves five
agreements to help rebuild Nicaragua, including campaign for professors
and other university employees in the region to donate one day's
salary. Sixth agreement denounces "direct and indirect North American
intervention, carried out through Israel, . . ." in Nicaragua.

GEN   Confederación Universitaria Centroamericana, 1948-1973. [Ciudad
49   Universitaria Rodrigo Facio: CSUCA, Secretaría General, 1973?].
      102 pp.
      At 1948 beginning of Confederation the five national uni-
versities had fewer than 6,000 students; now there are 75,000. Stages
of development of CSUCA with beginning of regional cooperation; progress toward regional faculties; enrollments, graduates. Establishment
of permanent secretariat in 1959. National and international pressures
on universities, military intervention in El Salvador's national university, an earthquake in Managua; but activity continues. A key
document. WKU

GEN   CONSEJO SUPERIOR UNIVERSITARIO CENTROAMERICANO (CSUCA). Actas de
50   la Cuarta Reunión de la Comisión Centroamericana en pro de los
      Estudios Generales. (Kansas, Estados Unidos - 8 al 12 de junio
      de 1964). Ciudad Universitaria Rodrigo Facio: CSUCA, 1964. 49
      pp.
      Representatives of five Central American universities study
and discuss organization of U.S. arts and sciences, departmentalization, honors programs, the teaching career at the University of
Kansas. KU

GEN   ------. Actas de la IX reunión ordinaria del Consejo Superior
51   Universitario Centroamericano. Ciudad Universitaria Rodrigo
      Facio: CSUCA, 1965. 83 pp.
      Need stressed for progress in comparative law, to solve
problems of Central American Common Market. Discussion of various
other research entities and policy questions, e.g. in social sciences,
and medicine, and financing projects. Question of rotating secretariat
to various countries to be investigated. Much discussion about preparing professors in basic disciplines, foreign universities, UNESCO
projects, and relationship with ROCAP. WKU

GEN   ------. Actas de la Quinta reunión ordinaria celebrada en San
52   Salvador del 20 al 26 de junio de 1960. San Salvador: Editorial
       Universitaria, 1960. 236 pp.
          Nearly 100 representatives, including observers from the
Universidad de Panamá, met to work on the unification of educational
systems of Central American universities and coordination of effort.
Welcoming speech by rector of the Universidad de El Salvador is
passionate in decrying "democratic immaturity of our people," denouncing
repressive governments which threaten universities for speaking up
against injustice and illegality. Other speeches are strong in calls for
unity, as are resolutions agreed upon. WKU

GEN   ------. Actas de la segunda reunión extraordinaria, celebrada en
53   San José, Costa Rica del 22 al 23 de junio de 1961. San Sal-
       vador: Editorial Universitaria de El Salvador, 1962. 135 pp.
          Work documents discussed: project of agreement of the
Central American universities for the regional integration of Central
American higher education; project of agreement of the Central American
universities for the development of exchange of professors,
researchers, students, graduates and administrative personnel;
recommendations of the technical commission regarding establishment of
General Studies; minimum requirements to be fulfilled by a professional
school preparing to establish graduate courses; recommendations for a
plan of integration, on a regional scale, of higher education based on
evaluations presented by the universities; recommendations for the
unification of titles and degrees awarded by Central American universities; recommendations regarding specialization of journals published by
the universities; study of criteria which should govern formulation of
general laws of private universities; resolution to link plans of
integration of higher education with project of the Committee of Economic Cooperation of the Isthmus for the formation of industrial
professionals. WKU

GEN   ------. Actas de la VI Reunión Ordinaria y de la III Reunión
54   Extraordinaria. Ciudad Universitaria Rodrigo Facio: CSUCA,
       1962. 60 pp.
          Regular meeting was held in Guatemala in December 1961 and
special meeting in Costa Rica in September 1962. Plan for Regional
Integration approved by all university consejos, but with some changes
proposed by UCR and USC, is discussed in some detail. Plans for CSUCA
secretariat for 1962-63 agreed upon; a coordinating commission for
Regional Integration Plan is created. Special meeting heard recommendations of this commission and reached accords on designating as
regional faculties those of Veterinary Medicine at San Carlos and
Microbiology at Costa Rica. Other related decisions were made. WKU

GEN   ------. Actas y resoluciones de la VIII reunión ordinaria.
55   Ciudad Universitaria Rodrigo Facio: CSUCA, 1964. 121 pp.
          Meeting in Tegucigalpa addressed by UNAH rector, who lists
problems: demand growing with demographic increases, inadequate
secondary school preparation, "vocationally disoriented" adolescents,
urgent need for General Studies. Business includes discussion of
contracts with foreign universities for research and need for safe-
guards, improving legal education; approval for statutes of the Central
American Medical Association; role of IIME in improving teacher

11

education. Revealing documents for understanding institutional and regional problems and anxieties. WKU

GEN ------. Acuerdos: II Reunión ordinaria del Consejo Superior
56 Universitario Centroamericano, Panamá, Panamá 18-19 noviembre de 1977, Documentos. [Ciudad Universitaria Rodrigo Facio]: CSUCA Secretaría Permanente, [1977?]. [110] pp.
Agreements approved include financial matters, strengthening student movement, development of social sciences, library collections of Central American materials, seminars on language and literature, research on human fertility, CSUCA publishing house EDUCA. Resolution backing National Autonomous University of Nicaragua in demands that Somoza government set free members of university community imprisoned for political reasons. Letter to President of United States backing Panama's need for solution to canal problem. WKU

GEN ------. Acuerdos, período 1978: V Reunión ordinaria, Consejo
57 Superior Universitario Centroamericano, San José, Costa Rica, noviembre 1978, Documentos. San José: CSUCA, Secretaría Permanente, 1978.
Resolutions of the fifth regular meeting of the Higher Council of Central American Universities (CSUCA), several of which are in response to governmental interference in university affairs in Guatemala and El Salvador. Report of staff activities, financial information on CSUCA. WKU

GEN ------. Acuerdos: III reunión extraordinaria del comité direc-
58 tivo de la Confederación Universitaria Centroamericana, 28 de Abril de 1973. Ciudad Rodrigo Facio: CSUCA, Secretaría Permanente, 1973. 12 leaves.
Rectors and student federation representatives from five universities meet with CSUCA staff, confront CSUCA's financial difficulties. Agreements on student matters, UNESCO cooperation; petition government of Nicaragua for university funds; condemnation of USAID for unauthorized (by CSUCA) contract with law school at University of Costa Rica and other maneuvers; resignation of CSUCA Secretary General Sergio Ramírez M.

GEN ------. Bases fundamentales de la organización del Consejo
59 Superior Universitario Centroamericano. Ciudad Universitaria Rodrigo Facio: Secretaría Permanente del CSUCA, 1963. 37 pp.
Council of rectors of five national universities of Central America ratify their by-laws, replacing ones of 1949, and leaving open access to membership in CSUCA by National University of Panama. KU

GEN ------. Boletín 2, no. 2 (January-March 1977). 45 pp.
60 Meetings, seminars related to human rights violations, Central American university student movement, social sciences, graduate studies in economics, university legislation, weed control, Central American history, agricultural and industrial workers, philosophy, Central American integration have been planned or held. Research on health of banana workers, economic and social development from Independence to 1930, urbanization are among the topics reported.

GEN ------. <u>Boletín</u> 2, no. 3 (April-June 1977). 45 pp.
61   University of Panama reintegrated in CSUCA, after suspension
during government intervention in its affairs; National University of
Costa Rica (Heredia) becomes new member and CSUCA makes plea to Costa
Rican government to finance its second semester of the year. Expression of solidarity with Autonomous University of Santo Domingo
against President Balaguer's intervention. Protest assassinations of
professor and former dean of law school at San Carlos University,
Guatemala. Announce seminars on child development and other topics.

GEN ------. <u>Boletín</u> 2, no. 4 (July-September 1977). 25 pp.
62   CSUCA signs agreement with SIECA, the Permanent Treaty of
Central American Economic Integration organization, to carry out joint
activities and programs related to regional development. Links also
with CLACSO, Latin American Council of Social Sciences. Seminars,
student affairs.

GEN ------. <u>Carta Informativa</u>, October 1978. 8 pp.
63   Celebration of the thirtieth anniversary of CSUCA in San José
includes approval of resolution condemning Somoza, supporting fight
against him, demanding respect for university autonomy, rejecting outside interference, including that of the U.S., in Nicaragua. Other
news of regional university development, e.g., accord between Universities of Panama and Havana.

GEN ------. <u>Carta Informativa</u>, November 1978. 16 pp.
64   Bulletin carries news of Guatemalan police assassination of
university student leader, with denunciation from Central American
university officials. CSUCA censures Somoza government's cutting
budget of Nicaragua's National University, reports "crimes" by government security forces in the University of El Salvador, and pays homage
to a Nicaraguan professor and former CSUCA staff member who died
fighting against Somoza.

GEN ------. <u>Carta Informativa</u>, January 1979. 16 pp.
65   Celebration of thirty-fourth anniversary of the winning of
autonomy of the Universidad de San Carlos de Guatemala, along with
description of invasion of campus of the Universidad Autónoma de
Nicaragua by the national guard and failure of the government to give
the money legally due the university. Also other regional university
news.

GEN ------. <u>Catalogo de centros regionales de enseñanza (niveles</u>
66   <u>pre- y post-grado) 1968-1969</u>. Ciudad Universitaria Rodrigo
      Facio: CSUCA Secretaría Permanente, 1969. 98 pp.
      The designation of regional centers was a major goal of the
Central American universities under the CSUCA Plan of Integration of
Higher Education. San Carlos University had the regional faculties of
sanitary engineering and veterinary medicine; Costa Rica was the center
for schools of chemistry, geology and microbiology. For each entity:
its history, organization, physical plant, course of study, course
descriptions, admissions requirements, degrees, professors. ROCAP and
AID helped finance data gathering for this volume. WKU

GEN   ------. Catálogo de estudios de las universidades nacionales de
67   Centroamérica, 1967-1968. San José: CSUCA, Secretaría Perma-
       nente, 1968. 399 pp.
          History, goals, administration, academic organization, en-
       trance requirements, student services, physical plant and laboratories,
       extension, student life, research, programs of study of the six
       national universities of Central America. KU

GEN   ------. Discursos, actas y resoluciones de la VII Reunión
68   Ordinaria. Ciudad Universitaria Rodrigo Facio: CSUCA, 1963. 94
       pp.
          Speeches by President of Costa Rica and rectors of the Uni-
       versidad de San Carlos de Guatemala and Universidad de Costa Rica, at
       opening of Seventh Regular Meeting of CSUCA, deplore past divisiveness,
       and praise CSUCA for its unifying force in Central America. General
       Studies lauded for its reforms in academia. Meeting on relationships
       among member institutions and between them and government. Universidad
       de Honduras will be seat of Central American Institute of Comparative
       Law; mechanisms for library exchanges decided; sports program, to
       include Panamá, is to be promoted; other important decisions made. WKU

GEN   ------. Discursos de la IX Reunión Ordinaria del CSUCA
69   pronunciados por los señores rectores de las universidades de
       Honduras y de Nicaragua. Ciudad Universitaria Rodrigo Facio:
       CSUCA, 1965. 20 pp.
          Rector Arturo Quesada of the Universidad Nacional Autónoma de
       Honduras passes on presidency of CSUCA to Rector Carlos Tünnermann
       Bernheim of the Universidad Nacional de Nicaragua in a ceremony in
       Leon, Nicaragua. Tünnermann has resigned CSUCA secretariat post and
       been elected rector of UNAN following death of Mariano Fiallos Gil.
       Some CSUCA accomplishment of past five years noted, plus UNAN's
       achievement of autonomy and a guaranteed income from the government.
       Historical links with university in Leon among 19th Century university
       founders in Central America recalled. WKU

GEN   ------. Encuesta sobre demanda de personal calificado en
70   Centroamérica. Estudio de Recursos Humanos en Centroamérica, no.
       7. Ciudad Universitaria, Costa Rica: CSUCA, 1966. 234 pp.
          Manpower studies, popularized by Frederick Harbison, were
       popular educational planning tools of the period. He and others,
       financed by the Ford Foundation, USAID and ROCAP, worked with national
       agencies and university statisticians to provide a diagnostic of public
       and private employment characteristics of 1962 and 1963. Data
       gathering and processing were difficult. Demand estimates to 1972
       made. In occupations normally requiring university education only some
       20 to 30 percent of employees have it; lack of education is conspicuous
       at all levels, but also there is no positive correlation between edu-
       cational level and productivity in higher level occupations. WKU

GEN   ------. "La Escuela de Estudios Generales y la Reforma Uni-
71   versitaria." In Primera reunión de la Comisión Centro-
       americana Pro-Estudios Generales. Ciudad Universitaria Rodrigo
       Facio Brenes (28-29 y 30 de Junio), pp. 37-43. Ciudad Universi-
       taria Rodrigo Facio: CSUCA, 1961.

Universities: General

In 1960 all five national universities had recommended establishment of General Studies, through CSUCA, as part of the Regional Integration Plan for Central American Higher Education. True institutional reform in structure and instruction is necessary to improve productivity and reduce failures. Plans of study, professors, students, economic problems, legislation, physical facilities are questions addressed. WKU

GEN 72 ------. *Estadísticas universitarias centroamericanas*. San José: CSUCA, 1978. 64 pp.
Data, mostly from 1970 to 1977, about Central American university enrollments by disciplines; graduates by career and years. University budgets and their relation to national budgets. WKU

GEN 73 ------. *Informe de labores de la Secretaría General, Período 1977*. II Reunión ordinaria del Consejo Superior Universitario Centroamericano, Panamá, Panamá 18-19 de noviembre de 1977: Documentos. [Ciudad Universitaria Rodrigo Facio]: CSUCA, Secretaría Permanente, 1977. 173 pp.
Activities of the secretariat, programs of health sciences and cultural affairs, publishing, student affairs. WKU

GEN 74 ------. *Lista de profesores de las universidades centroamericanas*. Ciudad Universitaria Rodrigo Facio, 1968. 288 pp.
Names, disciplines, educational background (for most) of some 2,500 professors; listed alphabetically, by faculties within each of the six public universities. Some are classified as full- or part-time, but pattern is not uniform. WKU

GEN 75 ------. *Memoria de la Primera Mesa Redonda Centroamericana de Derecho Penal (Tegucigalpa, 27 al 30 de abril de 1960)*. San Salvador: Editorial Universitaria, 1961. 446 pp.
Secretary general of CSUCA, Carlos Tünnermann Bernheim, speaks in the prologue of the "deplorable situation" of penal law, especially in the application of punishment. Meeting documents give panorama of "our repressive law," and present concrete proposals for reforms by the various governments. WKU

GEN 76 ------. *Memoria de la Primera Mesa Redonda Centroamericana de Educación Médica. (Tegucigalpa, del 23 al 27 de mayo de 1961)*. San Salvador: Editorial Universitaria, 1961. 423 pp.
Deans of medical schools and others examine present state of medical education in Central America and discuss General Studies and medical education; teaching of basic sciences, clinical sciences and preventive medicine. Especially useful for debates on minimum basic standards and views on the non-professional education traditionally limited to the secondary school in Latin America. Some are influenced by the U.S. liberal arts degree, while others argue against extending time to earn professional degree. WKU

GEN 77 ------. *Memoria de las actividades desarrolladas por la Secretaría Permanente, julio de 1960-diciembre de 1961*. Ciudad Universitaria Rodrigo Facio, Costa Rica: CSUCA, 1961. 189 pp.
Secretary General Carlos Tünnermann Bernheim presents report to CSUCA President Napoleon Rodriguez Ruiz of the Universidad de El

Salvador. Permanent Secretariat moves from Nicaragua to Costa Rica; other activities are related to implementing sixteen resolutions of CSUCA's Quinta Reunión, including holding of meetings on dental, legal, and medical education. Funds were secured from the Interamerican Development Bank for a study of land tenancy and agricultural labor conditions by the Central American Social and Economic Research Institute. An immense amount of productive activity. WKU

GEN ------. Memoria de las actividades desarrolladas por la Secre-
78 taría Permanente, enero-diciembre de 1962. Ciudad Universitaria
Rodrigo Facio: CSUCA, 1962. 130 pp.
    Report, presented to CSUCA President Jorge Arias de Blois of the Universidad de San Carlos de Guatemala, describes, among other events, success in obtaining funds from the Ford Foundation and USAID to promote regional integration and other CSUCA programs. Several meetings on professional education described. Chapter on "Central American University Solidarity" contains resolutions chastising government of Nicaragua for its inadequate financial support on UNAN, and vigorous denunciation of the government of Guatemala for its violation of the San Carlos campus and murder of several students and the capture of many professors and students. Details of destruction committed by government forces relayed to regional and international bodies. WKU

GEN ------. Memoria de las actividades desarrolladas por la Secre-
79 taría Permanente, enero-diciembre 1963. Ciudad Universitaria
Rodrigo Facio: CSUCA, 1963. 180 pp.
    Presentation, addressed to CSUCA President Carlos Monge Alfaro of the Universidad de Costa Rica, cites international recognition now accorded the five national universities for their progress in regional integration and academic reform. Some accomplishments: development of regional faculties, e.g. the Central American Institute of Comparative Law; a study of human resources in Central America; collaboration with U.S. National Academy of Sciences to improve basic sciences; increasing support from international agencies.

GEN ------. Memoria de las actividades desarrolladas por la Secre-
80 taría Permanente, enero-diciembre de 1964. Ciudad Universitaria
Rodrigo Facio: CSUCA, 1964. 190 pp.
    CSUCA President Arturo Quesada, rector of the Universidad Nacional Autónoma de Honduras, receives report from Permanent Secretary General Tünnermann. Steps toward regional integration and external collaboration; all five universities now have some form of General Studies, and departmentalization is under way; regional schools and courses; expanded external financial help. First meeting, in El Salvador, of Central American professors of the social sciences. WKU

GEN ------. Memoria de la Primera Reunión de los Bibliotecarios de
81 las Universidades Centroamericanas, 1, 2, y 3 de marzo de 1962.
Ciudad Universitaria Rodrigo Facio: CSUCA and UCR, 1962. 164
pp.
    Meeting in Costa Rica, with help from Ford Foundation and UNESCO, focuses on libraries related to higher education goals, the present status of library services in each university, possibilities for cooperation among them, and possibilities for creating a Central American library school. Philosophical and statistical material included. WKU

GEN ------. Organización y programas 1977. Documentos. [Ciudad
82 Universitaria Rodrigo Facio]: CSUCA, 1977. 59 pp.
History, organization, objectives; activities and programs
include student affairs, social science, agriculture, and transnational
companies. Study of armed forces in Central America, university structure. Details of major publishing efforts; list of regional centers.
WKU

GEN ------. Plan para la integración regional de la educación su-
83 perior centroamericana. Publicaciones de la Secretaría Permanente
del Consejo Superior Universitario Centroamericano. Ciudad Universitaria Rodrigo Facio [San José]: Secretaría Permanente del
Consejo Superior, 1963. 41 pp.
"An uncommon example in Latin America" of regional planning
for cooperation was ratified by all five national universities. Goals:
to selectively strengthen certain academic programs, avoid duplication;
to encourage General Studies, departmentalization in basic disciplines,
mobility of students among the national universities, increased scientific capability, economic integration. KU

GEN ------. Plan para la integración regional de la educación su-
84 perior centroamericana (aprobado por el Consejo Superior Universitario Centroamericano, en su II Reunión Extraordinaria,
celebrada en la Ciudad Universitaria de Costa Rica durante los
días 22 y 23 de junio de 1961). [San José] Ciudad Universitaria:
CSUCA, 1961. 50 pp.
Secretariat of CSUCA publishes work of the technical commission authorized in a 1960 meeting in El Salvador, to work with the
University of Honduras to draw up the plan for regional integration.
General education recognized as the "essential proposal"; plans quite
detailed. Participants in meetings are highest level educational
leaders in the region. WKU

GEN ------. Primer censo de la población universitaria centro-
85 americana, 1959. Publicaciones de la Secretaría Permanente del
Consejo Superior Universitario Centroamericano, no. 4. León,
Nicaragua: CSUCA, 1959. 21 pp.
Census of students, according to the pattern established by
the Union of Universities of Latin America, shows a total in five
countries of 12,327; 9,859 were men. See entry GEN 94. KU

GEN ------. Primer Coloquio Centroamericano de Professores de
86 Filosofía: Resoluciones y recomendaciones. Serie Informes no.
3. Ciudad Rodrigo Facio: CSUCA, 1964. 22 pp.
Sponsored by CSUCA, at the Universidad de San Carlos de
Guatemala, with help from the Ford Foundation, representatives of five
national universities discuss present state of teaching philosophy and
its relation to General Studies. Stress essential nature of the discipline to achieve goals of higher education; homage to Karl Jaspers.
WKU

GEN ------. Primera Reunión de Encargados de Programas de Becas de
87 las Universidades Centroamericanas: Resoluciones y recomendaciones. Serie Informes no. 4. Ciudad Rodrigo Facio: CSUCA,
1965. 30 pp.

17

Participant meeting of UNAH, sponsored by CSUCA and the Ford Foundation, proposed, among other matters, creation of the Instituto Centroamericano de Crédito Educativo (ICCE), modeled after Colombia's ICETEX; need for scholarships for graduates studying abroad and in the region. WKU

GEN ------. Primera Reunión de la Comisión Centroamericana de
88   Bienestar Estudiantil: Resoluciones y recomendaciones. Serie
     Informes no. 6. Ciudad Rodrigo Facio: [CSUCA?], 1965. 21 pp.
     Meeting at Universidad Nacional Autónoma de Honduras of new CSUCA commission addressed such student services as orientation, loans, housing, health, student government. WKU

GEN ------. Qué es el CSUCA. Ciudad Universitaria Rodrigo Facio:
89   CSUCA, [1980]. 4 pp. In English and French, also.
     Acronym stands for both Central American University Confederation and the Central American Superior Council of Universities. Members are national, public universities of all six Central American countries. Council, meeting three times a year, is composed of seven rectors and seven presidents of national student unions. (Costa Rica has two public universities.) Encourages creation of regional institutions, promotes research in regional problems, has its own publishing house (EDUCA). WKU

GEN ------. Revista Centroamericana de Ciencia y Tecnología 1, no. 1
90   (January-June 1978). 290 pp.
     Besides general articles on the role of science and technology in society, contains several essays on science and research in Central American universities, and a "who's who" in the region's scientific community. Offers insights into sensitivity of Latin American universities' research policies vis-à-vis more developed regions of the world.

GEN ------. Segunda Reunión Centroamericana de Registradores:
91   Resoluciones y recomendaciones. Serie Informes no. 5. Ciudad
     Rodrigo Facio: CSUCA, 1965. 15 pp.
     Meeting in the Universidad de San Carlos de Guatemala, representatives of five Central American national universities define office of university registrar as necessary for centralized admission, recognition of degrees, care of student records. Recommend sharing documents such as catalogues, admissions guides, statistical information among members; that statistical material be gathered; that universities lacking centralized registration departments create them. WKU

GEN ------. Seminario sobre admisión a estudios universitarios en
92   las universidades de Centroamérica, (6 al 9 de mayo de 1964).
     Serie "Estudios" no. 1. Ciudad Universitaria Rodrigo Facio:
     CSUCA, 1964. 195 pp.
     Sponsored by CSUCA, College Entrance Examination Board and IIME, seminar in Costa Rica had as themes admissions policies and problems of selection and retention, gifted students, evaluation and examination, aptitude measurement, and statistical analysis; the University of Puerto Rico model. WKU

GEN ------. El sistema educativo en Nicaragua, situación actual y
93   perspectivas. Estudio de recursos humanos en Centroamérica, no.
     4. [Ciudad Universitaria Rodrigo Facio], 1965. 115 pp.
          Past, present and projected statistical description of
Nicaraguan education. Some partial and inconclusive data on costs and
efficiency included. One of six studies of this type which cover the
Central American countries. AzU

GEN ------. Tercer censo de la población universitaria centro-
94   americana, año 1962. Ciudad Rodrigo Facio: CSUCA, Secretaría
     Permanente, 1963. 15 leaves.
          Matriculation in five countries totals 16,371. Data by
institution, by discipline, by sex, by year of study. Drop in numbers
between first and last years shows symptoms of severe attrition. See
entry GEN 85. WKU

GEN ------. Tercera Reunión de la Comisión Centroamericana Pro
95   Estudios Generales, 17 a 24 de Marzo de 1963, Universidad de
     Puerto Rico, Río Piedras, Puerto Rico. Programa de Actividades.
     Ciudad Rodrigo Facio: CSUCA, 1963. 4 pp. Folder.
          Puerto Rican university leaders in General Studies provide a
showcase of their activities for their Central American colleagues.
WKU

GEN ------. Universidades centroamericanas directorio 1968. Ciudad
96   Universitaria Rodrigo Facio, 1968. 118 pp.
          Public universities only, including Panama, with names, ad-
dresses and telephone numbers of chief officers. Data also for CSUCA
secretariat and personnel in its regional institutes and schools, its
advisors in each university, the Central American University Planning
Commission, and other CSUCA agencies. WKU

GEN ------, Comisión Centroamericana en pro de los Estudios Gener-
97   ales. Los estudios generales en Centroamérica. [Actas, trabajos
     y recomendaciones de sus tres primeras sesiones]. Publicaciones
     de la Secretaría Permanente del CSUCA. Ciudad Universitaria
     Rodrigo Facio, 1963. 402 pp.
          Persuaded, by Ortega y Gasset and others, of need for broader
base in university education, representatives of five Central American
national universities hold three meetings in 1962 and 1963 in Costa
Rica and El Salvador to consider General Studies policies and university reform. Detailed minutes of meetings reveal issues to be resolved
and profundity of commitment. A key document. KU

GEN "C[osta] R[ica] Attacks Guatemala for Deaths of Professors." San
98   Jose News, 28 March 1980, p. 4.
          San Carlos University professor assassinated after threats
from "secret Anti-Communist Army" and his criticism of military government. Central American University Superior Council (CSUCA) asks international agencies to investigate persecution of Guatemalan university
faculty and students as part of campaign to destroy the National University "piece by piece."

GEN CROSS, MALCOLM. Urbanization and Urban Growth in the Caribbean:
99   An Essay on Social Change in Dependent Societies. Cambridge:
     Cambridge University Press, 1979. 174 pp.

Analysis of forces conducing to rapid urbanization in populations with little control over their social and economic patterns, especially as result of plantation structures. Education marked the deepened incorporation of Caribbean societies into the web of European economic and political connections; it now consumes a high percentage of national income to benefit a few who then consume and behave as the wealthy in rich countries are perceived to do. An insightful perspective. Uk

GEN   CUMMINGS, RICHARD L., and LEMKE, DONALD H.   Educational Innova-
100   tions in Latin America.   Metuchen, N.J.:   Scarecrow Press, 1973.
       357 pp.
       Anthology covers dynamics of catalysts and planning for
change, with most case histories from Central America. Begins with
chapter on history of Latin American university. KU

GEN   CURLE, ADAM.   Education for Liberation.   London: Tavistock
101   Publications, 1973.   144 pp.
       Written in 1971, work by a thinker highly influential in
promoting education in the "developmental decade" of the sixties in
Latin America reflects disillusion and bitterness over failure of
education to contribute to national development. Refers to Pakistan,
but generalizes about abuse of poor nations by rich ones with their
"so-called aid, which is really exploitive," and propensity of those
benefitting from higher education toward "gratification based on consumption" and their competition for public sector jobs. Uk

GEN   ------.   The Role of Education in Developing Societies: An
102   Inaugural Lecture Delivered in the University College of Ghana on
       15 February 1961.   [Accra]:   Ghana University Press, 1961.   33
       pp.
       One of 1960s' most vigorous advocates of education as a key
to Third World development draws on literature of the period concerned
with social change, revealing prevailing faith in creation of a middle
class of scientists, engineers, agricultural experts, lawyers,
businessmen through education as means to more equitable societies. Uk

       CURTIS, S.J.   History of Education in Great Britain.   See entry
       GUY 22.

GEN   DE ABATE, JOHN.   "Información de GULERPE: resultados y con-
103   clusiones de la VI Reunión celebrada en la Universidad Autónoma
       de Guadalajara, México."   Universitas 2000 3, no. 1 (1978):   211-
       25.
       UAG not a Caribbean university but highly active in region;
the private university sponsors a meeting of present and former university leaders who set out conclusions on topics for work and plans
for future. Interest in "open" university and other innovations.
Several Caribbean countries represented by well known leaders.

GEN   DEAL, CARL, ed.   Latin America and the Caribbean: A Dissertation
104   Bibliography.   Ann Arbor, Mich.:   University Microfilms Inter-
       national, [1978?].   164 pp.
       The topic of education, covered by countries, extends from
pages 47 to 59. Reflects characteristic abundance of literature on
everything except universities. KU

GEN "Diez años del programa educativo de la OEA en América Latina y
105 el Caribe." La Educación, Revista Interamericana de Desarrollo
Educativo 22, nos. 78-80 (1978). 290 pp.
 Ten years of activities of Regional Program of Educational
Development (PREDE) of the Organization of American States (OEA) re-
viewed in thirteen articles. Topics include development of university
libraries, educational research, plans for multinational use of educational television.

GEN "Directorio APICE-UNESCO de la educación superior en América
106 Latina y el Caribe = Repertoire APICE-UNESCO del l'èducation
supérieure en Amérique Latine et dans la region Caraibe = APICE-
UNESCO Directory of Higher Education in Latin America and the
Caribbean = Repertório APICE-UNESCO da educação superior na
América Latina e Caribe." María Lucía Leyva de Barbosa, Comp.
Bogota: APICE, 1980. 2 vol.
 Lists undergraduate, graduate and research programs in
twenty-four countries; prepared to increase regional exchanges, di-
rectory is based on questionnaire data, is reasonably detailed.
Colombia contributes over 200 pages.

GEN DOMEYKO DE VERA, CECILIA. Bibliography on New Forms of Post-
107 Secondary Education-Bibliografía sobre nuevas formas de educación
postsecundaria. Washington, D.C.: IDB, Economic and Social
Development Department, General Studies Division, 1977. 282 pp.
 Part of Seminar in Caracas, on Open Learning Systems, 1976.
 TxU

 D'OYLEY, VINCENT, and MURRAY, REGINALD, eds. Development and
Disillusion in Third World Education with Emphasis on Jamaica.
See entry UWI 41.

GEN DORE, RONALD. The Diploma Disease: Education, Qualification and
108 Development. London: George Allen and Unwin, 1976. 214 pp.
 An example of growing body of literature challenging link
between education and national development. Calls current faith in
education for development akin to earlier faith in inevitability of
progress, with civilization moving toward perfection. Lively attack on
manpower planners in UN Development Decade of Sixties who were "fanning
out all over," especially in the Third World, attempting to measure
social rates of return, particularly on high-level training. Ties
education only to world of work, not to human development as intrinsic
value, hence faults degree-seeking as unproductive status-seeking. Uk

GEN DRAYTON, ARTHUR. "Caribbean Studies in the Western Caribbean"
109 and "Caribbean Studies at the University of the West Indies."
Caribbean Educational Bulletin 4, no. 2 (May 1977): 30-38, 50-
55.
 Reports hopes of University of Haiti's rector for Caribbean
studies, but institution lacks staff, facilities, and focus on other
than national concerns or relations with metropolis. Cuba's higher
education now problem-centered, not region-centered, but interest is
expressed. UWI's three campuses have had common program in their
faculties of Arts and General Studies; curriculum options, resources,
research and publications.

GEN   EDMONDSON, LOCKSLEY. "The State and Prospects of African Studies
110   in the Caribbean: A Preliminary Report and Assessment." Carib-
      bean Educational Bulletin 5, no. 2 (May 1978): 3-23.
           Survey of courses, research and academic programs pertaining
to Africa in Dutch, French, Spanish and English-speaking Caribbean
universities. Strongest is at University of Puerto Rico, Rio Piedras.

GEN   "En óbito de dos distinguidos universitarios." Gaceta/UDUAL,
111   August 1980: 7.
           Secretary General of the Federation of Central American
Private Universities, FUPAC, and long-time Secretary General of the
National University of Nicaragua were assassinated on the first and
fourth of September in Guatemala.

GEN   ENARSON, HAROLD L. "University Education in Central America. A
112   Report of the Ford Foundation." [n.p.], 1962. 97 leaves.
           Five universities and their regional agency CSUCA are visited
to learn about their prospects for program of Ford grants. Overview of
pattern, description of individual institutions, regional cooperation
risks and benefits, recommendations for program of assistance, review
of programs underway, prospects. Critical comments on uncoordinated
assistance strategies by U.S. universities hungry for contract money,
with example, and warning against imposing U.S. solutions. WKU

GEN   ESCOTET, MIGUEL. "Reponsabilidad de la universidad ante el
113   estudiante." Universitas 2000 4, nos. 2-3 (1980): 27-32.
           Venezuelan educator, addressing First Latin American Seminar
on Student Affairs, criticizes traditional antagonistic attitude of
professor toward student; cites need for change to more creative pedagogy. Very few Venezuelan aspirants to university post scored well on
entrance examinations, testimony to poor preparation, a common Latin
American situation. Failure to develop talent in erroneous quest for
the professional degree.

GEN   "Estudios postgraduados, problemática de la integración centro-
114   americana." Noticias del CSUCA 3, no. 7 (June 1966): 3.
           Graduate studies have begun in the Universidad de El Salvador
on juridical and institutional problems of Central American integration, sponsored by CSUCA, the Interamerican Institute of International Juridical Studies, the Central American Institute of
International Law, and the Institute for Latin American Integration.
The list of courses is given.

GEN   "Etapas del plan de integración regional." Noticias del CSUCA 3,
115   no. 7 (June 1966): 4-5.
           Chart displays objectives of plan; the thirteen stages, from
postgraduate level through relation to plan for regional economic
integration; the instruments and contents of each stage; and the
affected groups and/or projects.

GEN   The Europa Year Book 1978. A World Survey: Countries Outside
116   Europe.
           Some recent data on school enrollments and policies are
included for various Caribbean countries and territories, along with
historical and descriptive material. UkLU-IE

GEN   FEDERACION DE UNIVERSIDADES PRIVADAS DE AMERICA CENTRAL Y PANAMA
117   (FUPAC). Breve informe sobre la Federación de Universidades de
       América Central y Panamá, FUPAC. [Guatemala]: FUPAC, Secretaría
       General, 1977. 11 leaves.
         Goals, structure, members, history, finance, programs. Ac-
       tivities since 1970. WKU

GEN   ------. Identidad y realización de la universidad. Edited by
118   Roberto Mertins Marúa. Seminarios FUPAC, 3. Guatemala: FUPAC,
       1972. 211 pp.
         Discussion at 1971 meetings in Panama among seventeen private
       university rectors and other leaders on ideological principles--the
       role of the private university at time of inquietude and search for
       identity and idependence from the dominant metropolis. WKU

GEN   ------. El movimiento estudiantil: Informe general. Primer
119   encuentro estudiantil de las universidades de FUPAC, Santa
       Bárbara de Heredia, Costa Rica, 3-7 de junio de 1974. Guatemala:
       FUPAC Secretaría General, 1974. 95 pp.
         Some thirty-five Central American student leaders from pri-
       vate universities consider conditions in each country, analysis of each
       of their universities and its student movement, the role of the student
       movement, possibilities of regional action. Conclude they must engage
       in consciousness-raising, making people aware of their exploitation and
       oppression; agree that universities must play a role in "liberation of
       our people." Need to collaborate with student groups in public uni-
       versities also. WKU

GEN   ------. Teleducación universitaria: VI Seminario FUPAC, IX
120   Seminario Latinoamericano para Directivos de Teleducación, III
       Seminario Internacional de T.V. Educativa, Antigua, Guatemala 16-
       21 marzo 1975. Guatemala: FUPAC, 1975. 119 pp.
         Jointly sponsored by the Konrad Adenauer Foundation and
       FUPAC; twenty-five participants hear presentations and discuss
       problems. Some confusion over medium and messages in final session.
       WKU

GEN   ------, and UNIVERSIDAD CENTROAMERICANA JOSE SIMEON CAÑAS.
121   Pedagogía de la nueva Universidad. Seminarios FUPAC, 3.
       Guatemala: FUPAC, 1975. 173 pp.
         Seminar held in San Salvador in 1972 for leaders from Central
       America's private (chiefly Catholic) universities, with some speakers
       from other areas. Peruvian Augusto Salazar Bondy, intellectual god-
       father of the domination-dependency theme, sets tone. Unidentified
       Oscar Varsavsky elaborates consequences of following U.S. model in
       science policy, which, by emphasizing pure instead of applied research
       and education, conduces to exploitation of Latin America's human re-
       sources as well as its material ones by the imperialist U.S. Debates
       following presentations reveal most of the acute anxieties confronting
       university leaders of the period. A serious work. KU

GEN   FIALLOS GIL, MARIANO. Panorama universitario mundial: Crónicas
122   y comentarios de la Tercera Conferencia Mundial de Universidades
       celebrada en la Ciudad Universitaria de México, D.F.; contiene,
       además, un epistolario polémico con el señor Pablo Antonio Cuadra

sobre los mismos asuntos. León, Nicaragua: Ediciones de la
Universidad, 1961. 124 pp.
    Pressures on universities in Latin America in the post-World
War II era generated by rapid social, economic and political changes;
population growth; demand for broader educational opportunity, new
teaching methods, new careers, new relationships with governments and
societies. Brief descriptions of university systems in the U.S.,
Israel, Japan, Germany, France, Poland, Asia; some common problems of
higher education in Latin America. TxU

GEN   FIGUEROA, JOHN F. Society, Schools and Progress in the West
123   Indies. New York: Pergamon Press, 1971. 208 pp.
    Most interesting aspect is discussion of language problems,
and pre-World War II history. Problems of elementary and secondary
schools: discussion of priorities in education in the West Indies. KU

    FISHER, STEPHEN H. The Commonwealth Caribbean: A Study of the
    Educational System of the Commonwealth Caribbean and a Guide to
    the Academic Placement of Students in Educational Institutions of
    the United States. See entry UWI 49.

GEN   FOGEL, BARBARA R. Design for Change: Higher Education in the
124   Service of Developing Countries. A Handbook for Planners. New
    York: International Council for Educational Development, 1977.
    71 pp.
    Cautionary comments for donor agencies at time of competing
demands for alleviation of poverty and illiteracy. Very general,
elementary work. KU

GEN   FORMOSO, MANUEL. "Palabras pronunciadas por el Dr. Manuel
125   Formoso, Secretario General de la Confederación Universitaria
    Centroamericana (CSUCA)." Paper presented at the VI Triennial
    Meeting of the International Association of University Presi-
    dents, San José, 28 June-3 July 1981. Mimeographed. San José:
    CSUCA. 18 pp.
    Universities in Central America began as religious
institutions, from 1676 to 1847. First Central American University
Congress, held in 1948, created CSUCA. Common concerns: creation of
general studies to balance excessive "professionalism," study of
national realities, organization of departments and flexible study
programs. Second Congress, in 1968, produced declaration which included among goals promotion of social change in behalf of social
justice. Data on economic and population growth, poverty; comments on
recent events affecting universities in Nicaragua, El Salvador, Guatemala. Calls for more active role in fight for economic, political,
cultural independence in region. WKU

GEN   FRANCO ARBELAEZ, AUGUSTO. "El gobierno de los Estados Unidos y
126   las universidades latinoamericanas." (primera parte) Mundo
    Universitario, no. 1 (October-December 1972): 45-56.
    Paper by Colombian educational leader sums up agonies ac-
companying modernization efforts of Latin American universities and
consequent suspicions of practice and motivation of aid-givers from the
U.S. Illustrates differing philosophical frameworks in social science
research; analyzes "intellectual contradictions" between Anglos and
Latins. Insightful, rational approach.

GEN   "La función social de la universidad en América Latina."
127   Universidades˜ nos. 14-15 (November-March 1963-64): 115-17.
       Part of the report of the IV General Assembly of UDUAL de-
scribes the university as depository of culture and agent of social
change. Question is how to satisfy both functions in contemporary
Latin America. Among needs are studies about universities in the
social reality; developmental activities, such as preparation of professionals at high and intermediate levels; social action in "direct
contact with reality" through community development; creation of
"social conscience" regarding national and continental problems.

GEN   GALE, LAURENCE. Education and Development in Latin America.
128   London: Routledge and Kegan Paul, 1969. 178 pp.
       Touches on aspects of education from Mexico to Chile, with
emphasis on Colombia and Guyana; includes elementary, secondary, and
post-secondary levels. Universities, technical studies, vocational and
liberal education, research, university reform, standards or lack of
standards, faculty members. The role of education in forming opinions.
Last section includes adult education and community development, overseas aid, and the general balance sheet of education in Colombia. The
bibliographic sources are few, information limited. KU

GEN   GARCIA LAGUARDIA, JORGE MARIO. Legislación universitaria de
129   América Latina. Introduction by Secretary General of Unión de
       Universidades de la América Latina. Mexico: UNAM [y] UDUAL,
       1973. 210 pp.
       Report commissioned by UDUAL; gives legal basis for universi-
ties, including those in Haiti and Spanish-speaking Caribbean; their
government structure; discussion of autonomy, description of academic
programs, students, financial support, faculty, degrees, coordination
mechanisms. History of private universities; chapter on "myth and
reality" of university autonomy. WKU

GEN   ------. Tema I: Universidad y Constitución en América Latina.
130   Mexico: Ediciones UDUAL, 1975. 19 pp.
       A speech at the First Latin American Conference on University
Legislation, addresses question of university autonomy under proposed
Cuban constitution; five points of autonomy defined by International
Association of Universities contrary to Cuban fusion of government and
education. Question of university role in development raised. WKU

GEN   GARIBAY GUTIERREZ, LUIS. "Reflections and Perspectives of Higher
131   Education in Latin America." Docencia-Postsecundaria 9, no. 3
       (May-June 1981): 87-91.
       Sixteen general principles to improve higher education in-
clude more attention to content of education; improved research,
finance, administration, institutional stability.

GEN   GIRVAN, NORMAN. "The Approach to Technology Policy Studies."
132   Social and Economic Studies 28, no. 1 (March 1979): 1-53.
       Opening article in volume of essays on science and technology
policy in the Caribbean produced by the Institute of Social and Economic Research, UWI, and the Institute of Development Studies, UG.
Distinguishes between technology transfer which perpetuates dependence
and transfer of knowledge which may not. Stages of development defined
with reference to planning. Comment on propensity of Caribbean

countries to establish national councils of science and technology, a step which may be "...at best...ineffectual; at worst it may actually be harmful insofar as it creates the illusion that 'something is being done'." Implications for higher education policy.

GEN   GLASER, WILLIAM A. The Brain Drain: Emigration and Return. A
133   Study for the United Nations Institute for Training and Research
       (UNITAR). New York: Pergamon Press, 1978. 324 pp.
            "At least 30 percent of Trinidadians and Haitians...studying
       and working abroad say they plan to emigrate permanently....Colombians
       ...are close to this figure." Reasons for remaining abroad are ex-
       amined under such variables as language, nature of education, national
       development, employment. Implications for education, e.g., "prestige
       value of foreign degrees" in Colombia, are "...less compelling for West
       Indian and African countries with new universities, such as Trinidad
       and Tobago, Jamaica..." UkLU-IE

GEN   GONZALEZ BAQUERO, RAFAEL. Un nuevo esquema organizativo para la
134   universidad. [Valencia: Universidad de Carabobo?], 1977. 163
       pp.
            Although he points to the Venezuelan university as example,
       Venezuelan professor of higher education theory and administration
       addresses reforms sought for Latin American universities generally.
       Common pattern, the cluster of separate professional schools, has
       suffered from lack of institutional coordination ("too many auto-
       nomies"), scattering of effort, absence of unity, lack of dynamism,
       high costs, confusion of purposes, conflicts over administrative
       functions, and inflexibility of programs. Proposes organizational
       scheme putting emphasis on academic departments, as in the U.S. As-
       serts no scheme will work without good administrators. Indicative also
       of the special role aspired to for the Latin American university: high
       moral purpose directed toward social justice. WKU

GEN   GRACIARENA, JORGE. "Algunas sugerencias para la orientación de
135   los programas de postgrado en ciencias sociales en América
       Latina." Paper presented to Consejo Latinoamericano de Ciencias
       Sociales, Reunión del Programa Latinoamericano de Estudios de
       Postgrado en Ciencias Sociales, CLACSO, Mexico, 2-4 November
       1972. [Mexico, 1972] Mimeographed. 22 pp.
            Regional expert in social science research for UNESCO char-
       acterizes state of social science research as critical, with polari-
       zation of intellectuals and ideologues "obsessively worried" in trying
       to stir up social class agitation to effect revolutionary change of
       economic and social regimens, and those of bourgeois persuasion who
       "mask structural contradictions and fundamental social conflicts,
       blocking formation of revolutionary conscience." Carefully reasoned
       approach to practical and epistemological problems and implications for
       graduate studies. WKU

GEN   GUTIERREZ, CLAUDIO. "Comentarios al movimiento de la reforma
136   universitaria, actualmente en curso en el área de Centro
       América." (tomado de "Los Estudios Generales en Centroamérica,"
       Publicaciones de CSUCA). Revista de la Universidad del Zulia,
       no. 29 (January-March 1965): 243-64.

The dean of Faculty of Sciences and Letters of University of Costa Rica cites need for reform of Latin American universities for their lack of foundation in humanistic and scientific studies. Describes agreement among Central American universities to adopt General Studies, improve teaching, undertake self-evaluation and restructuring.

GEN   ------. La libertad académica: Sus paradojas. Serie Cuadernos
137   Universitarios, no. 21. Ciudad Universitaria Rodrigo Facio:
       Universidad de Costa Rica, 1964. 22 pp.
       Costa Rican philosopher and dean of Faculty of Science and Letters reports to colleagues on visits to German and French universities. Observations on professors, students, organizations compared with Latin American institutions. WKU

GEN   HARMAN, GRANT S. The Politics of Education: A Bibliographical
138   Guide. St. Lucia, Queensland [Australia]: University of Queens-
       land Press, 1974. 316 pp.
       Political scientist looks at interaction between government and formal education, chiefly in English-speaking countries. Five-page section on Latin America and the Caribbean is mainly on universities. UkLU-IE

GEN   HARRISON, JOHN P. "The Latin American University: Present
139   Problems Viewed Through the Recent Past." In The Task of Uni-
       versities in a Changing World, edited by Stephen D. Kertesz, pp.
       419-32. Notre Dame, Ind.: University of Notre Dame Press, 1971.
       Post-World War II reform efforts much affected by U.S. governmental and foundation efforts. Political ideologies and nationalism influenced decisions. Most examples from South America, but some from Central America and the Dominican Republic. KU

GEN   ------. The University versus National Development in Spanish
140   America. 1968 Hackett Memorial Lecture. Austin: University of
       Texas at Austin, Institute of Latin American Studies, [1968]. 26
       pp.
       History and structure of traditional university, its ties with its societies. University reform movement seen as more political than academic, with major structural changes still not accomplished. Acknowledges anti-U.S. sentiment but calls for research integrated with teaching on U.S. model. Touches on prevalence of weak societies and concludes university responsibility for national development is essentially internal to Spanish America. Author was Rockefeller Foundation representative in Chile. ICharE

GEN   HATCH, W. B.; LABBENS, J.; and TERLINGEN, J. H. Informe de la
141   misión consultora de la UNESCO para las universidades centro-
       americanas. Publicaciones de la Universidad de Costa Rica, Serie
       Misceláneas, no. 89. San José, Costa Rica: [UCR], 1962. 88 pp.
       Key document in early days of major university reforms in structure, teaching methods, academic offerings, physical facilities. Reports of conditions in national universities in Costa Rica, Guatemala, El Salvador, Honduras, Nicaragua, of a meeting of the General Studies Commission of CSUCA. Describes European, U.S., and Central American approaches to General Studies, problems and trends. KU

GEN   HAWKINS, IRENE. The Changing Face of the Caribbean. Bridgetown:
142   Cedar Press, 1976. 272 pp. plus maps.
        Short chapter on educational imbalances, plus comments on
"radical graduates" of UWI in leadership roles. Criticizes education
based on European metropolitan life style, lack of local history and
geography, lack of science and technology; education yielding unem-
ployable products at all levels. WKU

GEN   HERZFELD, ANA, and WAGGONER, BARBARA ASHTON, eds. Acotaciones a
143   problemas fundamentales en la educación superior en las Américas.
        Lawrence: Escuela de Artes Liberales y Ciencias, Universidad de
        Kansas, 1971. 67 pp.
        The role of the university confronting change and develop-
ment, comparative analysis of some aspects of U.S. and Latin American
universities, planning, pre-professional education (general studies).
Topics for Eleventh Seminar on Higher Education in the Americas at
Universities of New Mexico and Kansas. See entry GEN 322. WKU

GEN   ------, and WAGGONER, GEORGE R., eds. Autonomía, planificación,
144   innovaciones: Perspectivas latinoamericanas. Lawrence: Escuela
        de Artes Liberales y Ciencias, Universidad de Kansas, 1972. 220
        pp.
        Beginning at Universidad Simón Bolívar in Caracas, continuing
at Universities of New Mexico and Kansas, group discussed and produced
policy statements on topics of the Twelfth Seminar on Higher Education
in the Americas. Essays by Luis Manuel Peñalver, Carlos Tünnermann B.
and Jaime George. Last has useful history of efforts to coordinate
Colombian higher education. See entry GEN 322. WKU

GEN   ------, eds. La universidad y los universitarios: Carrera
145   docente, investigación, estudios postgrados. Lawrence: Escuela
        de Artes Liberales y Ciencias, Universidad de Kansas, 1974. 324
        pp.
        Valuable collection of papers presented and discussed in
Fourteenth Seminar on Higher Education in the Americas during meetings
in Universities of Costa Rica, New Mexico, Kansas. Reveals different
stages of development in producing university professionals in, among
other places, Colombia, Panama, Costa Rica, Venezuela. Some U.S.
comparisons, and exposure of Latin American educators to period of
pressure for change in U.S. universities. WKU

GEN   HIASSEN, CARL. "Last Chance Island: It May Be Where Your Next
146   Doctor Comes From." Tropic, The Miami Herald, June 7, 1981: 10.
        Some 11,000 U.S. students unable to enter U.S. medical
schools study medicine abroad. Description of St. George's University
School of Medicine, in Grenada (a contributing territory to U.W.I.),
indicates considerable academic success, as measured by test scores for
alumni of this private enterprise. Considerable criticism of other
such money makers in the Caribbean, in Montserrat, Dominica, and the
Dominican Republic.

GEN   HILL, GEORGE CLIFFORD, Jr. "Regional University Cooperation and
147   Reform in Central America: Its Development, Progress, and
        Promise." Ph.D. dissertation, Catholic University of America,
        1971. 239 leaves.

Examines cooperative efforts and results of Council of
Central American Universities, CSUCA, the Cultural and Educational
Council of the Organization of Central America and the Federation of
Private Universities of Central America, FUPAC.

GEN   HUGHES, ALISTER. "Grenada." Caribbean Monthly Bulletin, Vol.
148   15, no. 10 (October 1981): 28-29.
       St. George's University School of Medicine in Grenada, es-
tablished in 1976, refutes attacks on quality of its program by, among
others, Association of American Medical Colleges, Grenada Medical Association, and UWI. Cites high examination scores and role in training
doctors for developing countries.

GEN   INSTITUTO AJIJIC SOBRE EDUCACION SUPERIOR EN AMERICA (IASEI).
149   "Quantitative Evolution of Postsecondary Level Latin America
       (1960-1977): Summary and Projections for the Year 2000."
       Docencia-Postsecundaria 9, no. 3 (May-June 1981): 97-116.
       Review of bibliographies shows little or no information on
postsecondary education, hampering decision making in many countries.
Difficulties of access to primary sources, unreliable and contradictory
data. Efforts by IASEI for GULERPE part of five-year project. General
data on demography, literacy, enrollments 1960-77, plus country
figures. See entry GEN 154.

GEN   INTER-AMERICAN DEVELOPMENT BANK (IDB). Economic and Social
150   Progress in Latin America 1976 Report. Washington, D.C.: IDB,
       1976. 446 pp.
       Chapter 5, devoted to financing of education, notes growing
demand for middle-level and higher education. Data on enrollment rates
by country at all levels, some financial information. Clearly di-
minished activity by IDB in higher education compared to earlier years.
See entries GEN 152, 153. WKU

GEN   ------. La educación avanzada y el desarrollo de América Latina.
151   Mexico: IDB, 1965. 133 pp.
       Sixth meeting of Bank's Board of Governors produces papers by
some leading Latin American educators on role of Latin American universities in regional integration, higher education within framework of
national development plans, university as a production unit, external
financing of higher education, universities' contribution to solution
of national and regional development problems, role of UNESCO. Optimism, faith in assumption "that the pace of development is directly
proportionate to the impetus given to education." Golden age when IDB
was known as the Bank of the Latin American University, in full, living
color. Prologue by Felipe Herrera sums it up. KU

GEN   ------. Higher Education and Latin American Development:
152   Roundtables. Asunción: IDB, 1965. 141 pp.
       English version of GEN 151, without prologue.

GEN   ------. Socio-Economic Progress in Latin America: Social
153   Progress Trust Fund Seventh Annual Report 1967. Washington,
       D.C.: IDB, 1967. 441 pp.

IDB has administered Fund since 1961, in agreement with U.S. government. A goal has been aid to higher education. Part 3 (pp. 313-414) of report, devoted to present situation and outlook for higher education, has useful information, as do appendices. WKU

GEN ------. Socio-Economic Progress in Latin America: Social
154 Progress Trust Fund Eighth Annual Report 1968. Washington, D.C.:
     IDB, 1968. 409 pp.
          State of education of member countries in part 2 (pp. 49-329), which describes their conditions and progress, including some data on universities. Information on loans, some of which were made to universities. Shift in emphasis to sectors other than higher education. WKU

GEN ------, The Secretary to the Board of Directors. "Operating
155 Policy of the Bank in the Education Sector." GP-45-1. Mimeo-
     graphed. [Washington, D.C.]: IDB, 6 May 1976. 7 pp. Original
     in Spanish.
          Document for official use covers objectives, fields of operation, guidelines for policy implementation, criteria for project appraisal. Reflecting goals of member nations, bank policy acknowledges that "rapid extension of Latin American educational systems . . . still falls short of satisfying the legitimate aspirations of the national majorities to share in the dividends of economic and social growth." Training for manpower development is a high priority; higher education will emphasize "training the top levels of leadership required for the development process." Other criteria for project appraisal: equal education opportunities, and efficiency of the instruments. WKU

GEN International Encyclopedia of Higher Education. Knowles, Asa S.,
156 ed. 10 Vols. San Francisco: Jossey Bass Publications, 1977.
          Includes individual countries and regional organizations in the Caribbean region, which are described by well known educators. History, legal bases of educational systems, types of institutions, relationship with secondary education, admissions, administration, programs and degrees, financing, student aid, access to education, staff, research, trends and problems are covered. KU

GEN JALLADE, JEAN-PIERRE. "Education Finance and Income Distribution
157 in Latin America." Seminar on Financing Education in Latin
     America 15-19 November 1976. Mimeographed. Washington, D.C.:
     IDB [1976?] 35 pp.
          Senior economist of World Bank says conventional wisdom of recent past that education is economic investment gives way to uncertainties over its function as perpetuator of social inequity, as well as its role in economic development. Providing educational opportunities to underprivileged to improve income distribution has popular appeal but is an illusion in many Latin American countries. In Colombia, e.g., public financing of primary education benefits only 40 percent of poor families of the 87 percent cohort of poor. Publicly financed higher education redistributes income from poor and very rich to upper middle class. Suggests pricing and taxing systems to reduce inequities of publicly financed education. Useful data. WKU

GEN   JIMENES GRULLON, JUAN ISIDRO. <u>La problemática universitaria</u>
158   <u>latinoamericana: Raíces, rasgos actuales y soluciones revo-</u>
      <u>lucionarias (dos ensayos)</u>. Santo Domingo: Universidad Autónoma
      de Santo Domingo, 1970. 113 pp.
          Spanish colonial cosmology-theology, subsequent positivism
      and recent liberal idealism all contribute to backwardness of Latin
      American universities by being foreign to realities of their societies.
      Population explosion; gulf between rich and poor not addressed by
      students' romantic rebellion, as they seek personal profit in tra-
      ditional professions while peasantry remains outside educational
      system. Calls for Americanization of learning, applied research, de-
      velopment of social sense, nationalization of revolutionary emotion,
      research for new political model to replace failed democratic model,
      avoidance of U.S.-style overspecialization and intellectual imperial-
      ism. Second essay characterizes ideas of Risieri Frondizi as
      excessively formalistic, ignoring need for revolution. MoSW

GEN   JORDAN, ALMA THEODORA. <u>The Development of Library Service in the</u>
159   <u>West Indies through Interlibrary Cooperation</u>. Metuchen, N.J.:
      Scarecrow Press, 1970. 433 pp.
          Results of early 1960s study include university libraries.
KU

GEN   ------, ed. <u>Research Library Cooperation in the Caribbean</u>.
160   Chicago: American Library Association, 1973. 145 pp.
          Papers of First and Second Conferences of the Association of
      Caribbean University and Research Libraries; topics include acqui-
      sitions of materials in English-, Spanish-, French-speaking Caribbean,
      problems of communication, bibliographic control. KU

GEN   KEELY, CHARLES. "Lack of Schooling Cripples Latin Development."
161   <u>Copley News Service Argentine Report</u>, 23 March 1966. 3 pp.
          Lack of educated Latin Americans to administer development
      programs seen as hampering Alliance for Progress. Inter-American Eco-
      nomic and Social Council reports that in 1963 only 0.07 percent of 3.8
      million work force in Central America had university education. Other
      data.

GEN   KELLER, CAROL. "Educational Perspectives in the Caribbean." <u>La</u>
162   <u>Educación: Revista Interamericana de Desarrollo Educativo</u> 22,
      no. 81 (1979): 103-14.
          Sharp challenge to reexamine goals of education and concept
      of development, relationship between education and work (not job);
      comments on ways international system affects attitudes toward and
      organization of education. Paper presented at 1978 Workshop on Multi-
      national Educational Projects, sponsored by UWI and OEA.

GEN   KELLY, GAIL P. "The Relation between Colonial and Metropolitan
163   Schools: A Structural Analysis." <u>Comparative Education</u> 15, no.
      2 (June 1979): 209-16.
          Legacy of colonial systems: relationship between metro-
      politan and colonial schools was one of separate, unequal and related
      institutions within a single educational hierarchy. Efforts to adapt
      to local conditions only served to perpetuate the colonies' under-
      development.

GEN   LA BELLE, THOMAS J., ed. <u>Education and Development: Latin</u>
164   <u>America and the Caribbean</u>. Los Angeles: University of
      California, Latin American Center, 1972. 732 pp.
         Studies of complexities inherent in meeting individual and
national goals through schooling address value systems, societal structures, reform movements, political power. Background for understanding
Latin American and Caribbean education in general; and Trinidad,
Barbados, Jamaica, Haiti, Cuba, Colombia, Venezuela, Puerto Rico and
parts of Central America in particular. Section 8 on universities
includes essays on autonomy, reform, student attitudes. AzTeS

GEN   LA ROCHE, HUMBERTO. <u>Democratización de la educación universi-</u>
165   <u>taria en la América Latina</u>. Maracaibo: Universidad del Zulia,
      1964. 29 pp.
         Address for Fourth Assembly of UDUAL calls for university
people to exercise social responsiblility in building new social order;
urges that public opinion must convince leaders that university education is a necessary priority for national investment; necessity of
autonomy, but avoidance of partisan politics. WKU

GEN   LATAPI, PABLO. "Algunas tendencias de las universidades latino-
166   americanas: Problemas seleccionados y perspectivas." <u>Papeles</u>
      <u>Universitarios</u>, no. 14 (March-April 1979): 101-24.
         Mexican sociologist-educator describes developmental tenden-
cies, diverse theoretical-ideological positions governing reforms and
changes; second part deals with access to universities, employment,
graduate studies and research. Examination of issues most typically
discussed in recent decades of institutional soul-searching: role of
university vis-à-vis the state, university as social critic, effects of
international pressures and concerns.

GEN   ------. "Universidad y cambio social: Siete tesis reconstruc-
167   cionistas." <u>Universidades</u>, no. 77 (July-September 1979): 696-
      709.
         Address to FUPAC in Guatemala describes views of universi-
ties' role vis-à-vis social change, from purely academic to university
dissolution. Advocates "reconstructionist" role, continuing changes in
individual as a result of education, with design and carrying out of
model experimental projects to benefit less favored members of society.
"Doing is an essential part of thinking."

GEN   ------. "Universidad y sociedad: Un enfoque basado en las
168   experiencias latinoamericanas." <u>Universitas 2000</u> 3, no. 1
      (1978): 45-81.
         Focuses on universities and social justice at Latin American
Caribbean Conference on post-secondary education. Theoretical framework, tensions affecting universities and social change, a "reconstructionist position," experiences relevant in Latin America, the
university and social utopia.

GEN   THE LATIN AMERICAN SCHOLARSHIP PROGRAM OF AMERICAN UNIVERSITIES.
169   <u>LASPAU Alumni Survey</u>. Cambridge, Mass.: 1977. 72 pp.
         Since its 1964 beginning over 2,000 scholarships have been
granted. Recent goal: faculty development in Latin American and
Caribbean universities. High retention rate, little brain drain.
Lists of participating universities, scholars, fields of study. WKU

GEN LATORRE, EDUARDO. "El papel de la universidad en los países del
170 tercer mundo." Paper presented at the Forum de Organismos no-
Gubernamentales de Centro América y el Caribe, 9 February 1977.
Mimeographed. Santo Domingo: Instituto Tecnológico de Santo
Domingo. 15 pp.
Calls for new kind of university in Third World, not copy of
those of other time or place; must determine needs and create education
for immediate usefulness as well as for research. Should study prob-
lems of society but not itself try to remedy them. INTEC, of which
author is rector, has pioneered in graduate studies and has created the
Center for Technical Assistance to link industry and university, with a
UN agency's help. WKU

GEN LAUERHASS, LUDWIG; ARAUJO HAUGSE, OLIVIERA DE; and LUCIA, VERA.
171 Education in Latin America: A Bibliography. Los Angeles: UCLA,
Latin American Center Publications; Boston: G.K. Hall, 1980.
431 pp.
Designed as an introductory reference volume, its 9,866
entries range in time from pre-Columbian to mid-1970s; in space over
all areas of Latin America and the Caribbean. Emphasis on post-1945
materials. Entries arranged by areas: Middle America and the Caribbean, Spanish South America, and Brazil; general section also on Latin
America. Entries cover serials and reference sources, education in
general, in-school education, out-of-school education, educational
planning and administration. In-school sections contain high percentage of entries on colleges and universities. UCLA libraries now
hold some 50 percent of materials cited. Due note is taken of the fact
that education is a field with fewer publications and weaker bibliographic control than many others. A remarkable and necessary
contribution to scholarship. KU

LEMKE, DONALD A. "Education in the English Speaking Caribbean."
See entry GUY 38.

GEN LENARIS, JULIO. "Universidad, estructura intelectual y desar-
172 rollo social." Encuentro 3, no. 11 (1970): 1-12.
Universities fail to develop intellectual rigor in students,
largely because they devote too much time to strictly professional
training.

GEN LENT, JOHN A. "Mass Communication Research in the Caribbean:
173 Background and Problems." Paper presented at Caribbean Studies
Association Meeting, Martinique, May 1979. Mimeographed. 23 pp.
Research opportunities abound, but little has been done because in past Caribbean universities have had only four schools of
journalism, none before 1953. Some governments forbid or discourage
research. Bibliography of eight and one-half pages shows some research
topic possibilities. WKU

LEVINE, DANIEL H. "Thinking about Students and Politics:
Venezuela in the 1960s." See entry VEN 85.

GEN LEWIS, SYBIL FARRELL. "Caribbean Research Institutions: The
174 Institute of Caribbean Studies." Mimeographed. Rio Piedras:
University of Puerto Rico, Institute of Caribbean Studies, May
1979. 12 pp. plus 14 pages appendices.

Center for research and teaching in social sciences, history, humanities and arts related to Caribbean and circum-Caribbean described by editor of Caribbean Studies at Caribbean Studies Association conference. Details of activities, academic programs. Appendices: personnel, publications of researchers. WKU

GEN   LEWIS, [W.] ARTHUR. "The University in Less Developed
175   Countries." In Conference of Overseas Vice-Chancellors, Nigeria, January 1974, pp. 5-15. [London]: Inter-University Council (IUC), [1974].
        Examination of role of donor agencies to ICED project on Higher Education for Development questions role of universities. Princeton political economist, formerly of UWI, describes universities in LDCs as in disagreement about what culture they transmit, who gets what kind of education. Speaks of "British trap" at UWI of trying to combine research and undergraduate teaching; advocates non-partisan contribution to politics. KU

GEN   LIEBMAN, ARTHUR; WALKER, KENNETH N.; and GLAZER, MYRON. Latin
176   American University Students: A Six Nation Study. Cambridge, Mass: Harvard University Press, 1972. 296 pp.
        Comparative study of students in Colombia, Mexico, Panama, Paraguay, Puerto Rico and Uruguay based on 1964-65 questionnaire data. Description of historical and contemporary student roles in universities and national politics. DLC

GEN   LINTON, NEVILLE O. "UNICA V Survey: Guyana--Caribbean Studies."
177   Caribbean Educational Bulletin 4, no. 1 (January 1977): 38-42.
        Twenty-two courses in seven departments at UG have Caribbean content, with graduate students and staff doing research on Guyanese and/or Caribbean topics. Same survey shows virtually nothing in East Asian studies at University of Guyana. Interest in Caribbean studies just starting at University of Surinam; University of the West Indies in Trinidad and Tobago has some courses in Indian History.

GEN   LIPSET, SEYMOUR MARTIN. "The Political Behavior of University
178   Students in Developing Nations." Social and Economic Studies 14, no. 1 (March 1965): 35-75.
        Some examples from Latin America (but most from other nations) put student political activity in useful perspective on universities in their societies, as change agents and/or related to change.

GEN   LOPEZ YUSTOS, R. ALFONSO. "Education in the West Indies."
179   Revista/Review Interamericana 2, no. 2 (Summer 1972): 167-73.
        Compiled for UNICA. Nearly all on pre-university level education, and chiefly in English-speaking Caribbean. Excludes items recorded in Comitas and Baa.

GEN   LUCARELLI, ELISA, and DIAZ, JORGE. SICAPER: Una experiencia de
180   capacitación a distancia de administradores educativos en servicio, ponencia presentada al I Congreso Interamericano de Administración de la Educación, Brasilia 9-14 December 1979. Serie Textos y Documentos, no. 8. Panamá: Universidad de Panamá, ICASE, 1979. 51 pp.

Program of in-service training for supervisory personnel in education begun in 1977, sponsored by University of Panama, Ministry of Education and Panamanian Institute of Special Skills, with help of Organization of American States. Serves Panama and rest of Central America with self-teaching programs, group discussion using methodology of action-reflection-action. Each country arranges own structure and supervision. Panamanian participation reached 38.7 percent. Data, conclusions, recommendations.

GEN   MAIER, JOSEPH, and WEATHERHEAD, RICHARD W., eds. The Latin
181   American University. Albuquerque: University of New Mexico
      Press, 1979. 237 pp.
          Introduction by editors. Essays, apparently written before
1970s, on history and philosophy of Spanish-American universities,
European backgrounds, university reform, role of rectors and
professors. DLC

GEN   MAINGOT, ANTHONY P. "Mexico, Central America and Panama: The
182   Prospects for Caribbean Studies." Caribbean Education Bulletin
      4, no. 1 (January 1977): 49-53.
          ". . . no significant attention given to the Caribbean as a
field of scholarly and intellectual focus in the Universities of
Mexico, Central America and Panama," but area is "slowly becoming
familiar" to scholar and layman, in part with U.S. reaction to Cuba.
Organizations ANUIES, CSUCA, FUPAC show interest in communicating with
UNICA, possibly to foster Pan-Caribbean studies.

      MANLEY, MICHAEL. The Politics of Change: A Jamaican Testament.
      See entry UWI 85.

GEN   MARTIN BARO, IGNACIO; FERREIRA LIMA, JOÃO DAVID; GARRETON, MANUEL
183   ANTONIO; and SAMAME BOGGIO, MARIO. Elementos de concientización
      en los curricula universitarios. Guatemala: FUPAC, 1975. 179
      pp.
          Central American Association of Private Universities
sponsored second meeting of academics, at which chief topics were
socio-political awareness in university curricula, university education
and national reality. Educators from elsewhere in Latin America attended, made recommendations. KU

GEN   MATHEWS, THOMAS. "Caribbean Cooperation in the Field of Higher
184   Education." In Regionalism and the Commonwealth Caribbean:
      Papers presented at the Seminar on Foreign Policies of Caribbean
      States, April-June 1968, edited by Roy Preiswerk, pp. 151-56.
      St. Augustine: Institute of International Relations, University
      of the West Indies, Trinidad, 1968.
          Drive to create and expand universities is integral part of
Caribbean movements to decolonize and promote economic development.
Loss of students to metropolises after studying abroad; anti-
imperialism, extreme nationalism, and efforts to transcend it at UWI.
Strain on institutions to meet perceived manpower needs for development. Cooperation among universities of region difficult, but some
communication among scholars occurs; examples. OU

GEN ------. "Report for UNICA on a Visit to the Centre Universitaire
185 Antilles-Guyane in April 1976." Caribbean Educational Bulletin
4, no. 1 (January 1977): 24-29.
Campuses in Guadeloupe and Martinique; sciences and economics
at former, latter to have humanities and social studies; both have law;
chiefly offering two-year programs. Caribbean content of some courses
in law, economics, geography, history, modern literature. Tentative
plans to cooperate with UG and UWI.

GEN MAZO, GABRIEL DEL. El movimiento de la reforma universitaria en
186 América Latina: Síntesis explicatoria. Cinco conferencias.
Lima: Universidad Nacional Federico Villarreal, 1967. 94 pp.
Reviews history of reforms, including current moves such as
development of general studies, which he supports. Strongly urges
national solutions and sense of identity as Latin Americans. WKU

GEN "Meeting of Educational Planners of the Central American
187 Countries." Newsletter, no. 3 (January 1981): 6-7.
For first time in Central American area, planning directors
from Ministries of Education, national planning offices and planners
from private and public universities met for discussions. ICASE organized five-day meeting in Panama. Topics: increasing unemployment of
professionals and technicians and their prospects in Central America,
educational systems in the face of political and social change in the
region.

GEN MEJIA-RICART GUZMAN, TIRSO. La universidad en la historia
188 universal. Publicaciones de la Universidad Autónoma de Santo
Domingo, vol. 278. Collección Historia y Sociedad, no. 41.
Santo Domingo: Editora de la UASD, 1981. 417 pp.
Dominican scholar and educational leader surveys universities
as integral parts of their economic, political and ideological
matrices. Examines major issues, roles, expectations as universities
evolve into their contemporary forms. Useful perspectives on the Latin
American university; comments on the influence of positivism, observations on the Cordoba reforms. WKU

GEN MENDOZA DIEZ, ALVARO. El ciclo preprofesional universitario.
189 Maracaibo: Universidad del Zulia, 1965. 198 pp.
Strong, well documented statement of need for breaking
pattern of traditional, purely professional university. Advocate of
views of Ortega y Gasset, Atcon, Waggoner, others interested in general
education. WKU

GEN MESA REDONDA SOBRE LA ENSEÑANZA DE LAS CIENCIAS SOCIALES EN LA
190 AMERICA CENTRAL Y LAS ANTILLAS, SAN JOSE, COSTA RICA, 1954,
organizada por la UNESCO en Costa Rica. [Havana]: Universidad
de la Habana, [1955]. 185 pp.
A round table for social sciences in the Caribbean and
Central America with full detail of the various universities and their
programs. Each spokesman of the region and representatives of UNESCO
comment. TxU

GEN   MITCHELL, WILLARD H.   CSUCA: A Regional Strategy for Higher
191   Education in Central America.   Center of Latin American Studies,
        Occasional Publications, no. 7. [Lawrence, Kans.]: University
        of Kansas, Center of Latin American Studies, 1967. 66 pp.
        Tentative beginnings in forties and fifties established com-
munication among five Central American national universities; ambigui-
ties over goals, but impetus to university reform with General Studies
in sixties. Integration more difficult. Description and evaluation of
reforms for each university, recommendations. For critique and
corrections see item GEN 218. KU

GEN   MORLES SANCHEZ, VICTOR.   La educación de postgrado en el mundo.
192   Caracas: Universidad Central de Venezuela, Facultad de Humani-
        dades y Educación, Coordinación de Postgrado, 1980.   367 pp.
        Preliminary version of study undertaken to further develop-
ment of a national policy for graduate studies in Venezuela and the
Third World generally, with aid of CONICIT, Central University of
Venezuela, and the University of Kansas. Goal is to know but not copy
policies and practices of other societies, to recognize values and
interests inherent in graduate studies programs. Comparative presentation is descriptive, analytical, synthesized. Raises important
questions about goals, values, beneficiaries of research and graduate
education. Chapter on Latin American graduate programs. Useful basis
for discussion, evaluation of both developing and developed systems.
WKU

GEN   MYINT, H. "Education and Economic Development." Social and
193   Economic Studies 14, no. 1 (March 1965): 8-20.
        Cautionary comments on identifying education as the key com-
ponent needed for national development, a favorite strategy of several
countries in the 1960s. Urges research.

        NACIONES UNIDAS (UNESCO). See UNITED NATIONS EDUCATIONAL,
        SCIENTIFIC and CULTURAL ORGANIZATION (UNESCO).

GEN   NETTLEFORD, REX. "Foreword." Caribbean Quarterly 23, no. 4
194   (December 1977): iii-iv.
        Issue devoted to topic of development; with regard to role of
education: "It is precisely this need to socialise large numbers of
people into new values to meet new aspirations which makes the post-
colonial Caribbean such a vital target for 'development' today. The
building of factories, the search for appropriate technology,...the
regulation of population growth,...and the re-statement of values...are
all aspects of that challenging process which seeks to ensure to the
region ultimate release from a traditional socio-economic, political
and cultural dependency."

GEN   NILES, NORMA A., and GARDNER, TREVOR G. The Brain Drain from the
195   West Indies and Africa. East Lansing, Mich.: West Indian
        Student Association, 1977. 161 pp.
        First of projected annual conferences of the West Indian
Student Association. Fifteen papers analyze problems of the professional at home, the student abroad and the would-be returnee to home
country. Caribbean university-prepared people lack opportunities for
appropriate employment, and home countries lose needed skills and
leadership. WKU

GEN   OCAMPO LONDOÑO, ALFONSO. "Education: A Look Ahead in the
196   Caribbean." In The Caribbean: Its Hemispheric Role, edited by
        A. Curtis Wilgus, pp. 127-37. Caribbean Conference Series 1,
        vol. 17. Gainesville: University of Florida Press, 1967.
        Statistics for education in the Caribbean and observations
about quality of professors and teachers. KU

GEN   ------. Higher Education in Latin America: Current and Future.
197   Occasional Paper no. 7. New York: International Council for
        Educational Development, 1973. 52 pp.
        Former Colombian minister of education and university rector,
at seminar of CHEAR, addresses demographic and economic aspects, growing
specialization, research, finance, university reform and laws, relationships with governments in general terms. Seventeen tables with
demographic, economic, educational data. WKU

GEN   "La VIII asamblea de la Unión de Universidades de América
198   Latina." Gaceta/UDUAL, no. 26 (November 1979): 6.
        Resolutions of UDUAL that its members lend aid to the
reconstruction of Nicaragua and the National Autonomous University of
Nicaragua, and that they help the Autonomous University of Santo
Domingo after damage from a hurricane. Also demand that government of
Guatemala "guarantee the life and dignity of Guatemalan
universitarios."

        ORGANIZACION DE LOS ESTADOS AMERICANOS (OEA). See ORGANIZATION
        OF AMERICAN STATES (OAS).

GEN   ORGANIZATION OF AMERICAN STATES (OAS). Educational Deficits in
199   the Caribbean. Atlas Series, no. 2. Washington D.C.: OAS,
        Department of Educational Affairs, 1979. 128 pp.
        Illiteracy; population without schools. KU

GEN   ------. Latin American Higher Education and Interamerican Co-
200   operation: Report and Recommendations. Washington, D.C.: Pan
        American Union, 1961. 20 pp.
        Study requested by President John F. Kennedy dealt with tasks
and needs of Latin American universities, the U.S.-sponsored Alliance
for Progress, and the meaning of international cooperation in area of
higher education. KU

GEN   ------, Comité Jurídico Interamericano. Aspectos jurídicos
201   relativos a la armonización progresiva de los planes de estudio
        de los países americanos y sobre la validez y equivalencia de
        títulos y grados. Documento de antecedentes preparado por la
        División de Codificación e Integración Jurídica del Departamento
        de Asuntos Jurídicos de la Secretaría General. Washington, D.C.:
        OEA, Secretaría General, 1975. 108 pp.
        Inter-American convocation of 1902; regional American convo-
cations, 1889-1974; regional European convocations. DPU

GEN   ------, Secretaría Ejecutiva para la Educación, la Ciencia y la
202   Cultura, Departamento de Asuntos Educativos. El Programa Regional
        de Desarrollo Educativo (PREDE) en el bienio 1980-81. Washing-
        ton, D.C.: Secretaría General de la Organización de los Estados
        Americanos, 1980. 63 pp.

Establishment, reorganization, program orientation, budget, personnel, documents of PREDE. Attention focuses on serving disadvantaged populations, use of technology, regionalization. Some university projects involved. WKU

GEN   OTEIZA, ENRIQUE. "Reunión general de Centro Ajijic para el
203   Mejoramiento de la Educación Superior en América (CAMESA)." Docencia Post-secundaria 7, no. 1 (January-February 1979): 23-30.
Director of UNESCO agency Centro Regional para la Educación Superior en América Latina y el Caribe (CRESAL) describes its 1978 establishment in Caracas. Plans to develop and improve regional higher education; Regional Accord on Studies, Diplomas and Grades had been signed in Mexico in 1974. With Venezuelan financial support, program is planned to develop a library and publish a bibliography, provide advisory services, address such topics as research, human resources, planning.

GEN   THE PAN AMERICAN ASSOCIATION OF EDUCATIONAL CREDIT INSTITUTIONS.
204   APICE: What is it? Bogota: APICE, [1980]. 20 leaves.
Founded in 1969 with member institutions, public and private, from Latin America and the Caribbean, it fosters development of student loan programs. Has celebrated eight congresses, 1966-1979, published numerous directories. WKU

GEN   PAN AMERICAN UNION, Division of Intellectual Cooperation. Higher
205   Education in Latin America. Vol. 6: The Universities of Costa Rica, El Salvador, Guatemala, Honduras, Nicaragua, Panamá, by Theodore Apstein, Ben F. Carruthers, and Ellen Gut. Washington, D.C.: Pan American Union, Division of Intellectual Cooperation, 1947. 185 pp.
Useful profiles give history, governance, enrollment, courses of study, admissions requirements, budgets of these still small, traditional universities. See entry GEN 295. KU

GEN   PARKER, PAUL C. "Change and Challenge in Caribbean Higher Edu-
206   cation: The Development of the University of the West Indies and the University of Puerto Rico." Ph.D. dissertation, Florida State University College of Education, 1971. 536 pp.
Excellent source of historical and other information and viewpoints on both universities. Assesses changes in two systems with reference to adaptation away from colonial origins toward more indigenous character. Background for understanding separatist and racist tendencies among Crown Colonies, and Puerto Rico's different development from the rest of Latin America. Departure from British university governance system; emphasis on basic arts and sciences; on-going efforts to protect quality while democratizing opportunity at UWI. UPR's efforts to escape political turmoil in controversy over island's status. FTaSU

PELCZAR, RICHARD. "University Reform in Latin America: The Case of Colombia." See entry COL 50.

GEN   PEÑALVER, LUIS MANUEL. "A modo de editorial." Universitas 2000
207   4, nos. 2-3 (1980): 7-15.

Inaugural address to First Latin American Seminar on Student Affairs, in Barquisimeto, Venezuela, focuses on post-1918 university model and current reforms being attempted. Need to revise concepts of all education, given changed student population and demand. Mixture of races, cultures, classes in Latin America and Caribbean requires new structures, but university should not be direct instrument of social change. Poor yield of universities--only 10 or 15 per 100 graduate--an indicator of need for this seminar convoked by GULERPE.

GEN   ------. Análisis de las conclusiones de la Primera Conferencia
208   de la Unión de Universidades Latinoamericanas sobre planeamiento
         universitario. Santo Domingo: Universidad Autónoma de Santo
         Domingo, 1970. 34 pp.
         Discusses education, universities, and development, based on
a dynamic concept of the university in Latin America. Includes the six
conferences. MexCo

GEN   ------. "Información de GULERPE: Reflexiones preliminares e
209   informe de actividades." Universitas 2000 3, no. 1 (1978): 201-
         10.
         Venezuelan former rector and minister of education, now
president of the Grupo Universitario Latinoamericano de Estudios para
la Reforma y Perfeccionamiento de la Educación, addresses colleagues
from several Spanish-speaking Caribbean countries and others in South
America. History of university reforms, need for innovation. Stresses
nature of GULERPE (no non-Latin members), as contrasted with CHEAR, and
UDUAL (not representing institutions) and announces plans for
publishing GULERPE's works in Universitas 2000 in Caracas.

GEN   ------; GARIBAY GUTIERREZ, LUIS; and SORIA, OSCAR. "The Present
210   Situation and Future Perspectives of Higher Education in Latin
         America." Paper presented at VI Triennial Meeting, International
         Association of University Presidents, San José, Costa Rica, 28
         June-3 July 1981. Mimeographed. 34 pp. plus 23 statistical
         leaves.
         Description of socioeconomic context includes data on
population, economic stagnation, urbanism, political instability,
poverty. Educational, scientific, and technological framework; evolution of the university, reforms under way or needed. Broadening
objectives, relationship with state and society, organization, student
characteristics, access, developmental needs, finance are main topics.
Challenge to powerful nations set forth. Tables demonstrate need for
improved data collection on education in Latin America and the
Caribbean. WKU

GEN   PIÑERO, EUROPA GONZALEZ DE, and CLAUDIO, RAMON, eds. Crecimiento
211   del personal docente. UNICA Series on University Structure and
      Organization. [Washington, D.C.]: UNICA/OAS, [1980]. 81 pp.
         Chiefly works presented at a conference in the Dominican
Republic, 10-15 March 1980. Detailed descriptions of measures taken to
improve the quality of university professors, in a time of rapid growth
and insufficiently prepared young faculty, in Venezuela's Universidad
de Carabobo and Universidad del Zulia, Puerto Rico's Universidad Interamericana and Universidad de Puerto Rico, the Dominican Republic's
Universidad Católica Madre y Maestra and Universidad Pedro Henríquez
Ureña. Useful insights into problems and institutions. WKU

GEN   PINTO MAZAL, JORGE. La autonomía universitaria: Antología/
212   estudio preliminar y selección de textos. Mexico: Universidad
       Nacional Autónoma de México, 1974. 291 pp.
           Autonomy has always been discussed and argued, but almost
every university person accepts it as essential--especially for professors, students, and researchers. Includes essays by leading
Mexican and Dominican educators on the topic of universities and their
relationship to the state. KU

GEN   PORTANTIERO, JUAN CARLOS. Estudiantes y política en América
213   Latina: El proceso de la reforma universitaria 1918-1938.
       Mexico: Siglo Veintiuno, 1978. 461 pp.
           Contemporary Latin American university maintains backward,
dependent capitalist division of work, perpetuating social hierarchies.
With massification and academic programs for which no employment
exists, universities face more than structural crisis. Social and
political background of 1918 Cordoba reform as a middle class challenge
to oligarchy and its consequences described in detail. Nationalist,
populist student credos derived from Cordoba important in Cuba and
elsewhere. Valuable collection of documents and polemic of reform
movements and important perspective on the topic. KU

GEN   "Post-graduate Studies in Latin America and the Caribbean."
214   Higher Education 1, no. 3 (February-June 1980): 2.
           CRESALC preparing study of evolution of graduate studies to
determine characteristics, origins of programs. Most analysis will
focus on countries with greatest quantitative development: Brazil,
Colombia, Cuba, Mexico, Venezuela.

GEN   PRESIDENTIAL COMMISSION OF THE UNIVERSITY FOR PEACE. University
215   for Peace: Basic Documents. San José: Presidential Commission
       of the University for Peace, 1981. 267 pp.
           Speeches by President Rodrigo Carazo of Costa Rica at United
Nations meetings, reports and resolutions of the U.N. directed toward
establishment of university in Costa Rica. WKU

       PRESTON, ASTON ZACHARY. "The Caribbean: Changing Needs in a
       Changing Society." See entry UWI 99.

GEN   PRIETO FIGUEROA, LUIS BELTRAN. El estado y la educación en
216   América Latina. Caracas: Monte Avila Editores, 1977. [300] pp.
           Need for education of masses, not just of elite; need se-
lection by abilities. Government must finance universities while they
retain their autonomy. Importance of general, not just technical,
education. Comments on University of Costa Rica and some universities
in Venezuela, among others. DLC

GEN   "Primera mesa redonda de las facultades centroamericanas de
217   agronomía." Universidades, no. 14-15 (November 1963-March 1964):
       62-63.
           Sponsored by CSUCA, the Faculty of Agronomy of UCR and the
Ford Foundation, representatives of five public universities approved a
basic, minimum plan of studies for agronomy students. Recommended
General Studies for them; promotion of basic disciplines in universities with integration of the separate faculties, and work in agricultural extension.

GEN   RAMIREZ MERCADO, SERGIO. "Ref: SP-CSUCA-3272-67." Copy of
218   letter to Willard H. Mitchell, dated 19 June 1967, from Ciudad
      Universitaria Rodrigo Facio. 10 pp.
        Adjunct secretary general of CSUCA criticizes and corrects
errors in Mitchell's paper CSUCA: A Regional Strategy for Higher Education in Central America. Denies formative role Mitchell attributes
to North American consultants in CSUCA's development, chides him for
ignoring 1947 and 1957 actions before their visit. Refutes claim that
National Science Foundation and University of Kansas proposed structural changes in CSUCA; cites activities ignored or not comprehended by
author, whose condescending approach he finds unwarranted. See entry
GEN 191. WKU

GEN   RENNER, RICHARD R., ed. Universities in Transition: The U.S.
219   Presence in Latin American Higher Education. Gainesville, Fla.:
      Center for Latin American Studies, University of Florida, 1973.
      147 pp.
        U.S. influence on Latin American higher education was the
focus of a seminar in the University of Florida in 1970. Universities,
foundations, government involvement in Latin American universities
among topics covered in procedings. KU

GEN   "Report on Item 10 of the MINEDLAC Agenda: Responsibilities of
220   Higher Education vis-à-vis the Requirements of Development and
      the Democratization of Education." Higher-Education 1, nos. 1-2
      (June 1979-January 1980): 10-14.
        Special commission, chaired by Carlos Tünnermann Bernheim,
looks at whether massification since 1960 is indication of more democratization. Higher education expansion 1970-77 at 15.3 percent (3.8
percent for primary, 9.7 percent for secondary)plus rapid increase in
institutions has been unsystematic and unplanned. Main topics covered:
democratization, higher education and employment, reform of higher
education, role and place of scientific and technical education and
research in the service of integrated development, contribution of
higher education to analysis of problems of changing societies, responsibilities of higher education towards the educational system as a
whole.

GEN   "Representantes del CSUCA se reunieron con el Doctor Guillermo
221   Soberón," Gaceta/UDUAL, no. 25 (October 1979): 5.
        Several representatives from the Confederation of Central
American Universities (CSUCA) meet with the rector of the National
University of Mexico (UNAM) and the president of the Union of Latin
American Universities (UDUAL), to request "fraternal help and solidarity" in the process of reconstruction of Nicaragua's Autonomous University. Report on death threats to rector and violence against others
at University of San Carlos of Guatemala.

GEN   "Resoluciones de FEUCA." Presencia Universitaria, no. 46 (Oc-
222   tober 1978): 15.
        San Salvador meeting of Federation of University Students of
Central America passes thirteen resolutions on governmental problems in
Central America; also proposes formation of teams of medical and
nursing students to aid Nicaraguan war victims.

GEN "Reunión técnica sobre necesidades y perspectivas educativas para
223 América Latina y el Caribe en la década del 80." Acción y
Reflexión Educativa, no. 5 (June 1980): 248-51.
Meeting organized by ICASE and the Department of Educational
Affairs of the Organization of American States, 5-9 May. Themes:
development of the region as context for education, analysis of some
global problems affecting development of educational systems, formulation of lines of action, determination of kinds of international
technical cooperation for the region. Specialists inventoried problems
and prepared recommendations. Universities should be seen as one--but
not the only--kind of post-secondary education, should diversify
offerings to fit job market, contribute to development, pursue
decentralization.

GEN ROGGI, LUIS OSVALDO. ICASE, una filosofía en acción. Serie
224 Textos y Documentos, no. 5. Panamá: Universidad de Panamá,
ICASE, Asistencia Técnica Internacional OEA, 1978. 57 pp.
History of graduate-level Central American Institute for
Administration and Supervision of Education, designed to remedy lack of
qualified personnel, since 1967 beginnings at University of Panama.
OAS and UNESCO have helped with program of courses, research, consulting, publishing. Activities, structure, philosophy, interdisciplinary character described. WKU

GEN ROJAS, PEDRO. "Discursos que el Doctor Pedro Rojas, secretario
225 general A.I. de la UDUAL, pronunció durante la ceremonia de
clausura de la XI Conferencia de Facultades y Escuelas de Medicina de América Latina." Gaceta/UDUAL, no. 25 (October 1979):
2-3.
Secretary General of UDUAL addresses closing session of
meeting of medical schools in Puebla, Mexico, refers to Ninth Conference in Havana and Tenth in Santo Domingo. Present theme is "population policies in our America and their manipulation by shameless
interests alien to our autonomy." Calls for "the cultural integration
of Latin America with all its consequences."

GEN ------. "Reflexiones sobre la autonomía universitaria en
226 Latinoamérica, teórica y práctica," Gaceta/UDUAL, no. 25 (October
1979): 3-5
History of university autonomy from "the first general
studies of the Low Middle Ages" through nineteenth and twentieth century resistance to civil or ecclesiastical intervention in university
affairs. Secretary general of UDUAL asserts that now autonomy is
more than self-determination in academic matters, signifying "capacity
to exercise cognitive criticism in the field of culture and action
consequent to theory in the political terrain." Cuba a special case
vis-à-vis autonomy.

GEN ROSARIO, ANTONIO. "Lo que verdaderamente tenemos que hacer es
227 formular teorías y escuelas que corresponden con nuestra
auténtica realidad. Gaceta/UDUAL, no. 39 (December 1980): 2-4.
Rector of Autonomous University of Santo Domingo opens conference of schools and institutes of economics of Latin America with
vigorous, familiar plea that educators and researchers look to Latin
American problems and their autochthonous solutions and methodologies.

GEN   ROULET, JORGE, and RIZ, LILIANA DE. <u>Bases para programa latino-</u>
228   <u>americano de estudios de postgrado en ciencias sociales</u>. Buenos
       Aires: Consejo Latinoamericano de Ciencias Sociales, Programa
       Latinoamericano de Estudios de Postgrado en Ciencias Sociales,
       1973. 60 pp.
           Persistent concern that research needed to overcome under-
development is stalled by ideological disagreement, dependence on
foreign training and consequent brain drain. Proposes national and
regional development to achieve "critical mass" of scholars, focusing
on problems in their Latin American context. Role of CLACSO and history of project. WKU

GEN   SAMAROO, BRINSLEY. "UNICA V Survey, Caribbean and Asian
229   Studies.Â Commentarª bª Nevillí LintonÛ <u>Caribbean Educationaš</u>
       <u>Bulletin</u> 4, no. 2 (May 1977): 39-49.
           Afro-Indian stereotypes contribute to ill will; some uni-
versity regional studies in Trinidad and Guyana were begun, but there
is no interest in Surinam. Conflicts within East Indian community, and
with Africans, engendered by Indian academic visitors. African and
Asian studies by their constituents can be counter-productive. Importance of promoting African and Asian studies are "part of the
universal search for knowledge."

GEN   SAMMY, GEORGE M. "The Role of the Modern University." <u>Caribbean</u>
230   <u>Quarterly</u> 15, no. 4 (December 1969): 47-51.
           Central question facing universities in developing nations is
whether or not they should play a traditional academic role or in-
corporate social service functions which may affect their own integrity
and the quality of education.

GEN   SANCHEZ, LUIS ALBERTO. <u>La universidad latinoamericana: Estudio</u>
231   <u>comparativo</u>. Prologue by Carlos Martínez Durán. Guatemala:
       Editorial Universitaria, 1949. 220 pp.
           Analysis by Peruvian educator-politician of the Latin Amer-
ican university, published under auspices of the organizing committee
of the First Congress of Latin American Universities. Prologue contains data on Universidad de San Carlos de Guatemala. TxU

GEN   ------, and BARRIENTOS, IVAN. <u>La formación del estudiante uni-</u>
232   <u>versitario</u>. Occasional Publications, no. 11. [Lawrence, Kan-
       sas]: University of Kansas, 1968. 44 pp.
           Philosophical treatment of role of university in "formation"
of the university student by a Peruvian educator-politician and Guate-
malan-born professor, at time of considerable change and debate in
Latin American universities. KU

GEN   SANZ ARADOS, JUAN JOSE. <u>Educación liberación en América Latina</u>.
233   Bogotá: Universidad Santo Tomás, 1979. 272 pp.
           For use of students in philosophy of education program,
particularly to introduce "liberation pedagogy." Strong emphasis on
social and historical context of education, with analysis of economic
and social development models of 1960s. Educational themes of the "New
School," especially ideas of Illich. Dangers of North American educational technology and pedagogical models; both seen as militaristic
and capitalist-dependent. Relations between culture and popular education, and diverse tendencies in Latin America. TxU

GEN   SCHERZ GARCIA, LUIS. El camino de la revolución universitaria.
234   Santiago de Chile: Editorial del Pacífico, 1968. 180 pp.
      Sociological analysis of the Latin American university gives
useful picture of Napoleonic model; examines trends and changes, including the role of science, which author sees as appropriate to a
university, and technology, which lends itself to exploitation from
abroad. KU

GEN   "Se reunieron CSUCA y FEUCA en Managua." Universidad, no. 419
235   (30 November-6 December 1979): 7.
      Representatives of Central American universities and their
student federations (FEUCA) met with members of Higher Council of
Central American Universities (CSUCA) for the first time in CSUCA's
twenty year history. Support expressed for Sandinista revolution in
Nicaragua. El Salvador's representative failed to arrive "due to the
tense political situation;" the Honduran representative was warned by
his government not to mix in Central American student affairs, and was
taken prisoner on his return home from the meeting.

GEN   SEDOC-DAHLBERG, BETTY. "University Planning and Regional De-
236   velopment." Paper for Second Meeting of Planning Officials in
      the Caribbean, 28 May-2 June, 1980. Mimeographed. [Paramaribo]:
      Universiteit van Suriname, 1980. 18 pp.
      Caribbean realities compel questioning colonial heritage in
society and university. Both national and regional planning must
include universities as component, with closer look at social and
academic functions related to manpower needs.

GEN   SEMINAR ON HIGHER EDUCATION IN THE AMERICAS. Quinto Seminario de
237   Educación Superior en las Américas. Edited by George R.
      Waggoner. Lawrence: University of Kansas, College of Liberal
      Arts and Sciences, 1964. 152 pp.
      Nineteen Latin American educators in six-week seminar produce
individual essays and a set of conclusions on the topic of the university and national development. WKU

GEN   ------. Sexto Seminario de Educación Superior en las Américas.
238   Edited by George R. Waggoner. Lawrence: University of Kansas,
      College of Liberal Arts and Sciences, 1965. 151 pp.
      Discusses topics of university reform and universities and
national development. Individual essays by twenty-eight participants
from fifteen countries provide insights into differences and similarities of views, stages of development. Among Caribbean countries
represented: Colombia, Costa Rica, Guatemala, Honduras, Mexico, Panama,
Venezuela. Conclusions and recommendations. WKU

GEN   ------. Séptimo Seminario de Educación Superior en las Américas.
239   Edited by George R. Waggoner. Lawrence: University of Kansas,
      College of Liberal Arts and Sciences, 1966. 96 pp.
      General conclusions of five-week seminar on topics of uni-
versity and society, student welfare, general studies, university administration. More valuable are individual essays, including those
from seven Caribbean countries. Twenty-six educators from fifteen
Latin American countries participated. WKU

GEN   ------. Octavo Seminario de Educación Superior en las Américas.
240   Edited by George R. Waggoner and Ana Herzfeld. Lawrence: Uni-
       versity of Kansas, College of Liberal Arts and Sciences, 1967.
       113 pp.
       Twenty-two educational leaders from eleven Latin American
countries discussed and produced reports on university self-study and
university planning. Viewpoints on their circumstances and directions
of change. WKU

GEN   ------. Noveno Seminario de Educación Superior en las Américas.
241   Edited by George R. Waggoner and Ana Herzfeld. Lawrence: Uni-
       versity of Kansas, College of Liberal Arts and Sciences, 1968.
       117 pp.
       Twenty-four educators began seminar at University of Costa
Rica, continued at Universities of New Mexico and Kansas with topics on
university planning and evaluation. Most significant activities:
evaluation of Faculty of Sciences and Letters of University of Costa
Rica and of College of Liberal Arts and Sciences, University of Kansas.
KU

GEN   "Seminario sobre evaluación y mejoramiento de la enseñanza uni-
242   versitaria." Caribbean Educational Bulletin 7, no. 2 (May 1980):
       2-38.
       UNICA and OAS and five Dominican universities held a seminar
for representatives of fifty Caribbean institutions. Among the topics:
growth and evaluation of faculties, evaluating staff development
programs.

       SERRANO, AUGUSTO. "Situación Probable y deseada de las re-
       laciones entre universidad y ayuda externa para la década del 80:
       El caso centroamericano." See entry HON 14.

GEN   SHERLOCK, PHILIP. "Education in the Caribbean Area." Caribbean
243   Quarterly 1, no. 3 (1950): 9-18.
       Caribbean education lacks both purpose and quality. Com-
pulsory education not enforced and enrollment figures are misleading
because attendance rates are low. Feels emphasis should be placed on
primary education.

GEN   ------. "Growth Plan for the Eighties." Caribbean Educational
244   Bulletin 6, no. 3 (September 1979): 1-6.
       Describes UNICA with its forty-five member institutions, its
governance and finance; restructuring of organization and general
statements about program goals.

GEN   ------. "Race Against Time." Caribbean Educational Bulletin 8,
245   no. 1 (January 1981): 3-43.
       Caribbean Association of Universities and Research Institutes
(UNICA) programs for Caribbean self-sufficiency in energy, food, data
and technology transfer described. Efforts at faculty development,
regional university communications system, work plans. UNICA has
forty-five members, representing constituency of 350,000 students,
30,000 faculty members.

GEN   ------. "The Role of Education in the Process of Development and
246   Modernization of the Caribbean People." In Problemas del Caribe
      Contemporáneo/Contemporary Caribbean Issues, edited by Angel
      Calderón Cruz, pp. 17-28. Río Piedras: Universidad de Puerto
      Rico, Instituto de Estudios del Caribe, 1979.
        Probes conventional wisdom of development equated to growth,
lightly salutes accomplishments of University of Puerto Rico and University of the West Indies, invites inquiry into appropriateness of
form and content of contemporary Caribbean education during 1975-76
academic year. WKU

GEN   ------. "Strengthening Caribbean Universities and their Facul-
247   ties through Establishment of Institutional Faculty Development
      Programs." Caribbean Educational Bulletin 8, no. 3 (January
      1981): 33-43.
        UNICA-sponsored project for 1982-83 to begin with workshop to
help "chief academic officers develop an increased awareness of the
need for faculty development on their campuses and the strategies that
could be used to heighten awareness when they return." Other related
activities proposed.

GEN   ------. "Time is Burning." Caribbean Educational Bulletin 4,
248   no. 2 (May 1977): 2-29. Interleaved English and Spanish.
        Plea by long-time secretary-general of UNICA for greater
cooperation among universities for regional development. Describes
some decentralization of UNICA, and its need for funding.

GEN   ------. "UNICA Activities." Caribbean Educational Bulletin 3,
249   no. 2 (May 1976): 3-6.
        Secretary-general of UNICA gives rationale for its 1948
founding. Deplores continuation of fragmentation within region, and
importation of ideas and methods from colonial powers.

GEN   SHILS, EDWARD. "The Implantation of Universities: Reflections
250   on a Theme of Ashby." Universities Quarterly 22, no. 2 (March
      1968): 142-66.
        Good discussion of problem of metropolitan and peripheral
institutions and the debilitating effect of mimetic structure and
practice. Risk of withdrawing from world university community to
concentrate on meeting local needs for manpower and applied research
while contributing nothing to intellectual culture can be balanced by
creating new knowledge acquired by the universal canons of science and
scholarship.

GEN   SHOREY, LEONARD L. Caribbean Education: The Need for Relevance.
251   Inaugural Antonio Jarvis Memorial Lecture at College of the
      Virgin Islands. Cave Hill: UWI, 1973. 23 pp.
        Extra-mural UWI tutor defines education broadly, shows how
schooling fails to relate to the Caribbean context. Irrelevance in
basic structure apparent in extent to which secondary schools are
geared to prepare students for higher education, which few will
achieve. English university examination system, by implication, still
rules. Criticizes predominance of academic subjects as incompatible
with economic realities. Expression of a widely held viewpoint. WKU

GEN   ------. "Caribbean Education: The Need for Relevance." <u>Micro-</u>
252   <u>state Studies</u> 2 (1979): 1-17.
       Irrelevance in basic structure of Caribbean education in
extent to which secondary schools are geared to prepare students for
tertiary level, although few go on.

GEN   ------. "The Future of Extra-Mural Studies in a Changing Carib-
253   bean Context." <u>Bulletin of Eastern Caribbean Affairs</u> 3, nos. 11
       and 12 (January-February 1978): 1-3.
       Professor at UWI, Barbados campus, calls for more orientation
toward regional problems and non-university clientele. Acute need for
training teachers of adults.

GEN   SILVA MICHELENA, HECTOR, and SONNTAG, HEINZ RUDOLF. <u>Universidad,</u>
254   <u>dependencia y revolución</u>. Mexico: Siglo Vientiuno Editores,
       1970. 217 pp.
       A socialist view of the Latin American universities. Until
the end of the eighteenth century the church dominated, and in the
nineteenth and twentieth centuries the Napoleonic, bourgeois approach
prevailed. The 1918 change in the University of Cordoba helped establish co-government of faculty and students. Neo-colonial aspect of
the Third World vs. the capitalist U.S. is the problem; the dependence
of the Latin American world on the U.S. Detail of changes believed
necessary in the Central University in Caracas, specifically the hopes
for new plans for social sciences. KU

GEN   SILVERT, KALMAN H. <u>Essays in Understanding Latin America</u>.
255   Foreword by Joel M. Jutkowitz. Philadelphia: Institute for the
       Study of Human Issues, 1977. 240 pp.
       Insights by late internationally known social scientist in-
clude scattered comments on universities and intellectuals and a
chapter titled "The Unwitting Prototypes: Latin American Students"
makes use of some examples from the Caribbean region. Background for
understanding its universities in chapter "Frames for the Caribbean
Experience." KU

GEN   "Simposio para coordinar y divulgar estudios sobre América
256   Latina." <u>El Universal</u>, 9 May 1980, p. I-27.
       President of Institute of Higher Studies for Latin America at
University Simon Bolivar sees symposium on Latin American studies as
part of effort to collect and analyze data and "look for identity and
unity so that integration becomes a fact" for Latin America and the
Caribbean. Present lack of communication among centers and specialists
impedes research.

GEN   "Sixth Biennial meeting of the Association of Caribbean Universi-
257   ties Held at Miami." <u>Caribbean Educational Bulletin</u> 7, no. 1
       (January 1980): 2-8.
       More than 100 university officials focused on two topics:
the scarcity of regionally produced food for local consumption and the
population explosion.

GEN   SMITH, DAVID HORTON. <u>Latin American Student Activism: Partici-</u>
258   <u>pation in Formal Volunteer Organizations by University Students</u>
       <u>in Six Latin Countries</u>. Lexington, Mass.: Lexington Press,
       1973. 169 pp.

Calls for better (not more) comparative research on complex question of student activism. Includes universities in Panama and Puerto Rico. Colombian and Mexican universities studied are not from Caribbean region, but some common patterns and values pertain. KU

GEN   SOLARI, ALDO E. "Los movimientos estudiantiles universitarios en
259   América Latina." Encuentro 1, no. 2 (March-April 1968): 72-88.
        Sociologist points out complexities of describing nature of student movements in time of turmoil and change. Rational analysis in realm of overheated rhetoric calls for systematic study.

GEN   SORIA N., OSCAR. "Needs of Post-Secondary Education in Latin
260   America: A Forecast for the Decade 1980-1990 through a Delphi
        Approach." Docencia--Postsecundaria 9, no. 3 (May-June 1981):
        117-58.
        Summary of an unpublished research paper produced at ISAEI for 1980 GULERPE meeting. Among goals listed: synthesis of sciences and humanities; resultant changes in preparation of faculty, research, administration, finance, curriculum; need for different relationships between universities and their communities, improved channels for international communication. Some proposed research topics.

GEN   SOTO BLANCO, OVIDIO. La educación en Centroamérica. Serie
261   Monografías Técnicas. San Salvador: Organización de Estados
        Centroamericanos, ODECA, Secretaría Permanente. 1968. 144 pp.
        ODECA, working for Central American integration, publishes series of monographs on various aspects of region to achieve rational bases for decision-making. Education seen as agent of social change. Problem of 40 percent illiteracy, inadequate data. Primary and secondary systems in six countries; essential perspective for understanding universities. WKU

GEN   SPENCER, DAVID ERIC, ed. Student Politics in Latin America.
262   [Philadelphia]: U.S. National Students Association, 1965. 287
        pp.
        Collection of essays by social scientists giving various perspectives on student political behavior; hortatory commentary by Spencer at beginning, middle, end of work. WKU

GEN   "Statistics on Higher Education in Latin America and the Carib-
263   bean: Preliminary Study." Higher Education 1, no. 3 (February-
        June 1980): 3-5.
        CRESALC study shows information comparatively analyzed at regional level is not systematic, hence fails to meet administrative, planning or research requirements. Need for improved collecting and processing but even more for conceptual aspect. Some guidelines.

GEN   SUAZO, TOME; LARA LOPEZ, GUILLERMO; and ALVAREZ ALVARADO, JESUS.
264   Informe del Comité de Evaluación Preliminar, Ciudad Universi-
        taria, Guatemala, 28 Marzo de 1966. Ciudad Universitaria Rodrigo
        Facio: Secretaría Permanente del CSUCA, [1966]. 16 pp.
        Lists regional research institutes, undergraduate and graduate programs; descriptions based on visits to five universities to collect data. Concludes there is strong support for regional integration. KU

GEN   SUNKEL, OSVALDO. "Reforma universitaria, subdesarrollo y
265   dependencia." Mimeographed. [Guatemala]: Universidad de San
       Carlos de Guatemala, [1970]. 24 pp.
            Chilean author says with post-World War II development came
power concentrations and dehumanizing social and economic systems, with
university's role to produce their needed human resources. Reviews
upheavals of sixties, calls for "critical reinterpretation of our
historic process." TxU

GEN   SWALLOW, JOHN R. "Regional Cooperation: The Permanent Secre-
266   tariat of the Central American Higher Education Confederation
       (CSUCA)." Ph.D. dissertation, Indiana University, 1975. 347 pp.
            Study of institution-building examines establishment,
operation, evolution, image of CSUCA's permanent staff as function of
consortium of universities. Useful juxtaposition of failure of political union in Central America with efforts at educational cooperation;
strong nationalistic, often opportunistic, drives conduce to separatism. History of CSUCA from 1948 beginning. Development and/or
failure of inter-institutional collaboration. Details of medical
education, manpower studies, general studies illustrate relationship
between institutional commitment and outcome of regional effort. Outstanding in its documentation, well written, an essential work.

GEN   TANZI, VITO. "Taxation, Educational Expenditure, and Income
267   Distribution." Seminar on the Financing of Education in Latin
       America, 15-19 November 1976. Mimeographed. Washington, D.C.:
       Inter-American Development Bank, [1976]. 23 pp.
            Analysis by IMF staff member of social goal of more equitable
distribution of income and opportunities via educational expenditure.
Both general revenues and earmarked funds, as in Colombia, Costa Rica,
Guatemala, Dominican Republic, Panama, Venezuela, probably have made
income distribution less even, benefiting those with high incomes.
Higher education, costing ten to fifty times as much as primary, yields
higher personal than social returns, favors wealthier classes in urban
areas. Good supporting data for Latin America as a whole. Two concrete tax remedies proposed. WKU

GEN   THOMPSON, KENNETH W. and FOGEL, BARBARA R. Higher Education and
268   Social Change: Promising Experiments in Developing Countries.
       Vol. 1: Reports. New York: Praeger Publishers, 1976. 224 pp.
            Macrostudy of relationship of universities to development in
Africa, Asia, Latin America attempts to discover definition of development and role of universities in its process. Useful questions raised
about over-used slogans, role of donor agencies, making of policy.
Some critical insights into university development in Colombia and the
lack thereof. KU

GEN   TOBIA, PETER. "A Comparative Study of the Educational Systems of
269   the Five Central American Countries." Ph.D. dissertation, Ohio
       State University, 1968. 291 pp.
            First section gives historical, geographical and other back-
ground data. Goal is to identify factors which make Costa Rica's
system most productive. Regional problems, individual country systems,
comparison of primary systems, and analysis are other sections. Many
factors contributed to Costa Rica's paramountcy in Central American
educational systems. Many useful tables.

GEN   TRINIDAD, Central Secretariat. <u>A bibliography of Education in</u>
270   <u>the Caribbean</u>. <u>Bibliographie de l'enseignement dans la Caraïbe</u>.
[Port-of-Spain]: Kent House, 1959. 144 pp.
     Includes Caribbean countries except Spanish-speaking ones.
Presence of relatively few entries on higher education reflects its
weak condition. FU

GEN   TUÜNNERMANN BERNHEIM, CARLOS. "La autonomía y la enseñanza de la
271   medicina." <u>Universidades</u>, no. 76 (April-June 1979): 251-84.
     Internationally known Nicaraguan educational leader gives
history of universities and various kinds of autonomy, and their transfer to Latin America. Consequences of Napoleonic model: production of
professionals, no attention to sciences. Autonomy, after 1918, sometimes an excuse to avoid social responsibilities. Argues concept
should not be absolute, but give liberty of thought while enhancing
social change. Universities, including their medical schools, must not
be divorced from society. Speech at Eleventh Conference of Faculties
and Schools of Medicine of Latin America, organized by UDUAL, in
Puebla, Mexico. Wide ranging and valuable footnotes add much.

GEN   ------. <u>De la universidad y su problemática</u>. Mexico: UNAM [y]
272   UDUAL, 1980. 196 pp.
     Ten essays range over main issues under discussion in con-
temporary Latin American universities. Moving from the general to the
particular, author discusses topics from the missions of the university
to new concepts of university extension. Comments on ideas of many of
world's thinkers about universities and their societies. WKU

     ------. <u>Ensayos sobre la universidad latinoamericana</u>. See entry
NIC 51.

GEN   ------. <u>Exposición comparada de las leyes orgánicas de las uni-</u>
273   <u>versidades centroamericanas</u>. No. 5. León: [CSUCA] Secretaría
Permanente, 1960. 104 pp.
     Chapters on history, autonomy, goals, integration, govern-
ance, participation of students and alumni in university governance,
patrimony of the five Central American public universities. A basic
document. WKU

GEN   ------. "Integración universitaria centroamericana." <u>Universi-</u>
274   <u>dades</u>, no. 5 (July-September 1961): 38-40.
     Secretary general of the Superior Council of the Central
American Universities (CSUCA) describes the plans for university
regional integration; faculties in arts and sciences being developed;
assistance from the U.S. (the National Science Foundation); and important publications.

GEN   ------. <u>El nuevo concepto de extensión universitaria y difusión</u>
275   <u>cultural en América Latina</u>. Documentos. [Ciudad Universitaria
Rodrigo Facio]: CSUCA, 1977. 42 pp.
     As university moved from serving the Crown, the Church, and
the higher classes to republican, Napoleonic model, it continued to do
little to promote science and culture or to spread benefits of education broadly. Overview of efforts to democratize and disseminate
learning and culture through university extension, with analysis of

differing philosophies. Particularly useful in drawing on works of best known contemporary Latin American educational thinkers. WKU

GEN ------, [ed.]. Pensamiento universitario centroamericano.
276 Ciudad Universitaria Rodrigo Facio: Editorial Universitaria Centroamericana (EDUCA), 1980. 523 pp.
     "Historical unfolding" of the Central American university, its place in the regional reality, its nature and goals, autonomy, reform, teaching and research, regional integration, and student thought are topics. Papers by educational leaders and key documents, especially those of the Confederation of Central American Universities (CSUCA), comprise an essential book for understanding the institutions and their ambiente. Small flaw: authors not listed with their works in table of contents; they are, however, given short, useful biographical treatment in text. Editor: long-time Secretary General of CSUCA, later, Nicaragua's minister of education. WKU

GEN ------. "Planificación y autonomía." In Autonomía, planifi-
277 cación, coordinación, innovaciones: Perspectivas latino-
     americanas, edited by Ana Herzfeld, Barbara Ashton Waggoner, and George R. Waggoner, pp. 64-108. Lawrence: University of Kansas, College of Liberal Arts and Sciences, 1972.
     Sophisticated, rational examination of seemingly paradoxical juxtaposition of university autonomy and national planning, as well as analysis of concept of national development. Ideas of leading thinkers, members of international bodies of universities presented. Description of national and regional organisms, voluntary and official, for coordination of universities; critical appraisal of Colombian and Venezuelan systems. Achievements of CSUCA. See entries GEN 52-98. WKU

GEN ------. "The Problem of Democratizing Higher Education in Latin
278 America." Prospects 9 (1979): 78-84.
     A leader of higher education in Latin America attacks the complex problem of democratization. Real democracy must begin with the basic needs of the child from kindergarten on, not by simply changing higher education. A change in teaching methods in the university with participation of students rather than formal lectures. Need for flexibility in programs and smoother lateral changes. Higher education must be broader than the formal university. Tünnermann believes that student pressure for progressive change has been valuable, but is less certain of it than in some of his earlier works.

GEN ------. Sesenta años de la reforma universitaria de Córdoba,
279 1918-1978. Ciudad Universitaria Rodrigo Facio: Editorial Uni-
     versitaria Centroamericana (EDUCA), 1978. 103 pp.
     Sees university reform of 1918 in Cordoba, Argentina, as most original contribution by Latin American students to university governance. Significant aspect of reform was university autonomy with co-government of students and professors. From 1918 to World War II, increased autonomy and new, middle-class students. Shifts from traditional universities important but Napoleonic pattern continues. After World War II some changes toward less specialization; new emphasis on social mission of university. KU

GEN ------. Los Treinta años del CSUCA: Una aventura del espíritu,
280 1948-1978. San José: CSUCA, 1978. 15 pp.

The first secretary-general of CSUCA (1959-64), former rector of the National University of Nicaragua, and current CSUCA staff member describes development of federation of Central American public universities in three stages, and its relation to other unifying efforts in the region.

GEN ------. La universidad latinoamericana y el planeamiento uni-
281 versitario. Serie Discursos, no. 5. León: Universidad Nacional Autónoma de Nicaragua, 1969. 32 pp.
    Twentieth anniversary meeting of the Union of Latin American Universities, UDUAL, considers topic of university planning. FU

GEN ------, and MENDOZA MORALES, ALBERTO. Exégesis de los estudios
282 generales. León: Universidad Nacional de Nicaragua, 1965. 14 pp.
    Contribution to the Fifth Meeting of the Central American Commission general studies group. Report to a meeting in the University of the Andes, Bogota, at a time of major university reform in Latin America.

GEN TYLER, LEWIS. "Education Systems in Latin America." Paper
283 presented at NAFSA Conference, Asilomar, February 1981. Mimeo-graphed. 19 pp.
    LASPAU official gives historical, institutional overview. Most useful material, seldom described elsewhere, relates to measuring quality of Latin American university degrees. Grading philosophies differ greatly from the U.S. pattern, need interpretation; for example, grading practices generally offer no incentive for high achievement. High attrition rate means degree holders have demonstrated "phenomenal academic survival skills." Comments on LASPAU testing for graduate study candidates, some LASPAU accomplishments. WKU

GEN ------, ed. Guide to Graduate Programs in Latin America and the
284 Caribbean, in Development, Administration and Planning, Agri-culture, Education, and Public Health, with a list of Appropri-ate Technology Centers. Cambridge: LASPAU, 1981. 259 pp. Spanish, Portuguese, and English.
    Part of USAID Training for Development project, begun in 1977, for Latin American and Caribbean faculty members. Profiles of 332 programs at 114 institutions, listed by countries, under the topic headings of title. WKU

GEN "The UNESCO Regional Centre for Higher Education in Latin America
285 and the Caribbean--CRESALC." Higher Education 1, nos. 1-2 (June 1979-January 1980): 1-4.
    Origin of CRESALC in 1971 recommendation of ministers of education and others concerned with science and technology in region, to foster international cooperation. Center inaugurated in Caracas in 1978, with Enrique Oteiza as director. Objectives, organization, ad-visory committee, library and documentation services, contact with other agencies, technical assistance.

GEN "UNICA Activities." Caribbean Educational Bulletin 2, no. 2 (May
286 1975): 44-48.

Universities: General

Fourth biennial meeting of some thirty members of UNICA held in Santo Domingo, February 1975. Plans to develop a "Caribbean information chain," based in the Caribbean Regional Library on Río Piedras Campus, University of Puerto Rico, with terminals to be established in seven English-speaking and Spanish-speaking countries, plus Haiti and the French West Indies. Five-year training program in university administration planned.

GEN "UNICA 4." Caribbean Educational Bulletin 2, no. 2 (May 1975):
287 22-25.
UNICA met in the Dominican Republic, with general theme "Caribbean Food Supply and Caribbean Universities." Discussion also of role of African Studies in Caribbean universities. List of grants from various foundations and governments to UNICA, totalling over $244,000.

GEN "UNICA--Seven Years Later." Caribbean Educational Bulletin 4,
288 no. 1 (January 1977): 3-12.
Growth from sixteen to forty-six member institutions, list of financial contributions, activities, publications, juxtaposed with "350 years of separatism and rivalry" among Caribbean lands and the European metropoles.

GEN UNION DE UNIVERSIDADES DE AMERICA LATINA (UDUAL). Censo uni-
289 versitario latinoamericano, 1962-1965. Mexico: UDUAL,
Secretaría General, 1967. 844 pp.
Lists every university in Latin America, with careers, requirements for admission; number of students admitted; numbers graduating by careers; numbers of professors full-time or part-time; researchers; and budgets in terms of U.S. dollars. TxU

GEN ------. Censo universitario latinoamericano, 1972-1973. Mexico:
290 UDUAL, Secretaría General, 1976. 925 pp.
Sixth such census, carried out with questionnaires. Covers general data, physical facilities, personnel, students, budgets. KU

GEN ------. Planes de estudios de las universidades latino-
291 americanas. Biblioteca Universitaria Latinoamericana, vol. 2.
Guatemala: UDUAL, 1953. 1004 pp.
First Latin American University Congress, in 1948, charged UDUAL with producing this work. (Volume 1, a directory, has suffered a delay in its publication due to lack of receipt of some information, according to a footnote.) Hope expressed for student exchanges, improved quality of programs and professors through proposed pilot programs. Twelve Caribbean universities included. KU

GEN ------. "Reunión extraordinaria de rectores de Centroamérica y
292 el Caribe." Universidades, no. 76 (April-June 1979): 509-16.
"Physical injury, violence and threats" against authorities and students at University of San Carlos of Guatemala occasions emergency meeting at UDUAL headquarters in Mexico City of officials of CSUCA (national universities in Central America) and FUPAC (private universities), Caribbean representatives and others. Press release denounces death threats against San Carlos rector and deans with wide publicity, naming Guatemalan leaders held responsible. List of uni-versitarios already assassinated published; UDUAL demands end to government abuses against San Carlos.

GEN   UNION PANAMERICANA. Corrientes de la educación superior en
293   América. Washington, D.C.: Unión Panamericana, Secretaría
       General, OAS, 1966. 122 pp.
       Essays on key issues of university planning and universities
and national and regional development at a time of considerable optimism, rapid growth and change. Especially useful are descriptions from
Nicaragua, Colombia, the Central American region, Venezuela, by Carlos
Tünnermann Bernheim, Augusto Franco, Carlos Caamaño, Luis Manuel
Peñalver. WKU

GEN   ------. La formación del profesorado de las escuelas normales
294   latinoamericanas. Washington, D.C.: Unión Panamericana, Secre-
       taría General, OEA, Departamento de Asuntos Educativos, 1964. 43
       pp.
       French higher normal school model now being influenced by
U.S. pattern of university preparation of teachers for secondary
schools. Based on information supplied by each nation; thus, even
Haiti looks good. No data on percentage participating in or completing
these programs. WKU

GEN   ------. Instituciones latinoamericanas de enseñanza superior.
295   2d rev. ed. Washington: Pan American Union, Secretary General ,
       OAS, 1961. 93 pp.
       Name, founding date, sponsoring agency, address, offerings,
other data. See entry GEN 205. DPU

GEN   ------. La orientación educativa y profesional en Chile, Guate-
296   mala, Panamá y Venezuela. Washington, D.C.: Unión Panamericana,
       Secretaría General, OEA, Departamento de Asuntos Educativos,
       1967. 114 pp.
       Reflects intense concern over data cited in introduction:
about half the secondary students fail during their studies; an equal
proportion of law and philosophy students abandon studies in the first
years; about 40 percent of medical students do not complete their first
year. Remedy: earlier and better orientation to careers. UDUAL gave
impetus to holding the First Seminar on Secondary Education in Central
America and Panama, in 1953. Elaborate bureaucratic efforts, e.g., in
Guatemala, range from home visits to radio programs. Much testing and
handwringing evident all around, in effort to push students toward
appropriate career slots. WKU

GEN   ------. Planes y programas de las escuelas normales latino-
297   americanas. Washington, D.C.: Unión Panamericana, Secretaría
       General, OEA, Departamento de Asuntos Educativos, 1963. 122 pp.
       Preparation of primary school teachers: objectives, general
culture, pedagogical materials, and normal school teaching plans.
Notes urban-rural differences in curricula, and large number of
subjects required. Study, based on official documents only, does not
pretend to describe actual situation. WKU

GEN   ------. Repertorio de la asistencia técnica y financiera para la
298   educación en América Latina: Quiénes ofrecen, qué ofrecen, cómo
       ofrecen. Washington, D.C.: Unión Panamericana, Secretaría
       General, OEA, Departamento de Asuntos Educativos, 1966. 185 pp.

Handbook lists dozens of sources: governments, international and national organizations, universities, and businesses offering everything from scholarships to technical advisors. An example of the enthusiasm of the era for education as a component of national and regional development. WKU

GEN   UNITED NATIONS EDUCATIONAL, SCIENTIFIC AND CULTURAL ORGANIZATION
299   (UNESCO). Conference of Ministers of Education and those Re-
      sponsible for the Promotion of Science and Technology in Relation
      to Development in Latin America and the Caribbean, Caraballeda,
      Venezuela, 6-15 December 1971." Paris, 1971. Mimeographed. 44
      pp.
         A preliminary draft of the regional convention for the inter-
national recognition of studies, diplomas and degrees in higher education in Latin America and the Caribbean. UkLACU

GEN   ------, Oficina Regional de Educación para América Latina y el
300   Caribe. Repertorio de publicaciones periódicas de educación de
      América Latina y el Caribe. Santiago, Chile: [UNESCO], 1970.
      103 pp.
         List by country of more than 500 publications which deal with
education.

GEN   UNITED NATIONS. Educación, recursos humanos y desarrollo en
301   América Latina. New York: Naciones Unidas, Comisión Económica
      para América Latina, 1968. 250 pp.
         Data and remarks presented in aggregate include, without
specifying, Caribbean universities. Second half of book gives general
characteristics, including current crisis, distribution of matriculation, proportion of graduates, social make-up of university population, functioning of system. Conclusions: need for more realistic
reform schemes, reorientation of learning, incorporation of research,
planning, research for development. WKU

GEN   UNIVERSIDAD AUTONOMA DE GUADALAJARA. "GULERPE, CAMESA, IASEI."
302   Alma Mater, no. 89 (March 1978): 117-32.
         Describes three organizations founded at Universidad Autónoma
de Guadalajara: GULERPE (Grupo Universitario Latinoamericano de
Estudios para la Reforma y Perfeccionamiento de la Educación), 1965;
CAMESA (Centro Ajijic para el mejoramiento de la Educación Superior en
América), 1977; IASEI (Instituto Ajijic Sobre Educación Internacional),
1978. All have had some participation by Caribbean universities, most
strongly in GULERPE. Emphasis on needs for communication, lessening of
dependence on people, ideas and institutions outside hemisphere.

      UNIVERSIDAD DE ORIENTE, Comisión Organizadora. "Documentos uni-
      versitarios." See entry VEN 173.

GEN   UNIVERSIDAD DE PANAMA (UP); INSTITUTO CENTROAMERICANO DE
303   ADMINISTRACION Y SUPERVISION DE LA EDUCACION (ICASE); and
      ORGANIZACION DE LOS ESTADOS AMERICANOS (OEA). Regionalización
      educativa: Informe final de la Primera Reunión del Proyecto
      Multinacional de Regionalización Educativa, Panamá, 25-27 Febru-
      ary 1980. Serie Asistencia Técnica, no. 3. Panamá: UP;
      ICASE; OEA, 1980. 94 pp.

While dealing primarily with pre-university level education in Central America, Chile, Ecuador and Panama, activities involve directly some of the universities, and outcome of efforts will have consequences for higher education. ICASE is located in the University of Panama. WKU

GEN   UNIVERSIDAD DE SAN CARLOS (USC). Primera Mesa Redonda Centro-
304   americana de Educación Jurídica. Guatemala: USC, 1964.
        CSUCA sponsored three-day meeting in Guatemala in 1961 in which all five member universities participated. General theme: The present state of legal education in Central America and discussion of minimum basic studies prior to pursuit of professional studies. Discussion of legal education practices, research. WKU

GEN   ------. Resoluciones y recomendaciones votadas por el Primer
305   Congreso Centroamericano de Universidades. Celebrado en San Salvador, del 15 al 24 de septiembre de 1948. Guatemala: Imprenta Universitaria, 1948. 127 pp.
        Reflects early efforts by Central American university leadership to collaborate in academic development on a regional basis. LNHT

        UNIVERSIDAD NACIONAL AUTONOMA DE NICARAGUA. Cuadernos Universitarios. See entry NIC 60.

GEN   UNIVERSIDAD SIMON BOLIVAR. El Caribe: Un mar entre dos mundos.
306   Caracas: Editorial de USB, 1978. 297 pp.
        Twenty-three intellectuals, mostly from universities in ten Caribbean countries, discuss such themes as regionalism and independence, national and regional identity, creativity and viability; in French, Spanish and English. Background for comprehending some regional problems with direct and indirect implications for universities. WKU

GEN   "Las universidades de América Latina: América Central." Uni-
307   versidades, no. 75 (January-March 1979): 61-78.
        Account of activities planned for 1979 by Association of Private Universities in Central America, FUPAC; several 1978 and 1979 meetings on such topics as research and graduate studies in various universities; regional cooperation. Declaration of CSUCA against Guatemalan violence directed at San Carlos University.

GEN   "Unusual Cooperative Enterprise Sets Sail in the Caribbean." ETS
308   Developments 25, no. 3 (Fall 1978): 3.
        Fourteen countries served by UWI and University of Guyana work with ETS to develop tests to be given by Caribbean Examinations Council. Previously all tests reflected British perspectives; now desire is to reflect Caribbean history, literature, culture with exam system locally managed.

GEN   USLAR PIETRI, ARTURO. "La universidad y la revolución." El
309   Nacional, 7° día, 11 Marzo 1973.
        Challenges popular student rhetoric about the "university in the revolution," pointing out that is too often taken to mean revolution in and destruction of institution itself. Historical role of intellectuals in fomenting revolutionary change; student action therefore counterproductive to their own stated goals.

GEN   VERDEJO DE NORTHLAND, RUTH. "Atlas de los déficits educativos en
310   América Latina." La Educación 24, no. 82 (January-April 1980):
        49-64.
            Organization of American States Department of Educational
Affairs undertakes compilation of educational lacks, by region,
country, regions within countries, ethnic divisions and others to
permit statistical analysis of growing insufficiencies of educational
opportunity at all levels.

GEN   VILLAGREN KRAMER, FRANCISCO, and BUSTAMANTE, JORGE AGUSTIN.
311   Legislación universitaria latinoamericana: Análisis comparativo.
        México: UDUAL [y] UNAM, 1967. 177 pp.
            Legal framework of universities in countries with one nation-
al university, with several national universities, with one national
and one or more private universities, and with several of both kinds.
Analysis of norms compared, autonomy, regimens of public and private
institutions, coordination mechanisms such as CSUCA, FUPAC, UDUAL. WKU

GEN   WAGGONER, BARBARA ASHTON. "The Latin American University in
312   Transition." In Viewpoints on Education and Social Change in
        Latin America, Occasional Publication, no. 5, pp. 5-22.
        Lawrence: The University of Kansas, Center of Latin American
        Studies, 1965.
            Social stresses affecting universities in acute manner. De-
scription of traditional model of Latin American university; changing
goals and structures; Venezuela's University of Oriente as experiment
in reform. WKU

GEN   ------; WAGGONER, GEORGE R., and WOLFE, GREGORY B. "Higher Edu-
313   cation in Contemporary Central America." Journey of Inter-
        American Studies 6, no. 4 (October 1964): 445-61.
            Overview of problems, e.g., hostility toward universities for
their perceived political role, low productivity of educational systems, inadequacies of academic offerings. Description of governance,
careers available, costs. Role of Consejo Superior Universitario
Centroamericano (CSUCA) as regional agency.

GEN   ------. "The National Universities of Central America: Problems
314   and Prospects." Background paper prepared for the Central Ameri-
        can Subcommittee of the Committee for Economic Development, 1964.
        Mimeographed. 65 pp.
            Change and resistance to change in five Central American
countries as it affects universities. Growing demand, inadequate
response at all levels of education, poor preparation of teachers,
isolation of universities from society, the weight of tradition. Explanation of structural changes underway, regional integration efforts,
flow chart of foreign aid agencies contributing to universities. WKU

GEN   WAGGONER, GEORGE R. "La educación superior en los Estados Unidos
315   y Latinoamérica." Revista de la Educación Superior 3, no. 3
        (July-September 1974): 3-30.
            Despite obvious difficulties of comparing universities with
such different historical roots, useful lessons may be learned from
each set of public institutions by the other. U.S. universities question their social roles, and Latin American universities seek better
academic quality and productivity.

GEN   ------. "National Planning, University Autonomy, and the Co-
316   ordination of Higher Education: Latin American Points of View."
       Journal of Inter-American Studies 16, no. 3 (August 1974): 372-
       78.
           Examination of Latin American view, by questionnaire study of
thirty-seven respondents, of relations between need for government
planning, which is in potential conflict with need for university
autonomy. Paradoxes emerge in responses.

GEN   ------. "Problems in the Professionalization of the University
317   Teaching Career in Central America." Journal of Inter-American
       Studies 8, no. 2 (April 1966): 204-5.
           Summary with some examples of recent reforms in national
universities. Recommendations for policies needed to professionalize
the university career, moving it away from the tradition of the part-
time, secondary activity of practitioners of other professions.

GEN   ------. "Los programas de estudios generales y la educación
318   profesional en las universidades latinoamericanas." Universi-
       dades, nos. 14-15 (November 1963-March 1964): 58-61.
           Twenty-one university officials from twenty Latin American
countries attended the Fourth Seminar on Higher Education in the Americas at the University of Kansas, 26 January to 23 March 1963, focusing
chiefly on university reform. Besides general studies and professional
education, participants discussed student participation in university
governance, economic problems of universities, "excessive isolation and
separation" among professors in the different professional schools in
Latin American universities.

GEN   ------. "University Autonomy and National Planning in Latin
319   America: Some Implications for U.S. Practice." Revista/Review
       Interamericana 3, no. 1 (Spring 1977): 123-34.
           Latin American universities defend autonomy fiercely, yet
public institutions rely on strong central governments for funding.
They accede to national developmental goals, but often resist planning
needs. Perpetual paradox of conflicting values. Comparison suggests
much less nationally generated structuring of academic institutions in
U.S., but some writers anticipate more state efforts at control, with
concomitant resistance, e.g., by unionization. Author does not see
evidence from past to predict stronger centralized control in U.S.

GEN   ------, and HERZFELD, ANA, eds. Metodología de la evaluación
320   universitaria: Teoría y práctica. Lawrence: Escuela de Artes
       Liberales y Ciencias, Universidad de Kansas, 1969. 245 pp.
           Tenth Seminar on Higher Education in the Americas produced
handbook on methodologies for university evaluation, based on work of
Ninth Seminar in Costa Rica and U.S., and their own evaluation of
Faculties of Education, Law, and Medicine at University of Costa Rica,
and Schools of Education, Law, and Engineering at University of Kansas.
Orientation to U.S. system at University of New Mexico. Paper
presented by Carlos Tünnermann Bernheim to seminar calls for "new
university reform" with university as "critical conscience of the
nation." WKU

GEN   WAGGONER, GEORGE R., and WAGGONER, BARBARA ASHTON. <u>Education in</u>
321   <u>Central America</u>. Lawrence: University Press of Kansas, 1971.
       180 pp.
            "Well written, concise accounts of school systems of Guate-
mala, El Salvador, Honduras, Nicaragua, Costa Rica and Panama; plus a
general historical introduction and a concluding section on regional
cooperation. Essentially school oriented and cautious in examining
educational problems." (HLAS Entry 6104, 35) KU

GEN   WALKER, KENNETH N. "Castro Support among Latin American
322   Students." <u>Social and Economic Studies</u> 14, no. 1 (March 1965):
       88-105.
            Study primarily of National University, Colombia, focuses on
student attitudes; finds increased exposure in politically active milieu, in academic areas confronting inherent social problems, increases
favorable attitude toward political figure symbolizing radical
restructuring of society.

GEN   WALTERS, MARIAN C., ed. <u>Latin America and the Caribbean II:</u>
323   <u>A Dissertation Bibliography</u>. Ann Arbor: University Microfilms
       International [1980?]. 78 pp. Supplement to <u>Latin America and</u>
       <u>the Caribbean: A Dissertation Bibliography</u>, edited by Carl W.
       Deal, 1977.
            Scanty material on higher education for Caribbean region:
none for French Overseas Departments, for example. See GEN 105. KU

GEN   WILGUS, ALVA CURTIS, ed. <u>The Caribbean: Contemporary Education</u>.
324   Gainesville: University of Florida Press, 1959. 290 pp.
            Tenth Annual Conference on the Caribbean at University of
Florida produced twenty-one papers, mostly of a general nature. Most
useful is "Bibliographic Sources on Education in the Caribbean" by
Estellita Hart. Her conclusion: they are scarce and hard to find.
See entry GEN 106. FU

GEN   WILLIAMS, ERIC EUSTACE. <u>The University in the Caribbean in the</u>
325   <u>Late 20th Century, 1980-1990</u>. Port of Spain, Trinidad: PNM
       Publishing Co., [1974]. 34 pp.
            Scholar-politician (Trinidad and Tobago) summarizes the situ-
ation in the Caribbean universities with data and points of view. Area
described is the islands plus Guyana and Belize. Most important
issues: independence of the region, nature of the area, and race
relations. [Also in <u>Caribbean Educational Bulletin</u> 2, no. 1 (January
1975): 3-31.] WKU

GEN   <u>The World of Learning 1983-84</u>. London: Europa, 1983. 1,790 pp.
326   By countries, lists academies, learned socities, libraries,
museums, in addition to universities. For these there are founding
dates, officers of administration, faculties of schools, numbers of
professors and students, academic year, publications, attached research
institutes.

GEN   ZESTINA, ROMEO AUGUSTO. "Interesantes declaraciones de Fabio
327   Castillo, Rector de la Universidad Nacional de El Salvador."
       <u>Nuestro Pueblo y la Universidad</u> 1, no. 1 (August 1968): 8-10.
            Describes the importance of the Central American public uni-
versities, the fruits of regionalization. The value of work done by

the United States and North American business in Central America is questionable. Declares that universities cannot be nonpolitical, and they must work for scientific and economic change. Castillo was one of CSUCA's most active members.

GEN ZUBIRIA, RAMON DE. "Realidad y perspectiva de los asuntos
328 estudiantiles en América Latina." Universitas 2000 4, nos. 2-3
(1980): 19-26.
    Former Colombian university rector sharply criticizes, at First Latin American Seminar on Student Affairs, distortion of university which is not student-centered. Attacks "academic narcissism," failure to educate in Platonic sense. Changes in numbers and nature of student body create new problems; copying U.S. form of student service without its spirit has failed dismally. Concrete proposals to serve academic and other needs of students in coherent manner.

GEN ZYMEIMAN, MANUEL. "Patterns of Educational Expenditures in Latin
329 America." Seminar on Financing of Education in Latin America,
15-19 November 1976. Mimeographed. Washington, D.C.: Inter-
American Development Bank. 13 pp. plus leaves of tables.
    World Bank education advisor refutes philosophy fueling educational expansion of 1950s in Latin America and Caribbean, which related income or stages of development to educational expenditures and enrollments in primary, secondary, university levels. His formula show no significant relationship between total expenditure on education as percent of GNP and GNP per capita for South America; however, there is direct relation between these variables in Central America and Caribbean region. Expenditures on higher education as percent of GNP do not relate to income per capita or to enrollment rates. Concludes allocation of funds for education and between types of education not a planned process or process destined to achieve stated goals of universal primary school attendance. WKU

Universities: By Country

Colombia

COL ARNOVE, ROBERT F. "Education Policies of the National Front."
1 In Politics of Compromise: Coalition Government in Colombia,
edited by R. Albert Berry, Ronald G. Hellman, and Mauricio
Salaún, pp. 381-411. New Brunswick, N.J.: Transaction Books,
1980.
Alternatively sharing power, 1958-74, Liberals and Conservatives did little to change system favoring urban elites in all levels
of education; support of higher education further separated already
sharply divided social classes. International assistance, by focusing
on university development, aided elite structure. Useful data on
financing and distribution of educational opportunity. WKU

COL ASOCIACION COLOMBIANA DE UNIVERSIDADES. Mundo Universitario, no.
2 13 (January-March 1980). 177 pp.
Entire issue, except for five pages on history of the colonial Latin American university, devoted to new law for reform of higher
education. Addresses by Colombia's president, minister of education,
president of ASCUN. Analysis, text of law.

COL ------. Tercer Congreso Nacional de Universidades: Memoria.
3 Cartagena: Editorial Universidad de Cartagena, 1959. 84 pp.
Nineteen rectors and delegates emphasize collaboration among
Colombian universities but no practical methods proposed, with most
space devoted to autonomy and related juridical matters. TxU

COL ------, Fondo Universitario Nacional. Educación de graduados y
4 formación de profesorado universitario en Colombia (1965-
1968), Partes I, II, y Anexos. Nestor Hernando Parra E.,
director of study. Bogotá: ASCUN, 1965. 169 pp., 101 pp., and
138 pp.
Need for underdeveloped country to supply human resources for
development requires educational planning. Reluctance of universities
to engage in research--undertaken in Colombia only in recent years,
beginning with medical schools. Need to study abroad, lack of adapta-
bility to local reality. Lack of incentives in academic conditions to
prepare professional professors and researchers, or capable people for
public sector activities. Description of university teaching situation
and personnel, state of graduate studies, estimated demand, bases for
planning, supporting data. Unequal advantage now to larger inland
cities. Heavy reliance on foreign support. WKU

COL BARRIOS R., DARIO C., director of study. "Formación de recursos
5   humanos para el desarrollo regional en la Universidad del Norte,
     Colombia." In Universidad y desarrollo regional, pp. 223-97.
     Organization of American States, Serie Monográfica y Estudios de
     la Educación, no. 2. Santiago de Chile: OEA/CINDA, 1980.
          Research Center of Universidad del Norte (CIUN) does studies
for university, public, and private enterprises. Summary of studies on
human resources and development policies for Barranquilla and department of Atlantico done for this private university. Institutional
history; policies for enrollment: engineering to comprise 45 percent;
health sciences 25 percent; psychology, administration and finance 30
percent. Serious shortcoming is lack of national human resources
studies; those available are listed. Studies also scant for Atlantic
region. Information on university's own professional graduates,
recommendations. WKU

COL BORRERO CABAL, ALFONSO. "Palabras del presidente del Consejo
6   Nacional de Rectores de la Asociación Colombiana de Universidades
     en la sesión de instalación, Universidad del Cauca, Popayán, Nov.
     6, 7, 8, 9 de 1977." Mimeographed. [Bogotá]: ASCUN, [1977].
     74 pp.
          Decries slogan "universities for all" as demagoguery,
pointing out that universities are selective and should be demanding;
puts emphasis on "equity" of opportunity. WKU

COL BURGOS OJEDA, ROBERTO. Pensamiento y vida. Cartagena: Edi-
7   torial Universidad de Cartagena, 1959. 110 pp.
          Anthology of articles by founder and director of University
of Cartagena's Department of Humanities includes several on universities. Outrage at lack of financial support in face of rising demand by
frustrated secondary school graduates. KU

COL CASTRO Y., NARCISO. "La Escuela Naval será desde hoy universi-
8   dad." El Tiempo, 18 November 1977, p. 8.
          History of Naval School since 1810 founding; now will be
called Universidad José Prudencio Padilla and will have three faculties
in Cartagena.

COL CATAÑO, GONZALO, ed. Educación y sociedad en Colombia: Lecturas
9   de sociología de la educación. Bogotá: Universidad Pedagógica
     Nacional, 1973. 444 pp.
          Readings primarily for students preparing for teaching are
introduced by editor's comments on scarcity of sociological studies of
all kinds in Colombia. Caribbean region appears tangentially, with
serious educational deficits. TxU

COL "Colombian Structure of Higher Education: A National Education
10   Study System." In Higher Education and Social Change: Promising
     Experiments in Developing Countries. Vol. 2, Case Studies,
     edited by Kenneth W. Thompson, Barbara R. Fogel, and Helen E.
     Danner, pp. 372-95. New York, Washington, and London: Praeger
     Publishers, 1977.
          "Illogical" distribution of university education in
proportion to population, especially for coastal region. Research,
teaching, graduate study, extension appear weak, inadequate. KU

COL   CONSEJO NACIONAL DE RECTORES. "Declaraciones y recomendaciones."
11   <u>Mundo Universitario</u>, no. 4 (July-September 1973):   9-20.
         Providing education at all levels is the greatest problem of
our time, especially in peripheral and dependent countries.   In
Colombian universities crisis exists: in 1960, with 23,000 students,
received $8.63 per student; in 1973, with 130,000, received $6.44 per
student.   Student conflict of 1971-72 threatened some universities with
extinction.   Increased demand can't be met within traditional system.
List of financial proposals.

COL   ------. "La reforma universitaria: criterios." <u>Mundo Universi-</u>
12   <u>tario</u>, no. 1 (October-December 1972):   9-15.
         Response to proposed statute on higher education.   Stress
importance for each university to establish its own system for administration and finance; nothing should be conceded of their autonomy;
universities themselves are court of last resort to resolve own
problems; coolness toward regional integration except as it is con-
venient; acceptance of idea of national standards, within limits;
prefer ASCUN over ICFES as policy-maker.   Consejo believes national
education budget should be at least 25 percent of general budget, with
allocations to universities made well in advance of their own budget-
making.

COL   CONSUEGRA HIGGINS, JOSE. <u>Cómo se reprime la universidad en</u>
13   <u>Colombia: Informe a la comunidad de la Universidad del Atlán-</u>
         dDtico. 2d ed., rev. Barranquilla: Ediciones Perijá, Colección
Ideología y Testimonio, 1973.   197 pp.
         Rector of Universidad del Atlántico, deposed by government
after take-over of the campus by troops, explains his concept of university "as active agent in the promotion of social change."   Enrollment of disadvantaged students, abolition of entrance exams,
doubled size, physical growth; efforts to limit foreign dependence by
printing and selling books, fostering local and national culture and
arts, eliminating value attached to graduate degrees obtained abroad.
Governor's refusal to pay budgeted funds, violation of autonomy greeted
with anger in local and national press; collection of articles, commentary on the event reveal some acute philosophical cleavages of the
1971-72 era.   KU

COL   "Declaración del Consejo Nacional de Rectores--CNR." <u>Mundo Uni-</u>
14   <u>versitario</u>, no. 2 (January-March 1973):   11-17.
         National Council of Rectors of Colombian Association of Uni-
versities (ASCUN) urgently needs more and better organized financing.
Approves government decree curtailing "dangerous phenomenon of proliferation of institutions of higher education lacking indispensable
minimum conditions to offer serious academic programs."

COL   DIAZ, FREDERICK. "Colombian Education: Struggle for Renewal."
15   Ph.D. dissertation, Michigan State University, 1975.   168 pp.
         Education at all levels traditionally offered strictly aca-
demic courses of study which have no relevance to the needs of the
nation's developing economy.   Attempts to democratize and reform in the
direction of vocational, technical, and scientific education struggle
in the climate of "constant tension between progressive and retrograde
traditional elements of Colombian society."   Obstacles in rejection of

manual labor and country's politico-ecclesiastical oligarchic structure. Descriptive and evaluative study, though mainly focused on non-
coastal areas, provides insights into consequences of race and its role
in education, and the demands placed on universities. Useful history
of Colombian education.

COL EDICIONES EL TIGRE DE PAPEL. Crisis universitaria colombiana
16 1971. Medellín: Ediciones el Tigre de Papel, 1971. 319 pp.
     Chronology of 1970-71 conflict; some episodes in Cartagena
and Barranquilla. Denunciations of U.S. aid agencies, University
Council; cites accomplishments of student uprisings in changing national policy. Demands for a system not dominated by bourgeoisie and
imperialism. WKU

COL FRANCO ARBELAEZ, AUGUSTO, and BUSTOS, FABIO M. ¿Para qué la uni-
17 versidad colombiana? Análisis comparado de objetivos. Serie
Universidad Hoy, no. 4. Bogotá: ICFES, 1971. 50 pp. plus
fold-out.
     Sets forth stated objectives of institutions as of 1968.
Finds "image of ideal university," reflecting Ortegan concept, but
sacrificing aspects of reality; lip service to research but little
concrete accomplishment. Need more realistic strategies. WKU

COL ------, and TÜNNERMANN BERNHEIM, CARLOS. La educación superior
18 de Colombia en la perspectiva mundial y latino-americana.
Bogotá: Fundación para la Educación Superior, 1978. 503 pp.
     Useful background, more useful facts on Colombian higher
education: numerical and legal data, structure, coordination and
planning. Series of provocative questions on role of education, demand
and access, productivity, student conflicts, brain drain. Conclusions:
Availability of higher education badly distributed geographically; too
many small, weak institutions; lack of effective national policy;
traditional career choices exceed market, fail to meet national needs;
poor administration; other serious problems listed. Set of concrete
proposals for improvement. WKU

COL GALAN, LUIS CARLOS. Proyecto de ley por la cual se dicta el
19 estatuto de la educación superior y exposición de motivos.
Bogotá: Ministerio de Educación, 1971. 82 pp.
     Minister of education's presentation to Senate. Crisis in
Colombia as elsewhere in universities requires response. Strong commitment to regional needs; plight of rural poor and obligation of the
11 per 1,000 who receive higher education. Structural changes to be
made. Comparison chart between 1967 Basic Plan (created with help from
a University of California mission) and Reform Project. Significant
changes, including creation of links with Latin American universities
and declaration of independence regarding foreign aid. WKU

COL ------. "Reforma universitaria. ¿Reforma, ajuste o desajuste?"
20 Nueva Frontera, no. 256 (5-11 November 1979): 7-9.
     In 1957 Colombia had 22,000 university students; by 1979,
over 320,000. The 140 universities produce a "proletariatized professional" the socioeconomic reality cannot absorb, with resulting
frustration. Reform proposals.

COL   GARRISON, LLOYD. "Summary Report, USAID-ICFES Bogotá, May 8,
21   1970." In Annexes, Third Education Sector Loan, USAID/Colombia,
      Annex V, Exhibit A, pp. 1-15. Bogotá: USAID/Colombia, 1970.
           Appraisal of "financing of the university system which is not
a system but several subsystems that are poorly and loosely integrated." Growth in GNP but little per capita income increase; large
jump in university enrollment underway; 1967-68 Plan Básico not implemented. Lack of quality control with proliferating self-denominated
universities. Wastefulness of secondary school through attrition.
Need for financial management and accountability. Other suggestions.
WKU

COL   GONZALEZ GONZALEZ, FERNAN. Educación y estado en la historia de
22   Colombia. Serie Controversia, no. 77-78. [Bogotá?]: Centro de
      Investigación y Educación popular (CINEP), 1978. 156 pp.
           Historian and political scientist draws on variety of sources
to describe education from colonial era to present in social and political context. Inequalities of society have impact on educational
access; growth of private universities in response to political
pressures in public system. AzTeS

COL   "Informes de las comisiones y conclusiones emanadas del Consejo
23   Nacional de Rectores de Sochagota." Mundo Universitario, no. 10
      (January-March 1979): 182-96.
           Calls for complete reform of all post-secondary education in
Colombia, developing permanent seminars for leadership, improving research and graduate study, obtaining better financial base.

COL   INSTITUTO COLOMBIANO PARA EL FOMENTO DE LA EDUCACION SUPERIOR
24   (ICFES). Directorio de la educación superior en Colombia 1977.
      Bogotá: Ministerio de Educación Nacional, ICFES. 249 pp.
           Brief data on public and private institutions, including the
seven on the Caribbean coast; origins, programs, degrees, enrollment.
WKU

COL   ------. Directorio de universidades colombianas. Bogotá:
25   ICFES, 1970. 135 pp.
           Each public and private university described in terms of
origin, objectives, class of institution, enrollment, budget, admissions, academic structure. WKU

COL   ------. La educación superior en Colombia: Documentos básicos
26   para su planeamiento. 2 vols. Bogotá: ICFES, 1968. 355 pp.
      and 331 pp.
           Material compiled in 1966 and 1967, published as Plan Básico
de la Educación Superior Colombiana by Asociación Colombiana de Universidades, Fondo Universitario Nacional. Latter dependent entity
separated and recreated as ICFES in 1968. Study carried on with
technical help from University of California. Studies for purpose of
developing national plan and policies to overcome absolute and relative
deficiencies in present system. Low productivity impedes development.
Qualitative and quantitative information, history. WKU

COL   ------. Estadísticas básicas de la educación superior: Pobla-
27   ción estudiantil, 1976 primero y segundo semestres calendario,

1977 primer semestre calendario. Bogotá: ICFES, [1977]. 11 leaves.
Enrollment figures for public and private universities. WKU

COL ------. Estadísticas de la educación superior 1975. Bogotá:
28 ICFES, División de Planeación y Financiación, Sección de Estadística, [1976]. 287 pp.
Basic data on numbers, courses, long and short programs, enrollment by sexes, graduates for all Colombian universities, including those in Montería, Cartagena, and Barranquilla. WKU

COL ------. Estadísticas universitarias: Estudiantes, profesores,
29 personal administrativo 1960-1970. Bogotá: ICFES, 1972. 23 tables, 7 graph charts.
Data on coastal universities are included. WKU

COL ------. Informe anual 1976. Bogotá: ICFES, [1977]. 52 pp.
30 This agency, dependency of the Ministry of Education, but with considerable autonomy, has six divisions whose activities are briefly summarized. Not very helpful for regional information. WKU

COL ------. Manual para la educación superior: Recomendaciones y
31 disposiciones legales sobre procedimientos y prácticas. 2d ed.
Bogotá: ICFES, 1971. 146 pp.
Handbook on higher education defines terms; regulates admissions, degrees, recognition of institutions; contains laws, guide to relevant agencies. WKU

COL ------. Reforma de la educación superior, documentos de estudio,
32 Versión preliminar. 2 vols. Bogotá: ICFES, 1971. 286 pp.
(continuous pagination).
A work group, charged by Colombian President Misael Pastrana with producing a plan for the reform of higher education, has help from ICFES in gathering basic documents. There are twelve documents covering such topics as content of present programs, dependence on foreign aid, autonomy, finance, and social demand. Summaries of advisory committee findings by professional disciplines, 21 statistical tables and various suggestions for improving the system are followed by the proposed statute for governing higher education. Useful data, including those for coastal universities. WKU

COL ------. Reforma de la educación superior: Proyecto de dispo-
33 sición normativa de la educación superior. Bogotá: ICFES, 1971.
31 pp.
Working paper for drafting national law governing higher education. WKU

COL ------. Seminario de administración universitaria, Medellín--
34 nov. 18-20/70: Conclusiones y recomendaciones. Bogotá: UCFES,
[1971?]. 31 pp.
Representatives from universities, USAID, UNESCO make recommendations to improve administration. WKU

COL ------. Universidad a Distancia. Bogotá: ICFES, 1974. 88 pp.
35 Presents concept of the University at a Distance, i.e.,

teaching in new ways by correspondence, radio, television, audiovisual tools, to serve masses of people and reduce costs. Describes the Open University in Britain and other countries, proposes objectives and organizational structure for Colombia. KU

COL   ------, Oficina de Planificación del Desarrollo Universitario.
36   <u>Realizaciones y estado actual de la educación superior en Colombia. Versión preliminar</u>. Bogotá: ICFES, 1970. 89 pp. plus tables.

      Nearly 13 percent increase in enrollment 1960-70, but below minimum level proposed in 1963 for Colombia and below that of Latin America as a whole. Universities should be involved in national problem solving. Primary and secondary education show gross qualitative and quantitative deficiencies; universities should take role in improving and diversifying secondary education. Unbalanced regional growth but some hope for integration. Decreased government financial support causing problems. WKU

COL   INSTITUTO COLOMBIANO PARA ESPECIALIZACION Y ESTUDIOS TECNICOS EN
37   EL EXTERIOR (ICETEX). <u>El crédito educativo en América Latina</u>. Bogotá: ICFES, 1969. 339 pp.

      Colombia created the Institute of Specialization Abroad, ICETEX, in 1950, because of scarce university resources in Colombia with only traditional careers available and limited access thereto. Efforts to industrialize and democratize called for study abroad. Seminar in Peru, where material for book was collected, had participants from many countries, but none with equivalent programs. WKU

COL   LE BOT, IVON. <u>Educación e ideología en Colombia</u>. Bogotá: La
38   Carreta, 1979. 345 pp.

      Description and critical reflection on ideologies affecting education. Especially useful is careful analysis of R. Atcon's <u>La universidad latinoamericana</u>, which embodied chief reform philosophy in 1960s and 1970s of U.S. and international agencies aiding Colombian universities. Rejects assumption that university can be democratizing agent in a society in such economic and social disequilibrium. AzTeS

COL   ------. <u>Elementos para la historia de la educación en Colombia</u>
39   <u>en el siglo XX</u>. Monografía de Seminario de Problemas Colombianos, Departamento Administrativo Nacional de Estadística (DANE). Bogotá: DANE, 1978, pp. 123-202.

      Compares Colombian educational system with ideal "concept of a democratic educational system." Changes historically were designed to increase access to education but didn't face need for cultural revolution. Education was chiefly in hands of church and oligarchy; by law education was not to be obligatory; a separate rural school system was required. Post-1930 liberal bourgeousie called for literacy for national development; there was European and U.S. influence and resistance to it. Paper gains of thirties and forties were undone in fifties. Elite access to university was reinforced with creation of ICETEX, pressure of church, industrial sector, foreign foundations. Pressure grows for investment in primary education rather than higher education; advantages continue for the privileged. A book necessary to comprehend universities on the coast and elsewhere. Much useful data. PPT

Colombia

COL   LONDOÑO BENVENISTE, FELIPE, and OCHOA NUÑEZ, HERNANDO. Biblio-
40   grafía de la educación en Colombia. Serie Bibliografía, 12.
Bogotá: Instituto Caro y Cuervo, 1976. 678 pp.
Of the 447 entries under "Higher Education," only about 6
appear to be related to the Caribbean region; most of those are mimeographed. The University of Cartagena has 1 entry: a 1958 catalogue.
WKU

COL   LOPEZ COLLAZOS, JAIME, and GENSINI, FRANCISCO. "La eficiencia
41   del sistema universitario colombiano: Análisis y sugerencias."
Mundo Universitario, no. 5 (October-December 1973): 37-68.
System is quantitatively and qualitatively inefficient due to
lack of national university policy, planning, financial support, human
resources. Faults rigid academic and administrative organization.
Corresponding recommendations. Supporting statistics for country as a
whole.

COL   LOW-MAUS, RODOLFO. Compendium of Colombian Educational System.
42   Bogotá: Ministry of Education, 1971. 139 pp.
Historical-geographical setting, legal bases for training.
Useful tables on enrollment, retention, availability and demand.
Publication sponsored by Ford Foundation. WKU

COL   MEDELLIN, CARLOS. "El ICFES y la ASCUN." Mundo Universitario,
43   no. 5 (October-December 1973): 6-7.
ICFES is the Colombian Institute for Promotion of Higher
Education, and ASCUN is the Colombian Association of Universities.
First is public, part of Ministry of Education but with some autonomy,
distributor of budgeted funds. ASCUN is private, with eighteen public
and thirteen private universities as members, an advisory group with
funding provided by legislature.

COL   MINISTERIO DE DEFENSA NACIONAL, Armada Nacional, Escuela Naval
44   Almirante Padilla. Información general. [Cartagena: 1978]. 31
pp.
Naval School of Colombia (soon to be denominated university);
mission, history, physical plan, courses of study, admission. WKU

COL   MINISTERIO DE EDUCACION NACIONAL. Reforma de la educación
45   superior. Decretos números 80, 81, 82 y 83 (22 y 23 de enero de
1980). Bogotá: Ministerio de Educación Nacional. 118 pp.
Tight control over post-secondary education is vested in the
national Ministry of Education by the law for both public and private
institutions. Spells out details on creation of universities, their
governance, admission to, retention in. Duties and powers of the
Colombian Institute for Promotion of Higher Education, ICFES, as an
establishment of the ministry. WKU

COL   ------, Oficina Sectorial de Planeación, Grupo de Estadística;
46   and ICFES, División de Planeación y Financiación, Sección de
Estadística. La educación en cifras, 1970-1974, primaria, media,
superior: Número de establecimientos, población estudiantil,
egresados, personal docente. Bogotá: La Oficina, 1975. 112 pp.
Number of institutions, student population, graduates,
teaching personnel, percentages of school attendance, distribution of
schooling. WKU

COL   MORALES VILLAMIZAR, ADOLFO. "El conflicto en las universidades."
47   Mundo Universitario, no. 10 (January-March 1979): 85-98.
       Coastal universities Atlantico and Cordoba among Colombian
universities losing one and two entire semesters from 1974 to 1977.
Colombian society is and has been traditionally violent; universities
show "permanent tendency toward violence," total lack of communication
among groups in conflict. Calls for universities and ICFES to systematically study causes; until now no responsible research.

COL   OFICINA DE EDUCACION IBEROAMERICANA (OEI). La Educación en
48   Iberoamérica: Sistema de indicadores socio-económicos y edu-
       cativos. Colombia. Serie Estadística, nos. 1-3. Madrid Ciudad
       Universitaria: OEI, 1980. ca. 150 pp. in 3 volumes.
       Remarkably comprehensive, thorough, objective collection of
information, in folders, on the socioeconomic framework of education,
and on education itself. OASDC

COL   OLIVERAS MARMOLEJO, PABLO. "El rendimiento de la educación
49   superior." Mundo Universitario, no. 1 (October-December 1972):
       61-65.
       Director of ICFES says twenty public universities have, with
national, state and municipal funds, a deficit of 70 percent, due to
demands for new programs, increased enrollment, higher costs, administrative deficiencies and "a system of teaching which implies a low
yield of utilization of human, physical and financial resources." But
state has not increased financial support enough.

COL   PELZAR, RICHARD. "University Reform in Latin America: The Case
50   of Colombia." Comparative Education Review 16, no. 2 (June
       1972): 230-50.
       Cordoba reform little followed in Colombia, because of its
student leadership fragmentation into radical political movements and
unsympathetic government. Rapid growth of numbers of universities and
enrollments in post-1944 era characterized as haphazard. Formation of
coordinating bodies, various attempts to rationalize, centralize, resistance to them. Describes planning efforts in Atlantic region among
coastal universities, role of ICFES. Reforms such as general studies,
ensuing political turmoil; role of foreign agencies, crises. Concludes
universities reflect society more than they shape it.

COL   RAMA, GERMAN W. "Educación universitaria y movilidad social.
51   Reclutamiento de élites en Colombia." Revista Mexicana de Socio-
       logía 32, no. 4 (July-August 1970): 861-92.
       Aspirations of middle class to gain power as well as status
conditioned by access to universities. Sees resistance by elites to
expanded opportunity.

COL   RENNER, RICHARD. Education for a New Colombia. Washington,
52   D.C.: U.S. Department of Health, Education, and Welfare, Office
       of Education, Institute of International Studies, 1971. 199 pp.
       Valuable overview of institutions in their contexts of histo-
ry, the economy, and social stratification. Touches on reform efforts,
describes role and preparation of professors, the brain drain, and
other topics. Nothing specific on coastal universities per se.

Colombia

COL SERNA G., HUMBERTO. Plan de formación profesoral: Programa de
53   post-grado en metodología de la enseñanza universitaria.
     Barranquilla: Universidad del Norte, 1975. 23 pp.
        Relatively new, private university is concerned to improve
the quality of teaching. Over 80 percent of the professors are under
thirty-five years old. Eight sessions on methodology are proposed.
WKU

COL STEVENSON COLLANTE, JOSE; CHARRIS, ADOLFO; NEGRETE, RODRIGO; and
54   ARRAUT, LUIS. "Declaración conjunta de los rectores de las
     universidades oficiales de la costa norte." Mimeographed.
     Barranquilla, 7 December 1977. 1 p.
        Rare unity in plea by rectors of four Colombian universities
to local, regional, and national governments for funds to finish
buildings, pay staff in order to finish academic year. WKU

COL TORRES LEON, FERNAN. Trayectoria histórica de la universidad
55   colombiana: Modelo de interpretación. 2d ed. Bogotá:
     Ministerio de Educación, Instituto Colombiano de Pedagogía, 1975.
     168 pp.
        A brief history of universities in Colombia. A central
concern from the 1960s on was the role of government vis-à-vis
students, many of whom held socialist views. KU

COL U. S. AGENCY FOR INTERNATIONAL DEVELOPMENT (USAID). Education
56   Sector Loan III. Washington, D.C.: USAID, 1971. 171 pp. plus 5
     appendices of 87 pp.
        Educational sector overview, analysis, strategy and plans;
the loan, its analysis, implementation and evaluation. Well prepared
map of educational system and its ambience. Assumptions: education
improves labor force; positively affects economic growth, leads to
improved productivity, lower birthrate; has positive effect on income
distribution. Describes integration efforts among coastal universities
as one goal of loan strategy. Useful data. WKU

COL UNIVERSIDAD CORPORACION METROPOLITANA. Programa de enfermería.
57   Barranquilla: Universidad Corporación Metropolitana, [1978]. 4
     pp.
        Private university created by Acosta Bendek Foundation empha-
sizes health sciences. Nursing degree requires eight semesters. WKU

COL ------. Programa de filosofía y letras. Barranquilla: Uni-
58   versidad Corporación Metropolitana, [1978]. 4 pp.
        After eight semesters and over 140 credit hours , graduates
receive professional degree in one of six broad areas. WKU

COL ------. Programa de nutrición y dietética. Barranquilla: Uni-
59   versidad Corporación Metropolitana, [1978]. 4 pp.
        Professional degree requires eight semesters of study in five
areas, including the socioeconomic realities of the country and public
health. WKU

COL ------. Programa de odontología. Barranquilla: Universidad
60   Corporación Metropolitana, [1978]. 4 pp.
        Ten-semester degree program in dentistry includes clinical
experience. WKU

COL   ------. Programa de psicología. Barranquilla: Universidad
61   Corporación metropolitana, [1978]. 4 pp.
        Basic general science, health sciences, clinical experience
produce professional psychologist. WKU

COL   ------. Programa de trabajo social. Barranquilla: Universidad
62   Corporación Metropolitana, [1978]. 4 pp.
        Sets forth general and specific goals of social work career
and defines six areas of knowledge to be studied. WKU

COL   UNIVERSIDAD DE CORDOBA. Plan de Desarrollo 1973-1977: Análisis
63   de encuestas. Nestor Hernando Parra E., director of study.
        Cuaderno no. 5. Bogotá: Consorcio de Ingenierías e Investi-
        gaciones Ltda. (CDI), 1972. 44 pp.
        Questionnaires to students, dropouts, secondary students,
graduates, resident professionals in Cordoba. Results useful, but need
analysis, as director says. WKU

COL   ------. Plan de Desarrollo 1973-1977: Análisis del desarrollo
64   del programa de integración universitaria de la zona norte (costa
        atlántica). Nestor Hernando Parra E., director of study.
        Cuaderno no. 6. Bogotá: CDI, 1972. 27 pp.
        Universities of the Atlantic coast were first in Colombia to
initiate studies concerning their integration, but ideas were not
implemented. Now, with government policy support and some increase in
budget, ICFES is formulating plans and outlook is favorable. Analysis
of development of integration program for north zone, future of integration, conclusions and recommendations. WKU

COL   ------. Plan de Desarrollo 1973-1977: Aspectos socio-
65   antropológicos de la población cordobesa. Nestor Hernando Parra
        E., director of study. Cuaderno no. 1. Bogotá: CDI, 1972. 45
        pp.
        Novel approach to university planning begins with description
of people in this isolated region, their beliefs and values, ecosystem;
examines possible outcome from higher education as confrontation occurs
between "primitive cultural values" and scientific-technical viewpoint.
WKU

COL   ------. Plan de Desarrollo 1973-1977: Aspectos socio-
66   económicos de Córdoba. Nestor Hernando Parra E., director of
        study. Cuaderno no. 2. Bogotá: CDI, 1972. 38 pp.
        Potentially rich agricultural region with land, capital,
technology concentrated in few hands while "majority of cordobeses are
still subjected to misery, illiteracy, poor health." Examines technical and social role of university. Useful statistical and textual
material. WKU

COL   ------. Plan de Desarrollo 1973-1977: Diagnóstico insti-
67   tucional. Nestor Hernando Parra E., director of study. Cuaderno
        no. 3. Bogotá: CDI, 1972. 108 pp.
        History since University of Cordoba's 1962 founding, adminis-
trative and academic structure, quantitative aspects, fiscal management, physical plant. WKU

COL ------. Plan de Desarrollo 1973-1977: Evaluación de las
68   unidades académicas. Nestor Hernando Parra E., director of
     study. Cuaderno no. 4. Bogotá: CDI, 1972. 60 pp.
         Examines qualitative aspects of Universidad de Córdoba:
definition of objectives, "real" behavior of academic community,
logistical support available; besides institution as a whole, the
separate schools are studied, with conclusions and recommendations.
WKU

COL ------. Plan de Desarrollo 1973-1977: Plan quinquenal. Nestor
69   Hernando Parra E., director of study. Cuaderno no. 7. Bogotá:
     CDI, 1972. 90 pp.
         University of Cordoba will double in size to 2,000 students
shortly. Plan considers developmental factors, strategies, areas of
development, policies, structure, demand, programs, finance. WKU

COL UNIVERSIDAD DE LA COSTA ATLANTICA, Oficina de Planeación
70   Regional. Proyecto integrado de las universidades de la Costa
     Atlántica colombiana. Barranquilla: [Oficina de Planeación
     Regional de la Costa Atlántica], 1967. 38 pp. plus about 40
     fold-out charts and tables.
         Universities of Cordoba, Cartagena, Barranquilla, Atlantico,
and Magdalena (Santa Marta) prepared for Organization of American
States a plan for short and long range integration. Description of
coastal population, with low percentage obtaining education; costs of
and needs for technical and financial assistance. Cite lack of appropriate courses for regional development, overlaps which integration
could help remedy. Long range (1961-81) plan "will give . . . defini-
tive integration of the four official universities which function on
the Atlantic coast." Describes regional plan as part of national plan
tailored to fit "priorities of Alliance for Progress." TxU

COL UNIVERSIDAD DEL ATLANTICO. "Homenaje de los egresados de la
71   Facultad de Ciencias Económicas. Junio 3, 1940--junio 3, 1959."
     Mimeographed. Barranquilla: Universidad del Atlántico, 1959.
     31 pp.
         Celebrates contribution of business school graduates to
region. FU

COL ------. Universidad del Atlántico: Primer plan quinquenal de
72   desarrollo 1967-1971. Barranquilla: Universidad del Atlántico,
     Oficina de Planeación y Oficina de Planeación Regional Universi-
     taria de la Costa Atlántica, 1966. 158 pp.
         Evolution from museum to technical institute, to poly-
technical institution, to 1946 founding as university: historical
details. Overview of Colombian university system, need for planning
generally and for coastal region especially. Lack of data and planning
in private sector, lack of manpower studies nationally and regionally,
coastal university integration needed, structure of a plan. Present
structure of Universidad del Atlántico. Details for future. Charts,
graphs. ICarbS

COL UNIVERSIDAD DEL NORTE. Administración de empresas. Barran-
73   quilla: Universidad del Norte, [1978]. 5 pp.

Private university founded in 1966 with support of business community offers ten professional programs. Degree in business administration requires ten semesters. WKU

COL ------. De frente al porvenir, relaciones-proyecciones, 10 años,
74   1966-1976. [Barranquilla]: Universidad del Norte, 1976. 20
     leaves.
     Private university with some 1,600 students in thirteen disciplines is developing attractive, functional campus on coast. Acknowledges support of individual and corporate contributors, seeks funds for added facilities. WKU

COL ------. Enfermería. Barranquilla: Universidad del Norte,
75   [1978]. 5 pp.
     Nature of program and profession of nursing. Six semesters of theory and practice lead to diploma. WKU

COL ------. Ingeniería civil. Barranquilla: Universidad del Norte,
76   [1978]. 6 pp.
     Ten-semester program described, with some subspecialties transferring to Universidad de los Andes, Bogotá, after second year. WKU

COL ------. Ingeniería mecánica. Barranquilla: Universidad del
77   Norte, [1978]. 7 pp.
     Program and profession described, with emphasis on needs of northern coastal region. Ten semesters for degree. WKU

COL ------. Medicina. Barranquilla: Universidad del Norte, [1978].
78   6 pp.
     Twelve-semester program leads to M.D. degree. WKU

COL ------. Psicología. [Barranquilla: Universidad del Norte,
79   1978]. 8 pp.
     Ten semesters required to become practicing psychologist.
WKU

COL VELEZ V., GUILLERMO; BATISTA J., ENRIQUE; ORTEGA V., MANUEL; and
80   RAMIREZ C., MARIANO L. "Modelo tentativo para establecer pro-
     gramas de postgrado en las universidades colombianas." Mundo
     Universitario, no. 4 (July-September 1973). pp. 135-156.
     Planning model for establishing nationwide policy for gradu-
ate studies. Part II follows discussion of minimum bases for creation of graduate studies, minimum criteria, relation to undergraduate goals. Flow charts for analysis. WKU

COL VILLAREAL, JUAN F. Causas y consecuencias de los paros universi-
81   tarios. Serie Universidad Hoy, no. 5. [Bogotá]: ICFES, 1971.
     44 pp.
     Strikes and stoppages caused loss of days from 1966 to 1971:
national universities, 601; sectional universities, 1,257; private universities, 410. Financial loss per institution calculated; demonstrates need for reform to overcome anarchy, crisis. WKU

COL ------. Consideraciones sobre la crisis universitaria. Serie
82   Universidad Hoy, no. 1. Bogotá: ICFES, 1977. 44 pp.

An official of ICFES prepares memorandum for minister of education in response to previous month's "latest university conflicts." Finds many roots for conflict: structure of higher education system, with its internal and external contests for power, and differences among universities; crises of government and of politics; ill-defined autonomy. Some problems with foreign aid. Proposes changes in law. WKU

COL   VILLARREAL, JUAN F.; VALENCIA TOVAR, ALVARO; and MOLINA, GERARDO.
 83   La crisis universitaria: Tres aspectos/tres puntos de vista.
      Serie Universidad Hoy, 2. Bogotá: ICFES, 1971. 76 pp.
      Profound problems in Colombian universities unsolved by perpetual efforts at "sterile reformism," with continuing loss of best-prepared professors, political convulsions. Weak autonomy and leadership leave too many decisions to government. Comments on student rebellion and role of military and police. Violent and authoritarian society seen as being challenged by students seeking social mobility. Comments on nation and foreign influences on it. WKU

Costa Rica

CoR ARIAS SANCHEZ, OSCAR. <u>Significado del movimiento estudiantil en</u>
1 <u>Costa Rica</u>. Publicaciones de la Universidad de Costa Rica, Serie
Misceláneas, no. 144. Ciudad Universitaria Rodrigo Facio: UCR,
1970. 61 pp.
From nineteenth century precursor institution through contemporary University of Costa Rica, role of student movement is
described. KU

CoR "Autoridades serán penadas si no admiten a alumnos." <u>La Nación</u>,
2 21 May 1975, p. 2.
Applicants to medical school at UCR get court order for
admission after being denied entrance for lack of space. University
had to use grades to cut off excess demand; rector denies any legal
infraction.

CoR BARAHONA JIMENEZ, LUIS. <u>La Universidad de Costa Rica (1940-</u>
3 <u>1973)</u>. San José: Editorial Universidad de Costa Rica, 1976.
408 pp.
Fundamental changes in 1964 included a program of general
studies. In 1974 there was a movement toward democracy and social
action. During recent years new concerns for research, teaching,
extension, a broader base of participation in the university council
and a general concern for international affairs particularly in Central
and South America. KU

BARAHONA RIERA, FRANCISCO. "The University for Peace." See
entry GEN 25.

CoR "El colapso de la educación superior." <u>La Nación</u>, 13 June 1980,
4 p. 14A.
National University (Heredia) closed by rector for lack of
funds. Editorial faults government for lack of funding policy for
higher education as symptomatic of "runaway populism"; points out irony
of having four universities without power to finance any one of them.

CoR CONSEJO NACIONAL DE RECTORES (CONARE). <u>Estadística de la edu-</u>
5 <u>cación superior</u>. San José: Oficina de Planificación de la
Educación Superior (OPES), 1978. 131 pp.

Data, mostly between 1970 and 1977, on university student
populations, academic achievement, graduation, socio-economic characteristics of students and their families, loans and scholarships;
teaching personnel, their numbers, academic qualifications and teaching
status and scholarships awarded; administrative personnel; libraries,
and research. Tables also on other post-secondary systems. WKU

CoR ------. PLANES: Plan nacional de educación superior. Versión
6   preliminar, 1976-1980. San José: OPES, [1976]. ca. 700 pp.
        Post-secondary education in Costa Rica, its structure,
financing, access, demand, physical and personnel resources, student
population. Concludes with analysis of 1976-1980 problems, including
defining autonomy and redefining role of general studies. Over 150
charts and graphs. WKU

CoR ------, Oficina de Planificación de la Educación Superior (OPES).
7   Estadística de la educación superior 1979. OPES 19/80, October
1980. San José: CONARE, OPES, 1980. 162 pp.
        Data on public universities: student population, teaching
and administrative personnel, libraries and research projects. Chapter, for first time, on private Universidad Autónoma de Centro América;
last chapter on other post-secondary institutions. UNED became part of
CONARE in 1979 and its available data are included. WKU

CoR ------. Lista de publicaciones de la Oficina de Planificación de
8   la Educación Superior (1975-septiembre 1980). OPES 17/80. San
José: CONARE, OPES, 1980. 20 pp.
        There were three publications in 1975; sixty-four items are
listed for most prolific year, 1978. WKU

CoR ------. Plan Nacional de Educación Superior II: Planes 1981-
9   1985. Versión preliminar. OPES 13/80, August 1980. San José:
CONARE, OPES, 1981. ca. 270 pp.
        Director of Planning Clara Zomer enumerates many changes
since 1975 Plan I was developed, including creation of UNED and establishment of UACA. Chapters, with abundant supporting documents,
cover financial needs in personnel, research, extension, computers,
libraries, administration, physical plant, equipment; recommendations.
WKU

CoR CONSEJO SUPERIOR UNIVERSITARIO CENTROAMERICANO (CSUCA). El sis-
10   tema educativo en Costa Rica: Situación actual y perspectivas.
Ciudad Universitaria, Costa Rica: Secretaría Permanente del
CSUCA, 1964. 242 pp.
        Development of the population and economic aspects. Struc-
ture of the educational system: elementary, secondary, and university.
Data on students, professors, and buildings; costs by faculty per
student; projections. WKU

CoR CRONICA UNIVERSITARIA, no. 1 (January-February 1981). 84 pp.
11   Publication of private Universidad Autónoma de Centro America, founded in 1976, carries advertisements of the various professional
schools of which it is composed, interspersed with editorials, articles
on the economy, the state of crisis in Costa Rica, university news,
literary and performing arts criticism. Collegium Magister offers

careers in administration and computation; Collegium Academicum offers law, business administration, international relations and computation; Colegio Veritas lists business administration, architecture, organization sciences; Colegio Fidelitas advertises business administration. There are others. UACA follows the Oxford/Cambridge pattern. Discussion of projected law of private universities.

CoR DURAN AYANEGUI, FERNANDO. "No debe desmantelarse la universi-
12   dad." Speech at ceremony transferring Centro Regional en Taceres to Universidad de Costa Rica by Costa Rican President Rodrigo Carazo, December 1980. Mimeographed. 6 pp.
     Acting rector, and later rector of UCR praises transfer as recognition of UCR's preponderant role in planning and orienting country's higher education. Refers to support for other, ill conceived universities, whose support by politicians is inimical to sound policy, challenging their "blind provincialism" and asserting that "UCR will never tolerate academic subordination to institutions lacking proven scientific-teaching experience." WKU

CoR ------. "Problemas de la educación superior en Costa Rica."
13   Speech honoring late Dean of Education Emma Gamboa, in Faculty of Education, 27 March 1981. Mimeographed. 27 pp.
     Frank, far-ranging comments on UCR and its role, situation, and needs. Points out strong tradition in UCR of concentrating on formation of people dedicated to teaching, science, arts and letters, rather than on the obligation to create professionals. Addresses question of truly democratic admissions policies which offer student appropriate education, rather than some present practices neither democratic nor productive. Comments on finance, growth of other institutions, changes needed internally and in relation to total system, including secondary level. WKU

CoR ------. Propuesta para la definición de una política de centros
14   regionales. Ciudad Universitaria Rodrigo Facio: Universidad de Costa Rica, Vicerrectoría de Docencia, [1979]. 21 pp. plus 5 page resolution.
     University Council, directed by academic vice-rector, attacks regionalization plan devised by University Congress III in 1972 as nonviable, saying its obsolescence began when the government--against judgment of UCR--created other higher education agencies, namely UNA, ITCR, UNED, and university colleges. Recognizes demand for education outside main campus, but insists that quality control be centralized there for regional entities. Resolution No. 664-79 would regulate in detail course offerings, teaching, finance, grading, admissions in regional centers. WKU

CoR "En un triángulo se debate la enseñanza del derecho." Universi-
15   dad, no. 300 (30 March-6 April 1979): 17.
     Creation of the new Universidad Autónoma de Centro América raises many questions about legality of private education, especially in Faculty of Law. Universidad de Costa Rica traditionally functioned as only certifying agency; role now challenged.

CoR "La Escuela de Historia de la Universidad Nacional." Revista de
16   Historia, no. 1 (1975): i-ii.

School of History, founded in 1973, along with UNA, offers bachelor's degree in teaching social studies for secondary teachers and a bachelor's degree in American history. These degrees and ten licenciaturas break with tradition of historian as narrator and describer of facts; instead graduates will be "scientific professionals at the technical level" able to "confront problems of reality"; to be "an agent of change, an analyst of socio-economic, cultural, political, rural and urban facts in the continental and national reality."

CoR   FACIO, RODRIGO. Dos discursos del rector de la Universidad de
17   Costa Rica: I, Una universidad libre. II, La justicia en la
      pequeña república universitaria. San José: UCR, 1956. 34 pp.
      Year-end remarks for 1954 and 1955 of this relatively young university celebrate its autonomy and successful avoidance of political involvement. Comments on predecessor institution, Santo Tomás, and the nineteenth and early twentieth century ambiente of Costa Rican education; role of university in the body politic. FU

CoR   "Finance Minister Reveals Plan to Aid Universities." San Jose
18   News, 21 September 1979, p. 9.
      National Rectors' Council, CONARE, asks budget increase. National University, UCR, University at a Distance and Costa Rican Technological Institute discuss 1981-85 plan for financing universities, as legislators seek to revise entire educational code to replace 1957 Fundamental Education Law. Proposal to divide country geographically.

CoR   "Formación docente en Costa Rica." La República, 5 November
19   1980, p. 15.
      A national conference is being prepared at the National University on teacher preparation. Precursor institutions of UNA were Normal School of Costa Rica and Higher Normal School in Heredia. Lack of coordination exists among universities and Ministry of Education on teacher preparation.

CoR   FREELAND, GLORIA. "Panelists Debate Licensing at IAPA Mid-Year
20   Meeting." San Jose News, 21 March 1980, pp. 1-2.
      Example of the licensing function of national universities in Latin America, here of jounalists in Costa Rica. Challenge comes not only from Inter-American Press Association (IAPA) as restrictive of free expression, but from new, private Autonomous University of Central America (UACA) which has its own school of journalism. University of Costa Rica fights to hold licensing power now implicit in its degree-granting function.

CoR   GALDAMES, LUIS. La universidad autónoma. San José, Costa Rica:
21   Editorial Borrase Hnos., Publicación de la Secretaría Pública,
      1935. 519 pp.
      Dean of philosophy and education of the University of Chile describes for Costa Ricans the structure of his university as the Costa Rican president proposes that the Congress reestablish the national university. President's message describes previous emphasis on diffusion of elementary education and need to increase higher education; explains autonomy and university governance. Analysis of function of education in society pervades several chapters. TxU

CoR   GAMBOA, EMMA. <u>Omar Dengo</u>. Publicaciones de la Universidad de
22   Costa Rica, Serie Educación, no. 7. San José: UCR, 1964. 60
      pp.
            Biography of Costa Rican educator influenced by John Dewey
and European thinkers who had influence on Costa Rican teacher education, by dean of UCR's School of Education. TxU

CoR   GUTIERREZ, CLAUDIO. "Al Sr. Paul Bomemisza y compañeros del
23   Seminario Evaluativo de la Educación Agrícola." Letter, photo-
        copy. Ciudad Universitaria Rodrigo Facio: Rectoría, UCR, 30
      April 1979. 8 pp.
            Response by rector to questionnaire on autonomy and planning
in higher education. Describes philosophies of different kinds of
autonomy, especially now that Costa Rica has more than one public
university; pros and cons. Coordination with Instituto Tecnológico de
Costa Rica. Cites five years of progress in UCR's internal administration and improved faculty quality and student-professor ratio. WKU

CoR   ------. Letter to Professor Carlos Monge A., Rector, Universidad
24   de Costa Rica, 25 June 1963. Anexo no. 3, sesión no. 1298.
      Unpublished. 12 pp. plus 7 page untitled document on General
      Education, 1962.
            Dean of Faculty of Sciences and Letters conveys to rector and
members of University Council the report of the General Education
Commission on reform project. All students will have first year of
general studies, modified after earlier difficulties leading to compro-
mises among professional schools and Sciences and Letters. WKU

CoR   ------. <u>Perspectiva de un período universitario</u>. Publicaciones
25   de la Universidad de Costa Rica, Serie Cuadernos Universitarios,
      no. 19. Ciudad Universitaria Rodrigo Facio: UCR, 1964. 12 pp.
            Speech by dean of Faculty of Science and Letters in its Third
Congress of professors and student representatives discusses various
polarities of viewpoints, e.g. paternalism vs. the liberal academic
attitude, "pure" academics vs. professional pursuits. Most discussion
grew out of implementing General Studies. Useful recapitulations of
issues addressed by reformers--and counter reformers--of this period of
Latin American university evolution and change. WKU

CoR   "Hacia la Universidad de la Paz." <u>Gaceta/UDUAL</u>, no. 36 (Sep-
26   tember 1980): 4.
            Government of Costa Rica has ceded land for establishing
Peace University, a project of the International Association of University Presidents. The Organizing Committee will meet in San José in
June 1981 to discuss: the curriculum, Latin American education, worldwide education of women.

CoR   "Hay que salvar a la UNA." <u>La República</u>, 28 July 1979, p. 8.
27   Refers to beginnings of National University in Heredia, over
five years before, with goal of being a local institution, and its
subsequent character as a center of "extremist proselytizing." But
now, offering careers unavailable at UCR, it is filling a national
need: hence government is called on to give adequate funding, hitherto
denied.

Costa Rica

CoR INCER, ANA. "Reviviendo la figura del Rodrigo Facio que nadie
28 olvida." Universidad, no. 300 (30 March-6 April 1979): 3-8.
　　　Homage to the late rector on sixty-second anniversary of his
birth by a former and the present rector. Leadership of small groups
of intellectuals in late thirties produced profound influence on
character of University of Costa Rica, the country and the region;
Facio was a leader in university reform.

CoR INTER-AMERICAN DEVELOPMENT BANK. "Inter-American Bank Lends $30
29 Million to Foster Higher Education in Costa Rica." Washington,
　　　D.C.: IDB news release, 5 May 1978. 1 p.
　　　Funds to be used by University of Costa Rica, Technological
Institute and National University to decentralize higher education by
providing short courses of study for secondary school graduates. Goal:
to increase proportion of community students outside central region
from 15 percent to 35 percent. UCR would construct three regional
centers plus administration and library facilities at main campus. WKU

CoR LEON VILLALOBOS, EDWIN. Una universidad en una ciudad de
30 maestros: Orígenes de la Universidad Nacional, 1870-1973.
　　　[Heredia]: Universidad Nacional, 1981. 170 pp.
　　　Lively, well documented account of people and events tells
much of the society and its values. Emergence of UNA out of earlier
normal schools and urgency of providing teacher education. Especially
revealing of the role of UCR as seen by its critics, some still active
in higher education. Hints at but does not elaborate on the stormy
administration of first Rector Benjamín Núñez and subsequent difficulties of UNA; author, who was observer and participant in many of the
events described, says he runs the risk of lacking objectivity. WKU

CoR MALAVASSI VARGAS, GUILLERMO. Metodología de los Estudios
31 Generales. Serie Misceláneas, no. 94. Ciudad Universitaria
　　　Rodrigo Facio: Publicaciones de la Universidad de Costa Rica,
　　　1964. 28 pp.
　　　Presentation made at the Fourth Meeting of the Central American Commission for General Studies, held in Lawrence, Kansas, gives
short history of UCR. Major reforms in UCR, begun in 1946, described
in useful chronology. Specific proposals for teaching students in
large numbers point to some problems to be faced. WKU

CoR MONGE ALFARO, CARLOS. Acceso a la universidad: Un problema de
32 nuestro tiempo (discurso). Costa Rica: Ciudad Universitaria
　　　Rodrigo Facio, 1967. 14 pp.
　　　Rector presents the 1966-67 annual report to members of the
University Assembly. Emphasis on the problem of access to higher
education and the first discussion of the possibility of regional
colleges. TxU

CoR ------. En torno a algunos problemas de la educación y de la
33 comunidad. Ciudad Universitaria Rodrigo Facio: Publicaciones de
　　　la Universidad de Costa Rica, 1969. 65 pp.
　　　During 1969, rector gave several formal lectures including
the annual report, a lecture in Buenos Aires on "the University and
Development" in the Interamerican Congress, his inaugural speech for
the new Faculty of Art building, and his presentation at the close of
the academic year in December of 1968. TxU

CoR ------. Tradición y renovación de la universidad. Serie Cua-
34 dernos Universitarios, no. 31. Ciudad Universitaria Rodrigo
    Facio: UCR, 1967. 12 pp.
        Salutes graduates, professors in their twenty-fifth year of
teaching, since 1941 founding of UCR. KU

CoR ------. La universidad contemporánea: Análisis crítico,
35 principios, metas y objectivos. Ciudad Universitaria Rodrigo
    Facio, Costa Rica: UCR, 1970. 19 pp.
        A lecture on the occasion of the inaugural of the Central
American seminar on University Planning by the rector of the University
of Costa Rica. KU

CoR "No pueden estudiar 3,000 universitarios." Seminario Universi-
36 tario, no. 492 (June 1981): 19-25.
        Limitations on enrollments in several schools of UCR deny
entry to some aspirants. Confusion over grade point averages needed to
qualify; unfairness, financial waste for university require study, new
policies.

CoR OFICINA DE EDUCACION IBEROAMERICANA (OEI). La Educación en
37 Iberoamérica: Sistema de indicadores socioeconómicos y edu-
    cativos. Costa Rica, Serie Estadística, nos. 1-3. Madrid,
    Ciudad Universitaria: OEI, 1980. ca. 150 pp. in 3 volumes.
        Remarkably comprehensive, thorough, objective collection of
information, in folders, on the socioeconomic framework of education,
and education itself. OASDC

CoR OFICINA DE INFORMACION CASA PRESIDENCIAL. Educación nacional:
38 ideario costarricense 1977. San José: Unidad de Investigaciones
    Sociales, [1977]. 302 pp.
        Essays by twenty-three Costa Rican leaders and thinkers on
national education, responding to a questionnaire which includes sections on higher education. Topics include objectives, policies,
planning, demand, future perspectives. WKU

CoR PACHECO LEON, FREDDY. "La investigación en la universidad." La
39 República, 21 August 1980.
        Criticizes lack of research in universities, especially at
UCR, as fundamental weakness. Insufficient support in money and
people; topic should be discussed and acted on at Fourth Congress of
UCR. Questions usefulness of separate research institutes.

CoR PIVA M., ALFIO, and LEON, EDWIN. Programa de trabajo, 1980-1983.
40 Heredia: Universidad nacional, 1980. 53 pp.
        Rector and secretary believe UNA is emerging from nearly
disastrous past three years, when funds were unavailable from government to pay employees and activities were suspended part of the time.
Reorganization underway; plans for improving library, preparation of
professors, research, extension, student life. Decentralized programs
in education in collaboration with Ministry of Public Education.
Graduate programs proposed with other universities, as well as improved
functioning of CONARE to avoid interuniversity feuding and program
competition. WKU

PRESIDENTIAL COMMISSION OF THE UNIVERSITY FOR PEACE. University for Peace: Basic Documents. See entry GEN 216.

CoR   "Problems Threaten Major Universities." San Jose News, 6 June
41   1980.
        Rector of University of Costa Rica says funds available only to function through November, and closing of the National University in Heredia seems likely before end of school year.

CoR   QUESADA, AMPARO SOLANO DE. "Heredia y la Universidad Nacional."
42   La República, 25 October 1980, p. 9.
        Tribute to Rector Alfio Piva Mesén and his efforts to reorganize the university, which "has always been in crisis," in harmony with the community of Heredia and national needs.

CoR   RAMIREZ, CELEDONIO. "La función de la nueva universidad."
43   Repertorio Americano, no. 2 (January-March 1975): 1-2.
        New Costa Rican public university, Universidad Nacional de Heredia, seeks to synthesize knowledge, develop learning in community settings through interaction, making university "bridge between truth and existence." Begins with Latin American Studies and School of Literature and Language Sciences.

CoR   RAMIREZ, MARIANO. Crecimiento de la población estudiantil uni-
44   versitaria. [San Pedro]: Universidad de Costa Rica, 1959. 250
        pp.
        Analysis of education at all locales in rural and urban areas, with data on enrollment, buildings, teachers. Projections for university needs by 1970. TxU

CoR   "Reacción funda 'U' privada." Universidad, 26 May 1975, pp. 12-
45   14.
        Storm of criticism from UCR students, professors, liberal political figures. Charge that those founding private Universidad Autónoma de Centro América are conservatives whose actions "make more acute the separation of classes"; that creating private agency violates planning principles; that sooner or later state subvention will be needed, drawing money from public institutions. Government officials, including minister of education, unaware of action before reading decree in official gazette.

CoR   "Replantean funcionamiento de los centros regionales." La
46   Nación, 20 April 1981, p. 6A.
        University of Costa Rica, National University, Technological Institute of Costa Rica, and Student Federation of UCR will study problems of the various regional centers. Students worry about restricted offerings, not getting senior professors, lack of information.

CoR   ROMERO, MARIO. El estudiante universitario: La deserción estu-
47   diantil en la Universidad de Costa Rica. Guatemala: IIME, 1964.
        96 pp.
        Abandonment of studies, a serious economic and social problem, is studied by questionnaires and interviews. UCR retains about 50 percent of its matriculants, with highest retention in schools requiring full-time dedication to study rather than those permitting outside work. Several variables analyzed. WKU

CoR   ROMERO PEREZ, JORGE ENRIQUE. "El debate sobre UACA." La Nación,
48   22 May 1979, p. 15A.
      Lawyer argues legal right of new private Universidad Autónoma
de Centro América to exist within Costa Rican framework of higher
education. Sets forth criticisms and rebuttal.

CoR   RUMBLE, G[REVILLE] W. S. V. "The Open University, Centre for
49   International Co-operation and Services. A Case Study in
      Distance Learning Systems: Costa Rica's Universidad Estatal a
      Distancia." Mimeographed. [San José: Consejo Nacional de
      Rectores, 1980]. 48 pp.
      Data on Costa Rica's educational system and national plan,
1976-80, including university expansion. Details of radio and
television programs of study to be offered, with comments on over-
optimistic "workload assumptions." Information on course preparation,
administration, staffing. WKU

CoR   ------. "A Recommendation for a Methodology to be Used to
50   Evaluate Costa Rican Universities." Carbon copy of report pre-
      pared for the Special Commission on University Institutions,
      named by the Legislative Assembly. [San José], 1980. 42 pp.
      Consultant from England's Open University sets forth means
and techniques to achieve goal set for commission by legislature to
formulate recommendations on "the rationalization of the expenditure of
each university, restructuring of higher education system to avoid
duplication of careers and massive production of professionals with no
relation to national labor market." WKU

CoR   ------, and BORDEN, GEORGE A. "Meeting Educational Needs in
51   Costa Rica: The Role of Distance Teaching: Universidad Estatal
      a Distancia." Mimeographed. San José: UNED, 1980. 76 pp.
      Report of British and U.S. consultants gives background for
1977 creation of UNED. Study of student demand, demand from disadvantaged sections of society, needs for educated manpower. UNED indeed
offers an alternative to conventional university; it has not succeeded
in opening itself to people from lower socioeconomic classes, since it
requires secondary school diploma; its programs are directed to manpower needs identified by CONARE. Tables of important data about all
public higher education. WKU

CoR   SOTO, JOSE ALBERTO, and BERNARDINI, AMALIA. La educación actual
52   en sus fuentes filosóficas. San José: Editorial Universidad
      Estatal a Distancia, 1981. 496 pp. plus foldout charts.
      Costa Rica's educational philosophy derives from such diverse
sources as Italian neo-idealism, Marxism, positivism, pragmatism, and
Catholic humanism. In recent years, these thinkers have been influential: Skinner, Rogers, Illich, Freire, García Hoz, Summerhill.
Their positions are briefly stated. Useful chronology of Costa Rican
education since 1565 provides something of a history of a remarkably
open society. An important work; a university textbook. WKU

CoR   TORRES MARTINEZ, RAUL, and CHINCHILLA GUTIERREZ, SARAH, editors.
53   Especialismo y formación humana: Seminario, efectos humanos del
      avance científico tecnológico. Ciudad Universitaria Rodrigo
      Facio: UCR, Escuela de Estudios Generales, 1980. 98 pp.

Costa Rica

Affirming its almost unique commitment among Latin American universities to liberal education, UCR celebrates its fortieth anniversary with symposium on the human condition in a world of narrowing specialization. Students, professors read, discuss ideas of Ortega y Gasset, C. P. Snow, Lynn White, Jr., UCR's rector-philosopher Claudio Gutiérrez, among others. Academic Vice-rector Fernando Durán addresses problem in academic and social contexts; student Jacques Sagot pleads the case for the broadest possible humanistic education. WKU

CoR TORRES MOREIRA, LUIS. El Departamento de Registro y sus diez
54   años de labores universitarias. Ciudad Universitaria Rodrigo
     Facio: UCR, 1966. 37 pp.
     By 1966 the University of Costa Rica had made some funda-
mental changes: creation of departments of the faculty of sciences and
letters made it logical to develop flexible pattern of study. Creation
of the centralized registrar's office was a major organizational
change. KU

CoR TORRES PADILLA, OSCAR. Un estudio de utilización de los pro-
55   fesionales en servicio social y el mercado del trabajo. Ciudad
     Universitaria Rodrigo Facio: UCR, Oficina de Planificación Uni-
     versitaria, 1972. 46 pp. plus 35 pages of appendices.
     First of series by planning office on use of human resources.
Social worker's study considers demographic and academic framework,
socioeconomic and cultural characteristics, working conditions, evaluation of university preparation. WKU

CoR "UCR Congress Meets this Week." San Jose News, 25 April 1980.
56   Financial headaches and academic quality chief topics at
week-long meeting of 800 professors and student representatives to
discuss conditions of University of Costa Rica, first such congress in
nine years. One proposal: elimination of poorly performing students
and professors who miss classes.

CoR UNIVERSIDAD AUTONOMA DE CENTRO AMERICA (UACA). "Alumnos
57   matriculados durante el primer cuatrimestre de 1981." [San José:
     UACA], 1981. Mimeographed. 2 pp.
     Student numbers, by career and college; total: 4,059. WKU

CoR ------. Ordenanzas Universitarias. Anuario Universitario 1981.
58   San José: UACA, 1980. 384 pp.
     Private university, authorized in 1975, is composed of af-
filiated university colleges operating under strict rules. Minimum and
maximum size, number of careers, class size, student and faculty rights
and responsibilities set forth. Documents affirming UACA's standing
include details of controversy over rights of law students, claimed
exclusively by University of Costa Rica, challenged in courts. Issue
centers on UCR's traditional licensing function in the professions; the
thirteen colleges and their offerings; examination standards for various degrees. WKU

CoR ------. "Proyecto de ley general de universidades." Crónica
59   Universitaria, no. 2 [1981?]: 3.
     An editorial attacks proposed law as doing nothing to improve
higher education. Says that it puts too much power in hands of the
state to control education.

Costa Rica

CoR ------. "Stvdivm Generale Costarricense: Información general,
60 la Universidad Autónoma y los colegios universitarios." Crónica
Universitaria, no. 2 [1981?]: 6-8.
Stvdivm Generale is one of the several colleges comprising
UACA, none of which will exceed 1,000 students. High scores on examinations required for graduation; each student must be accepted by a
tutor. Details of tutorial system, emphasis on student responsibility.

CoR UNIVERSIDAD DE COSTA RICA (UCR). Anales de la Universidad de
61 Costa Rica, 1942. San José: (UCR). Costa Rica. 32 pp.
Essays on various topics, including the 1941 first anniversary of publication of the law reestablishing the University of Costa
Rica; a wide-eyed report on visit of the university's secretary general
to various universities in the U.S., to New York City and Washington
D.C.; 1936 comments and disputes on reorganization of the university.

CoR ------. Anales de la Universidad de Costa Rica, 1953. San José:
62 [UCR]. 416 pp.
Relationships of university and the secondary schools, plan
of the new faculty of humanities; report of department of student
affairs, on full-time and half-time faculty members, planning of the
university city, economic-legal relations between the government and
the university, planning of the school of medicine, third reunion of
the universities of Central America, first assembly of the Union of
Latin American Universities (UDUAL), and reports of communication between delegates of the university and the Higher Council of Education.

CoR ------. Anales de la Universidad de Costa Rica, 1960. Ciudad
63 Universitaria, Costa Rica, 1961. 909 pp.
The university council, rectory, general secretary, schools,
faculties, academic and administrative departments, student council.
University was growing rapidly in both numbers and quality. Reports
were very detailed.

CoR ------. Antecedentes, planes y primeras realizaciones para el
64 establecimiento de la Escuela de Medicina. San Pedro: UCR,
1957. 57 pp.
Rector Rodrigo Facio's preface explains careful development
of medical school, after creation of Faculty of Sciences and Letters;
details of development; enrollment by faculties 1941-56, from 740 to
2,179 students. DLC

CoR ------. Antecedentes, planes y primeras realizaciones para el
65 establecimiento de Escuela de Medicina. Segunda Parte. Ciudad
Universitaria: Universidad de Costa Rica, 1961. 68 pp.
An update of 1957 plans with opening of medical school, with
new building, pre-medical studies, clinical work. Represents break
with traditional Latin American pattern with its links with Faculty of
Sciences and Letters. History and other information on creation of
medical school. TxU

CoR ------. El departamento de bienestar y orientación. Serie
66 Miscelánea, no. 105. San José, [UCR] 1965. 50 pp.
Department of student affairs includes physical education,
orientation and student life, health, supervision of restaurants and

soda fountains, medical services, loans, student organizations and sports. KU

CoR ------. Estadística de los primeros años del curso lectivo 1956.
67 Estadísticas Universitarias, no. 1. San José: UCR, 1957. 42 pp.
      Eight hundred and thirty-nine students were enrolled in UCR's twelve schools; since 1950 there have been 1,049 graduates. Useful but limited data. KU

CoR ------. Equilibrio entre las ciencias y humanidades en la
68 enseñanza superior. San José: UCR, Editorial Universitaria, 1959. 69 pp.
      A report to the Union of Universities of Latin America. The Faculty of Sciences and Letters, created in 1957, reports on general studies program in the new faculty. The common first year was new for Central America. KU

CoR ------. Estatuto orgánico de la Universidad de Costa Rica. San
69 José: Imprenta Nacional, 1956. 28 pp.
      Law covers goals; governance; degrees; faculties; role of students, professors, alumni; university-wide academic calendar; finance. Significant departure from Latin American tradition in creating Faculty of Sciences and Letters as central faculty of the university. Section on "Transitory Dispositions" hints at some of the problems of complex reorganization. KU

CoR ------. Estatuto orgánico de la Universidad de Costa Rica. San
70 José: Departamento de Publicaciones, 1957. 48 pp.
      Essentially unchanged from 1956 version, except for "Transitory Dispositions." KU

CoR ------. Estatuto orgánico de la Universidad de Costa Rica.
71 Ciudad Universitaria Rodrigo Facio, 1971. 55 pp.
      Laws regulating UCR. DPU

CoR ------. Informe del rector. Publicaciones de la Universidad de
72 Costa Rica, Serie Miscelánea, no. 87. Ciudad Universitaria Rodrigo Facio: UCR, 1962-63. 298 pp.
      Because UCR Anales has grown to nearly 1,000 pages, new kind of report from rector for the University Assembly is required, in written and oral presentation. Idea is to encourage open discussion of university activities and policies. Period of great expansion, reform in structure, new relationships between students and professors. Raises issues now under discussion elsewhere in Latin America on relation between education and national development and pressures to expand career choices. Financial matters, relationship with USAID. WKU

CoR ------. Informe del rector, 1968-1969. Ciudad Universitaria
73 Rodrigo Facio: UCR, 1969. 214 pp.
      Rector Carlos Monge Alfaro presents narrative account, beginning with an essay titled "Wisdom and Prudence in the University's Work"; policies and practices in general studies, admissions, regional centers, various reforms, and other matters. WKU

Costa Rica

CoR   ------. Informe del rector, 1972-1973. Ciudad Universitaria
74   Rodrigo Facio: UCR, 1973. 230 pp.
       Comments of rector on academic, administrative, and financial
affairs; relations with government and organizations, the Higher Council of Central American Universities (CSUCA); planning activities.

CoR   ------. Interacción de sistemas y grupos en un modelo para la
75   administración de la Universidad de Costa Rica. Ciudad Universi-
       taria Rodrigo Facio: UCR, Oficina de Planificación, 1972. 89 pp.
       Study of statutes and regulations yields model for adminis-
tration expressed in various organograms. Description and analysis of
problems. WKU

CoR   ------. Reglamentos, servicios técnicos y administrativos. San
76   José: UCR, 1959. 199 pp.
       Rules, technical and administrative services spelled out.
LNHT

CoR   ------. Teoría de los estudios generales. Publicaciones de la
77   Universidad de Costa Rica, Serie de Filosofía, no. 2. San José:
       UCR, 1958. 97 pp.
       Strong commitment to general education as intrinsically good,
to contribute to producing "the cultivated man." Presentations by
Costa Rican educational leaders and Angel Quintero Alfaro of Puerto
Rico. Reports on debates and practices in U.S. universities, essays by
Ortega y Gasset and others. WKU

CoR   ------, Departamento de Registro. Informe preliminar. San José:
78   Departamento de Publicaciones, 1957. 54 pp.
       By years and schools; number of students in university is
2,474.

CoR   UNIVERSIDAD DE COSTA RICA, Facultad de Ciencias y Letras. Acto
79   de inauguración de la nueva facultad y su pabellón central,
       bienvenidos a los estudiantes del primer año. Discursos del Rec-
       tor de la Universidad, Rodrigo Facio; del Decano de la Facultad,
       José Joaquín Trejos. Ciudad Universitaria: UCR, 1957. 29 pp.
       Milestone in development of modern university with new
academic structure and related building for Faculty of Science and
Letters. Speakers: two of Costa Rica's most noted educational
leaders. FU

CoR   [UNIVERSIDAD DE COSTA RICA], III Congreso Universitario.
80   Proyectos de reglamentos, ponencias y mociones, 22 al 30 de oc-
       tubre de 1971. Primera etapa. [Ciudad Universitaria Rodrigo
       Facio]: UCR, Comisión Organizadora, [n.d.]. 220 pp.
       Working document for discussion by participants of new uni-
versity statute and these themes: goals of UCR, general plan for
higher education, function and structure of UCR, university and society, research and the national interest, social service, growth,
priorities. WKU

CoR   ------. Resoluciones definitivas. Ciudad Universitaria Rodrigo
81   Facio: UCR, Comisión Organizadora, 1972. 30 pp.

Conclusions reached by university professors, students, administrators in a congress. Statement of goals, analysis of higher education in Costa Rica and university's place in it, university and society, growth, evaluation of teaching and research, governance and administration, housing, student life. WKU

CoR UNIVERSIDAD DE COSTA RICA, Vicerrectoría de Docencia. Catálogo
82 universitario. 2 vols. 1st ed. Ciudad Universitaria Rodrigo
     Facio: [UCR], 1977.
        Catalog has a double purpose: to make it easy for faculty and students to understand this complex university, and to present the image of the University of Costa Rica to the country and the international community. Plans of study, lists of faculty members, organization of the university.

CoR UNIVERSIDAD ESTATAL A DISTANCIA (UNED). Cursos de la Universidad
83 Estatal a Distancia 1981. San José: UNED, Vicerrectoría de
     Planificación, 1980. 101 pp.
        All programs begin with basic cycle of language, natural and social sciences. Degrees in education, public and business administration offered. WKU

CoR ------. Información General. San José: UNED, Vicerrectoría de
84 Planificación, Centro de Información y Documentación Institucional, 1980. 55 pp. plus 2 maps.
        Description of distance education concept and UNED, its functions, governance, requirements, degrees, extension offerings, personnel; maps of facilities in San José and of "areas of theoretical influence of UNED academic centers" throughout Costa Rica. WKU

CoR ------. Plan de Desarrollo de la UNED, 1981-1985. No. 2. San
85 José: UNED, 1980. 177 pp.
        Rector Francisco Antonio Pacheco explains in introduction need for frequent revision of plan for new and novel kind of university; constant study of other open university systems; need to balance demands for qualitative and quantitative changes with available human and financial resources, especially with Costa Rica's present economic woes. Carefully detailed text covers general aspects of UNED, its objectives, organization and function, social and occupational demand, academic offerings, resources needed. Valuable data. WKU

     [UNIVERSIDAD NACIONAL ABIERTA (UNA)--UNIVERSIDAD ESTATAL A
     DISTANCIA (UNED)]. Experiencias UNA-UNED: La evaluación institucional, tema C. See entry VEN 191.

     ------. Experiencias UNA-UNED: La visión de conjunto, entre la
     práctica y la imagen objectiva, tema A. See entry VEN 192.

CoR UNIVERSIDAD NACIONAL AUTONOMA (UNA). Catálogo universitario.
86 Heredia: UNA, 1979. 533 pp.
        University authorities, student services, courses in six faculties, offerings in two regional centers, careers approved and awaiting financing. WKU

CoR "Universidad Nacional de El Salvador: Atraso científico,
87 cultural, saldo de un año de intervención militar." Seminario
Universidad, 26 June-2 July 1981, p. 19.
An example of constant concern for activities in other
Central American universities reported in UCR newspaper: Salvadorean
military, with tanks, heavy arms, helicopters, invaded National University campus, attacking the 8,000 students, professors, workers
there. Rector later assassinated. Archives, medical equipment destroyed; offices of student groups, library of Faculty of Social
Sciences and Humanities burned. Suspension of education for some
47,000 students; those finishing cannot graduate or be certified to
work at their professions, due to police occupation of offices holding
their records.

CoR VARGAS, MARIA EUGENIA DENGO DE. "Presentación para la apertura
88 del diálogo nacional sobre la educación costarricense." Acción y
Reflexión Educativa, no. 5 (June 1980): 101-19.
Costa Rica's minister of education describes participation of
parents, students, teachers, former president of the nation in discussions of problems and their solution in entire educational system.
Data on present situation, questions raised, plan of regionalization of
education, education and national development; university as integral
part of system in Costa Rica.

CoR ZELEDON, RODRIGO. La investigación en la universidad. Publi-
89 caciones de la Universidad de Costa Rica. Serie Cuadernos Universitarios, no. 20. Ciudad Universitaria Rodrigo Facio: UCR,
1964. 14 pp.
Arguing the point of view of Houssay, Zeledón insists that
fundamental research must be done in Costa Rica or the country and the
university will fall into "national suicide." TxU

CoR ZOMER, CLARA. La educación superior en Costa Rica. San José:
90 CONARE, 1981. 21 pp.
Director of CONARE Planning Office for Higher Education
addresses Sixth Triennial Meeting of International Association of University Presidents in San José. Higher education history since 1814;
early priority given to primary education closed university for a time
but achieved nearly 100 percent elementary schooling access for the
populace. Focus on rapid expansion of the seventies, with data for all
universities. Diversification, regionalization, planning, coordination, finance, constitutional reforms. Problem areas: employment
for graduates in shrinking economy, control of institutions, rationalization of structure and expenditures, massification and protection of
quality. WKU

Cuba

CUB   ALFONSO CABALLERO, MARIO. <u>Raíz, savia y aliento de la Universi-</u>
1   <u>dad Masónica</u>. Havana: Universidad Masónica de Cuba, 1955.   23
      pp.
           Author was secretary of the "then-named 'Universidad Nacional
Masónica José Martí'" at its 1952 founding, resigned in 1954 in policy
dispute with Masonic leadership, and published this 1953 speech at 1955
opening of Universidad Masónica de Cuba.   Impassioned defense of humanistic values, with long passages from Ortega y Gasset and others on
mission of the university.   Criticism of existing institutions for
over-emphasis on science, technology, specialization.   Begins with
history of universities in thirteenth century; mentions 1950 Cuban law
governing private universities.   DLC

CUB   ALMUIÑAS RIVERO, JOSE A. "El sistema de ingreso y su incidencia
2   en la eficiencia de la enseñanza superior." <u>Revista Inter-</u>
      <u>nacional de Países Socialistas</u> 4 (1977):   193-202.
           Official of Cuban Ministry of Higher Education proposes entry
requirements to system to optimize success rate; recognizes need to put
."limits to the satisfaction of individual desires which often don't
correspond to the goals of the society." (Contrasts with traditional
Latin American leftist student demands to admit even worst prepared
students.) Describes Cuba's post 1969-70 policies on access to higher
education, distribution for day students by area of study, entry into
workers' courses.

CUB   ANGULO MONTEAGUDO, MANUEL DE J. "VI Seminario InterAmericano de
3   Educación sobre 'Planeamiento Integral de la Educación.'" <u>Islas</u>
      2, no. 1 (September-December, 1959):   139-79.
           Dean of education in Cuba's Central University prepares docu-
ment based on a hemispheric conference in Washington, D.C., with help
from UNESCO and OAS leadership.   Data on lack of prepared teachers and
schools; calls for all of Latin American education to be developed by
each country in articulated, planned system "inseparable from the life
of society." Specifies tasks of his university to support philosophy
of conference; recommendations of conference.

CUB   ANGULO Y PEREZ, ANDRES. <u>Recurso de inconstitucionalidad,</u>
4   <u>establecido ante el Tribunal de Guarantías Constitucionales y</u>
      <u>Sociales por profesores, empleados y estudiantes de la universidad</u>
      <u>de la Habana</u>. Havana: [n.p.], 1950.   19 pp.

A lawyer and twenty-six others—students, employees, professors—charge two 1949 budgetary laws are unconstitutional, since they do not grant the University of Havana the 2.25 percent of the total national budget expenditures guaranteed by law. DLC

CUB   ANIDO ARTILES, AGUSTIN. "Política, educación y democracia."
5   *Islas* 1, no. 3 (May-August 1959): 457-62.
       Expression of outrage at U.S. universities for awarding honorary degrees to the dictators of Cuba and Guatemala; sees universities being compromised for political ends, warns against Latin American universities' being polarized in competition between U.S.S.R. and U.S., losing their democratic goals.

CUB   ANTUÑA, VICENTINA. "Juan Marinello: Maestro emérito de la
6   cultura cubana." *Universidad de la Habana* 201 (1974): 6-21.
       Student rebel of the 1920s, professor and revolutionary of the 1930s and 1940s, first rector of the "Revolutionary University" is made professor emeritus of University of Havana. Example of intertwined educational and political efforts to achieve reforms.

CUB   *La Autonomía universitaria.* Prologue by José Rafael Burgos.
7   Publicaciones de la Agrupación Universitaria Centroamericana
       (AUCA), no. 2. [Guatemala], 1962. 48 pp.
       Violations of University of Havana's autonomy by "communist hordes" vigorously denounced by Salvadoran Catholic University students' organization, AUCA. Describes split in Cuban student federation, purge of professors, police interference in student elections after 1959. TxU

CUB   BIBLIOTECA NACIONAL "JOSE MARTI." *Bibliografía Cubana 1959/62-64.*
8   Havana: Consejo Nacional de Cultura.
       The volume for 1963-64, compiled by Marta Dulzaides Serrate and Marta Bidot Pérez, notes that "imperialist blockade" tries to deny them access to world thought about Cuba. Little on education. By 1977, Bibliografía Cubana (published 1978) lists primarily textbooks, some few at university level. Shows changes in a bibliographic source following the Revolution. See entry CUB 101 for some effects on continuity of the series. KU

CUB   BOTI, REGINO. "La planificación y la educación tecnológica." In
9   *Economía y planificación*, Universidad Popular, 7° ciclo, parte 2,
       pp. 163-86. Havana, 1961.
       Economic minister describes Cuba's deficit in technology as worse than Portugal's, the poorest of Europe. Traditional enthusiasm for legal education instead of science and engineering to be replaced by planned technical development, predicted to be more successful in socialist than capitalist system. KU

CUB   BOWLES, SAMUEL. "Cuban Education and the Revolutionary Ide-
10   ology." *Harvard Educational Review* 41 (November 1971): 472-
       500.
       Four-part analysis of the interrelation between revolution and education in Cuba. Major points include campaign against illiteracy, "the school goes to the country," interest circles "oriented to productive activities," and student participation in teaching. Major

problems include the emphasis on basic rather than higher education, the development of rewards other than grades, and the ability-grouping of students in a supposedly classless society.

CUB   BOZA DOMINGUEZ, LUIS. La situación universitaria en Cuba.
11   Santiago de Chile: Editorial del Pacífico, 1963. 200 pp.
      Chronology, with documentation, of 1959 take-over by revolutionary government of Federation of Student Leaders (FEU) of University of Havana. Betrayal of moderate, anti-Batista students and professors when "People, Government, and University" are declared one entity, thus doing away with university autonomy. Details of public and private university events leading to repression, exile, closing of private institutions. KU

CUB   "A Brief Note on the Bibliography of Cuban Education" and "A
12   Brief Bibliography of Recent Works on Cuban Education." U.S.-
      Cuba: Educational Exchange Newsletter 2, no. 1 (April 1982): 8-
      10, 12.
      Excellent summary of bibliographic problems and sources. Most items are on non-university education. Anticipates late 1982 publication by Greenwood Press of Human Services in Cuba: An Annotated Bibliography by Larry R. Oberg, which will have over 960 citations on education [1984 publication].

CUB   BRYAN, PATRICK. "Review of University Students and Revolution in
13   Cuba, 1920-68. Jaime Suchlicki, University of Miami Press,
      Florida, 1969." Caribbean Quarterly 17, no. 1 (March 1971):
      54-57.
      Comments on Suchlicki's hostility to Fidel Castro's relations with university student leaders and his reliance on data from exiles; concludes book to be a useful work overall.

CUB   BUNN, HARRIET, and GUT, ELLEN. The Universities of Cuba, the
14   Dominican Republic, Haiti. Higher Education in Latin America,
      vol. 4. Washington, D.C.: Division of Intellectual Cooperation,
      Pan American Union, 1946. 102 leaves.
      The three national universities described; academic calendars, administration, admissions, capital cities, degrees, enrollment, history, student affairs, teaching staff, courses of study. The University of Havana had 13,146 students, the University of Santo Domingo had 1,241, the University of Haiti, 701. The Haitian study notes few women have been enrolled because until recent times they were not admitted to secondary schools. OT

CUB   CARNOY, MARTIN and WERTHEIN, JORGE. Cuba: Cambio económico y
15   reforma educativa (1955-1978). Mexico: Editorial Nueva Imagen,
      1980. 158 pp. Translation of Cuba: Economic Change and Educational Reform.
      Before 1959 education served class structure dominated by foreigners. Authors' analysis concludes Cuba's educational system is inextricably linked with economic system, including career choices in university. Examines consequences and problems of educational reform. FMU

CUB   CARRERAS, DELIO J. The Aula Magna of the University of Havana.
16   [Havana?: Universidad de la Habana?, 1978]. 9 pp.

Brief description of the salon for graduation and other formal ceremonies of the University of Havana, with its neo-classic buildings; a short history of the university, and a summary of the new revolutionary points of view. Major changes in 1923, role of students under Julio Antonio Mella, and the complete change of the revolution rhapsodically treated. WKU

CUB   CASTRO, FIDEL. A Educacão em Cuba. Lisboa, Portugal: Inicia-
17   tivas Editorials, [1973]. 148 pp. Translated from Spanish.
      Castro's fundamental comment on education in a communist society is that one cannot separate manual from intellectual labor. Comments on the Ministry of Education, the political-technical aspects of education. Latter half on higher education is very specific. KU

CUB   ------. La educación en revolución. Havana: Instituto Cubano
18   del Libro, 1975. 233 pp.
      In a prologue, Juan Marinello summarizes activities in education in Cuba. Great emphasis on all levels of education. One major success was elimination of illiteracy. Private schools closed, coeducation adopted, work and school combined, emphasis on schools throughout the island particularly in the "campo." Strong emphasis on applied aspects of education, including higher education. Includes remarks on past evils of the university torn by politics, warped by insufficiencies, and in need of reform. KU

CUB   ------. La experiencia cubana. Barcelona: Editorial Blume,
19   1976. 317 pp.
      Report to first congress of Communist Party (1975) describes and interprets pre-revolutionary history and subsequent economic and social development. Education, as part of matrix, described, including university reform. Abundant data. Useful prologue by Juan Martínez-Alier. KU

CUB   ------. Fidel habla a los estudiantes del mundo: UIE-FEU Re-
20   unión de la Habana, Cuba, 23 de mayo-8 de junio 1961. Havana:
      Universidad de la Habana, Departamento de Informatión, Publi-
      caciones e Intercambio Cultural, 1961. 43 pp.
      A major address for the International Union of Students, in defense of the Cuban revolution; attacks U.S., President Kennedy, and the Alliance for Progress. Praises students for the project for the elimination of illiteracy in Cuba and the great growth of education from the elementary to higher education systems. ICarbS

CUB   ------. "Main Report, Second Congress of the Communist Party of
21   Cuba." Cuba Update 2, 1 (March 1981). 48 pp.
      Some 80 million pesos per year invested in scientific and technological work carried out by 23,000 workers, including 5,300 university graduates. Data on educational growth at all levels include increase from 1975 to 1980 of 84,000 to over 200,000 in colleges and universities. Over 30,000 are workers in extension courses; over 20,000 graduates in 1979-80.

CUB   ------. Revolutionary Struggle 1947-1958. The Selected Works of
22   Fidel Castro, edited by Rolando E. Bonachea and Nelson P. Valdes,
      vol. 1. Cambridge, Mass.: The MIT Press, 1972. 471 pp.

Lengthy introduction by editors and section "The University Years," reveal much about social conditions and the role of university students before and during the revolution. KU

CUB ------, and HART DAVALOS, ARMANDO. Educación y revolución.
23 Havana: Imprenta Nacional de Cuba, 1961. 319 pp.
    A conference during the "Year of Education." Finished with first campaign against illiteracy, leaders now push further efforts from elementary through higher education. Castro advocates education in every way, asserts that revolution and education are one thing. CuHU

CUB COMISION SUPERIOR DOCENTE DE LA UNIVERSIDAD DE LA HABANA. Carta
24 Docente: Humanidades, ciencias, tecnología, ciencias agrope-
    cuarias, ciencias médicas. Havana, 1963. 7 pp.
    Speech of Cuban President Dr. Oswaldo Dorticos at Universidad de Oriente, in Santiago de Cuba, urges changes to support the revolution; needs for professionals and technicians, links between government and universities in behalf of the revolution. WKU

CUB COMITE CENTRAL DEL PARTIDO COMUNISTA DE CUBA. "El desarrollo
25 social: La educación." In Primer Congreso del Partido Comunista:
    Memorias, vol. 3, pp. 78-82. Havana: El Comité, [1976].
    Data on educational deficiencies in 1953 and 1958. Law no. 561 of 1959 creating 10,000 schoolrooms in Cuba, literacy campaign. Increase from 15,000 university students to 83,000 in 1976, including 50 percent increase in courses for workers. Work-study emphasis. Projection of 140,000 in higher education by 1980. WKU

CUB CONGRESO UNIVERSITARIO LATINOAMERICANO, 1ST, GUATEMALA, 1949.
26 Ponencias de la delegación de la Universidad de la Habana al
   Congreso Latinoamericano de Universidades de [sic] Guatemala.
   Havana: Universidad de la Habana, 1949. 35 pp.
   University of Havana representatives at the first Latin American university congress. FU

CUB CONSEJO SUPERIOR DE UNIVERSIDADES. La reforma de la enseñanza
27 superior en Cuba. Havana, 1962. 115 pp.
   Representatives of Universities of Havana, Oriente and Las Villas, with government representatives, set forth new structure: departments replace traditional cátedra, schools are placed with faculties, courses divided into semesters not years; hours, class attendance, size are fixed. Complete listing of traditional lacks and problems in curriculums for the three universities and degree requirements. KWiU

CUB "IV Reunión de la Comisión Mixta de Cooperación Científicotécnica
28 México-Cuba." Universidades 77 (July-September 1979): 838-39.
   Proposals for exchange of professors between National University of Mexico and Cuban institutions on specific subjects; includes request for Cuban help in veterinary medicine, geomorphology, early childhood stimulation and sex education.

CUB Cuban Studies Newsletter/Boletín de estudios sobre Cuba. Vol. 1,
29 no. 1- . December 1970- . Pittsburgh: Center of Latin American Studies, University of Pittsburgh.

Cuba

Each issue has several entries on education from a wide variety of sources, but not many deal with higher education.

CUB
30
Cuba, organización de la educación 1975-1977: XXXVI Conferencia Internacional de Educación OIE Ginebra Suiza, Septiembre 1977. [Havana]: Editorial de Libros para la Educación, 1977. 162 pp. Spanish, French, English.

Transition to completely restructured educational system underway, hence data presented not able to reflect emerging qualitative and quantitative aspects. Legislation, administration; little on universities per se. WKU

CUB
31
Cuba Update. Special Issue: Education in Cuba 1, no. 6, (January 1981). 16 pp.

Interview with Jose R. Fernandez, Cuba's minister of education, describes five years of activity, including growth in higher education, graduate studies, plans. Résumé of United Nations evaluation. Data on enrollment at all levels. Higher education information treats technical institutes and universities as a unit.

CUB
32
DAVIDSON, LUIS J. "Apuntes para una historia de la matemática en Cuba." Universidad de la Habana 207 (January-March 1978): 79-86.

Pre-Columbian knowlege of mathematics; colonial university curriculum, twentieth century influence of U.S., and international communication. Backward state of mathematics after 1945 and post-revolutionary efforts to catch up.

CUB
33
¿Debe mantenerse la autonomía universitaria? Ediciones del Directorio Magisterial Cubano (en el exilio), No. 17. Miami: Directorio Magisterial Cubano (en el exilio), [1965?]. 76 pp.

Eleven Cuban professionals, mostly former Cuban university professors, in exile, present facts and opinions in a forum on university autonomy. Useful history of Cuban higher education before Castro, history of university autonomy in Cuba, abuses after 1959, and criticism of leftists' exploitation of autonomy in Latin America in general. WKU

CUB
34
DIRECTORIO MAGISTERIAL CUBANO EN EL EXILIO. Destrucción de la escuela privada cubana. [Miami: El Directorio, 1961?]. 20 pp.

Elimination of private schools in Cuba, and the role of Communist party. The law of nationalization of private schools is in the Gaceta Oficial of the Republic of 7 June 1961. This included private universities. KU

CUB
35
DIRECTORIO MAGISTERIAL REVOLUCIONARIO. La educación y la subversión marxista-leninista en Cuba. [Miami: El Directorio], 1963. 36 pp. plus 21 leaves of photos, appendices.

Denounces communist philosophical indoctrination in the name of education. Political life 1940-59; educational reform before and after 1959; describes and criticizes literacy campaign of 1961. Section 5 criticizes changes in universities. KU

CUB
36
EL DIRECTORIO REVOLUCIONARIO ESTUDIANTIL. "La universidad en Cuba comunista." Este y Oeste 3, no. 69 (15-30 May 1965): 20.

Ten points related to higher education before and after communism; charges deterioration in everything from numbers of matriculants to preparation of professors.

CUB   DOMINGUEZ, JORGE I. Cuba: Order and Revolution. Cambridge,
37   Mass.: The Belknap Press of Harvard University, 1978. 683 pp.
       Education at all levels in the political context. Strong
central control of universities, ideological constraints on research;
student life, roles, problems interwoven throughout book. KU

CUB   La Educación en Cuba. Buenos Aires: Editorial Convergencia,
38   1975. 174 pp.
       Gaspar Garcia Gallo, Fidel Castro, Oscar Rego, Elio Enriquez
and others on topics ranging from expansion of educational opportunities during U.S. occupation through plans for 1975. In 1900,
Universidad de la Habana had 381 students; increases in numbers in
later decades, but access always favored privileged classes. Push
after 1959 to offer access to all, relate study to work and ideology at
all levels of education. Four-fold increase in university students
over 1957.

CUB   "Educación superior en Cuba." Caribbean Educational Bulletin 7,
39   no. 2 (May 1980): 39-50.
       Plan, progress of higher education from 1959-60 to 1978-79,
with figures on matriculation, graduates, teaching personnel.
Structure of higher education, integration of work and study.

CUB   "Educación y ciencia, informe de la Presidencia, acto, palabras
40   introductorias y resoluciones." In Primer Congreso del Partido
       Comunista de Cuba: Memorias, vol. 1, pp. 315-45. Havana:
       Comité Central del Partido Comunista de Cuba, 1976.
       Summary of working commission's discussion of Tesis sobre la
política educacional y sobre la política científica nacional which
Congress will approve. Acuerdo No. 1 calls for ongoing postgraduate
courses and development of a single system of scientific degrees.
Speech of educational leader Jose Ramon Fernandez Alvarez on national
educational policy, including teaching of Marxism-Leninism at all
levels. CuHU

CUB   Estudio de cambios e innovaciones en la educación técnica y la
41   formación profesional en América Latina y el Caribe. No. 9:
       Cuba by Joaquín Melgarejo. Santiago de Chile: Oficina Regional
       de Educación de la UNESCO para América Latina y el Caribe, 1979.
       70 pp.
       Historical background for the restructuring of education; the
change from traditional university organization and function to
specialized agencies. Good presentation, data.

CUB   Exposición del Consejo Universitario en defensa de la autonomía
42   de la Universidad de la Habana. Havana: Consejo Universitario,
       1953. 7 pp. plus 1 leaf addendum.
       A measure before national budget-makers threatens
constitutionally guaranteed 2 percent minimum of Cuba's annual budget
for University of Havana. Ringing denunciation of what is seen as
threat to university autonomy. Classic example of Latin American

governmental-university fiscal relationship, as quotations from
Peruvian Luis Alberto Sanchez indicate. Added leaf, produced a few
weeks later, reacts against proposal to change hospital costs to
present 2.25 percent now received. Mentions funding of other public
universities. KU

CUB   FORT, GILBERTO V. The Cuban Revolution of Fidel Castro Viewed
43   From Abroad: An Annotated Bibliography. Lawrence, Kans.: Uni-
      versity of Kansas Libraries, 1969. 139 pp.
          Fifty-plus entries on education, about half by Directorio
Magisterial Revolucionario of Miami, Florida, in opposition to Castro.
Some on university changes. KU

CUB   GARCIA FERNANDEZ, OSCAR. "La universidad como generadora de
44   autonomía nacional." Revista Internacional de Países Social-
      istas: La educación superior contemporánea 3, no. 18 (1975):
      67-81.
          Paper given by Cuba's vice minister of higher education at
VII Meeting of UDUAL attributes much of revolution's success to student
activism against the "neocolonialist republic" of Batista. Federation
of University Students made alliances with workers, embraced communist
cause in 1920s.

CUB   ------. "Las mutuas relaciones entre la educación superior y la
45   ciencia." Revista Pedagógica 2, no. 2 (April, May, June 1978):
      3-8.
          Publication of Universidad de Oriente, Santiago de Cuba, with
five articles by Russians and this one by a Cuban. Role of science,
function of higher education, and role of party. Marxist-Leninist
concept of political, socio-economic and philosophical problems must
occupy first importance for educators and scientists. Details plan for
assuring party control of their activity and for keeping them from
isolation from daily life.

CUB   GILLETTE, ARTHUR. Cuba's Educational Revolution. Fabian Re-
46   search Series, 302. London: Fabian Society, 1972. 36 pp.
          Diagram of Cuba's national education system, from preschool
through a large range of post secondary options, and adult education.
Some details of the activities in immediate post-revolutionary period;
the drive against illiteracy; priorities tilting toward science and
technology in university, away from traditional humanities and
philosophy. KU

CUB   GOODMAN, LOUIS WOLF. "The Social Sciences in Cuba." Items 30,
47   no. 4 (December 1976): 54-61.
          Meager efforts before 1959, followed by little interest until
1973. Universities less central to research than in U.S. Social
Science Institute described. Teaching practices in University of
Havana's department of psychology; limitations on source material and
ideological constraints. Examines consequences of state control of
social sciences, and effects of U.S. embargo.

CUB   HANDELMAN, HOWARD, and HANDELMAN, NANCY. "Cuba Today: Impres-
48   sions of the Revolution in its Twentieth Year." American Uni-
      versities Field Staff Reports, no. 8 (1979): 1-21.

Cuba

General background provides setting for description of educational development, including higher education. Emphasis on variety of opportunities, social goals.

CUB HARDIN, HENRY N. Evaluating Cuban Education. Coral Gables:
49 University of Miami, 1965. 95 pp.
    U.S. Office of Education sponsored study for use of U.S. institutions in determining academic equivalents for placement of Cuban refugees. No information on universities after revolution. Useful brief history includes 1951 U.S. study which notes "general deterioration" of education. DPU

CUB HART DAVALOS, ARMANDO. Message of the Minister of Education to
50 the People of Cuba. Havana: Ministry of Education, Department of Public Relations, 1959. 98 pp.
    Calls for articulation of all levels of education, without "obstacle" of university autonomy; need change in "non-revolutionary" attitude of many universitarios; need for fewer in "liberal" professions, more in technical education. KU

CUB HERRERA, HERMES. "Higher Education and Its Innovatory Role in
51 Society: Economic and Social Innovation." In Report of the Sixth General Conference of the International Association of Universities, Moscow, 19 August-25 August 1975, pp. 157-60. Paris, 1976.
    Rector of University of Havana describes university at time of 1959 revolution as unable to meet needs of country; creation of Higher Council for Universities as part of the Ministry of Education, with universalization of education and integration of all education. Universities will reflect aims of revolutionary system, and include political and ideological training. WKU

CUB ------. "Un orgullo para todos nosotros." Universidad de La
52 Habana, nos. 203-204 (1976): 161-63.
    "Twentieth Anniversary of Granma Graduation" class celebrates revolution with 4,207 graduates in different fields, with over a third from evening classes and directed study programs for workers.

CUB INSTITUTO SUPERIOR POLITECNICO JOSE ANTONIO ECHEVERRIA. Ciencias
53 técnicas--ingeniería electrónica, automática y comunicaciones 1 (August 1977). 131 pp.
    First issue of journal to be devoted to scientific and technical research carried on in this university-level institute. Abstracts in English. CuHU

CUB ------. Ciencias técnicas--ingeniería en geodesia y geofísica 1
54 (July 1977). 133 pp.
    First issue of journal to be devoted to scientific and technical research carried on in this university-level institute. Abstracts in English. CuHU

CUB ------. Ciencias técnicas--ingeniería en procesos químicos,
55 alimentarios y azucareros 1 (September 1977). 131 pp.

First issue of journal to be devoted to scientific and technical research carried on in this university-level institute. Abstracts in English. CuHU

CUB ------. <u>Ciencias técnicas--ingeniería estructural</u> 1 (September
56 1977). 113 pp.
First issue of journal to be devoted to scientific and technical research carried on in this university-level institute. Abstracts in English. CuHU

CUB KOZOL, JONATHAN. <u>Children of the Revolution: A Yankee Teacher</u>
57 <u>in the Cuban Schools</u>. New York: Delacorte Press, 1978. 245 pp.
Emphasis is on the literacy campaign for adults which reduced illiteracy to about 5 percent; pre-university programs described with goals of system which link education at all levels to the state. Ethical questions raised about rewards of professional education. Interviews with Raul Ferrer, a leader of literacy campaign, and Jose Ramon Fernandez, minister of education. WKU

CUB LANCIS Y SANCHEZ, ANTONIO. <u>Cuestiones universitarias</u>. Havana:
58 Editorial Lex, 1954. 36 pp.
Troubled times in Cuba and the world put in historical perspective and linked to need for university reform by professor of law school. DPU

CUB LE-ROY Y GALVEZ, LUIS FELIPE. <u>A cien años del 71: El fusila-</u>
59 <u>miento de los estudiantes</u>. Havana: Instituto Cubano del Libro, 1971. 452 pp.
Celebrates heroism of student martyrs from the 1871 uprising against Spain through battles of <u>universitarios</u> against Batista, all in abundant detail. FMU

CUB ------. <u>La Real y Literaria Universidad de La Habana: Síntesis</u>
60 <u>histórica</u>. [Havana, 1966?], 69 pp. Separata de la <u>Revista de la Biblioteca Nacional "José Martí"</u> 56, no. 4; 57, no. 1 (1965-66).
Secular university, in convent from which Dominicans were "dislodged," began in 1842. Academic affairs juxtaposed against Spanish domination and resistance, and U.S. occupation which ends in 1902. Useful background for understanding Cuban attitudes in this straightforward account.

CUB ------. <u>La Universidad de la Habana: Síntesis histórica. El</u>
61 <u>escudo de la Universidad: Su simbolismo</u>. Havana: Imprenta de la Universidad de La Habana, 1960. 24 pp.
Symbolism of the university seal. KU

CUB "Libros y folletos (de Juan Marinello): bibliografía activa."
62 <u>Universidad de la Habana</u> 201, (1974): 106-16.
Many of Marinello's writings were on university reform, from 1919 to 1960s. Dedicated Marxist, ex-rector of University of Havana, writer, literary critic.

CUB MALDONADO-DENIS, MANUEL. "The Situation of Cuba's Intellec-
63 tuals." <u>The Christian Century</u> (January 17, 1968): 78-80.

Most Cuban writers and artists siding with revolution are of bourgeois origin. Majority of intellectuals, including non-Marxists, made transition and are integrated with "the people." By contrast to Puerto Rican intellectuals, Cubans do not feel alienated from society. Freedom in context of a country in a hostile world.

CUB MARINELLO, JUAN. Revolución y universidad. La Habana: Gobierno
64 Provisional Revolucionario, 1960. 27 pp.
     Ideal of autonomy, traditional in Latin American universities since 1918 in Cordoba, Argentina, no longer useful here. In Cuban Revolution collaboration between state and university is necessary. TxU

CUB ------. "La Universidad destacamento revolucionario." Universi-
65 dad de la Habana 201 (1974): 23-34.
     Former rector recalls long fight after reform of Cordoba to reform University of Havana. Conviction that only social, political, economic reforms could change university; celebrates Cuban Marxist leaders.

CUB MEJIA RICART, GUSTAVO ADOLFO. A Message to the President of
66 Cuba. [Trujillo City, Dominican Republic : n.p., 1949]. 6 pp.
     "You must not continue to lead a life at once cultured and savage, filled with bitter group revenge, bandits and gangsters who operate through force, violence and death in order to solve all your problems." Dominican father holds Cuban president responsible for death of his student-leader son at University of Havana. TxU

CUB MELGAREJO, JOAQUIN. Bibliografías sobre educación técnica y
67 profesional: Cuba. No. 3. Santiago de Chile: UNESCO Regional Office for Education in Latin America and the Caribbean (OREALC). [n.d.] 3 pp.
     Thirty-one entries, used to prepare Estudios de cambios e innovaciones en la educación técnica y la formación profesional en América Latina y el Caribe: Cuba.

CUB MENDEZ PEÑATE, RODOLFO. Nuevas tareas culturales, docentes y
68 edificaciones en la Universidad de la Habana durante el período rectoral, 1940-1943. Havana: Universidad de la Habana, 1943. 180 pp.
     Rector's report on progress of university, including budget, schools and divisions. IU

CUB MESA DE ARMAS, ENRIQUE, et al. Provincia Matanzas. Santiago de
69 Cuba: Editorial Oriente, 1978. 170 pp.
     History, physical and geographical description of region. Education chapter with statutes. University Center, previously run by University of Havana, now has four faculties and several speciali- zations. Federation of University Students (FEU) described. WKU

CUB MESA LAGO, CARMELO. Cuba in the 1970s: Pragmatism and Insti-
70 tutionalization. Albuquerque: University of New Mexico Press, 1974. 179 pp.
     Little on universities per se, but much on significant parts of the matrix in which they exist. Shift from romantic to pragmatic practice affects education; short sections on youth and intellectuals

vis-a-vis government policy. KU

CUB   MINISTERIO DE EDUCACION. Cuba: Organización de la educación
71   1975-1977. Havana, 1977. 161 pp. Spanish, French and English.
        Report on 1974-76 period requested by the International
Bureau of Education was affected by major structural and content
changes underway, tied to national political development and revised
constitution, including establishment of Ministry of Higher Education
by law of 28 July 1976. Before and after diagrams of educational
system. Emphasis on ideology of the state. WKU

CUB   ------. La educación en Cuba, 1973. [Havana], 1973. 417 pp.
72   Post-revolutionary changes in quantity and quality of all
education, including universities. Brief history of universities; 1960
reform and restructuring, e.g., of departments. New disciplines,
decentralization, combined work and study, governance; political-ideo-
logical factors in admission, student participation, relation of universities to society. WKU

CUB   ------. Panorama de la educación en Cuba. Havana: Instituto
73   del Libro, 1969. 138 pp.
        Pedagogical themes and theories; details of programs and
organization, interweaving Marxist doctrine with daily tasks. Little
on universities per se. FMU

CUB   ------. El plan de perfeccionamiento y desarrollo del sistema
74   nacional de educaión de Cuba. Havana, 1978. 192 pp.
        Emphasis on Marxist-Leninist theory. Projections to be made
on needed research and resources. Data on enrollments, retention in
pre-university years; little information on higher education. WKU

CUB   ------. Report to the XXX International Conference on Public
75   Instruction Convoked by the OIE and the UNESCO, Geneva (Switzer-
        land) 6-15 of July, 1967. Havana, 1967. 83 pp. plus annex.
        Information about country, culture, school system. New
requirement of two years obligatory social work for all university
graduates. Higher education part of Ministry of Education, with separate budget (total budget 332,992,800 pesos, with 37,081,900 for universities). Plans for technical, professional education; increased
access for women. OASDC

CUB   ------. Report to the XXVIII International Conference on Public
76   Instruction Convoked by the OIE and the UNESCO, Geneva (Switzer-
        land) 12-23 of July, 1965. Havana, 1965. 47 pp. Bound with
        Spanish and French version.
        Changes in university structure in Faculty of Humanities and
Faculty of Technology reported. OASDC

CUB   ------. "Seminario documento de trabajo: Informe Truslow."
77   Havana, 20 February-3 November 1956. Mimeographed. 65 pp.
        International Bank of Reconstruction and Development mission
survey. "Alarming signs" that for preceding twenty-five years Cuba
was falling behind relative to other Latin American countries in school
matriculation. OASDC

Cuba

CUB   ------. XXXIV Conferencia Interenacional de Educación, OIE,
78   Ginebra, Suiza, Septiembre 1973. [Havana]: Ministry of Edu-
      cation. 212 pp. Spanish, French, English.
      Organization, data on enrollment, finance, 1971 revival of
National Council of Universities (CNU) within Vice Ministry of Education, "to establish and consolidate an adequate policy on the higher
level of our educational system, with the collaboration of political
and mass organizations." OASDC

CUB   MINISTERIO DE EDUCACION SUPERIOR. Especialidades en la educación
79   superior de Cuba, perfil del especialista y contenidos fundamen-
      tales de los ciclos de estudios. [Havana], 1978. 241 pp.
      Twelve different groups of specialties in higher education
are described, including number of years and places of study and list
of work opportunities. Heaviest emphasis on sciences and technology;
five specializations offered in Marxist-Leninist philosophy, and a law
graduate must study Russian language. English required for many programs, especially in science and technology. Every graduate studies
Marxism-Leninism. WKU

CUB   ------. "Indicación metodológica: Proceso de rendidción de
80   cuentas sobre el trabajo científico investigativo en los centros
      de educación superior." [Havana], October 1978. Mimeographed.
      76 pp.
      Forms and procedures to be used by all twenty-eight centers
of higher education in reporting on scientific and research tasks each
year. Descriptions, problems, foreign assistance, budgets, results.
Special emphasis on applications for solving national problems. Data
to be compiled for offices of research and graduate study, and of
statistics and automated systems of Ministry of Higher Education. WKU

CUB   ------. "Lineamientos generales para el desarrollo de las acti-
81   vidades culturales y deportivas de los estudiantes en los centros
      de educación superior." Mimeographed. [Havana]: El Ministerio,
      [1979]. 19 pp.
      Theoretical framework developed by the First Congress of the
Communist Party of Cuba for sports and arts in higher education for
1976-80; plans for activities in centers of higher education and for
local, regional, and national meets and competitions, and preparation
for international sports events. WKU

CUB   ------. Metododlogía del sistema de ingreso a los cursos, cursos
82   1979-80 y 1980-81. Havana, 1979. 60 pp.
      Pre-university graduates will enter directly into Active
Military Service (SMA) as part of entry into higher education. Organization of enrollment system, method of evaluating socio-political and
academic conduct; selection process for study abroad or in places with
special requirements; steps necessary for requests, evaluation,
decision. WKU

CUB   ------. Plan general de cursos de postgrado, año 1978.
83   [Havana], [1978]. 264 pp.
      National program of 605 graduate courses to be offered in
twenty-eight centers of higher education, intended for upgrading professionals in production and services, and "scientific-pedagogical
teams of higher education." Course descriptions, duration, location,

available places for "comrades" and others. Emphasis on applied
sciences; philosophy, history, economic courses emphasize solving
problems within Marxist world view. WKU

CUB   ------. Plan nacional de cursos de postgrado, año 1979.
84   [Havana], [1979]. 654 pp.
        Graduate programs of 20 to 120 hours; 652 courses, some given
for first time in agencies other than centers of higher education, but
with methodology under control of the ministry. Goal of professional
advancement related to work, in production, service, research,
teaching, or culture; based on survey of needs of government agencies.
WKU

CUB   ------. Plan nacional de estudios de postgrado, año 1979.
85   [Havana, 1979]. 34 pp.
        Twenty-nine programs to upgrade professionals in specific
jobs in the natural sciences, agriculture, social sciences. Hours
required, place of course, dates. Each states objective or "specialization," except three including "Historical Analysis of the Countries
of Asia, Africa, and Latin America," whose objectives are
"reorientation." WKU

CUB   ------. Reglamento del trabajo docente y metodológico. Havana,
86   March 1979. 22 pp. plus tabloid.
        System of activities in centers of higher education designed
for economic needs in accord with norms of socialist society. Rules of
organization, entry into system, leaving it, aid, evaluation, student
assistants, teaching, methodology, sports and culture, military
service, planning and control, procedures of control. WKU

CUB   ------. Reglamento general para los centros de educación su-
87   perior. [Havana], 1976. 50 pp.
        Nothing is left to chance and little to choice in control of
programs of study, methods, materials, research, administration, or
student selection in universities and other centers of higher education. All rules are made by minister of higher education. Marxist-
Leninist ideology required of faculty and administration along with
their professional knowledge. Reports and duties of all concerned
spelled out. Teaching departments are basic units of educational
structure (not professional schools). WKU

CUB   ------. Sistema de superación de los cuadros científico-pedagó-
88   gicos de la educación superior. [Havana, 1979]. 22 pp.
        Antecedents of integrated plan for upgrading leadership in
higher education included study abroad and foreign visiting professors;
creation in 1968 of vice-rectors for research, in 1974 for postgraduate study. Objectives of system; description of plans for degree
and non-degree programs, the former "selective," the latter "massive;"
structure and functioning of system. WKU

CUB   ------. El trabajo científico docente de los estudiantes en la
89   educación superior. [Havana], 1976. 52 pp.
        Guide to raise quality of scientific and teaching personnel
in ideology, relating theory to practice, uniting individual search for
knowledge with collective work. Sequence of study plans, methodology;
details of thesis defense. WKU

Cuba

CUB   ------. Dirección Docente-Metodológica. <u>Normas y metodología</u>
90   <u>para la elaboración de planes y programas de estudios</u>. [Havana],
        1976. 76 pp.
        To achieve social and political goals, Cuba needs immediate
revision of structure and organization of study process. Plan of
study, conduct of courses, bibliographic plan. Model calendar shows
classes, exams, practice periods, work projects, vacations. WKU

CUB   ------. <u>Sobre el trabajo metodológico, indicaciones pre-</u>
91   <u>liminares</u>. Havana, 1976. 33 pp.
        Marxist-Leninist definition of "method." Program of up-
grading teaching personnel in centers of higher education, relating
goals with theory and practice. Departments must have meetings on
methodology and demonstration classes. Details for classroom control.
WKU

CUB   NICOLA ROMERO, JUSTO. <u>El régimen de universidades y la Ley no.</u>
92   <u>11</u>. Santiago de Cuba: Universidad de Oriente, Departamento de
        Extensión y Relaciones Públicas, 1959. 17 pp.
        Law recognizes some universities as "official," disbands
others with resulting chaos. Denial that law is anti-Catholic or
intends destruction of private institutions. DLC

CUB   "Now No One's Intelligence is Lost." <u>Granma</u>, 10 September 1978,
93   p. 6.
        Full-page feature shows growth in education since 1959 revo-
lution. Map shows location of thirty-six centers of higher education
distributed through country, including the three universities. Increase from 15,000 plus students in higher education to over 130,000.

CUB   "Nuestro experimento en la educación universitaria." <u>Universidad</u>
94   <u>de la Habana</u> 32, no. 190 (April-June 1968): 63-67.
        Praise for university accomplishments.

CUB   OBERG, LARRY R., comp. <u>Contemporary Cuban Education: An An-</u>
95   <u>notated Bibliography</u>. (Revised). Stanford: Stanford University
        Libraries, 1980. 40 pp.
        Bibliography, designed chiefly as an aid to students and
faculty in School of Education, emphasizes English and Spanish language
materials available in the Bay Area. Broad in scope; thorough in
periodicals, indexes and bibliographies, statistical sources. Limited
number of items on higher education <u>per se</u>. KU

CUB   PARISEAU, EARL J., ed. <u>Cuban Acquisitions and Bibliography:</u>
96   <u>Proceedings of an International Conference held at the Library of</u>
        <u>Congress April 13-15, 1970</u>. Washington: Library of Congress,
        1970. 164 pp.
        Chapters on bibliographies and U.S. universities' library
acquisition problems especially useful. Post-revolutionary cuts in
communication never stopped exchanges but sharply hampered them.
Havana's Instituto del Libro lists catalogues, among other publications
of the Cuban universities, academies, and institutes. WKU

CUB   PARTIDO COMUNISTA DE CUBA, DEPARTAMENTO DE ORIENTACION REVO-
97   LUCIONARIA. <u>Política educacional: Tesis y resolución</u>. Havana:
        El Departamento, 1976. 71 pp.

Plans between 1981 and 1990, with goal of educating all youth through age eighteen. Fundamental Marxist-Leninist view of teaching. All teachers and professors to be qualified by 1980, and higher education to be available throughout the island. Graduate study plans and basic concern with research. KU

CUB   PARTIDO COMUNISTA DE CUBA. First Congress of the Communist Party
98   of Cuba, Havana, December 17-22, 1975. Moscow: Progress
       Publishers, 1976. 303 pp.
       In his Report of the Central Committee of the Communist Party of Cuba, Fidel Castro contrasts the deplorable state of the nation's educational system before the Revolution with the changes brought about by the first comprehensive Educational Reform (26 December 1959). Socialist regime has invested eleven times more resources in education than capitalist system; outlines plans for the future which will make education throughout the country even more all-encompassing. Fundamental Law on Education is planned which will make school attendance through the twelfth grade compulsory. TxU

CUB   PAULSTON, ROLLAND G. "Education." In Revolutionary Change in
99   Cuba, edited by Carmelo Mesa-Lago, pp. 375-97. Pittsburgh: Uni-
       versity of Pittsburgh, 1971.
       Panorama of education before and after 1959 focuses on changes, with brief comments on universities. KU

CUB   ------. The Educational System of Cuba. Washington: U.S.
100   Department of Health, Education and Welfare, [1976]. 13 pp.
       1962 Higher Education Reform Law consolidated the three national universities; substituted emphasis on technical education for humanistic and legal education. Diagram of education system leading to universities and alternatives. WKU

CUB   PERAZA SARAUSA, FERMIN, compiler. Anuario bibliográfico cubano.
101   Havana: Ediciones Anuario Bibliográfico Cubano. 1937-1966.
       Title 1953-1966: Bibliografía cubana. Last issue published in Havana (in mimeograph) in 1959; 1959-60 edition published in Medellin, thereafter in Gainesville and Miami; 1967 Anuario title changed to Revolutionary Cuba. Generally had items on universities. Revealing before-and-after views in prefaces, with expression of outrage over "the imperialist Russian invasion" of Cuba in 25th anniversary volume of 1961. See entry CUB 8. KU

CUB   PORTUONDO, JOSE ANTONIO. Tres temas de la reforma universitaria.
102   Cuadernos 51. Santiago de Cuba: Universidad de Oriente, De-
       partamento de Extensión y Relaciones Culturales, 1959. 42 pp.
       Twenty-second anniversary of Universidad de Oriente; themes: the revolution and the university, the idea of a provincial university and the significance of the humanities. TxU

CUB   PORTUONDO DE CASTRO, JUAN MIGUEL. Como los comunistas se apo-
103   deraron de la Universidad de La Habana. Ediciones del Magis-

terial Cubano (Exilio), No. 23. Miami: Ediciones del
Magisterial Cubano (Exilio), 1962. 56 pp.
    Charges that University of Havana, once "the maximum center
of culture and the firmest bulwark of Cuban democracy," is now an armed
camp. Euphoria at Batista's overthrow in January 1959 gave way by May
to shock, as nonuniversity people took over the medical school and
hospital; "cold war" against the university, takeover of student
government, impedence of reform. Documents "final attack," responses
and events through August 1960. LNHT

CUB   PUIG Y PUPO, JOSE RAMON ROLANDO. Apuntes sobre la Escuela de
104   Derecho y la Universidad de la Habana. [Havana]: Universidad de
      la Habana, 1959. 78 pp.
    Handbook for entering student who may be "too reserved" to
ask necessary questions for orientation, by student in School of Law
and Commercial Sciences. History, campus security, physical facilities, governance, entrance requirements. Explanation of three kinds of
matriculation; payment for ordinary "matriculation may be postponed due
to certain abnormalities being confronted at the present moment."
Although printed in August of 1959, time is stopped in its pre-
revolutionary tracks. Great sentimental enthusiasm for tradition. FMU

CUB   READ, GERALD H. "The Cuban Revolutionary Offensive in Edu-
105   cation." Comparative Education Review 14, (June 1970): 131-43.
    Fidel Castro and the Revolution are changing education at
every level, with Marxist orientation; education relates theory to
practice and incorporates the masses; in Cuba this is the end of the
traditional Latin American theoretical approach.

CUB   ------. "Persisting Problems in Cuban Education." Phi Delta
106   Kappan 53 (February 1972): 352-57.
    Summary of the successes and problems in Cuba at the time of
the first Congress of Education and Culture, April 1971.

CUB   RODRIGUEZ, MIGUEL CESAR. El estudiantado cubano: Víctima y
107   esperanza. Guatemala: Congregación Mariana Universitaria.
      Suplemento de "Septiembre", [1961]. 22 pp.
    Former press officer of the Cuban Federation of University
students describes student resistance to and counter measures of
government, and his disdain for Cuban communists who undermined democratic forces. Details of pro-Castro takeover of student movement.
TxU

CUB   RODRIGUEZ SOLVEIRA, MARIANO. "Nota." Islas 1, no. 3 (May-August
108   1959): 455-56.
    Rector of relatively new Universidad Central de Valle in Cuba
says the Revolution calls for reexamination of role of universities, of
professors and students; says that Fidel Castro promises increased
financial support, regulation of private universities; expresses optimism for great improvement.

CUB   ------. "Nota." Islas 2, no. 1 (September-December 1959): 5-6.
109   Rector of Central University of Cuba Addresses Third General
Assembly of Latin American Universities, describes "one of the most

beautiful moments of Cuba's history" as a corrupt dictatorship ends. Urges universities to remain "the conscience" of Hispano-America.

CUB "Sobre el Ministerio de Educación Superior, ley que crea el
110 Ministerio de Educación Superior." Universidad de la Habana 203-204 (1976): 171-79.
    Law No. 1306 creating Ministry of Higher Education sets forth duties of agency for controlling all post-secondary education, and Law No. 1307 establishes structure of specialties and specializations for higher education.

CUB STOLIK NOVYGROD, DANIEL. "Objetivos de la educación profesional
111 de postgrado." Educación Superior Contemporánea 4, no. 28 (1979): 143-50.
    Planned economy permits and requires consolidated system for higher education, with content, methodology, and organization determined by productive process. Terminology defined, purposes listed. Author is an official in Cuba's Ministry of Higher Education.

CUB SUCHLICKI, JAIME. "Cuba." In Students and Politics in De-
112 veloping Nations, edited by Donald K. Emmerson, pp. 315-49. New York: Frederick A. Praeger, 1968.
    Description of student activism from nineteenth century anti-Spanish movement through post-revolutionary reorganization of universities. Details of breakup of political groupings in University of Havana by Castro. KU

CUB ------. "El estudiantado de la Universidad de la Habana en la
113 política cubana, 1956-1957." Journal of Inter-American Studies 9, no. 1 (January 1967): 145-67.
    Student riots against Batista government began in 1956. The universities served as a central focus for revolutionary sentiments. All universities were closed in 1959.

CUB ------. University Students and Revolution in Cuba, 1920-1968.
114 Coral Gables: University of Miami Press, 1969. 177 pp.
    Focuses on student political activism in University of Havana, historically important center of resistance to dictatorship. Philosophy and practice of universities under Castro. KU

CUB Tesis y resoluciones: Primer Congreso del Partido Comunista de
115 Cuba. Havana: Departamento de Orientación Revolucionaria del Comité del Partido Comunista de Cuba, 1976. 673 pp.
    Total commitment to education essential for the revolution. Detailed plans for all levels, with emphasis on Marxist-Leninist philosophy. Universities part of post-secondary system; relating research and teaching, national needs, development of science and technology. CuHU

CUB TORRES HERNANDEZ, MIGUEL. "Los grados científicos y las cate-
116 gorías científicas en Cuba." La educación superior contemporánea [Sovremennaia Vysshaiashkola (Contemporary Higher School)], 13 January 1976: 219-225.

Requirements for the doctoral degree are spelled out in detail along with composition of the Comisión Nacional de Grados Científicos which controls the process of degree-granting. All candidates must master Marxism-Leninism, a foreign language (English or Russian), and a special discipline. Various categories of scholars listed.

CUB 117   TUROSIENSKI, SEVERIN K. Education in Cuba. Bulletin 1943, no. 1. Washington, D.C.: U.S. Office of Education, Government Printing Office, 1943. 90 pp.

Chapter 6 on University of Havana. History, organization and functioning, programs of study in its twelve schools. OASDC

CUB 118   U.S. DEPARTMENT OF HEALTH, EDUCATION, AND WELFARE, Office of Education. Educational Data: Cuba, compiled by Grace I. Krumwiede and Adela R. Freeburger, with Charles C. Hauch. Washington, D.C.: Division of International Studies and Services, November 1962 (OE-14034-67). 18 pp.

Pre- and post-revolutionary organization of education. Lists five public and four private universities with founding dates. All except three public universities closed after 1959-60. WKU

CUB 119   UNIVERSIDAD CATOLICA DE VILLANUEVA. Catálogo 1956-1958. Marianao. 113 pp.

Faculty, with their degrees, listed. First private Cuban university founded 1946 by North American Augustinians; growth from thirty students in five faculties to 1,032 in thirteen faculties. Rules, courses of study, fees. OASDC

CUB 120   ------. Universidad de Santo Tomás de Villanueva: Contribución a la Historia de sus diez primeros años. Havana, 1956. 189 pp.

Six faculties, four schools; from 34 to 1,224 students in ten years. Catholic university graduated 26 night commercial students, 20 in philosophy and letters, 17 in day commercial studies, 15 in art and decoration, and 47 others in various fields in 1956. Espouses equal opportunity for women students. History, especially efforts to get legislative and presidential sanction for "first modern Catholic university." Organization, academic offerings. DLC

CUB 121   ------. Curso 1960-1961. Marianao. 43 pp.

Notes elevation in 1957, by Holy See, to status of Catholic University. Library of 30,000 volumes. Courses of study, entry rules, fees. OASDC

CUB 122   ------. Las empresas cubanas y la Universidad de Villanueva en el desarrollo industrial de Cuba. [Havana: Universidad de Villanueva, 1954?]. 15 leaves.

Augustine fathers of North America created Cuba's first private university in 1946; Cuban congress passed Law of Private Universities in 1950. With 519 students, plans are made for greatly increased physical facilities to create chemical engineers, a new profession in Cuba; next will come mechanical engineering. Role of private philanthropy. DPU

CUB 123   UNIVERSIDAD CENTRAL DE LAS VILLAS. Aporte a la revolución. Santa Clara, Marta Abreu de las Villas: Departamento de Publicidad, 1959. 19 pp.

Mostly photos of student and faculty leaders of anti-Batista uprising in takeover of city of Santa Clara, which determined success of revolution. Work of clandestine university press. WKU

CUB ------. Boletín Oficial 3, no. 6 (1954). 81 pp.
124   Contains rules for university, programs of students; a catalogue.

CUB ------. Boletín Oficial 3, no. 6, edición extraordinaria (July
125   1954). 81 pp.
       Regulations of the university's six schools, includes govern-
ance, courses, degrees, staff selection, examinations.

CUB ------. Boletín Oficial 12-27 (January-December 1954). No con-
126   tinuous pagination.
       Legal decrees, financial data, professors appointed,
purchases of books and other equipment.

CUB ------. Boletín Oficial 54-73 (1959). No continuous pagination.
127   Last of regular bulletins before revolution, of which there
is no evidence. Mostly provincial information, including purchases of
U.S. tractors and conspicuousness of U.S. companies as suppliers.

CUB ------. Catálogo, 1962. [Santa Clara], 1962. 127 pp.
128   Goals, structure, courses offered. Facultad Obrera established for workers outside traditional system. Development of
courses of regional need, such as rice cultivation and agricultural
machinery. Library, sports, theater programs. CuSCUC

CUB ------. [Catálogo], 1969. [Santa Clara], 1969. 67 pp.
129   History includes efforts "to escape North American
imperialism" after 1952 beginning and pressing through 1959 revolution.
Enrollment by courses, growth of library from 1958 to 1968, from 14,600
to 139,913 volumes, and increase to 55,575 periodicals. CuSCUC

CUB ------. La ciudad universitaria "Abel Santamaría" avanza. Santa
130   Clara, 1961. 13 pp.
       Into the revolution; changes underway. CuHU

CUB ------. La educación rural en Las Villas. Havana: Departamento
131   de Relaciones Culturales, Escuela de Pedagogía, 1959. 220 pp.
       Research on rural education, with U.S. technical help, in
region served by relatively new university shows average years of
schooling to be three; about one-fourth of school-age children never
attended school. Background for understanding pre-revolutionary, pre-
university educational ambience. FMU

CUB ------. Indicadores generales de inicio de curso; curso 1978-
132   79. [Santa Clara]: Departamento Estadística, 1978. [19 pp.]
       Enrollment in three centers of 7,474 includes 3,299 in
courses for workers, by ages, faculties, origin; agencies sending
workers; numbers of teaching personnel by rank. WKU

CUB ------. Informe anual 1961-1962. [Havana?]: Junta Superior del
133   Gobierno. [n.d.] 38 pp.

Political-revolutionary aspects, teaching personnel (264 professors and instructors); first year for schools of Letters and History, Veterinary Medicine; 11,330 students. CuSCUC

CUB ------. *Informe del curso 1965*. [Santa Clara]: Rectoría. 36
134 pp.
Courses of study in faculties of sciences, social sciences, psychology, technology and engineering, agriculture, humanities, and education. CuSCUC

CUB ------. *Memoria inaugural de la Universidad Central de Santa*
135 *Clara*. Havana: Editorial "Selecta," 1948. 77 pp.
Founders of university, without official approval, set forth projected law for creation of Universidad Central, citing efforts since 1937 to get a university in central Cuba. Structure for administration and teaching. Speech before members of *Círculo de Profesionales Universitarios de Santa Clara*. CuSCUC

CUB ------. *XX Aniversario, 1952-1972*. Santa Clara: Departamento
136 de Estadística y Planeamiento del Vice-Rectorado Docente, 1972.
106 pp.
Initiatives in late 1940s by local leaders got 1952 start of courses, previously only available in Havana, in new university to meet needs of agricultural area. Anniversary publication says pre-revolutionary university "reflected interests and ambitions of yankee exploiters. . .", explains changes conducive to linking learning and production and to opportunities for workers. Administrative and academic structure, fields of study and service. WKU

UNIVERSIDAD CENTRAL DE SANTA CLARA. See UNIVERSIDAD CENTRAL DE LAS VILLAS.

UNIVERSIDAD CENTRAL "MARTA ABREU" DE LAS VILLAS. See UNIVERSIDAD CENTRAL DE LAS VILLAS.

CUB UNIVERSIDAD DE LA HABANA. *Acuerdos de la Comisión Mixta para la*
137 *Reforma Universitaria*. Havana, 1959. 60 pp.
Agreements on principles for reform. CuHU

CUB ------. *Boletín Oficial Universitario* 27, no. 1 (January 1960).
138 59 pp.
Minutes of meeting of University Council.

CUB ------. *Boletín Oficial Universitario* 3, no. 9 (1 September
139 1976): 1-16.
Text of Law 1306/76 creating Ministry of Higher Education. Stipulation of Marxist-Leninist doctrine for higher education.

CUB ------. *Crítica y reforma universitarias*. Havana, 1959. 382
140 pp.
Twenty-one essays and lectures from 1795 to 1959. The first attacks public education as "retarding the progress of arts and sciences by outdated scholasticism" demanded by Spain; says reform must begin with university. Humanistic values affirmed in most works; awareness of educational currents in U.S. and Europe. Final essay, on eve of Revolution, is plan for centralizing university libraries. TxU

CUB   ------. Del Consejo Universitario a la opinión pública. Havana,
141   1953. 18 pp.
        In praise of the university's survival, "in most rigorous
contrast with its ambience"; seen as "highest form of expression of the
national conscience." Chronology of various conflicts with government;
description of scientific accomplishments, many with U.S. universities;
growth in numbers, expansion of offerings. Denies fostering bonchismo
and partisan political activity. TxU

CUB   ------. Lápidas y monumentos: A Tour Around University Mon-
142   uments and Plaques. Havana, [n.d.] 14 pp.
        The "Royal and Pontifical University of Saint Jerome," later
the "Royal and Literary University of Havana" became in 1902 the University of Havana with its neoclassical campus. Monuments to heroes of
War of Independence and martyrs of the 1959 revolution, as well as to
scientists and educators. WKU

CUB   ------. Memoria: Curso anuario 1975-1976. Edited by the Gen-
143   eral Secretary. Havana: Impresora Universitaria "André Voisin,"
        1977. 403 pp.
        Government of the university, the National Center of Scien-
tific Research, the faculties (medicine, humanities, sciences, technology, agriculture), the Pedagogical Institute, military preparation,
student federation, and the committee of workers in the university.
Purchase of books from Spain and USSR. TxU

CUB   ------. La reforma integral de la Universidad de La Habana.
144   Havana: Federación de Empleados de La Universidad de La Habana,
        1960. 16 pp.
        Recounts deeds of students since 1871 through Batista regime
and opposition after 1952 culminating in 1959 revolution. Role of
Federation of University Students, accepted by University Council, is
rejected by employees of university and its hospitals, who demand voice
in governance. Denounces government of University of Havana to the
Revolutionary government and public opinion, demands voice in their
working conditions as their right. TxU

CUB   ------. "Texto de la Ley no. 1306/07 que crea el Ministerio de
145   Educación Superior." Boletín Oficial Universitario 3, no. 9 (1
        September 1976): 1-9.
        Ministry of Higher Education will exercise methodological
teaching and administrative control of universities, institutes, and
centers of higher education. Responsibility for planning, including
numbers of students in each career; development of national network of
centers and national research policy and practice of Consejo Nacional
de Ciencias y Tecnología. Outlines educational centers of Ministry of
Higher Education and also those of other ministries including Public
Health, Education, Armed Services, Sports, Foreign Relations and
Culture.

CUB   ------. La Universidad de La Habana, al Consejo Ejecutivo y a la
146   Asamblea General de la Unión de Universidades de América Latina.
        Havana, 1964. 83 pp.
        Response to UDUAL's expulsion of the University of Havana and
to charges brought by former professors now in exile. Strong attack on
evils of university in past, with blame on internal corruption and

inadequate structure, and flawed society outside. Need to fight old use of "autonomy," integrate university with government goals and policies. TxU

CUB ------. Vida Universitaria 4 (January 1953)-8 (December 1957).
147   Bimonthly, usually reporting celebrations of historical events, personages; meetings, conferences, research projects; conspicuous ties with the U.S. Though little on university per se, offers background view of styles, interests of university people in pre-revolutionary era.

CUB ------. Comisión Superior de Docencia. Carta Docente, nos. 1-17
148   (6 November 1962-28 November 1963).
       Seventeen papers on teaching methods, various aspects of higher education including humanities, science, technology, agriculture, medicine.

CUB   UNIVERSIDAD DE LA HABANA, Consejo Universitario. Exposición del
149   Consejo Universitario en defensa de la autonomía de la Universidad de la Habana. [Havana: Imp. Universidad de la Habana, 1953?]. 7 pp.
       Sets forth legal basis for university autonomy, established in Article 23 of the Ley Docente of January 8, 1937, which is construed as forbidding threats to its economic independence; since the 1940 Constitution, university had received 2.25 percent of national budget but in 1953, with inflation, is receiving less than in 1941 for larger enrollment. TxU

CUB   UNIVERSIDAD DE LA HABANA, Federación de Empleados. La reforma
150   integral de la Universidad de la Habana. [Havana], 1960. 16 pp.
       "Virile action" of Student Federation (FEU) responsible for progress; conflicts with rector, role of employees' associations and denunciation of pre-revolutionary university governance. TxU

CUB   UNIVERSIDAD DE LA HABANA, Secretaría General. Datos estadísticos
151   recopilados por el negociado de revisión de expedientes de estudios. Curso Académico de 1953-1954. Havana: [1955?]. 72 pp.
       Enrollment by schools and careers, public and private schools; the origins of students; courses and grades. TxU

CUB   UNIVERSIDAD DE LA HABANA, Vicerrectoría Docente. Información
152   profesional sobre las especialidades que se cursan en la Universidad de La Habana. Havana: Universidad de la Habana, [1978]. 33 pp.
       To help student choose career contributing to future development of socialist country and his personal qualities. Daytime courses for graduates of pre-university secondary program, who choose among seven faculties, engage in related work, fulfill military training obligation. Afternoon and evening courses for workers in four fields; correspondence opportunities for those in remote areas in three fields. Goals and content of each course of study. WKU

CUB   LA UNIVERSIDAD DE LA HABANA. Havana: n.p., [ca. 1967], 39 pp.
153   Short history, research, educational policies, governance and structure. Agrarian research, discussion of Cuba as "laboratory for social research;" list of university research units. PPiU

CUB UNIVERSIDAD DE LA HABANA, no. 200 (March 1973). 190 pp.
154 Example of current university quarterly starts with Fidel
Castro's speech on XX anniversary of attack on Moncada garrison, includes examples of university research in history and literature.
Documents on founding of University in 1728. WKU

CUB UNIVERSIDAD DE ORIENTE. Ciencias naturales y matemáticas, no. 2
155 (July-September 1977). 74 pp.
Example of research publication, with works by university
faculty members.

CUB ------. Revista Pedagógica: Sobre la Educación Superior 1, no.
156 1 through 2, no. 1 (April 1977 through April-June 1978).
Examples of beginning issues of quarterly devoted to Marxist-
Leninist philosophy in higher education, including Soviet practices on
the organization of entrance examinations, mostly by Soviet authors.

UNIVERSIDAD DE SANTO TOMAS DE VILLANUEVA. See UNIVERSIDAD
CATOLICA DE VILLANUEVA.

UNIVERSIDAD DE VILLANUEVA. See UNIVERSIDAD CATOLICA DE
VILLANUEVA.

CUB UNIVERSIDAD POPULAR (RADIO-TELEVISION PROGRAM). Conferencias.
157 Universidad Popular 1er ciclo. Havana, 1960.
Addresses by government officials and others, originally
presented on the television program "La Universidad Popular." FU

CUB ------. Defensa de Cuba. Universidad Popular 2° ciclo. Havana,
158 1960. 223 pp.
Speeches by seven officials, including Raúl Castro of the
Revolutionary Armed Forces, the vice-president of the Federation of
University Students, and Prime Minister Fidel Castro Ruz promoting the
Popular University, to reach especially the working classes, through
use of a national printing service and television. TxU

CUB ------. Economía y planificación. Universidad Popular, 7°
159 ciclo, parts 1-2. Havana, 1961. 270 pp. and 262 pp.
Transcription of radio and television programs by various
ministers explaining policies for planning and development. KU

CUB ------. Educación y revolución. Universidad Popular, 6° ciclo.
160 Havana, 1961. 319 pp.
Hortatory speeches and concrete plans for the Year of Education as vast literacy campaign is launched. Four thousand scholarships for university students announced and their participation in
building a campus described. Speeches are by Armando Hart Dávalos and
others. TxU

CUB VALDES, NELSON P. and BONACHEA, ROLANDO E. "Fidel Castro y la
161 política estudiantil de 1947 a 1952." Aportes, no. 22 (October
1971): 23-40.
Predilection to violence in Cuban society from late 1930s was
matrix for violence and power-seeking in University of Havana. Growth
of bonches (gangs) with and without ideologies, with Socialist Revolutionary Movement (MSR) in control of student government when Castro

entered law school in 1945. Rival Insurrectional Revolutionary Union (UIR), a kind of training-ground for Castro, "a product more than a cause of the deep and unresolved tensions of Cuban society." Careful documentation.

CUB   VALDES, NELSON P. and LIEUWEN, EDWIN. The Cuban Revolution: A
162   Research-Study Guide (1959-1969). Albuquerque: University of
      New Mexico Press, 1971. 230 pp.
      Twenty-nine entries on university education make this an especially useful work for the period covered. KU

CUB   VALDES RODRIGUEZ, J.M. La reforma universitaria y los medios
163   audiovisuales. Havana: Universidad de La Habana, Servicio de
      medios audiovisuales, 1963. 32 pp.
      Every field of knowledge from history to brain surgery can be taught with film, and university should supply them all. This reform is part of the fight against imperialism and the Batista dictatorship.
KU

CUB   VECINO ALEGRET, FERNANDO. "El primer congreso del partido
164   comunista de Cuba: Lineamientos para la educación superior."
      Revista Internacional de países socialistas 2, no. 18 (1977):
      105-33.
      Minister of higher education describes evolution of integrated system designed to meet planned needs of country in socialist ideological framework, relating study and work. Major structural changes after 1959-61 period, growth, programs for workers, technical education. Sending 1,000 students per year to socialist countries, especially to USSR; plans to send 5,000 in next five years. Increase from twenty-four careers in 1959-60 to forty underway, with emphasis on new agricultural specialties. Lists manpower studies needed, optimum size and kind of institutions for planned economy, the national network, types of higher education institutions and their locations, administrative organization, students, professors, research, physical facilities, international activity, the Ministry of Higher Education. A basic document.

CUB   ------. "La Universidad de La Habana sabrá decir presente." La
165   Universidad de La Habana 203-204 (1976): 163-71.
      Minister of higher education salutes graduates, of whom 45 percent are women and 50 percent members of the Communist Party and of the Union of Communist Youth. History and criticism of old university; new education laws explained, with problems of creating new specializations in higher education.

CUB   La voz de la Universidad de Oriente. Universidad de Oriente,
166   Departamento de Extensión y Relaciones Culturales, Cuadernos 47.
      Santiago de Cuba, 1959. 109 pp.
      Radio talks on role of university in Cuba, e.g., in fight for independence from Spain; talks on research and literature, also. Rebuttal to critics of Law No. 11, which abolished certain private universities: Belén, Candler, Masónica, de La Salle, and "José Martí." Indicative of conflicts of social and academic views. DLC

Dominican Republic

DoR ALENINO, ANDRES. "La educación superior y el desarrollo domini-
1   cano." <u>Ciencia</u> 1, no. 1 (May-June 1972): 17-32.
     Emphasizes university's role in transforming society by
stressing social change and analysis of revolutionary and socialist
doctrines.

ANTONINI, GUSTAVO A. and YORK, MASON A. "Integrated Rural Development and the Role of the University in the Caribbean: The
Case of Plan Sierra, Dominican Republic." See entry GEN 13.

DoR AYBAR, ANDRES MARIA. <u>La universidad y el desarrollo nacional</u>.
2   Colección Conferencias, no. 11. Santo Domingo: [UASD?], 1967.
     6 pp.
     Reflects belief that National Autonomous University of Santo
Domingo is essential for country's development. Rector is strong
supporter of university reform plans. WKU

DoR BATISTA DEL VILLAR, GUAROCUYA. <u>Universidad crítica y patria</u>
3   <u>soberana: Dos Años de gestión universitaria 1976-1978</u>. Colec-
     ción Educación y Sociedad, no. 7. Publicaciones del la Universi-
     dad Autónoma de Santo Domingo, vol. 261. Santo Domingo: Editora
     Alfa y Omega, 1978. 619 pp.
     Reappearance of the <u>Anales</u> in a different form, according to
rector, with date and a "methodological essay of rendering accounts."
Philosophy and activities designed to break with past dependency and
underdevelopment in capitalist system described in introduction.
Agreements signed with universities in Mexico, Puerto Rico, Cuba,
Panama, Venezuela. "Unitary" program of general reorganization; role
of planning office. Documents demanding budgetary support from Balaguer government; speeches on various occasions reflect militancy.
Enrollment data by faculties, 1976-77. WKU

DoR ------, and SOLANO, DARIO. "Docencia universitaria e inves-
4   tigación de la realidad nacional." <u>Ciencia</u> 1, no. 1 (May-June
     1972): 111-25.
     Argues that university research activities should address
themselves more to national needs, and include more students.

DoR BELTRAN DE HEREDIA, VICENTE. La autenticidad de la bula "In
5   Apostolatus culmine", base de la Universidad de Santo Domingo,
     puesta fuera de discusión. Santo Domingo: UASD, [1965]. 74 pp.
     Bound with La Bula "In Apostolatus culmine", by Agueda María
     Rodríguez.
        Research verifies authenticity of Papal Bull establishing
     forerunner of University of Santo Domingo and its claims to being the
     oldest university in the hemisphere, founded in 1538. KU

DoR BERGES, ROBERTO L. "La formación del arquitecto en la UNPHU; Una
6   década de experiencia." Paper read at seminar "La Formación del
     Arquitecto," at Universidad Nacional Pedro Henríquez Ureña, Sep-
     tember 1976. Mimeographed. 16 pp.
        Concern for social and cultural context of academic philoso-
     phy; need for broad education advocated by Ortega y Gasset; architec-
     ture as fusion of art and science. Special Dominican problems with
     change from rural to urban population, poverty. WKU

DoR BLANCO, SALVADOR JORGE. "Reglamento para la Educación Superior.
7   Privada, Numero 1255." Santo Domingo: [Oficina del] Presidente
     de la Republica Dominicana. 25 July 1983. Mimeographed. 10 pp.
        Proliferation of private universities in recent years
     prompted presidential decree establishing criteria for their existance.
     Henceforth to be recognized they must furnish, among other information,
     justification for their creation in terms of national or regional
     needs, congruence of their development plans with national socio-
     economic needs, and their uniqueness. Detailed requirements cover
     curricula, physical and fiscal matters, degrees. Creates Consejo
     Nacional de Educación Superior (CONES) to take charge of very strict
     comprehensive set of directives.

        BUNN, HARRIET, and GUT, ELLEN. The Universities of Cuba,
     the Dominican Republic, Haiti. See entry CUB 14.

DoR CABRAL DELGADO, CESAR RAUL. "Faculty Conditions of Service in
8   the Universities of the Dominican Republic: A Survey Study."
     Ph.D. dissertation, Saint Louis University, 1976. 141 pp.
        Hypothesis is that present conditions of science in the
     Dominican Republic are not adequate to retain and attract qualified
     Dominican or foreign academicians. Evidence: The great numbers who
     leave their universities and enter the government, industry, or a
     foreign university. Based on data from UASD, UNPHU, and Catholic
     University Madre y Maestra.

DoR COMISION ESPECIAL. Informe al Honorable Señor Presidente de la
9   República don Antonio Guzmán Fernández sobre la educación
     superior dominicana. Santo Domingo: [UNPHU], 1980. 82 pp.
        Presidential commission of secretary of education, fine arts
     and culture and five public and private university leaders studies
     legislation governing establishment and functioning of higher edu-
     cation. Problem: the proliferation of higher education institutions
     and quality control. Useful history and analysis followed by proposed
     model legislation. List of applicable laws given in notes. WKU

DoR   DAVID, HENRY P., ed. Higher Education in the Dominican Republic:
10   A Report of Academic Visits, Summer 1966. Silver Spring, Md.:
      American Institutes for Research, 1966. 129 pp.
          After grave problems in the Dominican Republic and with U.N.
      troops still in the area, the Autonomous University of Santo Domingo
      and the new private university, Pedro Henríquez Ureña, were offered
      help by USAID. Several U.S. faculty members were consultants. Useful
      general chapters: G. R. Waggoner, "Higher Education in the Dominican
      Republic: An Overview"; E. D. Duryea, "Organization and University
      Administrative Services"; and B. Waggoner, "Observations on Higher
      Education in the Dominican Republic." KU

DoR   "La educación superior en la República Dominicana." Appendix D
11   in Diagnóstico de la Educación. Santo Domingo: [Ministerio de
      Educación], 1978. 15 pp.
          Report prepared for USAID loan. Government expenditures on
      one public and four private institutions, matriculation 1965-76 and by
      institution, graduates 1971-76, entrance requirements, matriculants and
      graduates in education, libraries, areas of study by institution,
      tuition costs. Suggestions for improvement. WKU

DoR   FONDO PARA EL AVANCE DE LAS CIENCIAS SOCIALES. Las Ciencias
12   Sociales en la República Dominicana: Una evaluación. Santo
      Domingo: Asociación para el Desarrollo, 1977. 77 pp.
          Before the opening of the School of Sociology in the Uni-
      versidad Autónoma de Santo Domingo in 1962, the social sciences "be-
      longed to philosophy, literature, common sense, and speculation." In
      1977, a meeting was held in Santo Domingo to help formulate policies
      for research to cope with areas of neglect and to define roles of
      universities, government, and national and international agencies.
      These seven papers were presented there. WKU

DoR   ------. Fondo para el Avance de las Ciencias Sociales en la
13   República Dominicana: Información general. Santo Domingo, April
      1978. 15 pp.
          Independent agency designed to help encourage research and
      publication in applied social sciences for benefit of Dominicans.
      Weakness of disciplines in universities to be remedied by better sup-
      port, communication, preparation of professionals. Aid from Ford
      Foundation. WKU

DoR   FUNDACION UNIVERSITARIA DOMINICANA (FUD). Informativo. Santo
14   Domingo: FUD, 1977. 6 pp., flyer.
          Sponsoring agency for the National University Pedro Henríquez
      Ureña urges contributions to its fund. List of members of adminis-
      trative boards and the corporations or professions they represent. WKU

DoR   "Grullón destaca logros en desarrollo de UCMM." Listín Diario, 9
15   June 1981, p. 12.
          President of Catholic University's development council, at
      inaugural ceremony for extension center in Santo Domingo, points out
      achievements in ten years since beginnings in an old building in San-
      tiago de los Caballeros. Contribution of training personnel for
      mining, hotels, business, government. Pride in government and private
      support for scholarships for less privileged but able students.

DoR INSTITUTO SUPERIOR DE AGRICULTURA (ISA). Descripción, logros y
16 perspectivas. La Herradura, Santiago: ISA, 1981. 31 pp.
     Since 1968 an affiliate of UCMM, ISA was created by group of
entrepreneurs in 1961 when country had only twelve professionally
trained agronomists. History, principles and objectives, analysis of
academic programs, foreign advisors, new programs. Collaboration with
UASD and UNPHU and Ministry of Agriculture with USAID help. List of
twenty-eight full time professors, eleven more training abroad and
plans for additional nineteen in selected specialties; projected enrollment growth. WKU

DoR INSTITUTO TECNOLOGICO DE SANTO DOMINGO (INTEC). Curso de post-
17 grado en ingeniería mecánica con mención en factoría
   azucarera. Santo Domingo: INTEC, [1977?]. 15 pp.
     State Sugar Council and INTEC design experimental program for
mechanical engineers specializing in sugar processing, the country's
major source of income. No such program exists here or abroad. WKU

DoR ------. Documentos: INTEC, no. 1 (1976), 122 pp.
18   INTEC began academic life in 1970 with postgraduate and short
courses, research and publication. Founded by a group of young professionals "rebelling" against traditional university structures, it
later began offering licenciatura degree and short programs in social
sciences, engineering and health sciences. Financing is by students
and professors who serve without renumeration. Different cycles
serve technical and professional students to avoid loss of time and
questions of social status. Efforts to overcome dependency on exterior, and underdevelopment. History and philosophy of INTEC
culminate in an evaluation session.

DoR ------. Documentos: INTEC, no. 2 (1977), 211 pp.
19   Innovative institution has graduated three classes in five
years of existence, now has several graduate programs. Essays on its
educational philosophy and practice.

DoR ------. Estatutos. Santo Domingo: INTEC, [n.d.] 18 pp.
20   These statutes, in force since August 1974, govern the private, university-level entity created in 1973, in part "to orient its
scientific tasks toward the search for solutions to crucial problems of
the Dominican Society, as an academic institution located in a dependent and underdeveloped nation." Governance is by a board of
regents, the rector, and the academic council. WKU

DoR ------. Programas de grado. Santo Domingo: INTEC, 1976. 30
21 pp.
     Courses to be offered, requirements in several programs; new-
style university structure. IU

DoR ------. Proyecto del ciclo propedéutico. Santo Domingo: INTEC,
22 1981. 31 pp.
     More than strictly remedial project, designed to improve
success rate in later work, concentrates on basic language, math and
science. Costly traditional high failure rate in universities in
Dominican Republic and other underdeveloped countries must be corrected. Goals, programs, administration, costs. WKU

Dominican Republic

DoR 23 ------. Reglamentos académicos, usos, costumbres. Santo Domingo: INTEC, [n.d.] 36 pp.
Rules for admissions, grading, class attendance, and transfers from other institutions are given; a system of monitoring is provided for superior students to assist professors in tutorials. Rules for professors in organizing and presenting their material were approved by the Academic Council in 1975. WKU

DoR 24 ------. "Resumen del programa de consolidación y expansión del INTEC para la década de los 80." Mimeographed. [Santo Domingo]: INTEC, February 1981. 10 pp.
Program of consolidation and expansion will offer new and modified careers in engineering, social sciences, public health and development of common propaedeutic cycle for all students. Plans for twenty-seven graduate programs in 1981-86 period, plus 195 courses in continuing education. Research requires expanded library (for 300,000 volumes), thirty more classrooms, other facilities. Greatest increase to be in areas needed for national development, science and technology. List of possible specialties, cost estimates. WKU

Dor 25 LA FONTAINE, JOFFRE ALBERT DE. "The First University in the New World: The University of Santo Domingo (1538-1965)." Ph.D. dissertation, Southern Illinois University, 1979. 165 pp.
Straightforward historical account concludes with advocacy of assumption of leadership by university in all aspects of Dominican life.

DoR 26 LATORRE, EDUARDO. "Educación y sociedad: El caso de la República Dominicana." Ciencia y Sociedad 2, no. 1 (January-June 1977): 83-96.
The rector of the Instituto Tecnológico de Santo Domingo gives a panorama of current Dominican education, with its roots in the colonial past producing an inadequate product for modern development. Recent increase in educational expenditures by government shows a miserly per-pupil investment. Rectors of universities have recently been made members of the national Educational Council as part of an effort to reform the national system of education.

DoR 27 ------. "Principales objetivos del Instituto Tecnológico de Santo Domingo." Mimeographed. Santo Domingo: INTEC, September 1977. 23 pp.
Rector describes founding of the private Institute of Santo Domingo by group of young Dominican professionals and scientists, who basically have in common academic training abroad at the postgraduate level, with goals of social betterment. Opposition to traditional university dictated the name, yet it is more than a technological institute. Seeking new model for Dominicans and third world countries, one that is not "primitive" or "based on emotional criteria." Begun with graduate level work in 1972 "recycling" existing professionals for new, more needed careers. WKU

DoR 28 ------. Sobre educación Superior. Serie Educación, no. 2. Santo Domingo: INTEC, 1980. 234 pp.
Compendium of speeches, articles under three main topics: Dominican education, higher education for the third world, the INTEC

model. INTEC rector appears to be ideologically neutral, concerned with general observations. WKU

DoR   MAQUETE, CLODOMIRO. "Definen antinacional proyecto alfabeti-
29   zación en la región sur." La Noticia, 28 May 1981, p. 14.
      Department of Pedagogy, UASD, rejects USAID project to serve illiterate children with radio lessons, in cooperation with Dominican secretary of education, calling it "one more instrument of imperialist penetration and an attack against the national character of the education we ought to give our children." President and secretary of education called on to reject plan. An example of continued suspicion in UASD of U.S. government.

DoR   MARINO HERNANDEZ, FRANK. El sistema educativo dominicano. Santo
30   Domingo: Editora Taller, 1975. 213 pp.
      General socio-economic aspects of primary, secondary, vocational, technical and special education; but most emphasis on higher education. The seven universities are described, the academic structures, matriculation, professors, programs, capacity of the university system, program needs and general conclusions about both basic education and higher education. This thorough study is up-to-date and useful. KU

DoR   ------. Recursos humanos de nivel superior en la República
31   Dominicana. Santo Domingo: Ediciones Sargazo, 1972. 128 pp.
      Study of human resources trained at university level. Concludes that insufficient data make it difficult to make an accurate estimate of supply and demand. Data from 1964-65 include university enrollments. TxU

DoR   MARTIN, JOHN BARTLOW. Overtaken by Events: The Dominican Crisis
32   from the Fall of Trujillo to the Civil War. Garden City:
      Doubleday and Company, 1966. 821 pp.
      Scattered but revealing comments of his perceptions of universities and their students in the civil war context, by former U.S. ambassador; typifies U.S. policy of suspecting intellectuals in Latin America for leftist rhetoric. WKU

DoR   MARTINEZ RICHIEZ, RAFAEL. Coordinación entre las instituciones
33   de educación superior y la Secretaría de Estado de Agricultura.
      Santo Domingo: Secretaría de Estado de Agricultura, Oficina de Coordinación Universitaria, [1980]. 13 pp.
      Report on coordination activities among three Dominican universities to improve agriculture and serve rural population, especially with efforts to link students with farm life. Sixteen research projects listed, various extension services. WKU

DoR   MEJIA-RICART GUZMAN, TIRSO. Diez ensayos sobre reforma y planea-
34   miento universitario. 2 vols. Colección Historia y Sociedad,
      no. 22. Santo Domingo: UASD, 1975. 446 pp.
      Scholar, university reform leader produces essays on planning and reform, compiled ten years after restructuring of the national university. Carefully developed work culminates in plan for new statutes covering all aspects of university. WKU

DoR ------. La universidad, la iglesia y el estado en la República
35 Dominicana. Publicaciones de la Universidad Autónoma de Santo
Domingo, vol. 274. Colección Historia y Sociedad, no. 39. Santo
Domingo: Editora de la UASD, 1980. 116 pp.

With degrees in medicine, psychiatry and philosophy earned in
UASD and in Germany, author was active in post-Trujillo era university
reform efforts and a vigorous supporter of public university concept.
Presents chronology of events, varied points of view, personae in the
evolution of UASD, and the proliferation of universities after 1961.
Second half of book, especially, is essential to understanding current
situation in higher education. U.S. role in support of conservative
sectors is clear. A useful social history of a nation plagued by
social and political problems and rivalries. WKU

DoR "Mensaje de despedida del doctor Antonio Rosario, rector de la
36 Universidad Autónoma de Santo Domingo, con motivo de la termi-
nación de su período académico 1978-1981, pronunciado en el acto
de investidura celebrada el 25 de Febrero de 1981." Universidades 3d ser., no. 84 (April-June 1981): 25-31.

Sentimental farewell to graduates preceded by description of
two major problems he leaves behind: chronic economic insufficiencies,
and lack of "mystique" of the old days. Prior to presidential election
of 1978, UASD was a body united against the government. Now, without
need for hostility, political fragmentation and infighting weaken the
university's mission.

DoR MOYA PONS, FRANK. "La investigación social y el desarrollo
37 dominicano." Mimeographed. Santo Domingo: Cámara Americana de
Comercio, 1978. 25 pp.

Trujillo-era university had no social scientists; after 1962
had to develop professionals abroad to learn national reality, needs
for development. Creation of Fund for the Advancement of the Social
Sciences, sponsored by the Association for Development, Inc., receives
monies from local and multinational companies, foundations. Growth of
social sciences in universities. WKU

DoR NAMIS, ARMANDO JOSE. El desarrollo y los colegios universitarios
38 regionales. [n.p.] Colección Conferencias, no. 10. 1967. 11
pp.

With increased number of secondary graduates, need for
regional higher education opportunities exists. Sees initial cycles of
university education outside main campus as advantageous for both
students and university; benefit especially to teachers. IU

DoR NUÑEZ COLLADO, AGRIPNO. La UCMM: Un nuevo estilo universitario
39 en la República Dominicana. Santiago: UCMM, 1977. 348 pp.

Prologue by Héctor Incháustegui Cabral gives history of
Dominican educational vicissitudes occasioned by foreign interventions,
and effects of secular philosophies on Catholic education. Monseñor
Núñez compiled his speeches and writings about UCMM, founded in 1962,
before and during his period as rector (1970-). Chapter Las Crises
covers not only UCMM but others in period of turmoil; other chapters
describe growth and changes in his institution. WKU

DoR ------. La Universidad Católica Madre y Maestra y el desarollo
40 dominicano. Santiago: UCMM, 1975. 36 pp.

Speech before American Chamber of Commerce in Santiago stresses UCMM contributions to national development. Information on its students, professors, economic condition. Many photos of campus. WKU

DoR   OFICINA DE EDUCACION IBEROAMERICANA (OEI). La Educación en
41   Iberoamérica: Sistema de indicadores socioeconómicos y edu-
      cativos. Dominican Republic. Serie Estadística, nos. 1-3.
      Madrid, Ciudad Universitaria: OEI, 1980. ca. 150 pp. in 3
      volumes.
         Remarkably comprehensive, thorough, objective collection of
information, in folders, on the socioeconomic framework of education,
and education itself. OASDC

DoR   PACHECO, ARMANDO OSCAR. La obra educativa de Trujillo. La Era
42   de Trujillo, 25 Años de Historia Dominicana, vol. 5 Ciudad
      Trujillo: Impresora Dominicana, 1955. 299 pp.
         General Trujillo has created an ideal educational system,
including physical education exercises. KU

DoR   PEREZ, MAXIMO MANUEL. "La UCMM anuncia nuevas carreras." Listín
43   Diario, 9 June 1981, p. 1.
         Rector Agripino Nuñez Collado inaugurates new center of UCMM
in Santo Domingo which will specialize in public, business and hotel
administration; philosophy courses for clergy also to be offered.
Backing from Dominican government, Inter-American Development Bank,
United Nations.

      PIÑERO, EUROPA GONZALES DE, and CLAUDIO, RAMON, eds.
      Crecimiento del personal docente. See entry GEN 211.

DoR   "Policía dona a la UASD 300 galones de pintura." El Caribe, 11
44   June 1981.
         Delivery of paint is both symbolic and substantive event,
Police, traditional enemy of student body, are welcomed on campus by
rector and other functionaries with first part of gift of 1,700
gallons. Shabby buildings, long neglected by government, are to be
painted by student volunteers.

DoR   "Programa intensivo de administración de la educación superior."
45   Universidades 76 (April-June 1979): 529-35.
         Five Dominican Republic universities undertake five year
(1979-84) intensive study of higher education administration, led by
the Technological Institute of Santo Domingo. Formation of National
Council of Institutions of Higher Education (CONIES). Rector of INTEC
calls for analysis of university models, to find what is best suited to
third world.

DoR   "Primer congreso dominicano de historia." Listín Diario, Suple-
46   mento 4 June 1983, p. 7.
         A meeting is planned "for the first time in over a quarter of
a century" for Dominican historians. Among topics to be addressed:
historical sources, research methodologies, teaching, preparation of
history professors. Rectors of the major Dominican universities are
expected to participate. WKU

126

DoR RODRIGUEZ DEMORIZI, EMILIO. Cronología de la Real y Pontificia
47   Universidad de Santo Domingo, 1538-1970. Universidad Autónoma de
     Santo Domingo [Publicaciones], vol. 144. Colección Historia y
     Sociedad, no. 1. Santo Domingo: Editora del Caribe, 1970. 109
     pp.
         Early sixteenth century efforts to develop schooling at all
     levels, with 1538 Bull of Pope Paul III creating forerunner of UASD.
     Competitions in the 18th century with the Jesuits, interruption of
     university with Haitian invasions, development of association of
     students and their role in politics and international affairs, petition
     for and granting of autonomy; 1962 and 1966 foundings of private
     universities. FU

DoR SANCHEZ, JUAN FRANCISCO. La Universidad de Santo Domingo. La
48   Era de Trujillo: 25 Años de Historia Dominicana, vol. 15.
     Ciudad Trujillo: Impresora Dominicana, 1955. 414 pp.
         Chiefly celebrates twenty-five years of the Trujillo era.
     History of university emphasizes reforms and progress after 1930;
     discussion of liberal arts education and adoption of U.S. university
     pattern; budget, enrollment, faculty 1931-54. Anexo covers regulations
     of ancient predecessor institutions; has laws, decrees, resolutions
     1884-1954. MoU

DoR SANCHEZ HERNANDEZ, ANTONIO; MARTINEZ, RAMON; ARVELO, RAFAEL; and
49   JAKOWSKA, SOPHIE. Perspectivas de la investigación en la Uni-
     versidad Autónoma de Santo Domingo. Publicaciones de la
     Universidad Autónoma de Santo Domingo, vol. 276. Colección
     Educación y Sociedad, no. 12. Santo Domingo: Editora de la
     UASD, 1979. 85 pp.
         Research first regulated at UASD in 1969; Office of Scien-
     tific Research created in 1970, with Council of Scientific Research
     composed of administrators and faculty and student representatives from
     the seven faculties. Post-1965 research chiefly in social area; be-
     cause of conflicts with government, activity of UASD was "more politi-
     cal than academic." Applied research in natural sciences listed.
     Priorities developed by commissions, along with policies for finance,
     administration; role of university planning. Institutional research
     tasks listed. WKU

DoR "Se crea la Asociación de Bibliotecas Universitarias Dominicanas."
50   Gaceta, no. 31 (April 1980): 5.
         All Dominican universities except the Universidad Autónoma de
     Santo Domingo form an association to coordinate development, planning
     and use of their libraries.

DoR SECRETARIA DE ESTADO DE AGRICULTURA, Programa Nacional de
51   Desarrollo para el Pequeño Agricultor (PPA), Proyecto de Edu-
     cación Profesional (PEP). Guías para presentación, aprobación,
     administración y financiamiento de propuestas de investigación.
     Santo Domingo: Secretaría de Estado de Agricultura, 1980. 17
     pp.
         Prepared for interuniversity coordinating committee. WKU

DoR SECRETARIA DE ESTADO DE AGRICULTURA, Projecto de Educación Pro-
52   fesional. Resumen de las principales actividades del Proyecto

de Educación Profesional. Santo Domingo: Secretaría de Estado
de Agricultura, 1977. 12 pp.
    Participant universities: UASD, UNPHU, and UCMM's Higher
Institute of Agriculture, ISA. Report prepared for UNICA meeting
describes development project to help small farmer, with USAID funds
administered by secretary of Agriculture and universities. Activities
and budget. WKU

DoR   SECRETARIA DE ESTADO DE EDUCACION, BELLAS ARTES Y CULTURA.
53   Diagnóstico del sector educativo en la República Dominicana.
     Santo Domingo: Editora Educativa Dominicana de Santo Domingo,
     1979. 343 pp.
    Pages 275-88 contain basic data on higher education. The
socio-economic context of education, demography, general aspects of
educational administration, are followed by sections on reforms,
problems, conclusions and recommendations for each level of education.
USAID gave technical and financial help for study. WKU

DoR   TOLENTINO DIPP, HUGO. "El logro de una educación integral y el
54   plan de estudios del colegio universitario." Mimeographed.
     Santo Domingo: UASD, 1967. 11 pp.
    A goal of reform movement was achievement of broader edu-
cation than strictly professional, which necessitates structural and
other changes. LNHT

DoR   TRUJILLO MOLINA, RAFAEL LEONIDAS. Discurso del generalísimo
55   Rafael L. Trujillo Molina . . . primer doctor honoris causa de la
     Universidad de Santo Domingo, pronunciado en el acto académico
     celebrado el 28 de octubre con motivo del cuarto centenario de su
     fundación, 1538-1938. Ciudad Trujillo, Distrito de Santo
     Domingo: Publicaciones de la Universidad de Santo Domingo, 1938.
     18 pp.
    Four hundredth anniversary of founding of first university in
the Americas produces appropriate ceremony starring General Trujillo.
FU

DoR   UNIVERSIDAD AUTONOMA DE SANTO DOMINGO (UASD). Anales. Vol. 28,
56   nos. 97-100, 1961-67. Santo Domingo: UASD, 1974. 203 pp.
    After 1960 the annals of UASD were unpublished. This one
summary includes reports by the four rectors of the period; documents
which gave the University its autonomy in 1961; which responded to a
police invasion in a time of civil strife; which gave UASD title to its
experimental farm; which defined the constitutional jurisdiction of the
University. Copy of an 1887 letter urging reestablishment of the
university, report of a fossil collection, and university statistics on
graduation are included. WKU

DoR   ------. Anales. Vol. 28, nos. 101-6, 1967-72. Santo Domingo:
57   UASD, 1975. 598 pp.
    Continuing government pressures keep UASD in precarious eco-
nomic condition as it pursues academic reform in the post-Trujillo era,
at the time of worldwide university turmoil. Reports by the three
rectors of the period include financial data, activities of departments
and schools and enrollment figures, as well as a list of UASD publications, 1963-73. WKU

DoR   ------. Anales. Vol. 29, no. 107, 1973-74. Santo Domingo:
58   UASD, 1975. 439 pp.
       National government policy leaves university lacking money to
buy paper and repair windows and classroom chairs; administrators
struggled to allocate funds to pay creditors and professors. Norms
were developed for evaluation of academic personnel. Speeches by
rector included denunciatory remarks on the ninth anniversary of U.S.
military intervention in the Dominican Republic, and the fiftieth
anniversary of the departure of U.S. troops from the first intervention. Enrollment data and a list of 1964-74 graduates. Research
papers (on bacteria in frozen seafood and on dental treatment) are included in report. WKU

DoR   ------. Anales. Vol. 30, no. 108, 1974-75. Santo Domingo:
59   UASD, 1977. 403 pp.
       According to the rector, UASD survives despite the national
government's "incomprehension, mockery, and aggressions" towards it,
the only public university in the Dominican Republic. Fiscal star-
vation is blamed on President of the Republic Belaguer's fear of
"international communism" at UASD. Contains data on present enrollment
and courses of studies, graduates by careers since 1883, work of the
Development and Reform Commission, the agreement between UASD and the
Universidad de la Habana, and a list of the 1976 graduates. See also
item DoR 3. DLC

DoR   ------. "Análisis de ingresos." Mimeographed. [Santo Domingo]:
60   UASD, 1981. 5 pp.
       Funds from Dominican government and university's own re-
sources have increased 34.16 percent from 1979 to 1981. But enrollment
increased 46.84 percent. Decreased per student income from state is
aggravated by failure of government to pay its January and February
quotas, putting UASD back in precarious situation of pre-1978 (under
President Belaguer). WKU

DoR   ------. Un año de labor por el desarrollo y reforma universi-
61   tarios 1966-1967. Santo Domingo: UASD, Comisión para el
       Desarrollo y Reforma Universitarios, 1967. 229 pp.
       Post-Trujillo era struggle to create a model for the uni-
versity occurs in midst of conflict between those in favor of and those
opposing academic and social change. Feudal structures, archaic
teaching methods, isolated faculties, cronyism in faculty selection
cited among problems from 1961-1965, especially for adopting General
Studies. Renovation movement, after 1965 civil war, produces strong
statement about goals, philosophy, details of the reform. WKU

DoR   ------. Catálogo General 1970-1971. Santo Domingo, [1970]. 460
62   pp. plus diagram of university organization and map of campus.
       University Reform and Development commission tries to system-
atize information and stimulate improvement in publications; history in
colonial and republican eras followed by attempts after 1961 to overcome defects of the Trujillo era; 1966 reform law made fundamental
structural changes; 1968 report of rector. Administration and academic
organization; plans of study; rules; and statistical data, including
enrollment figures and voting results of student elections by party and
faculty for 1969. WKU

DoR   ------. Documentos. Serie OPLAU, no. 1. Colección Universidad
63   y Planificación, vol. 221, no. 1. Santo Domingo, 1977. 202 pp.
      When the Office of University Planning (OPLAU) was created in
1976 it replaced the Commission for Development and University Reform
of 1966. As an advisory unit to the rector and University Council,
OPLAU's duties and personnel posts are detailed here along with the
System of Information on Students (SIE) (a kind of registrar's office),
the Office of University Comptroller, and procedures for budgetary
administration. WKU

DoR   ------. Edición homenaje en conmemoración de la investidura del
64   generalísimo doctor Rafael L. Trujillo Molino como doctor honoris
      causa en leyes de la Universidad de Pittsburgh, Pennsylvania,
      E.E.U.U. de América, 1942. Ciudad Trujillo: [n. p.], 1942. 80
      pp.
      In Spanish and English. A University of Pittsburgh trustee
nominated Trujillo for "his meritorious achievements . . . not only in
the field of domestic policies, but . . . actions furthering the improvement of international relations and his endeavors to relieve the
moral sufferings of humanity." TxU

DoR   ------. Estatuto orgánico. Publicaciones de la UASD, vol. 122.
65   Santo Domingo: UASD, 1966. 34 pp.
      Continuation of the Real y Pontificia Universidad de Santo
Thomás de Aquino; rules include prohibition against political participation by the university, its organisms and its functionaries;
goals; structure, including Development and Reform Commission; governance, including duties of its officers; students' matriculation, rights,
duties, participation in governance. University grounds are inviolable
and no public official may enter unless required to by the University
Council. FU

DoR   ------. Facultad de Filosofía. [2d. ed., rev.] Ciudad
66   Trujillo: Universidad de Santo Domingo, 1946. 73 pp.
      Bases for reestablishing the Faculty of Philosophy as the
seat of theoretical (as contrasted to applied) studies of the liberal
arts and sciences. Proposal to model it after North American universities made by rector in 1939. Requirements for degrees, including the
doctorate, and other laws. LNHT

DoR   ------. Guía de carreras 77. Serie OPLAU, no. 2. Colección
67   Universidad y Planificación, vol. 222, no. 2. Santo Domingo,
      1977. 77 pp.
      All careers are designed to meet needs of Dominican society
besides demands of labor market. University structure, degrees
available in each of seven faculties, certificates in the three regional centers, and the goals and courses of the University College for
entering students at UASD are given. WKU

DoR   ------. Homenaje de los estudiantes universitarios al General-
68   ísimo Trujillo. (3 dic., 1956). Ciudad Trujillo: Editora del
      Caribe, 1957. 57 pp.
      One of many ceremonies offering opportunity for General
Trujillo to don academic robes and hear himself praised for
benefactions. FU

DoR   ------. <u>Memoria de las actividades universitarias corres-</u>
69   <u>pondientes al período 1979-1980</u>. Santo Domingo: UASD, 1980.
      306 pp.
         Report presented to the October session of the University
Council by Rector Antonio Rosario reminds leaders of university's 1538
founding, of 1961 law establishing its public, autonomous character,
and of its role as defender of liberty and humane values. UASD participation in activities of UDUAL seen as significant; ties developed
with Central American universities through CSUCA and FUPAC. Deplores
assassinations of university people in Guatemala. Importance of
hosting First Conference of Dental Schools of Latin America. Growth of
physical plant and programs reported but pleads case for funds from
government to serve its expected 60,000 students. Detailed reports by
all units of UASD. WKU

DoR   ------. "Número de investidos, según facultad, departamento y
70   carrera, estructura por la sede central de la UASD. Período
      Académico enero-diciembre de 1980." Mimeographed. [Santo
      Domingo]: UASD, Unidad de Estadísticas, January 1980. 9 leaves.
         Current enrollment data; also academic performance in Uni-
versity College, 1975-76 to 1979-80, showing 55.5 percent success. WKU

DoR   "Número de secciones, número de asignaturas y cantidad de alumnos
71   inscritos por asignaturas en la sede central y los centros
      regionales, total UASD. 1° 1980-1981." Mimeographed. Santo
      Domingo: [UASD] OPLAU, Unidad de Estadísticas, July 1981. 11
      leaves.
         Figures from the departments in seven faculties. WKU

DoR   ------. <u>Para el desarrollo y la reforma universitarios.</u>
72   <u>Memoria, 1971-1972</u>. [Santo Domingo]: Comisión para el
      Desarrollo y Reforma Universitarios, [1972?]. 336 pp.
         Introduction, i-ix, describes post-1966 breaking of the domi-
nation of traditional <u>profesores titulares</u>, modernizing and
democratizing structure and academic functions, struggles to develop
coherent plan. Development plan; organization of Reform Commission;
academic reforms, from details of restructurings to proposed emblems of
the different schools; plans of studies, regional centers; statistical
procedures; administrative reforms. WKU

DoR   ------. "Población estudiantil por unidad académica y carrera en
73   la sede central y los centros regionales, 2° 1979-80." Mimeo-
      graphed. Santo Domingo: [UASD] OPLAU, Unidad de Estadísticas,
      August 1981. 5 leaves.
         Of 50,787 students in UASD, 43,135 are in the main campus in
Santo Domingo; the rest are in four regional centers. WKU

DoR   ------. <u>Políticas universitarias para la formulación del presu-</u>
74   <u>puesto, 1981</u>. Santo Domingo: UASD, 1981. 25 leaves.
         Document, approved by University Council in 1980, covers
general policies on curricular, institutional and welfare matters.
Second part has policies and criteria for formulating budget. Goal is
to reestablish fundamental university activities and correct "ac-
cumulated dysfunctions" of recent years in line with demands of growth.
WKU

DoR   ------. "Reglamento sobre promoción, retiro y baja estudiantil."
75   Mimeographed. Santo Domingo: [UASD] Office of the Rector. 8
       pp.
       Regulations governing students' progress toward degree,
eliminating those who fail, rewarding regular and honor students. A
perennial and sometimes politically touchy issue in Latin American
public universities. WKU

DoR   ------. Resolución del claustro universitario de la Universidad
76   de Santo Domingo. Ciudad Trujillo: Universidad de Santo
       Domingo, 1959. 18 pp.
       A brief resolution censuring the rector of the University of
Caracas for authorizing the collection of funds to overthrow the
Trujillo regime in the Dominican Republic, followed by lists of professors' signatures arranged by faculties. FU

DoR   ------. Universidad Autónoma de Santo Domingo: 430 aniversario
77   de su fundación; cuatro discursos académicos. [Santo Domingo],
       1968. 32 pp.
       With world wide student unrest, Rector Aybar Nicolas looks
back on emergence of universities following the overthrow of Trujillo's
tyranny in 1961, and forward to problems of developing country. Vice-
rector Tolentino Dipp deplores inheritance of university as "cultural
superstructure of colonialism." TxU

DoR   UNIVERSIDAD CATOLICA MADRE Y MAESTRA (UCMM). Información general.
78   [Santiago de los Caballeros]: UCMM, Facultad de Ciencias,
       Sociales y Administrativas, [1977]. 8 pp. Flyer.
       Academic organization; finance; programs in accounting, busi-
ness administration, law, social work; matriculation. WKU

DoR   ------. Un nuevo estilo universitario. Santiago de los
79   Caballeros: UCMM, [1976]. 6 pp. Flyer
       History, objectives, seventeen four-year and five-year
careers, admission requirements, services, library, map of campus. WKU

DoR   ------. La UCMM: Un enfoque evaluativo. Santiago de los
80   Caballeros: UCMM, Oficina de Planeamiento, 1976. 30 pp.
       From 357 students in 1965-66, to 4,128 ten years later
indicates local and national demographic and social pressures for
university education. Forty-five percent of UCMM students from lowest
socio-economic stratum, most from regions away from capital. Educational credit data: high cost effectiveness ratios--40 percent of
matriculants graduate. WKU

DoR   UNIVERSIDAD CENTRAL DEL ESTE (UCE). Historia y Trayectoria. San
81   Pedro de Macorís: UCE, 1980. 92 pp.
       Brief biographies of founder-rector and present rector,
father and son, of university founded in 1970. Legal status granted by
government in 1971. Goals, affiliations, philosophy. San Pedro de
Macorís, flourishing sugar industry center in nineteenth century with
vigorous cultural life, fell into abrupt decline; poverty and government neglect now being countered by creation of UCE. Administration,
list of careers for expected 15,000 students. Plans of study. WKU

DoR   ------. "Noticias." Anuario Científico 1, no. 1 (1976): 187-
82   205.
        Six years after UCE founding, new journal carries news of
activities: a course in cooperatives, creation of science faculty, a
socioeconomic study carried out by medical students in San Pedro de
Macorís, student community services. Speech by rector-founder José A.
Hazim Azar at inauguration of first campus classroom building emphasizes policy of free education for youth in a poor region. Private
university receives some government funds.

DoR   ------. "Noticias del UCE." Anuario Científico 3, no. 3 (1978):
83   261-85.
        Reprints, chiefly, from Santo Domingo press include news of
new classroom buildings, a library for 400,000 volumes, an auditorium
for 600. Some 6,100 Dominican and 2,600 foreign students bring prosperity to community; foreign students pay $1,400 per semester. Gradu-
ation of eighty-five doctors, six lawyers, and eight teachers in first
graduation of year; seventy-two doctors plus other professionals in
second. Research and publishing strong in fields of medicine and
archaeology.

DoR   ------. "Noticias del UCE." Anuario Científico 4, no. 4 (1979):
84   150-200.
        Plans to construct 150-bed hospital to serve local populace
and train medical students. Three percent of the 12,300 students pay
full fees, rest of funds from government and private sources. Vigorous
response, reprinted from El Caribe, to Wall Street Journal article
casting doubt on quality of medical education calls UCE "a beautiful
academic reality." WSJ called San Pedro de Macorís "a primitive, dusty
village," outraging students who cite great progress in this once
impoverished, neglected region.

DoR   ------. "Noticias de la UCE." Anuario Científico 5, no. 5
85   (1980): 171-209.
        Rector José Hazim Frappier, son of founder-rector, reviews
accomplishment of UCE on its tenth anniversary, as do newspapers of
Santo Domingo. Some 15,000 students, 2,000 from abroad; benefits to
community, development of campus praised. Graduation of 326 doctors,
opening of dental laboratory, research, service, new rectory building.

DoR   ------. Recursos humanos de la región: Trabajo presentado por
86   la Universidad Central del Este en el Primer Seminario de
        Desarrollo Integral de la Región Este. San Pedro de Macorís:
        UCE, Facultad de Ciencias Económicas y Sociales, Escuela de
        Economía, 1978. 66 pp.
        Region comprising some 16 percent of Dominican Republic's
land area and 10 percent of its population suffers from economy which
had declined with collapse of sugar industry; 71 percent of its heads
of households had emigrated. Great impulse to development with establishment of UCE, both direct and indirect, especially in employment.
Data on employment, characteristics and income for various occupations.
Recommendations for a policy for human resources include improvement of
skills, family planning, urban-rural population distribution, just
remuneration for workers. WKU

UNIVERSIDAD DE SANTO DOMINGO.   See UNIVERSIDAD AUTÓNOMA DE SANTO DOMINGO.

DoR   UNIVERSIDAD NACIONAL PEDRO HENRIQUEZ UREÑA (UNPHU).   Catálogo
87   general UNPHU 1980. Santo Domingo: UNPHU, 1980. 569 pp.
        First university-wide catalog produced (1,000 copies) since 1966 founding of this private university. History, statutory base, objectives, governance, administration, academic structure, general information, academic programs. WKU

DoR   ------. Estatuto Orgánico. Santo Domingo, 1975. 19 pp.
88   Founded in 1966, this private university spells out, as one of its articles to assure fulfillment of its objectives, its apolitical character, forbidding any partisan political activity within its precinct, or political activity by the university itself, or of its members in their capacity as members. Departments will be its basic units in the disciplines or professional schools. University governance, determined by the Fundación Universitaria Dominicana, Inc., is carried on by the rector and the academic council. WKU

DoR   ------. Estatuto orgánico de la Universidad Nacional Pedro
89   Pedro Henríquez Ureña. Santo Domingo: UNPHU, 1979. 24 pp.
        Juridical status, goals, functions, administration of private university. Revision of earlier statutes. WKU

DoR   ------. Gobierno, estructura académica, carreras ofrecidas 1970-
90   1971. Santo Domingo: UNPHU. 25 pp.
        Dominican University Foundation, mostly composed of industries, commerce and banking interests, created and finances private university in accord with its rules. Academic structure, governance, careers; projected enrollment of 6,970 by 1974-75. WKU

DoR   ------. Guía de admisión, 1977-1978. Santo Domingo: UNPHU. 8
91   pp.
        Admission information includes list of professional and technical level careers offered. WKU

DoR   ------. Guía de estudiante, 1977-1978. Santo Domingo: UNPHU.
92   9 pp.
        Matriculation information. WKU

DoR   ------. "Reglamento del régimen estudiantil." Mimeographed.
93   Santo Domingo: UNPHU, August 1975. 12 pp.
        Rights, responsibilities, offenses, penalties. Tight regulations for student groups and their activities, including broadcasting and publishing. WKU

DoR   ------. "Reglamentos de exámenes, pruebas y sistemas de evalua-
94   ción." Mimeographed. Santo Domingo: UNPHU, August 1975.
        14 pp.
        Rules for tests, matriculations, graduation, academic honors.
WKU

DoR   ------. Facultad de Arquitectura y Artes, Escuela de Arqui-
95   tectura y Urbasnismo. "Plan de funcionamiento de las Escuelas de

Arquitectura y Urbanismo." Mimeographed. [Santo Domingo]:
UNPHU, [1976?]. 37 pp.
　　　History, goals of university. Emphasis on education in the
Dominican context; program of studies, including work in community
development. WKU

DoR　WEDGE, BRYANT. "The Case Study of Student Political Violence:
96　Brazil, 1964 and Dominican Republic, 1965." World Politics 21
　　　(January 1969): 182-206
　　　Study aims at predicting probable behavior in time of stress.
Individual interviews following U.S. intervention in Dominican
Republic.

French Antilles

FrA 1   "Antilles-Guyane Françaises." <u>Caribbean Monthly Bulletin</u> 12, no. 6 (June 1978): 10.
     University officials want complete course of study at the Centre in Guadeloupe. Rector opposes on grounds of decreasing secondary graduates and student attitude favoring off-island education.

FrA 2   BIENAYME, ALAIN. <u>Systems of Higher Education: France</u>. New York: International Council for Educational Development, 1978. 144 pp.
     Despite reforms since 1968 there are still problems in the universities: decision-making power for professors, the role of students, the rector. Continuing discussion over centralization and Ministry of Education. Overseas departments are legally identical to those of metropolitan France. KU

FrA 3   BRASSEUR, GERARD. <u>La Guyane Française: Un bilan de trente années</u>. Paris: La Documentation Française: 1978. 184 pp.
     General work providing data on geography, administrative and financial organization, and economic and social activities of French Guiana. Short chapter on education and research reveals there is relatively little of either. Post-secondary: a two-year program for electronic technicians and a program broadcast from Martinique for first-year law. KU

FrA 4   CAUMER, ANTOINE DE. "Oublier créole; parler français." <u>L'éducation</u>, no. 344 (February 1978): 8-10.
     Questions whether the people of the Antilles are French or Creole. Children are embarrassed speaking Creole in school but in practice use the language.

FrA 5   CENTRE UNIVERSITAIRE ANTILLES-GUYANE (CUAG). <u>Année Universitaire 1972-1973</u>. Pointe-à-Pitre, Guadeloupe and Fort-de-France, Martinique: [Centre Universitaire, 1972]. 40 pp.
     History, locations, administration, programs of centers in Guadeloupe and Martinique, with 2,500 students. University structure regulated by the Academy of Bordeaux and French law. WKU

FrA ------. Année Universitaire 1974-1975. [Pointe-à-Pitre, Guade-
6 loupe and Fort-de-France, Martinique: Centre Universitaire,
1974]. 52 pp.
    Summary of most aspects of the university centers in
Guadeloupe and Martinique. General plan of administration, services,
libraries, preventive medicine program, research, teaching and
students. Convention between Antillean university centers and University of the West Indies for communication and exchange. In 1972-73
there were 2,789 students; in 1973-74, 2,823; and in 1974-75, 3,088.
Programs included law, economics, letters, and natural and physical
sciences [several are now in different locations from those given
here]. See also item FrA 13. WKU

FrA ------. Enquête sur les nouveaux étudiants de première année à
7 l'UER de Lettres et Sciences Humaines 78-79. [Fort-de-France/
Pointe-à-Pitre?]: CUAG, Cellule Universitaire d'Information et
d'Orientation, [1979]. 8 pp.
    Questionnaire results show relationships among university
programs chosen and secondary school areas of specialization, geographic origins of students, participation in CUAG information meetings
at secondary schools, other university choices, professional and educational goals. Majority of 111 entering students are from Martinique,
where faculty in question is located. Ninety-eight percent have chosen
studies designed for professional goals. Half of the science students
would prefer to study in another institution. WKU

FrA ------. Enquête sur les nouveaux étudiants de première année à
8 l'UER de Sciences Exactes et Naturelles (78-79). [Fort-de-
France/Pointe-à-Pitre?]: CUAG, Cellule Universitaire d'Information et d'Orientation, [1979]. 10 pp.
    Questionnaire results show relationships between choice of
university program and secondary school attended for 123 of 133 entering students. Proximity to parents an important consideration for
most, but some 50 percent come from Martinique to campus in Guadeloupe.
Over half had another kind of education as first preferences, e.g.,
short technical courses; over half have chosen career, with teaching as
their goal. WKU

FrA ------. Livret de L'Etudiant. [Fort-de-France]: CUAG, [1980?].
9 179 pp.
    Description of Center's organization, goals, operation, in-
cluding location of various faculties and facilities on the Fort-de-
France and Pointe-à-Pitre campuses. Admissions policies, degrees and
programs offered, student services. WKU

FrA ------. Cellule d'Information et d'Orientation. Bulletin d'In-
10 formation, numéro spécial futurs bacheliers (March 1977), 4 pp.
with mimeographed insert of 4 pages.
    Bulletin for prospective students. Guadeloupe and Martinique
university centers both offer first cycle of law and economics, then
specialties are divided between them. Letters and humanities are
taught in Fort-de-France, exact and natural sciences in Pointe-à-Pitre;
after two years and earning the diploma, student could do next degrees
in metropolitan France. Four page mimeographed insert describes seven-
year medical degree program in Bordeaux, Montpellier, Toulouse.

FrA   ------. Bulletin d'Information, no. 3 (1978-79), 4 pp.
11   Account of recent and coming events, programs. Comments by
president of CUAG on status and goals; charges that French government
has done little to help develop coherent program suited to French
Antilles and Guyane. Problems: buildings without professors, incomplete educational programs; lack of disciplines related to local
environment, insufficient research facilities. Cites obstacles to
progress toward "antillanization" of personnel and education.

FrA   ------. Bulletin d'Information, no. 4 (April-May 1979), 4 pp.
12   Account of recent and coming events, programs, scholarships
available. President of CUAG describes student disturbances; charges
that buildings were planned, built, and turned over to university
without participation of users, who could have discovered errors of
planners; difficulty of trying to share insufficient facilities and
personnel on two campuses. Summary of last University Council meeting.

FrA   ------. Rapport d'Activités 1977-1978. [Martinique and/or
13   Pointe-à-Pitre?: CUAG], 1978. 25 pp.
          Enrollment of 3,757 students, with 2,237 in law. Others in
humanities, exact sciences, economics, medicine and anthropology. Record of services (consultations) performed by office of information and
orientation, studies carried out, visits to secondary schools. Some
research on retention of students. WKU

FrA   "Centre Universitaire Antilles Guyane, 1977-1978." Mimeo-
14   graphed. Pointe-à-Pitre: Cellule d'Information et d'Orientation
du CUAG, [1977]. 17 pp.
          Campus in Guadeloupe offers degrees in general studies, law,
economics; in Martinique, the same plus arts and the humanities.
Physical and natural sciences in Guadeloupe. No mention of French
Guiana. WKU

FrA   COHEN, HABIBA S. Elusive Reform: The French Universities, 1968-
15   1978. Boulder, Colorado: Westview Press, 1978. 280 pp.
          Although Caribbean university centers are not included in
this careful description and evaluation of the French university system, they are to a degree products of changes--and resistance to
change--in metropolitan France. Reform efforts toward democratization
and more local autonomy were up against traditional elitist practice
and centralized authority. Useful data; good chapter notes; twenty-
page, up-to-date bibliography. KU

FrA   COMPERE, DANIEL. "Antilles-Guyane Françaises." Caribbean
16   Monthly Bulletin 12, no. 9 (September 1978): 20-22.
          Although creation of an educational and research unit in
medical science in the Antilles was authorized in 1975, conflict persists over implementation. Nineteen medical students from Guadeloupe
and Martinique were in metropolitan France by 1978. Conflict over
location and kind of facility needed, between doctors in Guadeloupe and
Martinique, islanders and metropolis.

FrA   CULTURAL SERVICES OF THE FRENCH EMBASSY. New York. "The French
17   System of Education." Education in France, special issue
([1963]), 29 pp.

Free compulsory education to age sixteen; degrees and diplomas granted by state after public examinations. Diagram of system.
Universities in each académie ["also Algeria"]. Nearly 7,000 (of
212,000) university students from "countries in French community"
studying in metropolitan France.

FrA   ------. "The Orientation of Higher Education Act No. 68-978,
18   Nov. 12, 1968." Education in France, no. 38 (January 1969): 1-
       29.
       Aims, structure of new system, provisions for implementing
the reform. Stress on autonomy and participation, increased science
and technology. Diagram: the university of tomorrow.

FrA   DELION, ANDRE G.; LE VEUGLE, JEAN; and LABORIE, SUZANNE. L'édu-
19   cation en France: Problèmes et Perspectives. Paris: La Docu-
       mentation Française, 1973. 207 pp.
       Section on higher education points out combinations of "ex-
treme centralism" and "extreme liberty"; describes structure of various
types of institutions. No mention of overseas universities per se.
UkLU-IE.

FrA   DREYFUS, F. G. "Problems of the French University." In The Task
20   of Universities in a Changing World, edited by Stephen D. Ker-
       tesz, pp. 287-305, 2d ed. South Bend: University of Notre Dame
       Press, 1972.
       Background for understanding French university system over-
seas. Useful comments by Philip E. Mosely on range of problems, especially those related to rapid growth and demand. KU

FrA   DUKE, ROSAMUNDE, and GRUYADINE, HONORE. "Harsh Realities of Our
21   Caribbean Experience." Caribbean Contact, (December 1979): 12.
       "French colonialism" blamed for recent violence against
Dominican refugees, with educational system viewed as a chief agent of
"cultural alienation." Comments on role of intellectuals; emigration
to mainland France, e.g., to complete university studies; independence
movement.

FrA   "Education in Martinique." The Caribbean 11, no. 6 (January
22   1958): 126-28.
       Seventy-fifth anniversary, in 1956, of the inauguration of
general education in Martinique, with same methods and principles as in
metropolitan France. Nearly one-fourth of the island's population in
school, with a higher rate of school age population in school than in
metropolitan France. Describes ties to metropolitan France, e.g., in
staffing schools. Implications for higher education important.

       EINAAR, J. F. E. "Education in the Netherlands and French West
       Indies." See entry NeA 6.

FrA   GAUSSEN, FREDERIC. "The Human Cost of French University Ex-
23   pansion: Academics without Careers." Minerva 11, no. 3 (July
       1973): 372-86.
       Lack of planning, hierarchical teaching staff conduce to lack
of career fulfillment for great percentage of aspirants to teaching
profession. Enrollment expansion rate now constant, surplus of lower-

level lecturers. Detail of advanced degree requirements and lengthy
waiting for completion.

FrA   GEIGER, ROGER L. A Retrospective View of the Second-cycle Reform
24   in France. Yale Higher Education Research Group Working Paper
      (YHERG), 18. New Haven, Conn.: Yale University, Institute for
      Social and Policy Studies, 1977. 19 pp.
         Tangled themes of politics, ideology, power struggles, di-
      vided authority and responsibilities, centralization and autonomy,
      employability of university graduates, loss of quality and diminished
      reputation of institutions set forth. Efforts to democratize fall on
      hard times with 1976 reform, intended to fit university education to
      labor market. Depreciation of degrees hurts middle and lower-middle
      class aspirants. WKU

FrA   GRESLE, FRANÇOIS. Les Enseignants et l'école; une analyse socio-
25   démographique des instituteurs et des professeurs de la Martinique.
      Les Cahiers du CERAG, no. 19 [Fort-de-France]: Centre d'Etudes
      Régionales Antilles-Guyane, 1969. 157 pp.
         Overview of Martinique's educational system reveals special
      problems: youthful population; greatly expanded primary system; young,
      insufficiently prepared teachers; older, conservative teachers; social
      system reflected in educational system which perpetuates class differ-
      ences, leaves poor at a disadvantage. Concludes that entire system
      needs "rejuvenation," especially to improve entry into, retention in
      and better performance of secondary schools. DLC

FrA   HALLS, WILFRED DOUGLAS. Society, Schools and Progress in France.
26   Oxford, New York: Pergamon, 1965. 194 pp.
         Movement after World War II to democratize education, but
      still small percentage of laborers' or farmers' children get to uni-
      versities, especially compared to British. Conflicts over democrati-
      zation vs. quality. Battle to meet overwhelming increase in student
      numbers in recent years. Information on French educational structure;
      overseas departments not specifically mentioned. DLC

FrA   HEARNDEN, ARTHUR. Paths to University: Preparation, Assessment,
27   Selection. Basingstoke and London: Macmillan Education Ltd.,
      1973. 165 pp.
         Efforts to democratize French education focused on change
      from selection of academically able children at age eleven for the
      lycée as being "classist," irrevocable. Development of (and resistance
      to) new type of comprehensive school, collège d'enseignement secon-
      daire, in 1963, designed for eleven- to fifteen-year-olds, should give
      more chances for university entry to less advantaged. Chapter one has
      diagrams and explanations of difficulties at university level.
      Chapters six through eight compare British practices and problems,
      including the external written examinations, most of which prevail in
      the West Indies. (Other chapters are on West Germany, Sweden, the
      U.S.A., and the U.S.S.R.). DLC

FrA   KING, EDMUND JAMES. Other Schools and Ours: A Comparative Study
28   for Today. 3d ed. New York: Holt, Rinehart Winston, 1967.
      360 pp.
         Chapter 3, "France, the Central Light of Reason," describes
      organization of French educational system, changes, problems. KU

FrA   LEGENDRE, BERTRAND. "Le baccalauréat: Un examen à toute
29   épreuve..." Le Monde de l'Education (June 1976): 6-8.
       Debate over national baccalaureate examination used since
1968 and due for 1980 change. Impact on university attendance.
Problems of lycées and socio-economic class distinctions.

FrA   "Letter from Guadeloupean Student." Caribbean Contact, (March
30   1980): 9.
       "Patriotic young intellectuals" studying in France denounce
"French imperialism in Guadeloupe and the Caribbean region in general."
Part of growing resistance to metropolitan control of overseas
departments.

       MATHEWS, THOMAS. "Report for UNICA on a Visit to the Centre
       Universitaire Antilles-Guyane in April 1976." See entry GEN 185.

FrA   MCCLAY, SHELBY T. The Negro in the French West Indies. Lexing-
31   ton: University of Kentucky Press, 1966. 278 pp.
       Few pages on education indicate some normal school studies in
certain lycées in 1950s. French government "wisely" sends "capable"
youth to Paris for post-secondary education. Some comparison with
Haiti. KU

FrA   MOODY, JOSEPH N. French Education Since Napoleon. Syracuse,
32   N.Y.: Syracuse University Press, 1978. 252 pp.
       Example of interrelatedness of education with social and
political values and events. Nothing on French Antilles per se but
indications of patterns to prevail there. KU

FrA   MURCH, ARVIN. Black Frenchmen: The Political Integration of the
33   French Antilles. Cambridge, Mass.: Schenkman Publishing Co.,
       1971. 156 pp.
       Post World War II push for full French citizenship for people
in French Antilles, resultant retention of metropolitan patterns and
control of education. Growth from 98 to 1,500 students in Martinique's
University Center and similar growth in Guadeloupe. Nearly double the
proportion of students to population in French islands to those in
British territories in West Indies. Praises French social justice in
promoting racial harmony. KU

FrA   PATTERSON, MICHELLE. "Governmental Policy and Equality in Higher
34   Education: The Junior Collegization of the French University."
       Social Problems 24, no. 2 (December 1970): 173-83.
       Problem of equity of access not solved by expansion of lower
level, vocationally oriented post-secondary system. Necessary background for understanding inquietudes affecting French Antilles
university professors, administrators, students.

FrA   Problèmes universitaires des Antilles-Guyane Françaises. Les
35   Cahiers du CERAG, no. 18. [Fort-de-France]: Centre d'Etudes
       Régionales Antilles-Guyane, 1969. 112 pp.
       Editor comments on various aspects of university problems in
French Antilles. New (1968) law on orientation of education raises
important issues for the university. Vice President, Jean Rosaz, takes
global perspective on school-society relations, emphasizes regional

needs: importance of Creole language study; Caribbean biological, economic and social science development with applied research and student involvement. University seen as development leader; calls for cooperation with other research units such as one in Trinidad at UWI. Studies about students in university centers in Martinique and Guadeloupe. DLC

FrA "University Reform in France: Statement of Principles of the
36 Higher Education Bill" and "The Higher Education Law of 12 November 1968." Minerva 7, no. 4 (Summer 1969): 706-12.
    Bill addresses flaws in current system and proposes changes for structural reorganization. Text of law describes mission of higher education, university institutions, governance, autonomy, finance, teaching staff.

Guatemala

GUA "Actividades del Instituto de Investigaciones Económicas y
1 Sociales de Occidente del Centro Universitario de Occidente,
Quezaltenango, de la Universidad de San Carlos de Guatemala."
Universidades 77 (July-September 1979): 798-802.
 Research, since 1973, directed at problems of this largely
indigenous population in western Guatemala on such topics as capital
formation, role of different institutions, use of resources. Current
topics include the agricultural crisis, food sanitation, health and the
psychological study of popular movements.

GUA "Acuerdo de Solidaridad." Presencia Universitaria, no. 46 (Oc-
2 tober 1978): 15.
 The Federation of University Students of Central America
(FEUCA), meeting in Panama, passes resolution deploring assassination
of the secretary general of Guatemala's Association of University
Students by paramilitary bands operating with government tolerance.
Victim was participating in anniversary celebration of the 1944 revo-
lution in Guatemala. Reported in Honduran university publication.

GUA BAUER PAIZ, ALFONSO. La penetración extranjera en la universi-
3 dad. Versión grabada de la disertación pronunciada por el autor
el 2 octubre de 1968, con ocasión del II Congreso Jurídico de
Estudiantes Centroamericanos en el Salón Mayor de la Facultad de
Ciencias Jurídicas y Sociales de la Universidad de San Carlos de
Guatemala. [Guatemala, 1968]. 71 pp.
 Economic domination determines Central American political and
cultural dependency, especially on the U.S. Attacks Inter-American
Development Bank and Organization of American States as supporters of
non-democratic university system; calls Consejo Superior Universitario
Centroamericano (CSUCA) an agent of U.S. penetration, along with USAID,
CARE, the Ford Foundation and several U.S. universities. Example of
polemic which aborted General Studies program at San Carlos. TxU

GUA BEACHY, DEBRA. "Guatemalan Academics in Exile Describe Threats,
4 Terrorist Attacks." The Chronicle of Higher Education, 12 January 1981, p. 21.
 Rector and dean of school of education resigned, fled to
Mexico; among few academics to escape right-wing terrorist attacks
which rector says are part of violence against University of San Carlos
ever since 1954 CIA-backed coup against elected government.

GUê   BRANAS, CESAR. <u>Jalones en el camino de la reforma universitaria</u>.
5   Prologue to <u>Discursos universitarios, 1945-1955</u> by Carlos Martí-
      nez Durán. [Guatemala: Universidad de San Carlos de Guatemala,
      1950]. 13 pp.
            Milestones cited in this introduction to a collection of
      speeches by Rector Carlos Martinez Duran of the Universidad de San
      Carlos begin with the 1918 university reform movement in Cordoba,
      Argentina. San Carlos remained traditionally fragmented in its sepa-
      rate faculties and backward. The 1944 Youth Movement helped achieve
      autonomy. Strong leadership of Martinez Duran described and praised.
      [Bound separately from <u>Discursos, 1945-1955</u>.] TxU

GUA   CONGRESO UNIVERSITARIO LATINOAMERICANO (1st: 1949: Guatemala).
6   <u>Actas del Primer Congreso de Universidades Latinoamericanas (15
      de septiembre de 1949)</u>. Guatemala: USC, 1949. 146 pp.
            Eight Caribbean countries were represented in hemispheric
      meeting sponsored by San Carlos' Rector Carlos Martinez Duran. Topics
      for discussion included autonomy and relations of universities and
      governments, academic and administrative organizational problems, co-
      ordination among Latin American universities and within systems of
      education, social action, and others. After ten days of work, approved
      resolutions to have considerable impact over next decades. DLC

GUA   CUEVAS DEL CID C., RAFAEL. <u>Discursos universitarios, 1970-1974</u>.
7   Guatemala: [Universidad de San Carlos de Guatemala], 1974.
            Speeches by rector on public occasions with themes such as
      university reform, social change, finance, autonomy, sports, mission of
      the university. Nothing specific, controversial, or illuminating. TxU

GUA   "Decreto Número 10." <u>El Guatemalteco</u> 141, no. 86 (7 July 1954).
8   Autonomy enjoyed by University of San Carlos is incomplete,
      lacking guaranteed money from national budget. Decree of governing
      junta orders Ministry of Budget to set aside annually 2 percent of the
      amount of the general budget for USC. Lt. Col. Castillo Armas also
      lifts state of siege after earlier overthrow of government.

GUA   FERNANDEZ, ALFREDO. "Los estudios generales: El principio del
9   final." <u>Nuestro Pueblo y la Universidad</u> 1, no. 1 (August 1968):
      15.
            Vigorous attack by students against the general studies
      program of the University of San Carlos in Guatemala made likely the
      end of the program. Objection was that the basic general arts and
      sciences program was brought from the U.S. All of the universities in
      Central America were influenced, but the attack had most impact on the
      University of San Carlos.

GUA   FERRUS ROIG, FRANCISCO. <u>General Mayor de la Universidad de San
10   Carlos en Guatemala de la Asunción: Reseña histórica, años 1778-
      1961</u>. Guatemala: Universidad de San Carlos, 1972. 92 pp. plus
      12 pages of photographs.
            Chiefly architectural history of principal building of Uni-
      versity of San Carlos, but interwoven with political and geological
      events. KU

GUA   FRIEDMAN, BURTON DEAN. El estudiante universitario: Progreso
11   académico de los estudiantes de la Universidad de San Carlos de
      Guatemala. Guatemala: IIME, 1964. 84 pp.
         Collaborating with the office of the registrar, IIME used
data collected in 1963 to analyze academic progress of 5,036 reenrolled
students. Average student requires 13.32 years to complete degree
programs designed for 6.14 years duration. Poor productivity is evident: in 1963, only 3.82 percent of San Carlos students graduated.
WKU

GUA   GONZALEZ ORELLANA, CARLOS. Historia de la educación en Guatemala.
12   México, D.F.: Colección Científica Pedagógica, 1960. 462 pp.
         Education in Guatemala from the Maya-Quiché through 1524
Spanish conquest to 1954, and from elementary to higher education.
Especially useful material covers the democratic revolution from 1944
to 1954. Gonzalez has sympathetic point of view to ideas of Juan Jose
Arevalo, the president who had been teacher and professor during his
years of exile in Argentina. WKU

GUA   ------. Principales problemas de la pedagogía universitaria.
13   Guatemala: Universidad de San Carlos, Biblioteca de Estudios
      Pedagógicos, 1962. 111 pp.
         Sees university as having responsibility in national life,
with need for change in methods of teaching/learning. Essays on
science and humanities, research, improving pedagogy. TxU

GUA   GUZMAN BOCKLER, CARLOS. "Colonialismo, violencia y universidad."
14   América Latina 13, no. 1 (January-March 1970): 3-17.
         Using University of San Carlos as example, argues that uni-
versities can make few academic improvements because colonialized,
"servile bourgeoisie" see university as source of social mobility
rather than knowledge.

GUA   LANNING, JOHN TATE. The University in the Kingdom of Guatemala.
15   Ithaca, N.Y.: Cornell University Press, 1955. 331 pp.
         Valuable for understanding the sixteenth century institution
implanted and controlled by the Spanish crown not only in Guatemala but
elsewhere in Latin America. Many of its patterns persist; as evidence,
see Lanning's glossary for terms still in use. Reveals much about
attitudes and value systems within and without the university, in very
agreeable prose. WSU

GUA   MARTINEZ DURAN, CARLOS. Discursos universitarios, 1958-1962.
16   Guatemala: Universidad de San Carlos de Guatemala, 1962. 229
      pp.
         Prologue by Alberto Velazquez describes and lauds Rector
Martinez Duran's career on occasion of his 1962 retirement. Over
thirty of his speeches show strong humanistic values, breadth of
knowledge, dedication to ideals. Describes, especially in last speech,
rifts within the university and tensions with the government; cites
rising enrollments, lack of funds. One of founders and promoters of
Consejo Superior Universitario Centroamericano (CSUCA), he urges
regional universities to collaborate. TxU

GUA   ------. Dos conferencias. Guatemala: [Universidad de San
17   Carlos de Guatemala], Imp. Sánchez y de Guise, 1939. 16 pp.

Urges graduating medical students to "research the biotypology of the criolla race" which has "reproduced the sexual miracle of Attica," with the superior men of Spain mated to the pure Indian maidens. Lavish seventeenth century ceremonies at San Carlos described in detail of costume, decor, personae. TxU

GUA ------. "La universidad." Mundo Hispánico extraordinario no. 10
18 (1957): 49.
"The virile and eternal voice of the students always proclaims [the university's] autonomy. And on the first of December 1944, the tradition was being reborn." The former rector of San Carlos waxes enthusiastic over the end of the dictatorship and coming of Guatemala's new president, universitario Juan Jose Arevalo.

GUA MATA GAVIDIA, JOSE. Docencia en forma de investigación. Es-
19 tudios Universitarios, vol. 2. Guatemala: Universidad de San Carlos de Guatemala, 1967. 62 pp.
Advocates combining research with teaching function in contrast to traditional methods in Latin American universities, which are dominated by attitudes of professional schools. Research is not a luxury or an extra function within the cultural being, but a necessity for the scientific, economic, socio-political, educational, and esthetic character of a nation. TxU

GUA ------. Fundación de la universidad en Guatemala, 1548-1688.
20 Guatemala: Universidad de San Carlos, Consejo Superior Universitario, 1954. 388 pp.
Philosopher weaves together chronology of events with their cultural complexities in relating the creation of the forerunners of contemporary Universidad de San Carlos. Cultural and social factors of sixteenth and seventeenth centuries, such as the Indian presence, power of crown and church, rise of Creole culture taken into account of university's organization, student body, academic offerings. Good documentation, illustrations. WKU

GUA MINISTERIO DE EDUCACION, Oficina de Planeamiento Integral de la
21 Educación (OPIE). Plan Nacional de Educación para la República de Guatemala (Cuadrienio 1969-1972). Guatemala: Editorial "José de Pineda-Ibarra," 1969. 391 pp.
Section on higher education, pages 162-72, presented in context of entire national system of education. Much useful data. Universidad de San Carlos Instituto de Investigación y Mejoramiento Educativo, IIME, discovers that 13.4 percent of its enrollees graduate, that a degree program of six years requires an average of fourteen years to complete. KU

GUA MONTOVANI, JUAN. Misión de la universidad en nuestra época.
22 Publicación no. 1, serie A. Guatemala: Universidad de San Carlos, Facultad de Humanidades, 1946. 32 pp.
Eloquent statement by Argentine educator in support of university autonomy: "Only to the dictators, generally strangers to high personal culture, does it occur to limit university scientific work and teaching." Praises democratically elected President Arevalo and his support for humanistic education, which guarantees that human beings are more than technicians. First anniversary of achievement of autonomy for University of San Carlos. NmLcU

GUA   OSORIO PAZ, SAUL. "Educación y empleo." <u>Universidades</u> 77 (July-
23   September 1979): 678-95.
         Rector of Universidad de San Carlos de Guatemala, speaking to
UDUAL General Assembly in Mexico, describes economically "backward and
dependent" society which graduates enter. Data show concentrations of
wealth; graduates by field, 1965-78. Problems of unemployment, under-
employment; financial and political difficulties of university which,
along with "restrictions of democratic liberties," impede formation of
professionals needed by country.

GUA   PETERSEN, JOHN HOLGER. "Student Political Activism in Guatemala,
24   a Research Note." <u>Journal of Inter-American Studies and World
       Affairs</u> 13, no. 1 (January 1971): 78-88.
         Types of behavior among students in Guatemala in the Uni-
versity of San Carlos. Most political students are the oldest, in the
longer university careers, independent from parents, and from the lower
classes. Students from law, economics, and humanities are more active
than those in medicine, engineering, pharmacy, agronomy, architecture,
and veterinary medicine.

GUA   "Problemas financieros de la USAC." <u>7 Días en la USAC</u>, 26
25   February-4 March 1979, pp. 6-7.
         Round table in Faculty of Economic Sciences focuses on insuf-
ficient funds from the national budget to provide physical space for
students or to meet requirements for research. Tables show percentages
of national budget for universities in five Central American countries,
and relation between university budgets and numbers of students.

GUA   RODRIGUEZ CABAL, JUAN. <u>Universidad de Guatemala: Su origen,
26   fundación, organización</u>. Guatemala: Universidad de San Carlos
       de Guatemala, 1976. 522 pp.
         Part of tricentennial collection by Spanish priest, with
introduction by Carlos González Orellana, deals with sixteenth and
seventeenth centuries. IU

GUA   "Siguen las muestras de repudio al asesinato del Lic. Manuel
27   Andrade Roca." <u>7 Días en la USAC</u>, 26 February-4 March 1979, pp.
       4-5.
         Entities inside and outside the university protest assassi-
nation of an advisor to the secretary general and a law professor, as
part of a process of violent repression by rightists who control the
government against the country's intellectuals.

GUA   "Televisión educativa en Guatemala." <u>Repertorio Centro Ameri-
28   cano</u>, no. 1 (December 1964): 1-31.
         Dental School of San Carlos University begins first use of
closed circuit TV for scientific education in Central America.

GUA   TORGERSON, DIAL. "Teachers Become Targets of Guatemalan As-
29   sassins." <u>Miami Herald</u>, 15 June 1981, p. 3A.
         Thirty-four teachers killed in 1980, thirty-six so far in
1981. At San Carlos University many classes not offered because professors are targets. Military officer calls university "life breath of
the guerrilla movement." Most antigovernment leaders from educated
middle, upper middle classes.

GUA UNIVERSIDAD DE SAN CARLOS DE GUATEMALA (USC). Características
30 socio-económicas de los estudiantes del primer ingreso, 1971-
1973. Guatemala: Departamento de Registro y Estadística, Editorial Universidad, 1975. 109 pp.
Report on first-year students from the office of the registrar includes these data: father's education, mother's education,
housing, numbers in the family, economic dependency of the student,
monthly income, salary, relationship between study and work. KU

GUA ------. Catálogo de estudios 1963. Guatemala: USC, 1963. 369
31 pp. plus photos.
Courses of studies, by years, in the ten faculties, "a first
step for construction of a future volume" with more detail. Table of
organization. TxU

GUA ------. Catálogo 1967-1968. Guatemala: Oficina del Registro,
32 1967. 279 pp.
In 1964, Consejo Superior Universitario created Department of
Basic Studies (actually School of General Studies) which integrated the
first two years of seven of the ten faculties. Explained as an "up-to-
date move" in the university reform; describes resultant major changes
in programs, structures, teaching methods. General academic aspects;
description of faculties and schools, with their history, plans of
study; and description of courses in ten different faculties. Ten
pages on general studies. TxU

GUA ------. Catálogo 1974-1975. Guatemala: Departamento de Regis-
33 tro y Estadística. [1974]
There are ten faculties. No mention of general studies;
programs of study given according to professional schools. TxU

GUA ------. Catálogo de estudios 1976. Guatemala: Departamento de
34 Registro y Estadística, 1976. 483 pp.
Introduction by Registrar Felipe J. Mendizabal mentions
impact on populace of recent earthquake. History focuses on 1945
achievement of university autonomy. Complete information on academic
programs, professors, policies. General studies gone; students enter
directly into faculties, in accord with their already chosen vocation.
WKU

GUA ------. Catálogo de estudios 1979. No. 6. Guatemala: De-
35 partamento de Registro y Estadística. 555 pp.
History, goals, organization, programs of study, professors.
Seven regional university centers, most of them recently begun, are
described. (Last catalogue produced by long-time Registrar Lic. Felipe
J. Mendizábal before his assassination, victim of ongoing political
violence directed at university officials.) WKU

GUA ------. Comisión de Transformación Universitaria. Informe
36 final. Guatemala: Universidad de San Carlos de Guatemala, 1974.
95 pp.
To carry out functions of aiding national identity, over-
coming dependence, broadening base of education, university needs to be
more dynamic in its organization and administration. Commission proposes many changes, e.g., smaller top administrative unit,

decentralization of teaching function, inter-disciplinary centers, avoidance of excessive specialization, research linked to national needs, abolition of cátedras en propiedad. Organizational diagrams and flow chart. WKU

GUA ------. En torno a la universidad. Guatemala: Facultad de
37 Humanidades, 1967. 51 pp.
        Essays by three professors: "Goals of the University," "Basic Factors in Higher Education," and "The University and the Public Welfare," by Hugo Cerezo Dardon, Carlos E. Pomes, and Carlos Gonzalez Orellana respectively. This was an era of reform and counter reform-- at San Carlos. TxU

GUA ------. Guía orgánica de la Universidad de San Carlos de Guate-
38 mala. Guatemala: Imprenta Universitaria, 1952. 103 pp.
        The administrators of the university; a brief historical summary; academic calendar; the faculties of law and social sciences, medicine, engineering, chemistry and pharmacy, economics, dentistry, humanities, and agronomy; plans for new campus. KU

GUA ------. Labores realizadas durante el período 1950-1954.
39 Guatemala: USC, 1954. ca. 100 pp.
        Photos, from rector's office to children's wading pool. Enrollment in the eleven professional schools increased between 1950 and 1953 from 2,443 to 3,517 students. There were 459 graduates during this period. TxU

GUA ------. Labores realizadas durante el período 1954-1958.
40 Guatemala: USC, 1958. 156 pp. plus photos.
        Despite political turbulence (overthrow of the nation's e-lected President Arbenz), improvements continued, with a guarantee of 2 percent of national budget. New and expanded programs, including strengthened basic disciplines in humanities faculty. Considerable data on finance; 4,280 students; 449 graduates. TxU

GUA ------. Leyes, estatutos, y reglamentos generales de la Uni-
41 versidad de San Carlos de Guatemala, vigentes en la actualidad.
Guatemala: USC, 1961. 115 pp.
        Ten professional schools comprise the university, one of whose stated goals is "that it shall contribute to the spiritual linking of the peoples of the Central American isthmus, and to that end it will promote the exchange of professors and students." WKU

GUA ------. Ley orgánica y estatutos de la Universidad de San Car-
42 los, 1947. Guatemala: USC. 48 pp.
        Article I proclaims the university's autonomy; Article III says it will "contribute to carrying out the union of Central America . . . and will obtain the exchange of teachers and pupils . . ." Rules for governance and function of the seven faculties are given. TxU

GUA ------. Memoria de labores, 1962-1966. Guatemala: USC, 1966.
43 222 pp.
        Humanities faculty report details major structural reforms, function of departments, duties of professors, students, administrators. Emphasis on organization, systematizing. TxU

GUA   ------. 1963 Boletín estadístico universitario. No. 2. Guate-
44   mala: Oficina de Registro, 1963. 84 pp.
          Felipe Mendizabal describes activities of his office: pro-
duction of first San Carlos University catalogue; first university-wide
enrollment, with collection of socioeconomic data about students; first
statistical study of technical, teaching and administrative personnel;
publication of data for internal use and for international agencies.
Statistics presented with useful interpretive text. WKU

GUA   ------. 1976 Boletín estadístico universitario. No. 15.
45   Guatemala: Departamento de Registro y Estadística, 1976. 147
      pp.
          Tables, charts, complete description for year of San Carlos
and the rest of the Central American universities. WKU

GUA   ------. 1977 Boletín estadístico universitario. No. 1. Guate-
46   mala: Departamento de Registro y Estadística, 1978. 165 pp.
          Enrollment since 1945, by faculties, in San Carlos. Current
student population characteristics, including some demographic data on
1977 matriculating group; financial aid. Section IV gives graduates by
disciplines since 1950. Financial and staff information. Section VIII
has data on enrollment and budgets of both public and private universities for all of Central America. WKU

GUA   ------. Segundo censo estudiantil universitario, enero de 1963.
47   Guatemala: USC, Oficina de Registro, 1963. 20 pp.
          Personal, academic, familial, housing, income, work,
transportation information about the 6,183 students enrolled, compiled
by Felipe Mendizabal. Over one-third are heads of families, over one-
half are working, two-thirds are over 21 years of age. WKU

GUA   "Universidad de San Carlos inicia plan de estudios básicos
48   total." Repertorio Centro Americano, July 1965: 48 pp.
          All students will study basic sciences and humanities for two
years before entering professional schools. Represents a major reform
in university structure and function.

GUA   UNIVERSIDAD MARIANO GALVEZ DE GUATEMALA. Boletín estadístico
49   1980. Guatemala: Universidad Mariano Gálvez de Guatemala, 1981.
      36 pp. plus 8 graphs.
          Shows, among other things, rapid growth. Business adminis-
tration, law, engineering draw 1,437 of its 2,276 students. WKU

GUA   ------. Proyectos de desarrollo, 1980. Guatemala: Universidad
50   Mariano Gálvez, Oficina de planeamiento, 1980. 21 leaves.
          Demographic and geographic background, enrollments for all
Guatemalan universities. Evangelical university describes its organization, academic programs, financial resources for building new campus,
projects for teacher training, graduate study. WKU

GUA   UNIVERSIDAD RAFAEL LANDIVAR. Boletín Informativo, no. 1 (May
51   1968). 19 leaves.
          Planning office publication of Catholic University founded in
1961 gives student population data to 1968 and projections through
1978. Report on faculty of humanities. KU

GUA ------. Catálogo general de estudios 1973. Guatemala: URL,
52 1972. 376 pp.
First complete description of Catholic university, founded in
1961, giving history, academic, administrative, financial structure;
courses offered in six faculties; programs of study in capital and
outside. Statistical section shows growth from 318 to 2,414 students.
Plans for new campus. WKU

GUA ------. Una institución con 16 años de servicio a Guatemala.
53 Guatemala: URL, 1978. 8 pp.
Summary of accomplishments, data on new campus, careers
offered in seven faculties and departments in Guatemala City; four
regional centers offer various programs ranging from education to
technical training in agriculture. WKU

GUA ------. Facultad de Derecho. Cara Parens 1, no. 1 (July 1967).
54 First in series of trimestral publication pays homage to
Rafael Landivar and Ruben Darío; announces plan for students to work
with illiterates who comprise 87 percent of population in rural areas;
articles on general topics.

GUA ------. Cara Parens 2, no. 3 (March 1968).
55 Articles on lack of nationally written texts, dependence on
foreign sources; humanism in Guatemala; need for new economic policies.

GUA ------. Oficina de Relaciones Públicas. Boletín Oficial, no. 1
56 (20 May 1971)-no. 7 (20 January 1972).
Official bulletin of the university covers recent change in
rectors, selection of beauty queens, dates of enrollment in different
faculties. The ten-year-old university had 1,300 scholarship students
in 1971 out of a total of 2,230. Rules for examinations given.

GUA "University Official Murdered." San Jose News, June 20, 1980.
57 Registrar Felipe de Jesus Medizabal of University of San
Carlos shot near his home. Rightist groups killing people at university because they claim it is breeding ground for leftists. Mendizabal
produced annual statistical reports on San Carlos and Central America,
among best available in Latin America.

GUA VASQUEZ MARTINEZ, EDMUNDO. La universidad y la constitución.
58 Estudios Universitarios, vol. 1. Guatemala: Universidad de San
    Carlos de Guatemala, 1966. 46 pp.
Lectures, one on the occasion of his becoming rector of the
University of San Carlos, during which he argues the importance of
autonomy in the university, and the other a paper on the importance of
national problems to the university. TxU

GUA "El Vicepresidente de Guatemala solicitará protección para el
59 rector de la Universidad de San Carlos." Gaceta, no. 20 (May
    1979), p. 7.
Text of telegram to Guatemalan vice president seeking protection for rector of San Carlos, whose life is threatened, from representatives of the Unión de Universidades de América Latina (UDUAL), the
Confederación Universitaria Centroamericana (CSUCA) and the Federación
de Universidades Privadas de América Central (FUPAC).

Guyana

ASHBY, ERIC. Universities: British, Indian, African, A Study in the Ecology of Higher Education. See entry UWI 3.

GUY THE ASSOCIATION OF COMMONWEALTH UNIVERSITIES (ACU). Awards for
1   Commonwealth University Staff 1978-80. London: ACU. 228 pp.
     Sources of financial aid for academic and administrative
staff to do research, study, or teach in a commonwealth country other
than that in which they live. Companion to Scholarship Guide for
Commonwealth Postgraduate Students and Grants for Study Visits.
Examples of strength and continuity of links with England for University
of the West Indies and University of Guyana. UkLACU

      ------. Commonwealth Universities and Society: The Report of
      the Proceedings of the Eleventh Congress of the Universities of
      the Commonwealth, Edinburgh, August 1973. See entries UWI 4, 5.

GUY ------. Scholarship Guide for Commonwealth Postgraduate Students
2   1980-82. London: [1980], 326 pp.
     Over 1,100 award plans, including ones for postdoctoral
study, in commonwealth universities and non-university institutions,
for people studying in commonwealth countries other than their own.
Example of strong ties of English-speaking Caribbean territories with
metropolitan institutions. UkLACU

GUY BACCHUS, M. KASSIM. Education and Socio-cultural Integration in
3   a "Plural" Society. Occasional Paper Series, no. 6. Montreal:
     Centre for Developing-Area Studies, McGill University, 1970. 41
     pp.
     Differences in educational opportunities and cultural values
between post-slavery blacks and East Indians contributed to polarized
society. Using educational data of 1920-65, sees rapid changes after
1945 with more social integration resulting, and conflicts of 1960s as
part of a transition phase to greater integration. Says education has
reduced cultural cleavages. Important implications for understanding
University of Guyana. CaOTU

GUY ------. Education for Development or Underdevelopment? Guyana's
4   Educational System and its Implications for the Third World.

155

Development Perspectives, 2. Waterloo, Ontario: Wilfrid Laurier University Press, 1980. 302 pp.

Government of Guyana "like those in other LDCs, held the view that education in some unclear, unstated, and even miraculous way would by itself produce economic and social development." It did not. Carefully documented history of education from early colonial era into vastly expanded present system. Disaffections; effects on social relationships and expectations; analysis of and comments on economic factors to be faced in making reforms. KU

GUY   ------. "Education, Social Changes and Cultural Pluralism."
5   Sociology of Education 42, no. 4 (Fall 1969): 368-85.
        As structural changes took place in the society with increased social and political acceptance by East Indians, participation in all levels of education increased. Increase in British-educated East Indian lawyers and doctors eventually leveled off, with other ethnic groups entering professional education.

GUY   BAKSH, AHAMAD. "The Contribution of the Guyanese Educational
6   System to Socio-cultural Integration." Mimeographed. [Turkeyen]: UG, Department of Sociology, 1972. 18 pp.
        The "homogeneity function" of education is not realized at any level of education, including the university. Opines that what goes on in wider society has repercussions at school level. Parties formed at UG with openly "racial" bias, reflecting social and political reality of wider society in 1970. WKU

GUY   ------. "Education and Economic Development: The Relevance to
7   Guyana." Mimeographed. [Turkeyen]: UG, Department of Sociology, 1973. 41 pp.
        Accepts concept of education as means to development rather than for personal fulfillment, finds secondary and university levels still too weighted with British-derived "academic" subjects. Problem of educated unemployed possibly due to lack of skills needed for development and failure of economy to expand rapidly enough to use skilled people. High cost of producing arts and social sciences graduates perhaps an overly heavy burden in a poor country. WKU

GUY   ------. "The Mobility of Degree Level Graduates of the Universi-
8   ty of Guyana." Comparative Education 10, no. 1 (1974): 65-86.
        Indo-Guyanese and Afro-Guyanese value education for upward mobility. Common Entrance Exam discriminates against rural and lower income children. UG catering primarily to lower income groups, possibly because it has been an evening institution. Ratio of Indo-Guyanese to Afro-Guyanese graduates decreased between 1968-70 and 1970-72, from 66.9 percent to 57 percent, but Afro-Guyanese were more mobile before and after graduation; 67.6 percent of the sample of graduates feel they experienced a rise in status and prestige.

GUY   ------. "The Pattern of Higher Education at the University of
9   Guyana, 1963-1964 to 1971-1972." Mimeographed . [Turkeyen]: UG, [1973]. 35 pp.
        Analysis of data on enrollment, academic programs, populace served, national origins of faculty in context of egalitarianism and national needs. Predominantly Indo-Guyanese teachers and civil servants during most of the period, but more secondary school graduates

entering. Graduates have relevant qualifications, with degree and diploma programs, but economy not expanding fast enough to employ them. WKU

GUY   BRITISH GUIANA. "Memorandum by the Ministers of Education and
10   Social Development on Higher Education." First Legislature under
       the British Guiana (constitution) Order in Council, 1961. Ses-
       sional Paper no. 2, 1963. Mimeographed. 10 leaves.
          Needs for the establishment of a separate university in
British Guiana: example of 500 secondary teachers, of whom 366 were
unqualified, and the average cost of graduates of the University of the
West Indies in Jamaica, based on the Guyanese government contribution
to the UWI, is estimated to be $80,000 (Guyanese dollars). Plans for
development began with the College of Arts and Sciences in 1963.
Criticism of the existing higher education in the West Indies. UkLU-IE

GUY   ------. Suspension of the Constitution, A Report Presented to
11   the Secretary of State for the Colonies and Parliament. London:
       HMSO, 1953. 20 pp.
          Previous April's election under the new constitution led to
class war and "racial hatred." Cheddi Jagan was minister of agriculture; Forbes Burnham, the minister of education. Ideological and
economic split. Fear of Communist ties of Dr. Jagan and his wife;
their activities documented. Broadcast by Governor followed by singing
of "God Save the Queen." Same actors on the stage in the '80s, shaping
ambiance of UG. UkLU-IE

GUY   ------. "White Paper on Educational Policy." Mimeographed.
12   [Georgetown], 1963. 16 pp.
          Stresses equality of opportunity; aim to establish secondary
comprehensive schools throughout the country, as resources permit,
beginning in September 1963. Successful completion of five-year course
would have academic examination qualifications for admittance to higher
education at University of Guyana. Effort to end Christian denominational control (with government subsidy) of school system. October
1963 date for establishing a College of Arts and Sciences as first step
to establishment of the University of Guyana. UkLU-IE

GUY   CAMERON, NORMAN E. 150 Years of Education in Guyana (1808-1957).
13   Georgetown: University of Guyana, 1968. 91 pp. Reprinted 1971.
          Foreword by Lancelot Hogben identifies author as first pro-
fessor of mathematics at UG. Well researched, humanely written account
of education in its social dimension, reflecting value systems in a
slave and post-slave culture. Essential for understanding milieu out
of which local institutions developed into UWI and UG and the roles of
churches and governments. WKU

GUY   CARIBBEAN EXAMINATIONS COUNCIL (CXC). Report for 1976.
14   [Bridgetown]: The Council, 1976. 24 leaves.
          Fourth anniversary of establishment of Caribbean Examinations
Council (CXC). Duties: Preparation of examination regulations, development of syllabi, matters relating to appointment of examiners, and
other matters. Goal of 1979 examinations, locally developed, with help
from official examining bodies in Scotland, Cambridge, University of
London, Princeton. UkLACU

"CXC Grows." See entry UWI 36.

GUY ------. Report for 1978. [Bridgetown]: The Council, 1978. 38
15 leaves.
Vast task of preparing for first exams in 1979, with most
significant accomplishment being the setting up of question papers,
with one British and one Caribbean moderator for each subject. List of
Council and Committee members, and national committees; staff and
budget. UkLACU

GUY ------. Secondary Education Certificates Fact Sheet. St.
16 Michael's, Barbados: The Council, [1978]. 16 pp.
Introduction, by Dennis Irvine, vice-chancellor, University
of Guyana, and chairman, Caribbean Examinations Council (CXC), explains
the Caribbean Secondary Education Certificate Examinations, to be
offered for the first time in 1979. Fourteen governments' representatives attempt common syllabi in English, history, geography, mathematics, integrated sciences. Exams for completion of five years of
secondary school; general proficiency in one, or more than one, 'O'
level. Will be accepted for university entry as equivalent of the
traditional General Certificate of Education (GCE) (originating in
Britain). A milestone on the way to more Caribbean control of its
higher and secondary education. UkLACU

GUY "Committee of Concerned Educators Attack New Move at UG."
17 Caribbean Contact, Vol. 6, no. 3. (July 1978): 6.
Resistance of University of Guyana faculty members and officers to "politically controlled" Admission Council for Higher Education
(ACHE). Council proposes lowering admissions standards and requiring
"desirable social attitudes" for matriculants, which critics see as
political loyalty test to Burnham government.

THE COMMONWEALTH FOUNDATION. Reports on Visit of a Working Party
to Universities in Ghana, Nigeria, and Sierra Leone, January-
February 1973. See entry UWI 31.

GUY "Commonwealth Universities today: A Special Report": Times
18 Higher Education Supplement (12 August 1983): pp. 15-23.
Good overview on occasion of Commonwealth Universities
thirteenth Congress, in England. UG's "most recent sign of discontent"
against Guyanese government's political control plus the economic crisis lead to academic staff's boycott of graduation ceremony and resignation of Vice Chancellor Dennis Irvine.

GUY Commonwealth Universities Yearbook. London: Association of the
19 Universities of the British Commonwealth. 1958 .
After 1962 separation of the University of Guyana from UWI,
the Yearbook began entries on UG. In the 1980 issue, e.g., it had
information on administration and teaching staff, greater Georgetown,
UG's constitution, income, site, library (115,000 volumes), first
degrees, diplomas, academic year, publications. Statistics for 1977,
degrees awarded. KU

GUY The Co-operative Republic of Guyana. A Digest of Educational
20 Statistics, 1973-1974: With a Ten Year Review. Georgetown, The

Planning Unit, Ministry of Education and Social Development, 1975. 207 pp.
    Since founding in 1963 University of Guyana has graduated 610 people in degree courses and 557 in certificate and diploma courses. Data on courses, enrollment, staff, and costs. UkLU-IE

GUY   CRITCHLOW, GLADSTONE O. <u>A Digest of Educational Statistics 1974-</u>
21   <u>1975</u>. Georgetown: Ministry of Education and Social Development Planning Office, 1976. 183 pp.
    One hundred years of education, ten years of independence from Britain, fourteen years of the University of Guyana. For 1974-75: 185 degrees, 203 certificates and diplomas, for total of 1,557 since 1966. Chronology of events in higher education. UkLU-IE

GUY   CURTIS, S. J. <u>History of Education in Great Britain</u>. 7th ed.
22   London: University Tutorial Press, 1967. 774 pp.
    Comprehensive description from before the Reformation to 1960 shows structures and implicit values carried on through education at all levels. Useful for understanding education in the Commonwealth, though there is no mention of overseas territories. Chapter seventeen, on recent developments, including problem of eleven-plus exam and increase in numbers with access to universities, is enlightening. UkLU-IE

GUY   DAVID, WILFRED L. <u>The Economic Development of Guyana, 1953-1964</u>.
23   Oxford: Clarendon Press, 1969. 399 pp.
    Points to high unemployment, insufficient investment in education for adequate development: 1952, over 3 million dollars (Guyanese) for education; 1964, 10.8 million. Greater Georgetown (the capital) with more than one-fourth of the population has two-thirds of the pupil population. "The country is paying for its past neglect of teachers and professional training." Absolute increase at University level of public funds for public service training. UkLU-IE

GUY   DESPRES, LEO A. "Cultural Pluralism and Nationalist Politics in
24   British Guiana." In <u>Studies in Political Change</u>, Edited by Myron Weiner. Chicago: Rand McNally, 1967. 310 pp.
    Contemporary polarized society derived from racial and cultural rivalry during independence movement, with roots in African slavery and East Indian indentured servitude. The educational system is largely Christian denominational with government support; the alienated, largely rural Indian population has remained outside the system. UkLU-IE

    FIGUEROA, PETER M. E., and PERSUAD, GANGE, eds. <u>Sociology of Education, A Caribbean Reader</u>. London: Oxford University Press, 1976. 284 pp. See entry UWI 48.

GUY   GOMES, L. H. B. "Strategy and Constraints in Educational
25   Planning: The Case of Guyana." Mimeographed. [Georgetown]: [n.p.], 1969. 10 pp.
    The strategy was to develop free secondary education after 1962 to '0' level; constraints were financial. Description of increased demand, insufficiency of prepared teachers. UkLU-IE

GREAT BRITAIN. Commission on Higher Education in the Colonies. Report of the Commission on Higher Education in the Colonies. See entry UWI 58.

------. West Indies Committee. Report of the West Indies Committee on Higher Education in the Colonies. See entry UWI 59.

GUY 26 "Guyana." Caribbean Monthly Bulletin 13, nos. 1-2 (January-February 1979): 23-28.
    Includes paragraph about University of Guyana. The Association of Professional Engineers complains of lack of any engineering graduates for two successive years, and two newspapers call for investigating charges of University of Guyana admissions based on race and politics.

GUY 27 HAMMOND, S. A. Memoranda, British Guiana--Education. Georgetown, Demerara: The Authority of the Governor, 1942. 61 pp.
    Highest level of education is secondary; Queen's College (for boys) is maintained by the government, the Bishop's High School (for girls) is grant-aided. All references to British structures; needs for local references. Queen's College is the only university prep school. Urges a "considerable degree of education" for girls in addition to homemaking courses. UkLU-IE

GUY 28 INGOLD, C. T. "The overseas Postgraduate." Overseas Universities, no. 20 (November 1973): 14-17.
    Dennis Irvine, vice-chancellor of the University of Guyana, comments on the Working Party of Inter-University Council Report. Asks definition of "breadth of training" recommendation for Ph.D., and questions changing content of the program. Not a brain drain but inadequate facilities overseas hamper research, urges "related work experiences for a student prior to his postgraduate training"; agrees on importance of "special training for persons who are likely to end up as university teachers."

GUY 29 INTERNATIONAL COMMISSION OF JURISTS. Racial Problems in the Public Service. Report of the British Guiana Commission of Inquiry. Geneva: International Commission of Jurists, 1965. 199 pp.
    Complaints originated with Indians against Africans. Rapid demographic increase after 1946, literacy improvement, increased education; now 50 percent of the population wants fairer treatment. British troops called in to quell racial disorders. Education especially needed to cope with racial/political turbulence. Good background for understanding UG's early years. UkLU-IE

GUY 30 INTER-UNIVERSITY COUNCIL FOR HIGHER EDUCATION OVERSEAS (IUC). IUC and Related Services, A Guide. 2nd ed. London: ACU, 1978. 53 pp.
    British government established the IUC in 1946 to aid universities in developing countries and foster cooperation among United Kingdom and territorial universities. London-based staff channels aid, technical assistance. Main focus: help in staffing overseas universities. Provides strong, conspicuous link with metropolitan power. UkLACU

GUY   ------. Reports of the Vice-Chancellors' Conference, March 1979,
31   Jamaica. London: ACU, [1979]. 30 pp.
       Guyana and the University of the West Indies were repre-
sented. Keynote address: need for international cooperation, problems
of food, inaction; importance of Third World; universities and development. UkLACU

GUY   ------. Vice-Chancellors' Conference, Summer 1976, Aspen,
32   Colorado. [London]: ACU, 1976. 77 pp.
       Carnegie Corporation and U.S. State Department sponsored
conference, with topics centered on universities and national development in Africa, Asia and the Caribbean. Common problems: access,
financing, staffing, research and graduate study. UkLACU

GUY   IRVINE, DENNIS H. Address on the Occasion of the Official
33   Opening of the University Campus at Turkeyen, ECD, on Tuesday,
       24th February 1970. Turkeyen: University of Guyana, 1970. 8
       pp.
       Vice-chancellor celebrates opening of campus with thanks to
Governments of Guyana, Canada, United Kingdom, and Bookers Group of
Companies for financing it. Remarks center on need to balance
teaching, research, service. WKU

GUY   ------. "The University and National Development: Case History
34   Guyana." Typescript. Turkeyen Campus, Georgetown: University
       of Guyana, 20 September 1977. 14 pp.
       Vice-chancellor and principal describes university's concept
of its role in society; moves away from traditional metropolitan model,
serving older clientele with half of students earning certificates and
diplomas in areas related to work. Autonomy in traditional sense
foregone in order to collaborate with government to meet national needs
and gain necessary financial aid. WKU

GUY   ------. "Vice-Chancellor's Address to the Graduates of the
35   Thirteenth Convocation Ceremony on Saturday, 10th November 1979."
       Photocopy of typescript. Georgetown, Turkeyen Campus: Universi-
       ty of Guyana. 11 pp.
       "If 1978-79 has taught us anything it is that a university in
a developing country is a fragile entity. . . ." Survival and even
some successes in the face of economic deprivation and other vicissitudes. National role and regional participation in Caribbean Examinations Council, Association of Commonwealth Universities and other
entities. WKU

GUY   JAGAN, CHEDDI. The West on Trial: My Fight for Guyana's Freedom.
36   London: Michael Joseph, 1966. 471 pp.
       Autobiography of one of Guyana's two most prominent leaders
has useful information on universities, especially Howard University
and Northwestern University, which he attended in the U.S.; more on
aspects of education in Guyana in his youth and after his return to
Guyana. UkLU-IE

GUY   KABDEBO, THOMAS, and STEPHENSON, YVONNE. "The University of
37   Guyana Library: Past, Present and Future." Library Association
       Record 72, no. 7 (July 1970): 258-60.

University born when country, attaining nationhood, lived with turmoil, uncertainty. Details of building both university and its library presented in useful detail by librarian from University College London and UG reference librarian.

GUY   LEMKE, DONALD A.   "Education in the English Speaking Caribbean."
38   Preliminary version, prepared for UNESCO. Mimeographed.
      Santiago de Chile: UNESCO Regional Education Office for Latin
      America and the Caribbean, June 1975. 84 pp.
      Effects of the colonial legacy on the educational system; national education programs in Barbados, Guyana, Jamaica, Trinidad and Tobago; regional educational movements. Problems created by tying curriculum and teaching methods to examination system. Private school patterns dominated all education, and there is little vocational education.

GUY   LEWIS, [W.] ARTHUR.   Installation Address by the Chancellor.
39   Georgetown: University of Guyana, 1967. 15 pp.
      Economic component of education in development demands university preparation, even in small institution such as UG. Goals of excellence, autonomy, democracy. FU

GUY   LOGAN, DOUGLAS.   "The Commonwealth Scholarship and Fellowship
40   Plan." Overseas Universities no. 11, (November 1966: 7-9).
      Outgrowth of 1958 Commonwealth Trade and Economic Conference in Montreal and 1959 Oxford Conference was the establishment of the Commonwealth Scholarship Commission with over 500 current scholarships at any one time in the United Kingdom and 250 new awards each year. Quotes definition of the Commonwealth as a "loose association of states held together by the University of London."

GUY   MINISTRY OF EDUCATION AND SOCIAL DEVELOPMENT.   "Education and
41   Training." In 1972-1976 Development Plan, pp. 325-37. Mimeo-
      graphed. Georgetown: Ministry of Education and Social
      Development, [1972].
      Summary of plans for primary, secondary, higher education. University of Guyana to maintain internationally acceptable standards, meet local needs. Establishment of extramural studies, continued overseas preparation for faculty. Projected capital expenditures. WKU

GUY   ------.   "Regional Cooperation in Education, Meeting of Edu-
42   cational Planning Officers, November 6-8, 1974: Background
      Information and Materials." Mimeographed. Georgetown, 1974.
      115 pp.
      Useful insight into practices and policies for teacher education--which ignore the existence of the University of Guyana and apparently duplicate some of its functions. WKU

GUY   ------.   The Planning Unit. The Co-operative Republic of Guyana,
43   a Digest of Educational Statistics, 1973-1974. Georgetown: The
      Ministry, 1975. 207 pp.
      Teacher preparation in the University of Guyana and other programs. Organization of Guyana's educational system with enrollment and staff data. Nine faculties with nine-fold increase in staff since 1963. Relations with University of the West Indies for certain

degrees. Since 1966, University of Guyana has produced 1,167 graduates, about half in certificate and diploma courses. UkLU-IE

GUY ------. Education Makes a Nation: A Digest of Educational
44 Statistics 1974-1975. Georgetown: The Ministry, 1976. 183 pp.
Commemorates 100 years of compulsory elementary education and tenth year of independence. Diagram of educational system from pre-primary through university levels, statistics on all levels, chronology of educational developments since 1964-65. WKU

GUY "None to Stop Academies Enrolling University Students." Carib-
45 bean Contact, Vol. 5, no. 12 (April 1978): 1.
"Desirable social attitude" proposed as entry requirement to University of Guyana by Guyana government. Reduction in number of '0' level subjects also proposed, in name of "democratization."

PENSON, LILLIAN M. Educational Partnership in Africa and the West Indies. See entry UWI 98.

GUY POTTER, R. C. G. "History of Teacher Training in British
46 Guiana." Typescript carbon copy. [Georgetown], 1953. 21 pp.
Speech reviewing 100 years since the first students were in the first training scheme. British Parliament made grants to various missionary societies in England in 1835 "to be used in educating the children and the slaves, most of whom were then apprentices waiting to be freed." Description of a monitorial system, with the use of child teachers. Denominational controversy. Emphasis on evangelizing with some competent to teach, "to those who are utterly illiterate." UkLU-IE

PRESTON, ASTON ZACHARY. "The Caribbean: Changing Needs in a Changing Society." See entry UWI 99.

ROBERTSON, AMY; BENNETT, HAZEL; and WHITE, JANETTE, comps. Select Bibliography of Education in the Commonwealth Caribbean, 1940-1975. See entry UWI 105.

GUY "Ruthlessness vs. Resistance." Caribbean Contact Vol. 7, no. 6,
47 (October 1979): 9.
Opposition to authoritarian rule of Forbes Burnham, Guyana's prime minister for fifteen years, led to seizure of passports of some University of Guyana professors, violence against others, and announcement of closing of university until January 1980 for "financial" problems. Formation of "Committee for Academics in Peril" by West Indians in Los Angeles.

GUY SINGH, PAUL. "In Defense of Academic Freedom." Thunder 4, no. 1
48 (January-March 1972): 1-14.
Appendix supplies context: University of Guyana's Board of Governors yielded to Ministry of Education right to admit degree candidates, university funds were frozen, Board of Governors was reconstituted with people connected to ruling party, staff members were threatened with murder. Succinct, eloquent definition and defense of academic freedom by dean of Faculty of Social Sciences.

GUY   SUKDEO, FRED. "The Impact of Emigration on Manpower Resources in
49   Guyana." Mimeographed. Georgetown: University of Guyana,
      Faculty of Social Sciences, 1972. 16 pp.
          Professionally educated people needed for national develop-
ment emigrated increasingly, mostly to North America, leaving both
public and private sectors underserved in areas as diverse as geology
and medicine. Political and economic factors blamed. WKU

GUY   UNITED NATIONS. EDUCATIONAL, SCIENTIFIC AND CULTURAL ORGANI-
50   ZATION. Report of the UNESCO Educational Survey Mission to
      British Guiana, 4 November 1962 to 28 March 1963, prepared by C.
      L. Germanacos, H. Wander, G. S. Congreve, (WS/0663.22), [1963].
      102 pp.
          Environmental, historical, social determinants, demographic
and economic factors, problems of finance, and the educational system.
Discussion of historic dual control of church and state as a major
obstacle to modernization and social integration; government plan to
take control. "White Paper on Higher Education" of 1962, in which
British Guiana minister of education decides to pull away from the
University of the West Indies and establish an independent College of
Liberal Arts and Sciences, summarized in paragraphs 92-98.

GUY   UNIVERSITY OF GUYANA. Bulletin 1975-77. Georgetown, [1975].
51   259 pp.
          History, governance, admission, programs of study in five
faculties. WKU

GUY   ------. "1973-1983 Publications of Members of University of
52   Guyana Staff." Mimeographed. Turkeyen Campus, Georgetown:
      Library, University of Guyana, 1980. 31 leaves.
          Includes over a dozen titles relating to higher education.
WKU

GUY   ------. "1963-1973 Publications of Members of University of
53   Guyana Staff." Mimeographed. Turkeyen Campus, Georgetown:
      Library, University of Guyana, 1973. 67 pp.
          Large number of works in chemistry, social sciences; several
useful titles on universities and other aspects of education. WKU

GUY   ------. "Serials." Mimeographed. [Georgetown]: University of
54   Guyana, [1980]. 3 pp.
          Some fifty-plus UG serial publications are listed, mostly
beginning in the late 1970s, such items as departmental reports,
student handbooks, regulations. WKU

GUY   "The University of Guyana." Overseas Universities, February
55   1967: 5-7.
          First students admitted in 1963 in faculties of art, science,
and social sciences. Classes had met for three and one-half years in
Queens College, from 5 p.m. to 10 p.m. Land for campus given by the
Booker group of companies; capital grants from the United Kingdom and
Canada. The technical institute is to continue in the university with
advanced training; university will offer diploma courses for para-
professionals. Guyana makes annual contribution to the University of
the West Indies for places in medicine, engineering and agriculture.

Guyana

Chancellor, Sir Arthur Lewis, was vice-chancellor of UWI. Of the full-time staff, 55 percent are West Indian or Guyanese.

Haiti

HAI
1
AGENCE CANADIENNE DE DEVELOPPEMENT INTERNATIONAL. "Rapport de la mission d'identification effectuée à la Faculté d'Agronomie et de Médecine Vétérinaire, à Damiens, République d'Haiti, du 7 au 19 Juillet 1974." Mimeographed. [n.p.: ACDI], October 1974. 30 pp.
A 1960 decree by President François Duvalier placed the University of Haiti under control of the Ministry of National Education, with the rector as administrator; the medical school was placed under the Ministry of Health and the faculty of agronomy and veterinary medicine (FAMV) under the Department of Agriculture, Natural Resources and Rural Development (DARNDR). FAMV is not well coordinated within the university, which has no central campus. A project to restructure the entire FAMV is proposed, with provision for departments, upgrading faculty, improved curricula, and student selection and retention. WKU

HAI
2
ASSOCIATION OF CARIBBEAN UNIVERSITIES AND RESEARCH INSTITUTES (UNICA). Vers une politique structurelle pour l'enseignement superieur en Haiti. [Port-au-Prince]: UNICA, 1977. 83 pp. Also in Spanish.
Recommendations made by Rudolph P. Atcon and Ernani Braza. A tentative master plan for higher education in Haiti. Plan includes a description of national characteristics; a definition of objectives of the university; the structure of the university, the formation of a central administration, preparation of personnel, needs in laboratories. Planning of a campus, budget and general recommendations. KU

HAI
3
BALLANTYNE, LYGIA MARIA F. C. "Haitian Publications: An Acquisitions Guide and Bibliography." Mimeographed. Washington, D.C.: Library of Congress, Processing Services, Hispanic Acquisitions Project, 1979. 53 pp.
Addresses problems of acquisition of Haitian publications, publishing, and book trade. Describes problems of illiteracy, Creole-speaking population, few publications and small editions. "Outside the government agencies, very few Haitian institutions publish material of interest to scholarship and research. The University of Haiti does not have a press." A journal of ethnology, published since 1958, is personally financed by the dean of the school. Academic libraries in agriculture and veterinary medicine and pharmacy are well organized. DLC

BUNN, HARRIET, and GUT, ELLEN. <u>The Universities of Cuba, the</u>
<u>Dominican Republic, Haiti</u>. See entry CUB 14.

HAI   CACERES, HUGO. <u>Analyse de la Bibliothèque de la faculté d'agron-</u>
4   <u>nomie et de medécine vétérinaire d'Haiti et recommendations pour</u>
    <u>l'amélioration de son organization et de ses services</u>. Port-au-
    Prince: Institut Intéraméricain des Sciences Agricoles de l'OEA,
    Representation en Haiti, 1975. 6 pp.
       School of Agriculture and Veterinary Medicine holdings are
studied and given recommendations for improvement. Described by Ballantyne
as two university faculties with well organized libraries. WKU

HAI   <u>Haiti: A Report of the Research and Information Commission of</u>
5   <u>the International Student Conference</u>. Leiden: Coordinating
    Secretariat of National Union of Students (COSEC), 1962. 27 pp.
       Repression, imprisonment, or exile await students and faculty
members deemed troublesome by Duvalier regime. Bloody history, before
and during current dictatorship, including founding and functioning of
University of Haiti, its loss of autonomy and partial dismemberment;
the sorry, starved condition of all levels of education. Conclusion:
a denunciation by Tenth International Student Conference of "the
Duvalier tyranny." WKU

HAI   [Inter-American Development Bank] (IDB). "Rapport sur l'édu-
6   cation en Haiti." Mimeographed. [1975]. 62 pp.
       Comprehensive review of Haitian schools from 1960 to 1974.
Consists mostly of statistics on past enrollments, projected enrollment
expectations for all levels of education. Also includes figures for
urban and rural sectors and a breakdown of public and private schools.
Final recommendations for the university are: a central coordinating
office, an information exchange with other universities abroad and a
revamping of present programs so as to meet standards of foreign
universities. WKU

HAI   ------. <u>Resumen del documento Haiti: Análisis y perspectiva</u>
7   <u>para una nueva educación</u>. Borrador. Washington: IDB, [1976],
    41 pp.
       An in-house document based on a UNESCO study gives relevant
demographic data, a description of formal and non-formal education,
discusses the Creole language problem. The University of Haiti is seen
as weak and its reform not a priority item. Costs per pupil at
different levels of education and recommendations of IDB mission. WKU

HAI   [JONES, WILLIAM]. "Memo de l'Ambassadeur Américain à Jean-Claude
8   Duvalier." Supplement to <u>Caribbean Monthly Bulletin</u> 13, nos. 1-2
    (January-February, 1979): 5-12. Reprinted from Haiti Obser-
    vateur 8, no. 31 (28 July-4 August 1978).
       U.S. aid proposal for Haiti calls for modernization, major
national policy changes. Literacy rate given as 10 percent, compared
with 64 percent in Dominican Republic, 78 percent in Cuba, 82 percent
in Jamaica; Haiti spends $1.00 per year per capita on education, while
the above noted countries spend, respectively, $13.00, $31.00 and
$82.00.

HAI   LESPINASSE, RAYMOND.   <u>Bibliothèque de la faculté d'agronomie et</u>
9   <u>de Médecine vétérinaire</u>.   Port-au-Prince: Institut Inter-
      américain des Sciences Agricoles de l'OEA, Représentation en
      Haiti, 1977.   7 pp.
      Description of library of Faculty of Agriculture and Veteri-
nary Medicine.   WKU

HAI   MOROSE, JOSEPH P.   "Pour une réforme de l'éducation en Haiti."
10   Ph.D. dissertation, Faculty of Letters, University of Fribourg,
      Switzerland, 1969.
      Divisive language differences deprive many of education.
Urges radical reforms in society and education, including bilingual
education and changed national attitudes and values.   UkLU-IE

HAI   REMY, ANSELME.   "Economic Dependence: U.S. Solutions to Haiti's
11   Economic Problems."   Supplement to <u>Caribbean Monthly Bulletin</u> 13,
      nos. 1-2 (January-February 1979):   1-4.
      Attack on U.S. proposal to aid Haiti (see "memo de l'Ambassa-
deur Américain à Jean-Claude Duvalier" in same publication, pp. 5-12)
on grounds it serves only Haiti's bourgeoisie in league with multinational companies.   Indirect implications for educational policy.

HAI   ROMAIN, J.B.   <u>Etude ethno-socio-psychologique et linguistique</u>
12   <u>du milieu haitien, en vue d'une réforme de l'université d'état</u>.
      [Washington, D.C.?]:   UNICA/OEA, 1978.   130 pp.
      Behavioral scientist acknowledges uniqueness of Haitian
person and milieu, with a special value system underlying all cultural
characteristics.   Nature of Haitian culture must be starting point for
reforming university.   Analysis of material, social, spiritual life
according to four social classes shows great differences between traditional and modern classes, has significance for University.   University as seen by common people and professionals reveals need for
coordination of all of education.   Committee to be formed.   Language
factor in educational failure assessed.   Recommendations for reform:
autonomy, change in teaching method; aid programs, creation of public
relations office, international communication and exchange, increased
public service, research on Haitian reality.   WKU

HAI   RONCERAY, HUBERT DE.   "Algunos aspectos de la ideología edu-
13   cacional en Haiti."   <u>América Latina</u> 11:4 (October-December 1968):
      49-84.
      Questionnaire-study of all levels of Haitian education which
attempts to relate value orientation and expectations about education
to such factors as socioeconomic status and income.   Rather vague
conclusions.

HAI   U.S. AGENCY FOR INTERNATIONAL DEVELOPMENT (USAID).   <u>Development</u>
14   <u>Assistance Program, F[iscal] Y[ear] 1979, USAID HAITI</u>.   Washing-
      ton, D.C.:   U.S. Department of State, 1977.   179 pp. plus 34 page
      statistical appendix.
      Education and human resources development is hindered by
poverty, illiteracy and Creole language barrier to formal system.
Educational administration, including university, is fragmented among
various ministries, with separate pre-university systems for rural and
urban sectors.   University enrollment increased from 1,530 to 2,028

between 1969 and 1974 but careers are ill suited to Haiti's needs, with consequent emigration. WKU

HAI   UNIVERSITE D'ETAT. "Effectif des étudiants de l'Université
15   d'Etat pour l'année académique 1972-1978 par année, par sexe,
       nombre de professeurs haitiens et étrangers." Mimeographed.
       Port-au-Prince, [1978]. 6 pp.
       Medicine and pharmacy have consistently highest enrollment of
ten faculties, with law in second place. Total number of students grew
from 2,028 in 1974 to 2,926 in 1978. Number of Haitian and foreign
professors not given for 1973-74. WKU

HAI   WIESLER, HANS. La scolarisation en Haiti. Port-au-Prince:
16   République d'Haiti, Département des finances et des affaires
       économiques, Institut haitien de statistique, 1978. 112 pp.
       Very comprehensive demographic and school enrollment data,
including students in the national university, 1951-77; 1977 enrollment
by schools and institutes, diplomas for 1971-72. In 1960 and 1973, 0.6
percent of population attended university. Over half of education
expenditures paid for by foreign funds. DLC

Honduras

HON ATCON, RUDOLPH P. <u>Principios de la reforma universitaria</u>.
1   Tegucigalpa: Universidad Nacional Autónoma de Honduras, 1960.
     39 pp.
          Recommendation for the modern university: general studies,
adequate preparation for professionals, technology, scientific research, postgraduate work, cultural and scientific extension. In
general, uses a U.S. approach rather than traditional Latin American
pattern; as consultant to Honduras' National University, outlines appropriate structure for accomplishing reform. The university must
avoid <u>politiquería</u>--an unhealthy concern with national politics. WKU

HON CONSEJO SUPERIOR UNIVERSITARIO CENTROAMERICANO (CSUCA). <u>El sis-</u>
2   <u>tema educativo en Honduras</u>. Estudio de Recursos Humanos en
     Centroamérica, no. 3. Ciudad Universitaria Rodrigo Facio, Costa
     Rica: CSUCA, 1965, 119 pp.
          In 1962 the University of Honduras had 1,731 students in eight
faculties; of the 204 professors, some were full-time, some part-time,
some engaged hourly. WKU

HON "La crisis de la Universidad de El Salvador." <u>Presencia Uni-</u>
3   <u>versitaria</u>, no. 51 (March 1979): 6.
          University of Honduras periodical describes history of dispute
between state and university people since the 1841 founding of the University of El Salvador, which culminated in military intervention in
1972. Rightist control has led to deaths and repression; cites polarized
society as problem. Indication of awareness of events in neighboring
country.

HON Declaración." <u>Presencia Universitaria</u>, no. 51 (March 1979): 1.
4   Universidad Nacional Autónoma de Honduras protests government's
jailing one professor and pursuing another.

HON ESPINOZA M., DAGOBERTO. "incidencias de las políticas de población
5   en América Latina." <u>Universidades</u> 76 (April-June 1979): 379-88.
          Dean of Faculty of Medical Sciences of National Autonomous
University of Honduras speaks about his faculty's policy of refusing to
participate in birth control efforts under rubric of "family planning"
(although government does). Cites role of international agencies, e.g.,
AID and U.S. foundations, in pushing for birth control. Contends root of

trouble is socioeconomic, at UDUAL's XI Conference of Faculties and Schools of Medicine of Latin America.

HON   GALVEZ, CARLOS M. "La función telúrica de nuestra universidad."
6   Revista de la Universidad 3, no. 1 (January-December 1964): 85-87.
      Calls for universal education to serve the spiritual and material needs of the nation.

HON   GUARDIOLA, ESTEBAN CUBAS. Historia de la Universidad de Honduras
7   en la primera centuria de su fundación, seguida de un estudio crítico de las pastorelas del doctor José Trinidad Reyes.
      Tegucigalpa: Talleres Tipográficas Nacionales, 1952, 207 pp.
      First half of the volume describes the university from 1847 to 1947; the second half is devoted to description of the first rector, Father José Trinidad Reyes, and his pastoral verse. KU

HON   HIDALGO, FERNANDO ROBERTO. "Education in Honduras: A Case Study
8   of an Underdeveloped Latin American Republic." Thesis, Master in Education, Lynchburg College, 1969, 160 pp.
      Recent governments have given increased support to education and reforms have been introduced. Description of national university includes course requirements. Concluded that improved education requires democratic government with more equitable distribution of resources.

HON   Ley orgánica de la universidad. Decreto no. 170. [Tegucigalpa]:
9   Imp. Calderón, [1958?], 22 pp.
      Law governing structure and operation of university and its relation to the state. DPU

HON   LOPEZ VILLAMIL, HUMBERTO. "Vinculación de la Universidad Nacion-
10   al Autónoma de Honduras a la tierra." Revista de la Universidad 3, no. 1 (January-December 1964): 89-94.
      Law school students produce model law for creation and function of a school of agronomy and veterinary medicine with details of university and governmental roles.

      "Nicaragua: La agonía de una dictadura." See entry NIC 38.

HON   "Plan de desarrollo. Se abre una nueva etapa en el CURLA."
11   Presencia Universitaria, no. 51 (March 1979): 10-11.
      Regional Center of the Atlantic Coast (CURLA) established in 1967 by Universidad Nacional Autónoma de Honduras began to function first in Tegucigalpa, then in La Ceiba. Political infighting, strikes, violence among competing student groups delayed development but center now has 1,200 students. Emphasis on agriculture; forthcoming AID loans; projections to 1983.

HON   QUESADA, ARTURO. "La ciudad universitaria [de Honduras]." Extra
12   1, no. 1, August 1965, pp. 26-27.
      Comments of rector on beginning of construction of university campus reflect pride in reforms such as general studies.

HON   ------. La universidad y el desarrollo. Tegucigalpa: Imprenta
13   Soto, 1968. 45 pp.
       Discussion of the concept of the university and of develop-
ment by the rector of the National University of Honduras. Concern for
technical work and science, need for engineers, economists, doctors,
dentists, and administrators. The need for cooperation among Central
American universities. WKU

HON   SERRANO, AUGUSTO. "Situació probable y deseada de las re-
14   laciones entre universidad y ayuda externa para la década del
       80: la década del 80, (segunda parte) posibles estrategias de
       desarrollo, edited by Luís Scherz García, pp. 135-47. Ediciones
       CPU, no. 38. Santiago, Chile: Corporación de Promoción Uni-
       versitaria, 1976.
       Despite title, Honduras is the case used to show growing
resistance to foreign aid with conditions imposed by outside agencies.
Scarcity of national resources requires aid, but "Central American
people reject cultural, political and economic exploitation."
Mentions role of CSUCA; data on University of Honduras, list of
agreements between CSUCA and AID/ROCAP, 1964-68. NIC

HON   "La UNAH y la crisis del Somocismo." Presencia Universitaria,
15   no. 46 (October 1978): 7.
       The Universidad Nacional Autónoma de Honduras asserts its
anti-Somoza stance, linking the Nicaraguan government to forces in the
Honduran university rectory, editorial office, and the office of the
Federation of University Students.

HON   "La unidad en la UNAH." Presencia Universitaria, no. 51 (March
16   1979): 7.
       Editorial calls for unity of the democratic sectors in forth-
coming university elections; mentions threat to Honduran university
autonomy in time of political tension.

HON   UNIVERSIDAD JOSE CECILIO DEL VALLE. UJCV: Una alternativa
17   diferente. [Tegucigalpa]: Universidad José Cecilio del Valle,
       [1979], 4 leaves.
       Pamphlet cites need for new university, with only 1.3
percent of labor force having some kind of higher education in 1974.
Private university offers business administration and engineering;
political activity forbidden. WKU

HON   UNIVERSIDAD NACIONAL AUTONOMA DE HONDURAS (UNAH). Acuerdo No.
18   11." Mimeographed section of work, title unknown. [Tegucigal-
       pa]: UNAH, [1977?], pp. 30-51.
       Background and evolution of General Studies Plan since 1960.
Much dense prose on injustice of present colonial, backward, dependent
society and need for changing students' basic formation so they can
change society. Apparently some pressure from professional schools,
yearning for ideal interdisciplinary models of learning; centralized
quality control, decentralized performance. Adds up to New Plan of
General Studies, with two pages of courses and electives in languages
(not literature), social and physical sciences, nothing in humanities.
WKU

HON   ------. <u>Boletín de la Secretaría General de la Universidad
19   Nacional Autonoma de Honduras, 1969-70</u>. Tegucigalpa: UNAH, 42
       pp.
       Resolutions of the governing council; reports of rector's
office on chiefly financial matters; 1970 matriculation by careers;
reports of some thirty academic entities.

HON   ------. <u>Estadísticas 1976</u>. No. 8. Tegucigalpa: UNAH, [1977?],
20   104 pp.
       Student populations, graduates, personnel, academic and other
matters. Eighty charts and graphs. WKU

HON   ------. <u>Memoria de la Universidad Nacional Autónoma de Honduras
21   1960-1961</u>. Tegucigalpa: UNAH, 1961. 717 pp.
       Among most important activities reported was creation of
Department of Basic Sciences, which all students in medicine, pharmacy,
and dentistry will enter, instead of their respective professional
schools, as in past. Later, engineering students will do the same.
The University Center of General Studies and Humanities was also
created. Consultations on reform being carried on with Rudolph Atcon;
participation in CSUCA meetings and support for regionalization of
higher education; financial data: information on student welfare and
academic units. WKU

HON   ------. <u>Memoria de la Universidad Nacional Autónoma de Honduras
22   1963-1964</u>. Tegucigalpa: UNAH, 1964. 728 pp.
       A major problem: medical school has inadequate facilities
for its limit of forty first year matriculants, and student federation
demands places for eighty. Administrators hold the line. Plans under
way for university campus, beginning with General Studies. Efforts to
match Ford Foundation funds. Strong participation in CSUCA and reform
movements. Reports by administrative and academic units in detail.
WKU

HON   ------. <u>Memoria de la Universidad Nacional Autónoma de Honduras
23   1976</u>. 2 vols. Tegucigalpa: UNAH, 1976. 505 pp. and 88 pp.
       Despite financial problems, many improvements in
administrative and academic aspects are listed. Per-pupil support by
government is less than in 1960, and appeals to private enterprise were
unfruitful. The library has about 100,000 volumes; projected enrollment of 22,275 students by 1980 calls for increases in physical
plant and professors. Various academic and administrative reforms
planned for 1977. Detailed statistical information on all parts of the
university, down to names of students with amounts of student loans
repaid. WKU

HON   ------. <u>Primer encuentro de la comunidad universitaria</u>.
24   Tegucigalpa: Editorial Universitaria, 1977, 29 pp.
       Meeting of students, professors, employees held 12-16 No-
vember 1974 to discuss the nature and role of university in an "underdeveloped and dependent" country. Calls for structural and academic
change, social action. WKU

HON   ------. <u>20 años de autonomía</u>. [Tegucigalpa: UNAH], 1977, 20
25   leaves.

Honduras

Academic programs; enrollment 1958-77, totals per year and by careers, before and after 1957 autonomy; teaching personnel, financial data.   WKU

Mexico

MEX
1
ALEGRIA, PAULA. La educación en México antes y después de la conquista. México: Secretaría de Educación Pública, Instituto Federal de Capacitación del magisterio, 1963. 175 pp.
     Carefully written, balanced presentation of pre-conquest and post-conquest educational institutions and practices. Useful perspective on contemporary reality. WKU

MEX
2
BAEZ-JORGE, FELIX. "La antropología, el desarrollo capitalista y el nacionalismo mexicano." Boletín de la Escuela de Ciencias Antropológicas de la Universidad de Yucatán 4, no. 24 (May-June 1977): 2-22.
     Militant action of Mexican anthropology ought to be oriented to design models permitting ethnic groups to conserve their patrimonial rights and language. Criticizes university education which continues colonial values and dependency, ties with foreign universities and their approach to research.

MEX
3
BARRON TOLEDO, JESUS. La enseñanza superior en México, 1970-1976. México: ANUIES, 1976, 382 pp.
     Data on enrollments, teaching personnel, incomes, calendars, careers, numbers of faculties and schools. Seven-fold increase in federal government funds to University of Yucatán in five years. WKU

MEX
4
DIAZ DE COSSIO, ROGER. "El futuro de las universidades mexicanas." Universidades, 2d. ser. 10, no. 42 (October-December 1970): 46-56.
     After decade of explosive growth in all levels of education, universities cannot meet demand with present structure and programs of study. Proposes "cellular model" for growth, better basic education in university, new careers, shorter time in universities, work experience.

MEX
5
"Editorial." Boletín de la Escuela de Ciencias Antropológicas de la Universidad de Yucatán 4, nos. 22-23 (January-April 1977): 1.
     Development of anthropology as a major academic career in province is encouraging, with new agreements signed with other agencies, by which students may go on to graduate studies. But benefits are mostly for social anthropology; archaeology's progress is slow, lacking institutional articulation on an equal footing. Prevailing university mentality is too centralized and given to "internal colonialism."

MEX   "Editorial." Boletín de la Escuela de Ciencias Antropológicas de
 6   la Universidad de Yucatán 5, no. 25 (July-August 1977): 1.
       Pleased with fifth anniversary of publication, which remains
open to all ideological currents, without permitting "official manipulation or that of pressure groups who see only their own interests."
Before, much research was unknown, data were taken away in spirit of
"intellectual colonialism." Now quantity of local research requires
separate works, enabling wide dissemination and exchange of materials.

MEX   Educación y realidad socioeconómica. [1st ed.]. [México]:
 7   Centros [sic] de Estudios Educativos, [1979], 562 pp.
       Volume two of documents of International Congress of Edu-
cation, Mexico, March 14-18, 1978, organized by Center of Educational
Studies of Mexico and International Society of Comparative Education of
the U.S. Higher education, education and employment, materials and
systems of instruction. CEE

MEX   ESTRADO R., GERARDO. "Universidad y cambios sociales y políticos
 8   en México: Los antecedentes de la 'apertura' 1958-1968." Paper
      presented at Latin American Studies Association Meeting, Houston,
      2-5 November, 1977. Mimeographed, 34 pp.
       Although detailing political tensions and conflicts over the
role in society of the National Autonomous University of Mexico (UNAM),
paper touches central issues in all Latin American universities, including those in Mexico's provinces. UNAM important as model and
symbol. WKU

MEX   FLORES, EDMUNDO. "Mexico's Program for Science and Technology,
 9   1978 to 1982." Science 204 (22 June 1979): 1279-82.
       Director of National Council for Science and Technology
(CONACYT) describes increased commitment to research and education in
basic and applied sciences, up from present 0.6 percent to 1.0 percent
of GDP by 1982. Inventory being made of all agreements with other
countries and agencies, of human resources, of needs. Seventeen
thousand scholarships for post graduate study, with half in country.
Consequences for universities include strengthening research centers in
state universities and better integration of effort.

MEX   GALVEZ A., ELIOTH; VILLAGOMEZ V., RAFAEL; and VALDEZ G., ALFONSO.
 10   La población escolar de educación superior en México--Licencia-
      tura--1970-75. México: ANUIES, 1976, 234 pp.
       Tables show numbers entering Universidad de Yucatán in 1970
and 1975, and total numbers enrolled, 1970 and 1975, by areas and
careers. Total enrollment grew from 1,920 to 4,486 students. WKU

MEX   GONZALEZ AVELAR, MIGUEL, and LARA SAENZ, LEONCIO, comps. Legis-
 11   lación mexicana de la educación superior. México: UNAM, Insti-
      tuto de Investigaciones Jurídicas, 1969, 613 pp.
       National legal basis for universities. Legislation for each
institution. In case of Yucatán, juridical status of antecedent
schools began in 1624 with royal charter. Laws governing present-day
university of Yucatán. KU

MEX   GUEVARA NIEBLA, GILBERTO, compiler. La Crisis de la educación
 12   superior en México. México, D.F.: Editorial Nueva Imagen, S.A.,
      1981. 334 pp.

Papers presented at a 1979 seminar with the same title, at the Universidad Autónoma Metropolitana in Xochimilco. Violence by and against students in 1968 and following years viewed variously as result of flawed university system, a process of political deterioration, and economic crisis. Introduction by compiler offers microcosm of Latin American university weighted with tradition and attempting change. Although UNAM is focus, problems are general and to some degree affect all Mexican universities. KU

MEX GUTIERREZ R., LUIS. "Se aprobó la adición al artículo tercero."
13 Uno Más Uno, 18 December 1979, p. 1.
    Chamber of Deputies approves, by 200 to 53, controversial addition to constitution reaffirming university autonomy, in effect including the university's right to limit power of labor unions to paralyze university activities. Chiefly a response to ideological battles at National University of Mexico but applicable nationwide to public higher education.

MEX KING, RICHARD G., with ALFONSO RANGEL GUERRA, DAVID KLINE, and
14 NOEL F. MCGIVEN. The Provincial Universities of Mexico: An
    Analysis of Growth and Development. New York: Praeger Pub-
    lishers, 1971, 236 pp.
    Covers nine universities, not including University of Yucatán. However, useful background on history of universities, relation to state and national governments; comparison with other Latin American autonomous universities; after Mexico's revolution less "automatic hostility" existed between university and state. KU

MEX LATAPI, PABLO. Comentarios a la reforma educativa. México:
15 Prospectiva Universitaria, A.C., 1976, 85 pp.
    Description of reform: its philosophy, legal status, administration, research and planning, pedagogy, new secondary and higher education alternatives. Commentary concludes education has not produced social change promised in political rhetoric. Poses six major problems, all rooted in impoverished state of populace. WKU

MEX ------. "Misión de la universidad en México como país en desar-
16 rollo." CEE Folleto de Divulgación, no. 4 (15 April 1969): 5-
    15.
    Paper for seminar on national university reform addresses current turmoil and disorientation, defines development as "process of humanization" and university as place for "seeking truth." Elaborates on concepts in Mexican context, calls for leaders in universities to be disinterested and endowed with spirit of service.

MEX LEVY, DANIEL C. "Limits on Government's Financial Control of the
17 University of Mexico." Yale Higher Education Research Group-
    Working Paper Series 22 (December 1977), 32 pp.
    Mexican universities received most of their funds without any strings; government gives as much as the year before and often extra, but there is no implication of governmental control.

MEX ------. "University Autonomy Versus Government Control: The
18 Mexican Case." Ph.D. dissertation, University of North Carolina
    at Chapel Hill, 1977, 580 pp.

Using operational definition of "autonomy," study examines government-university relations and university autonomy under different regimes, concludes "'reconciliation' model approximates Mexican government-university relations far better than an 'authoritarian' model does."

MEX   LLINAS-ALVAREZ, EDGAR. "Revolution, Education, and Mexicanidad:
19   The Quest for National Identity in Mexican Educational Thought."
       Ph.D. dissertation, Columbia University, 1977, 338 pp.
       Exploration of two turn-of-the-century currents of educational thought in Mexico--hispanizante and americano-europeizante--how they clashed and mirrored national struggle for identity that culminated in 1910 Revolution. Study describes administrative turmoil in educational institutions; the appearance and eventual ascendance of José Vasconcelos and followers; and events leading to creation of a Secretariat of Public Education. Higher education seen as part of a whole.

MEX   MOSELEY, EDWARD H., and TERRY, EDWARD D. Yucatán: A World
20   Apart. University, Ala.: The University of Alabama Press, 1980,
       335 pp.
       Ten U.S. scholars and one from Yucatán cover history, geography, society, archaeology, literature, relationship of Yucatán with federal government. Problems of university related to physical and social ambiente and rest of education briefly described. Enrollment data for 1972. KU

MEX   OSBORN, THOMAS NOEL II. Higher Education in Mexico: History,
21   Growth, and Problems in a Dichotomized Industry. El Paso, Tex.:
       Texas Western Press, 1976, 150 pp.
       Includes both private and public institutions with some emphasis on their economic problems. Describes the various regions and their universities. Mentions the University of the Southwest in Campeche and the University of Yucatán, the area included in this bibliography, but makes no important differences between this area and others. Osborn has a tendency to take for granted that the U.S. view is the natural one. KU

MEX   Perspectivas de la educación en América Latina. [1st ed.].
22   [México]: Centro de Estudios Educativos, [1979], 381 pp.
       Volume one of documents of International Congress of Education, México, March 14-18, 1978, organized by Center of Educational Studies of Mexico and International Society of Comparative Education of the U.S. Priorities in educational research, rural and indigenous.
CEE

MEX   RANGEL GUERRA, ALFONSO. La educación superior en los estados:
23   Sus Proyecciones a 1980. México: ANUIES, [n.d.], 40 leaves.
       Present and projected enrollments. Most data in aggregate.
WKU

MEX   ------. La educación superior en México. México: El Colegio de
24   México, 1979, 146 pp.
       History, description, objectives, administration, efficiency of the system. University of Yucatán, created in 1922, had nineteenth century antecedents. Mexican universities lack research, planning, relationship to national needs. Discussion of needed improvements. KU

MEX   ------. "Situación actual de la educación superior en los es-
25   tados. Sus proyecciones a 1980." Revista de la Educación
Superior 3, no. 2 (April-June 1974): 3-57.
Secretary General of ANUIES addresses problem of rapid growth
of secondary and tertiary levels, lists various meetings of and
declarations by rectors on the topic, presents much statistical information in aggregate. All very general. IU

MEX   REPETTO MILAN, FRANCISCO. "Reforma educativa a nivel universi-
26   tario." Revista de la Universidad de Yucatán, Memoria 13, no. 73
(January-February 1971): 13-18.
Proposed reforms for University of Yucatán.

MEX   Revista de la Universidad de Yucatán. No. 1- . January-Febru-
27   ary 1959- . Mérida: Universidad de Yucatán.
Bimonthly publication has occasional articles on some aspect
of the University of Yucatán itself--a speech, ceremonial event, a
report--but chiefly emphasizes literature, history, archaeology of the
region. Useful background for understanding strong sense of local
identity.

MEX   RUZ MENENDEZ, RODOLFO. Aportaciones para el estudio de la histo-
28   ria de Instituto Literario de Yucatán. Edición conmemorativa de
la Universidad de Yucatán. Mérida: Zamna, 1967, 278 pp.
Primarily celebrates the hundredth anniversary of the creation of the Instituto Literario de Yucatán. Benito Juárez and Justo
Sierra supported this work in Yucatán. José Vasconcelos, minister of
public education, supported the shift to its becoming the Universidad
Nacional del Sureste in 1922. Most of the work in the instituto was
in the secondary and the preparatoria but there were aspects of higher
education. By World War II the Universidad de Yucatán is responsible
for the entire peninsula's higher education. KU

MEX   SANCHEZ, GEORGE ISADORE. The Development of Higher Education in
29   Mexico. New York: King's Crown Press, 1944, 140 pp.
Good account of events and ideological forces shaping higher
education. Post-revolutionary period; with schooling part of social
reform, finds universities in Napoleonic Latin America pattern except
for practice of incorporating preparatory schools as part of many
universities. Inventory of extant institutions by regions shows University of Yucatán with Instituto Literario del Estado (preparatoria),
Faculty of Medicine and Surgery and School of Nursing and Midwifery,
Faculty of Jurisprudence, Faculty of Chemistry and Pharmacy. Useful
and still valid observations on Mexico and Latin American values and
practices. KU

MEX   TORRES MESIAS, LUIS. "La Universidad de Yucatán en 1968."
30   Revista de la Universidad de Yucatán 11 (February 1969): 50-52.
Report to state congress lists enrollment in ten schools, for
total of 3,609; over half are in the preparatory school. Various
equipment added.

MEX   U.S. EMBASSY, Educational Counselling Center, Mexico. "The
31   Structure and Comparison of U.S. and Mexican Education." México:
U.S. Embassy, [1978], 1 leaf.

Mexico

Parallel diagrams, preschool through postdoctoral, showing ages and years of schooling. WKU

MEX   UNIVERSIDAD DE YUCATAN. Bosquejo histórico y vida académica.
32   Mérida: Universidad de Yucatán, 1963, 39 pp.
      Short history, description of functions, structure, government, degrees, facilities. WKU

MEX   ------. Leyes y reglamentos. Mérida: [UY] 1948, 100 pp.
33   Statutes granted by state of Yucatan state purposes, governance, structure, degrees. University will be in conformity with the national constitution. Plans of studies in the several faculties. DLC

MEX   ------. Memoria de la semana de la literatura en Yucatán: LV
34   aniversario de la fundación de la Universidad de Yucatán.
      Mérida: Universidad de Yucatán, 1977, 216 pp.
      Fifty-fifth anniversary of university's founding is occasion for week-long celebration of regional literature and song. Cultural history full of sense of Yucatecan separateness, uniqueness reflected in university itself. Various essays, including one on "The Doctor and Arts." WKU

MEX   ------. Memoria de las fiestas inaugurales del nuevo edificio de
35   la Universidad de Yucatán, diciembre, 1941. [Mérida: Pluma y
      Lápiz, 1942], 134 pp.
      New building to house university is cause for celebration with music, dance, speeches. Mention of wartime interruption in getting laboratories from U.S. Describes Jesuit beginnings of first yucateco priests; first purely clerical University of Yucatan (established 1624), created in 1861 with some scholarships for indigenous youths. Church-state conflict; lack of institutional unity with growth; failure of efforts to unify national higher education reflected in university's name changes. Social, political, economic elements in region affect university. DLC

MEX   ------. Monografía de la Universidad de Yucatán. Mérida: Uni-
36   versidad de Yucatán, 1977, 165 pp.
      Antecedents of university; its creation approved by state government in 1918, with cooperation of federal government. Chartered as National University of Southwest Mexico with cooperation of federal government. History, governance, growth (to 8,000 students by 1976), academic programs in fourteen faculties and schools. WKU

MEX   VILLA, KITTY MAKER. Mexico: A Study of the Educational System
37   of Mexico and a Guide to the Academic Placement of Students in
      Educational Institutions of the United States. World Educational
      Series. [Washington, D.C.]: American Association of Collegiate Registrars and Admissions Officers, 1982. 277 pp.
      Comprehensive, well presented reference document.

MEX   "Yucatán." In Instituciones de educación superior, directorio
38   1977-1978, pp. 231-34. México: ANUIES, 1979.
      Origin, character, statistics on only Mexican university considered to be in Caribbean region. University of Yucatán lists thirteen schools plus its preparatory school. Merida also has three technical institutes and a higher normal school. WKU

Netherlands Antilles

NeA CURIEL, W. J. Kooperativisme meer dan een ideaal. Vol. 7.
1 [Willemstad, Curaçao: Hogeschool van de Nederlandse Antillen,
1977]. 51 pp.
Seventh in series of essays issued by the Law School of the
Netherlands Antilles. The notion of "cooperativism" as a form of
society is introduced, and possible applications, e.g., in the field of
economics are discussed, as well as recent developments of cooperativism in Latin America and Caribbean. The history and future of
cooperativism in the Netherlands Antilles also considered. WKU

NeA DEPARTMENT OF EDUCATION. Education in the Netherlands Antilles.
2 [Willemstad]: Department of Education, [1969?]. 12 pp. Also in
Spanish and French.
Structure of educational system; mentions scholarships for
university attendance (in the Netherlands). Most significant datum
indicates potential for university attendance is small: in 1968, there
were 43,000 primary students, 2,189 in secondary schools. WKU

NeA "Development of Surinam Educational System." Memorandum prepared
3 by staff member, Cultural Affairs Office, U.S. Embassy. Paramaribo: U.S. Embassy, CAO [1977]. 6 pp. Photocopy of typescript.
First secondary school begun in 1951; in 1958, forty-five
graduates. First teacher training college begun in 1953. Entrance
examinations bar many from higher education in Holland. Thirty percent
passing sixth grade go to junior high level; about one-third of high
school graduates go to Holland. Diagram of system. WKU

NeA DIP, CARLOS E. De Ontbinding van de Staten. Vol. 4. Willem-
4 stad, Curaçao: Hogeschool van de Nederlandse Antillen, 1975. 48
pp.
Fourth in series of essays from the Law School of the Netherlands Antilles. Discussion of right of governments to "de-integrate,"
e.g., the parliament, the senate. The introduction of this right in
Dutch law is explained, along with the impact of its introduction in
the law of Surinam and the Netherlands Antilles. Analysis of practical
applications. WKU

NeA ------. "Tirso Sprockel and Higher Education in the Netherlands
5 Antilles." Caribbean Educational Bulletin 3, no. 3 (September
1976): 41-45.

Tirso Sprockel was responsible for the initiation of higher education in the Netherlands Antilles. He advocated cooperation and coordination of institutions to avoid duplicating facilities.

NeA   EINAAR, J. F. E. "Education in the Netherlands and French West
6   Indies." Journal of Negro Education 15, no. 3 (Summer 1946):
      450-61.
      Description of the Dutch and the French activities in the
islands and the mainlands in the 1940s. Some elementary schools but,
except for some study in medicine, pharmacy and dentistry in Surinam,
there was no higher education.

NeA   HASHAM, M. F. Careers Index of the Netherlands Antilles. St.
7   Augustanus: Hogeschool van de Nederlandse Antillen, 1978. 156
      pp.
      Employment opportunities in such fields as banking, pe-
troleum, trade, insurance, government. Educational requirements and
available resources in law, engineering, administration. WKU

NeA   HELLINGA, W. G. "Education in Surinam (Dutch Guiana) and the
8   Linguistic Situation." Mimeographed. Amsterdam: Department of
      Cultural and Physical Anthropology of the Royal Anthropological
      Institute, 1951. 29 pp.
      History from 1760, first school for children of the free
mulattos and blacks. Problems of several languages other than official
Dutch, "colonial system which has always tried to economize on education," poor teacher preparation, poor attendance, rural-urban differences, lack of books. UkLU-IE

NeA   HENRIQUEZ, N. E. Enkele Aspecten van Collectieve Arbeidsver-
9   houdingen. Vol. 8. Willemstad, Curaçao: Universiteit Neder-
      landse Antillen, 1979. 30 pp.
      Eighth in series of essays from the Law School of the Nether-
lands Antilles. Analyses of various aspects of collective labor relationships. The right of organization, recognition of labor unions,
the collective labor agreement, the right to strike are discussed in a
general (international) context, and applied as well to the Netherlands
and the Netherlands Antilles. WKU

NeA   KUNST, A. J. M. Receptie en Concordantie van Recht: De invloed
10   van het Nederlandse Recht op dat van de Nederlandse Antillen.
      Rechtshogeschool van de Nederlandse Antillen, [n.p.] 1973. 39
      pp.
      Second in series of essays from the Law School of the Nether-
lands Antilles. Speech given on annual Rechtshogeschool anniversary
celebration provides analysis of influence of Dutch law on the laws of
the Netherlands Antilles. WKU

NeA   NETHERLANDS ANTILLES. "Government Programme, 1977-1981." Mimeo-
11   graphed. [Willemstad, Curaçao 1977]. 34 pp.
      Covers political restructuring, employment and economic de-
velopment, public finance, revising of educational system, cooperatives. More participation in educational policy by islands in future.
Papiamento is official school language in Leeward Islands, English in
Windwards. Institute of Higher Studies to become university. WKU

NeA   RÖMER, R. A.   "Education in Caribbean Perspective: The Sprockel
12   Period." Caribbean Education 3, no. 3 (September 1976):   47-51.
       Brief historical analysis of education in the Netherlands
Antilles.   Discussion of Tirso Sprockel's role in establishing higher
education.   Major effort is being made to tailor curriculums to elementary social needs.

NeA   SCHILTKAMP, J. A.   Bestuur en rechtspraak in de Nederlandse An-
13   tillen ten tijde van de West-Indische Compagnie. Vol. 1.   Wil-
       lemstad, Curaçao: Rechtshogeschool van de Nederlandse Antillen,
       1972.   71 pp.
       First in series of essays in the fields of law, law history
and other disciplines that play a role in the program of the Recht-
schogeschool (Law School) of the Netherlands Antilles.   Historical
survey of rule and jurisdiction in the Netherlands Antilles during the
period of the West-Indische Compagnie, the Dutch trade organization for
the West Indies, until 1972.   WKU

NeA   SEDOC-DAHLBERG, BETTY.   "De universiteit in de Derde Wereld."
14   Speech on the occasion of the proclamation of the Faculty of
       Social-Economic Sciences of the University of Surinam, on No-
       vember 1, 1975. Paramaribo: Publicatie S.E.F., 1975.   19 pp.
       Highlights common characteristics and problems with the past
of the development process, which provides information on the degree of
social self-sufficiency/self-reliance of the underdeveloped countries.
References used are recent, with emphasis on native (Third World)
academics.   Importance of the Faculty of Social-Economic Sciences for
Surinam is discussed.   Rapid rise in costs for universities in Third
World countries but graduates lack employment; people seek status and
wealth associated with university degree, and high schools prepare
students for university entry.   Alternatives needed.   WKU

NeA   "Shete dia de actividad: Apertura ofishal di Universidad di
15   A.N." La Prensa, 6 September 1979.
       Papiamento-language newspaper reports week-long festivities
for opening of University of Netherlands Antilles in Willemstad,
Curaçao.   Rector magnificus will open 1979-80 academic year.

NeA   TORFS, JACQUES.   Evaluation of the Education System and Plans of
16   Surinam. Paris: UNESCO, 1969.   30 pp.   Photocopy.
       Dutch system imposed without regard to Surinam's own geo-
graphy and culture.   Low productivity of both secondary and primary,
but "system qualitatively and quantitatively better than Latin American
systems." Cites need for national, long-range education plan, locally
designed.   University enrollment of 527, with law having 382 students;
medicine 29; and training school for civil servants, 116.   UkLU-IE

NeA   "Universidad de Antiyas: Puente entre cultura Hulandes y region
17   di Caribe y America." Nobo Dialuna, 10 September 1979.
       "A bridge between Dutch science and culture and the area of
the Caribbean and Latin America": the University of the Netherlands
Antilles.   Hopes students will now study in Curaçao, following their
preparations adapted to local needs.   Help from Dutch government,
contribution of land by Shell Curaçao for campus.

NeA   <u>Universidat di Aruba Bulletin 1973-1975</u>. [Oranjestad]: 1973.
18   92 pp.
         Founded in Aruba in 1952 by Carlin I. Browne, still
president, as private secondary academy, it developed into a community
college. Chartered 1970 by laws of Netherlands Antilles as institution
of higher learning. Opportunities for non-degree-seeking adults, high
school equivalency program. College of liberal arts, education,
business administration, preprofessional social work. Language of
instruction is English. WKU

NeA   "The University of the Netherlands Antilles Curaçao, Netherlands
19   Antilles." Mimeographed. Jan Noorduynweg: University of the
       Netherlands Antilles, [1980]. 9 leaves.
         Established in 1970 as Institute of Higher Studies, with
local two-year law program and completion of studies in Holland. In
1973 full law program began; public administration was added later;
1978 merger with Engineering School of the Antilles. Organization,
admissions, courses, degrees. Language of instruction is Dutch. WKU

NeA   VAN BOHEEMEN, H. "Educational Troubles in Surinam." Mimeo-
20   graphed. Distributed by Royal Tropical Institute, 3 pp. Reprint
       translated from <u>De West-Indische Gids</u> 32 (1951): 65-91.
         Instruction begins in Dutch, when many children at primary
level have never heard the language; spoken languages: Negro English,
Dutch, Javanese, Dutch-Hindi. High rate of dropping out, by contrast
to East India with more gradual use of Dutch. UkLU-IE

NeA   VAN DER HORST, GERARD. "The Dutch Way of Development: Cooper-
21   ation in the Field of Higher Education." <u>Overseas Universities</u>
       no. 24 (October 1977): 20-22.
         Twenty-five years earlier Dutch universities had set up the
Foundation for International Cooperation, NUFFIC, offering aid rather
than encouraging students from developing countries to go to Holland.
Dutch universities are working with the "still very small" University
of Surinam, "which is socially and culturally more a part of the Caribbean [than of South America]." NUFFIC asks if a program could be
worked out with Surinam, the University of Guyana and the University of
the West Indies.

Nicaragua

NIC "Acta de fundación y estatutos de la Universidad Católica
1 Centroamericana." La Gaceta, 22-24 (March 1961): 634-638.
　　　Statutes establish what will be known as "La Universidad
Católica Centroamericana, Sección de Nicaragua" or "Universidad Católica Centroamericana de Nicaragua." Four faculties, governance, legal
obligations.

NIC ALVAREZ ALVARADO, JESUS. Evolución y desarrollo de la Universi-
2 dad Nacional Autónoma de Nicaragua: Los obstáculos al desarrollo
universitario. Seminario. 25 años de actividades universitarias centroamericanas, Tegucigalpa, Honduras, 17-20 octubre
1973. León: [n.p.], 1973. 58 leaves.
　　　Description of the university in León, Nicaragua. Until 1958
the university was either closed or static, between 1958 and 1965 the
university was dynamic and open, between 1966 and 1971 the university
worked on technical and planning problems, and from 1971 to 1973 it was
concerned with social problems. KU

NIC ARELLANO, JORGE EDUARDO. Historia de la Universidad de León.
3 Vol. 1: Epoca colonial. León: UNAN, 1973. 305 pp.
　　　Background for all Central American universities, beginning
with granting of royal charter for University of San Carlos de
Guatemala in 1676. DLC

NIC ------. Historia de la Universidad de León: Epoca moderna y
4 contemporánea. Colección "Documento," no. 3. León: Editorial
Universitaria UNAN, 1974. 208 pp.
　　　The institution whose existence was interrupted in 1824,
1827, 1869, 1896 and 1912 became the Universidad Nacional de Nicaragua
in 1947, and the Universidad Nacional Autónoma de Nicaragua in 1958.
KU

NIC [ARRIEN, JUAN BAUTISTA.] "La experiencia de la planificación
5 educativa en el marco de la revolución popular sandinista."
Carbon copy of memorandum with handwritten note. [Managua], June
1981. 3 pp.
　　　Outline shows efforts to integrate education and economic
recovery, respond to social needs. Objectives: expansion, improvement, transformation of education. Steps to follow literacy

crusade include national consultation, basic education for adults, workshops, evaluation, development of national plan for education. WKU

NIC ------. Nicaragua: Revolución y proyecto educativo. Managua:
6   Ministerio de Educación de Nicaragua, 1980. 203 pp.
    Former rector of Catholic Universidad Centroamericana, now director of planning and educational development of Ministry of Education, writes: "true education is always revolutionary and a true revolution is always educative." Elaborates his thesis in the Latin American theoretical-practical framework, insisting that there need be no regnant ideology to explain the national reality and to arrive at a just society and "the new man." Out of the Latin American historical and dialectical reality arise Latin American philosophy and education with their own unique characteristics, the Sandinista roots of the new educational project, pedagogical principles, methods of carrying out goals in neatly ordered formulation. WKU

NIC ------. El papel de la universidad en la educación no formal.
7   Managua: UCA, 1977. 49 pp.
    Rector of Catholic University calls for it to direct its efforts to those outside its precincts unserved by conventional programs, in effective social service. Use of radio, theater, television. WKU

NIC ------. La universidad ante el cambio social. Lección inaugural
8   año académico 1977-1978. Managua: UCA, 1977. 39 pp.
    Does not insist overmuch on ascribing all ills to dependency, but acknowledges reality in country. Tensions inherent in university vis-à-vis society in the selection process, value judgments. Lists action alternatives for Latin American universities generally, against unmentioned pressures in Nicaragua on eve of revolution. WKU

NIC ------. "Universidad, cambio y cristianismo." Encuentro:
9   Revista de la Universidad Centroamericana, (April-September 1976): 3-18.
    In May 1976 Rector Arríen gave his inaugural lecture in the Universidad Centroamericana in Managua--the church, the community, and the university.

NIC ------, and KAUFFMANN, RAFAEL. Nicaragua en la educación: Una
10 aproximación a la realidad. Managua: Ediciones Universidad Centroamericana, 1977. 423 pp.
    Rector and academic director present general philosophical statement, present historical context of Nicaragua, description and analysis of education, socioeconomic structure and educational demand, problems, projections, policy for preparing human resources for development. Careful documentation. WKU

NIC ARRIEN, JUAN BAUTISTA, and LOPEZ, CAIRO MANUEL. Relaciones jurí-
11 dico-políticas entre el estado y las universidades privadas de Nicaragua. Managua: UCA, 1978. 44 pp.
    Rector of Catholic University (UCA) and law professor list post-secondary institutions, distinguish among them in their relation to the state, define autonomy as it affects the two major universities. Recent growth of private universities in Latin America with

politicización and lack of capacity of public ones. Nicaragua now has the Polytechnic University (UPOLI) and two other specialized schools which, with UNAN and UCA, make up the Nicaraguan Association of Institutions of Higher Education (ANIES) created in 1970. UCA autonomy recently somewhat disturbed by government accusation, e.g., teaching Marxism. Cautionary comments. WKU

NIC CASTILLA URBINA, MIGUEL DE. "Autonomía universitaria hoy en
12 Nicaragua. ¿Ante quién? ¿Para quién?" Acción y Reflexión Edu-
     cativa, no. 5 (June 1980): 173-79.
     Concept of university autonomy belongs to a "glorious past" when it was part of the fight for liberty. Still to be studied is role of university "sometimes as personage, sometimes as scenario" in the war, to see it in terms of the political movement and class warfare. Critical of UNAN for past performance in serving the dominant class, calls for change in its nature, conception, goals and functions in the popular revolutionary state of workers and peasants.

NIC ------. Educación para la modernización en Nicaragua. Buenos
13 Aires: Editorial Paidos, 1972. 162 pp.
     Prize-winning book, chiefly descriptive; covers all levels of education with history, enrollments. Illiteracy conduces to back-wardness; recommends agrarian reform, educational reform, financial support, planning, expansion of teacher training. KU

NIC ------. Universidad y sociedad en Nicaragua. La UNAN 1958-
14 1978: 20 años de asedio a la palabra libertad. 2 vols. León:
     UNAN, Editorial Universitaria, 1979. 315 pp.
     Schooling seen as mechanism for selection and social control by dominant class. History of universities in general and UNAN in particular, in great detail; well documented. Evolution of concept of autonomy and its meaning for Nicaragua's national university; autonomy weakened by dependent, underdeveloped character of nation and conse-quent dependency of university on foreign aid. Stormy 1944-58 period seeking autonomy from Somoza hegemony; various "sub-stages" include reform movement of late sixties. Defines autonomy in a capitalist setting as "social peace" or "conditional liberty," with suspension of university's critical function. Examples of 1958-78 "siege" and response. WKU

NIC CHAVEZ, LIGDANO. Anteproyecto de programa de estudios generales
15 para las facultades de Managua. Managua: UNAN, 1965. 46 pp.
     Philosophy of general studies, plan of the courses, develop-ment of the plan, the method of teaching, grades. Effort to reorganize university, avoid its being only a group of separate professional schools which students entered directly from secondary level.

     "La Confederación Universitaria Centroamericana (CSUCA) prepara sistema de cooperación universitaria para la reconstrucción de Nicaragua." See entry GEN 48.

NIC CONRADO, EDUARDO. "Higher Education in Nicaragua." Photocopy of
16 unpublished speech at meeting in El Paso, Texas, [November 1978]. 5 pp. plus 5 leaves on higher education and facts about Nicaragua.

Background; current problems at UNAN include polarization of populace, government three months in arrears in its payments to university, two military interventions into university, killing and wounding students. Writer is dean of Faculty of Letters and Science at Managua Campus of UNAN, on leave in U.S. WKU

NIC CONSEJO NACIONAL DE LA EDUCACION SUPERIOR (CNES). Estadísticas
17 de la educación superior (Informe correspondiente al inicio del curso 1980-1981). Managua: CNES, Oficina de Planeamiento, 1981. ca. 40 leaves.
Over a 17 percent enrollment increase over previous period with 81.5 percent of total in UNAN. Rest are in UCA and technical schools. Student-professor ratio at thirty-eight to one. Majority of students at UNAN are in the evening classes and hold jobs outside (98.6 percent). Distributions by age, sex, academic areas of study for all institutions. WKU

NIC ------. Lineamientos del Plan de Desarrollo 1981-1985 (primera
18 versión). Managua: CNES, Oficina de Planeamiento, 1980. 165 pp.
Consejo Nacional de Educación Superior was created in 1980, with goal of developing higher education as a "true subsystem" of the educational, economic, social development of Nicaragua. Estimates of needs for various careers, development of new ones; efforts to increase and improve teaching, measure efficiency. Resources available and projected. Creation of preparatory school for disadvantaged youth; tightening requirements for retention in universities. WKU

NIC ------. Logros de la educación superior, julio 1980-mayo 1981.
19 Managua: CNES, Dirección de Política Económica e Inversiones, 1981. 28 pp.
Greatly increased state support for universities since the Revolution helps accommodate rapid growth; full time professors increased from 47.9 percent to 61.9 percent; building expanded, along with replacement of equipment destroyed in battles. Figures for 1975-81 show evolution of higher education. Twelve professors from socialist countries and ninety-eight from non-socialist countries taught there in 1980. Enrollment by field of study. WKU

NIC ------. Reglamento del régimen docente, del sistema de evalu-
20 ación del aprendizaje, y del movimiento de alumnos-ayudantes en todos los centros de educación superior de la república. [Managua]: CNES, 1980. 24 pp.
Evaluations and requirements for academic promotion of students, of their graduation; rights, duties, eligibility for student teaching assistant program (a new program in the universities); policies for transitional period in higher education. WKU

NIC ------. Reglamento del registro académico estudiantil.
21 [Managua]: CNES, 1980. 8 leaves.
Rules to assure completion of academic work in systematic manner, with new controls and record-keeping--of a kind common in U.S. universities. WKU

NIC CONSEJO SUPERIOR UNIVERSITARIO CENTROAMERICANO (CSUCA). El
22 sistema educativo en Nicaragua: Situación actual y perspectivas.

Ciudad Universitaria, Costa Rica: Secretaría Permanente del
CSUCA, 1965.   115 pp.
    Population growth and economic aspects related to structure
of educational system: elementary, secondary, and the university.
Data on students, professors, and buildings, and cost by faculty per
student; projections.   KU

NIC   CORRALES MUNGUIA, JULIAN.   "El docente en la Universidad Nacional
23   Autónoma de Nicaragua."   In *Tres problemas universitarios*, edited
by Marshall R. Nason, Dinko Cvitanovic, and Jaysuño Abramovich.
Albuquerque: University of New Mexico, 1975.   pp. 40-46.
    Vice-rector outlines university teaching structure, chief
feature of which is the academic department.   Procedures for recruitment to teaching; rules, responsibilities, numbers; efforts to improve
quality hampered by scarce resources.   WKU

NIC   "Creación del Consejo Nacional de la Educación Superior."   *Uni-*
24   *versidades* 3d ser., no. 84 (April-June 1981):   123-24.
    New body created by governmental decree no. 325 lists its
functions and characteristics, affirming administrative, economic, and
academic autonomy of the various higher education centers.   It will
also carry out national education policy, assigns funds, formulate
uniform statutes, create or eliminate faculties or careers and centers,
and authorize degrees.

NIC   *Educación y dependencia: El caso de Nicaragua*.   Colección
25   Estudios Sociales.   [Managua]:   INPRHU, 1977.   477 pp.
    Papers from 1976 seminar sponsored by Christian, non-denomi-
national organization.   Seven essays on general topics of education and
liberation and education and dependency, by Miguel Obando y Bravo and
other Nicaraguan educators and scholars.   Coherent presentations,
useful information--including some statistical data, analysis, conclusions.   Strong antipathy toward U.S. influence on education and
culture.   YUS

NIC   FIALLOS GIL, MARIANO.   *A la libertad por la universidad*.   León:
26   UNAN, 1960.   143 pp.
    Speeches, articles by Rector Fiallos on "interpretations of
university life" between May 1957 and June 1959 show breadth and depth
of his view of mission of university in Nicaragua, Central America and
Latin America.   Forthright demands for autonomy and adequate financing
from government; relationship with Consejo Superior Universitario
Centroamericano; comments on weaknesses of Nicaraguan social structure.
KU

NIC   ------.   "Carta del rector a los estudiantes,"   "Homenajes," y
27   "Discurso del rector."   *Cuadernos Universitarios* 9 (May 1959):
3-11.
    Rector writes of good relations between university and
students, of autonomy, of relation with the Ministry of Education of
Nicaragua.

NIC   FIALLOS OYANGUREN, MARIANO.   "La reforma universitaria en
28   Nicaragua."   *Cuadernos Universitarios* 4 (September 1968):   27-34.

Dean of the Faculty of Sciences and Letters of the Universidad Nacional de Nicaragua at the opening session of academic year 1968-69. Recounts changes in the university since autonomy was granted in 1958, traces the increasing importance of the faculty in training scientists.

NIC   FUNDIS, RONALD JAY. Población estudiantil 1960-1967. Managua:
29   UNAN, 1967. 112 pp.

Planning document for new branch of National University in Managua, where demand is growing much faster than in León. Data on student population (for both National University and Catholic University), evolution and efficiency of the system, demographic aspects, and projections. KU

NIC   ------, and CHAVEZ, LIGDANO. "Resumen de la información presen-
30   tada en el 'Documento preliminar de estudio' del manual de infor-
      maciones y principios." Mimeographed. Managua: [UNAN] Recinto
      Universitario "Rubén Darío," 1968. 33 pp.

School desertion/retention at all levels; highest loss in primary. Growth rates in enrollment, León and Managua, 1960-68. University admissions policies, reform and general studies, demand for higher education. Data on full-time, part-time students; some problems with more rapid increase of students in Managua than in León. KU

NIC   LINARES, JULIO L. "Universidad estructural intelectual y
31   desarrollo social." Encuentro 3, no. 1 (1970): 1-12.

Country entered the "infancy of modern capitalism" with new government of 1967, required technical capacity to cope with complexity of emerging commerce and agriculture. Defines ideal intellectual leader for this ambience, by contrast with literary types who now influence public opinion. Need for "intellectualized technocrat" rather than poetic types who "have instituted romantic solutions to social problems." There is little research and publication in and out of universities. Universities lack intellectual rigor, suffer from need of students to work full time, from professors teaching part time. Excessive professional orientation of universities precludes general education found in U.S. liberal arts requirements. Lack of communication among various elites and isolation from real problems. University reform is urgent.

NIC   MENDOZA, ALBERTO. Metodología del planeamiento universitario.
32   Managua: 32 UNAN, 1967. 131 pp.

Guide used in planning for UNAN begins with 1965 study and formulation of academic and administrative plan, concludes with 1967 physical plan. Sets forth principles to be followed and step-by-step procedures for development of Managua campus, with technical assistance from Inter-American Development Bank. WKU

NIC   MINISTERIO DE EDUCACION. Consulta nacional para obtener cri-
33   terios que ayuden a definir los fines y objetivos de la educación
      nicaragüense. Documento de base. Código D-1. Managua: El
      Ministerio, 1981. 15 pp.

"National consultation" asks for information on needs and problems at all levels of education from members of popular organizations, labor unions, private business, political parties, and from

the non-organized. Training discussion leaders, data collection
method. Main themes of inquiry listed. WKU

NIC   ------. Consulta nacional para obtener criterios que ayuden a
34   definir los fines y objetivos de la educación nicaragüense.
Mensaje del compañero Ministro de Educación Doctor Carlos
Tünnermanan Bernheim. Código E-1. Managua: El Ministerio,
1980. 3 pp.
New educational system, based on carrying out Sandinista
government goal of "humanistic transformation of the Nicaraguan society," undertakes national discussion to compare Somoza past with hopes
for future and to find ways of democratizing education and society.
WKU

NIC   ------. Consulta nacional para obtener criterios que ayuden a
35   definir los fines y objetivos de la educación nicaragüense.
Cuestionario guía de discusión. Código C-1. Managua: El
Ministerio, 1981. 26 pp.
"We are in the process of forming the new Nicaraguan, saving
what is good in ourselves and discarding the evil, consolidating our
own cultural values and seeking the best of the universal culture."
Education is to be the means for fulfilling goals of the Sandinista
Revolution: popular democracy, nationalism, anti-imperialism. Discussion guide to be used by groups in all parts of country asks open-
ended questions about education and access to it in Somoza era, at
present, and in the future. Reflects optimism of national leaders in
participatory process for policy making and building national
consensus. WKU

NIC   ------. La educación en el primer año de la Revolución Popular
36   Sandinista. Managua: El Ministerio, 1980. 238 pp.
A celebration of the single most important commitment of the
new government: the extension of educational opportunity to all
Nicaraguans and a vast increase in enrollments at all levels. Data
show record of spending before and after Revolution; policy changes;
shifts in emphasis, particularly in broadening the base of education.
Abundant scorn heaped on Somoza regime. A record of attitudes, goals,
activities, plans. WKU

NIC   ------, División de Planificacion y Desarrollo Educativo. "Docu-
37   mentos sobre el marco teórico del diagnóstico, su metodología o
aspectos importantes del mismo." Photocopy of typescript.
[Managua]: El Ministerio, División de Planificación y Desarrollo
Educativo, 1981. 6 pp.
General and particular problems are covered in this bibli-
ography, chiefly by Nicaraguan theoreticians and practitioners; some
UNESCO and other international sources. WKU

NIC   "Nicaragua: La agonía de una dictadura." Presencia Universi-
38   taria, no. 38 45 (October 1978): 1.
Cable sent to General Somoza by Rector of UNAH protesting
"economic aggression" against Universidad Nacional de Nicaragua in
cutting its budget. Also protest against National Guard violence and
vandalism at Catholic Universidad Centroamericana in Nicaragua and
threats against life of its rector.

NIC   PALLAIS, LEON. "Ser y misión de la Universidad Centroamericana."
39   Encuentro 1, no. 1 (January-February 1968): 6-12.
      "Pluralism" of this Catholic university affirmed, along with
its social and cultural roles. Proposed reforms for seven-year-old
institution with departmentalization and student participation.

NIC   RAMIREZ MERCADO, SERGIO. Mariano Fiallos, biografía. León,
40   Nicaragua: Editorial Universidad, UNAN, 1971. 203 pp.
      Revealing, well-written account of a man, a country, and a
university by a former secretary general of the Central American
Council of Universities (CSUCA) who became a member of Nicaragua's
ruling junta in 1979. In 1958, with Rector Fiallos' leadership,
University of Nicaragua won its autonomy. Discusses individual and
institutional survival in the Somoza years and growth of regional
university cooperation. KU

NIC   ------. Mis días con el rector. [León]: Universidad Nacional
41   de Nicaragua, Ediciones Ventana, 1965. 43 pp.
      Commemorative collection of articles honoring Dr. Mariano
Fiallos Gil at the time of his death. Influence of an educational
statesman on a young student at time of crisis and change in Universidad de Nicaragua; symbolic importance of university against dictatorship of Somoza. KU

NIC   "Rector de UNAN da su opinión: Autonomía se adapta al proceso."
42   La Prensa, 19 June 1981.
      Rector Mariano Fiallos Oyanguren describes university autono-
my in the Somoza years as "an autonomy of defense" against a hostile
government, by contrast to "an autonomy of presence in the Revolution,"
in which the university is involved in "transforming our society."
Distinguishes between academic freedom, which prevails, and concept of
carrying out agreed-upon programs and policies of the institution where
individual deviation is not acceptable.

NIC   "Revolución sandinista y educación." Encuentro, no. 15 (27
43   August-10 September 1979): 191.
      Political and educational seminar on point of view of
sandinismo and the process of education. Objectives are orienting the
university community towards a new political education, a revolutionary
point of view corresponding to social and educational needs of
Nicaragua. Supported by the Rector of the Universidad Centroamerica
and members of governing junta.

NIC   RODRIGUEZ, INDALECIO. "Universidad, investigación agropecuaria
44   y desarrollo social." Encuentro, no. 13 (January-June 1978): 5-
      10.
      Importance of agricultural research. The university must put
development high on the list of needs.

NIC   SERRANO CALDERA, ALEJANDRO. Interpretaciones en torno al proceso
45   histórico de la universidad nicaragüense: Trabajo preparado para
      el Seminario Centroamericano sobre la Universidad con motivo del
      XXV aniversario del CSUCA. León: [n.p.], 1973. 61 leaves. On
      cover: Seminario: 25 años de actividades universitarias
      centroamericanas, Tegucigalpa, Honduras 17-20 Octubre 1973.

Evolución y desarrollo de las universidades nacionales: Los obstáculos al desarrollo universitario.
Generalizations about universities in their historical contexts in Latin America. Growth of liberal humanism in Nicaragua, problems of internal and external dependency, the reform efforts. A useful social and educational perspective. KU

NIC STANSIFER, CHARLES L. "The Nicaraguan National Literacy Crusade.
46 American Universities Field Staff Report, no. 6, South America (1981): 1-14.
Former rector of National Autonomous University of Nicaragua, Carlos Tünnermann; former professor at UNAN, Miguel de Castilla Urbina and former rector of Nicaragua's Catholic Universidad Centroamericana, Juan Bautista Arríen, now minister of education and vice-ministers, respectively, provide leadership for literacy crusade of March-August 1980 with mostly secondary school students as teachers. Claimed reduction of illiteracy from 50 to 13 percent and national "conscientizing", with involvement of some 180,000 in Army of Cultural Liberation.

NIC TABLADA, TULIO BENITO. "Factors Related to College Graduation
47 and Professional Status of the Nicaraguan University Graduates." Ph.D. dissertation, University of Colorado at Boulder, 1978. 141 pp.
Survey of characteristics--type of college degree, salary, job, and vocational satisfaction--of 1970-74 (mainly five-year-degree) graduates of Nicaraguan universities. Questionnaires revealed few differences among respondents, e.g., most had attended day shift high schools with academic curricula; slightly over half attended public schools, the others, private; parents' education and income similar. Important factors in career decisions: vocational interest, opportunity to work while studying, and location of university. Twenty percent of respondents self-employed, 48 percent employed full-time, 5 percent employed part-time, 27 percent held more than one job.

NIC TIRADO, VICTOR; CABEZAS, OMAR; and NUÑEZ, CARLOS. Primer semi-
48 nario político Miguel Bonilla: La universidad y la revolución. [Managua]: UNAN, Comisión Política Universitaria, 1980. 139 pp.
Session for professors by "commanders" of Frente Sandinista de Liberación Nacional sets forth revolutionary policy. Alteration of concept of autonomy, shift away from education in careers formerly needed by private sector, adherence to revolutionary ideology, restructuring of university governance, among other matters. WKU

NIC TÜNNERMANN BERNHEIM, CARLOS. Breve reseña de la conquista de la
49 autonomía universitaria en Nicaragua. [León: Ediciones de la Universidad Nacional de Nicaragua, 1958]. 62 pp.
On March 25, 1958 Nicaraguan President Somoza Debayle approved the decree granting university autonomy. Nicaragua was the last of the Central American public universities to achieve this relative freedom from political domination. TxU

NIC ------. En inauguración del edificio de ciencias básicas.
50 León: UNAN, 50 1966. 15 pp.

This general science building is for support of the first year of general studies and represents collaboration among several faculties with courses in sciences. Important development because of regional concern of national universities for the general studies approach, with impulse from Council of Central American Universities (CSUCA).

NIC   ------. Ensayos sobre la universidad latinoamericana. San José:
51   EDUCA, 1981. 223 pp.
      Science, technology, society and university; research; new concept in extension and policies of cultural development; democratization; autonomy in Nicaragua in the dictatorship. First secretary-general of CSUCA, former rector of UNAN, past president of UDUAL, Nicaraguan minister of education after 1979, writes clearly, realistically, without cant. Useful history of UNAN in the usually turbulent context of Nicaragua's internal strife and external pressures. WKU

NIC   ------. Estudios sobre la teoría de la universidad. San José:
52   EDUCA, 1983. 534 pp.
      Previously published papers, except for "Apéndice. La autonomía universitaria: el caso de Nicaragua," which gives a brief, useful recounting of foreign interventions from 19th and early 20th centuries. Juxtaposes history of University of Nicaragua and its antecedent institutions with these "perpetually violent" political events into present era, with 1958 winning of autonomy and continuing struggles. Watershed of the Revolution of 1979 and a new relationship of the university and the state, as part of national philosophy of "la Nueva Educación." Asserts that creation of the Consejo Nacional de Educación does not weaken university autonomy, but changes it from a "defense" against the state to a "presence" of active participation in the revolutionary process, "without losing its character as guarantee of critical and independent thought." WKU

      ------. Exposición comparada de las leyes orgánicas de las universidades centroamericanas. See entry GEN 273.

NIC   ------. Hacia una nueva educación en Nicaragua. Managua:
53   Ministerio de Educación, 1980. 187 pp.
      Minister of education begins with speech at Universidad Centroamericana (Catholic), stating that educational philosophy of revolution is concerned with human values. Plan to integrate all education, under comprehensive law, with all sectors participating within principles of the Popular Sandinista Revolution. Democratization of society to be carried out through education. Credits university autonomy (1958) with contributing much to political development of those later participating in the Sandinista Revolution. Data on high illiteracy, poor physical facilities. Formation of National Council of Higher Education. Contributions of universities to nation. WKU

NIC   ------. La universidad: Búsqueda permanente. Colección Ensayo,
54   no. 3. León: UNAN, 1971. 173 pp.
      Collection of essays by then-rector on university in national life, its reforms, general studies, planning. Tributes to late Rector Fiallos Gil and Rubén Darío. WKU

Nicaragua

NIC ------. <u>La universidad latinoamericana y el planeamiento uni-</u>
55 <u>versitario.</u> 55 Serie Discursos, no. 5. León: Ediciones de la
UNAN, 1969. 32 pp.
    Twentieth anniversary meeting of the Union of Latin American
Universities, UDUAL, considers topic of university planning.

"La UNAH y la crisis del Somocismo." See entry HON 15.

NIC UNIVERSIDAD CENTROAMERICANA (UCA). "Datos estadísticos, curso
56 1967-68." Mimeographed. León: Centro de Cálculo y Estadística,
1967. 30 leaves.
    Of its 1,787 students, over 70 percent are male night
students; over half are from private secondary schools and less than 30
percent graduate in three largest faculties. Fifty-seven percent of
professors are part-time (<u>tiempo convencional</u>), 15 percent are half-
time. Other socioeconomic, academic, financial data on this Catholic
university. KU

NIC ------. <u>UCA, una universidad para Nicaragua.</u> Managua: [UCA],
57 1977. 17 pp.
    Explanation of and appeal for funds to invest in education to
overcome underdevelopment. Financial and other data. WKU

NIC UNIVERSIDAD NACIONAL AUTONOMA DE NICARAGUA (UNAN). "Auto-evalu-
58 ación de la Universidad: Análisis y cuadros." Mimeographed.
León: Comisión de Planeamiento Universitario, 1965. 19 pp. plus
17 pages appendices.
    Responses to questionnaire sent to professors show very
strong support for major restructuring and reform of university, with
move to more full-time faculty, greater use of library as teaching
tool, full-time students, departmentalization, general studies prior to
professional studies. Copies of questionnaire, results tabulated. KU

NIC ------. <u>Catálogo de estudios 1965.</u> León, 267 pp.
59   History after 1670 beginning with "embryo" seminary,
illustrates tight Spanish control and post-independence conflict with
governments; 1958 winning of autonomy and student participation in
university governance. Organization of university; courses, degrees,
professors in its eight faculties make up this first catalog for the
whole university.

NIC ------. <u>Cuadernos Universitarios</u> 2d ser., no. 1 (November 1966),
60 145 pp.
    Essays by twelve writers on topics such as the university and
the community, research, educational failures. Two essays on modernization and reorganization of the contemporary Nicaraguan university.

NIC ------. <u>Guía de carreras de la UNAN.</u> Managua: UNAN, Departa-
61 mento de Orientación Profesional, 1981. 49 pp.
    Expansion of courses in numbers and in their places of
offering. Plans for major changes by 1985. Each professional school
(five in León and eight in Managua) describes its occupational profile,
plan of study, degrees awarded. Students in "basic semester" may
choose careers in accord with available openings; these will be determined by assessing national needs. WKU

NIC ------. "Informe de la Universidad Nacional Autónoma de
62   Nicaragua sobre su situación después del terremoto de Managua."
      Mimeographed. [León]: UNAN, [1974]. 10 pp.
         Grim statistics for city of dead, displaced, unemployed; loss
of services, public offices, hospitals, schools. Inventory of damages
suffered by UNAN campus and personnel. Loss of half of library
holdings, damage to laboratories, equipment. Nearly 20 percent of
students lost families, many will have to quit education and/or move
away from Managua. University, already suffering from inadequate
funding from government, lists costs of repairs. WKU

NIC ------. "Informe de matrícula al 1-10-80, curso lectivo 1980-
63   1981." Mimeographed. [León]: UNAN, Departamento de Registro, 1
      October 1980. 4 pp.
         Campuses at León, Managua, Estelí have total of 27,616
students. Conspicuous change from past is lack of general studies; the
"basic semester" is entry point. WKU

NIC ------. "Informe general de matrícula, primer semestre 1979-
64   1980." Mimeographed. León: UNAN, Departamento de Registro, 29
      September 1979. 2 pp.
         Enrollment shows 3,997 students in León, 17,440 in Managua,
517 in Carazo, 161 in Bluefields. Student numbers by faculties. WKU

NIC ------. "Informe general de matrícula, segundo semestre 1979-
65   1980." Mimeographed. León: UNAN, Departamento de Registro, 20
      February 1980. 3 pp.
         Of 14,979 students in four núcleos, 6,332 are in general
studies. Largest enrollment in Managua, smallest in Bluefields. WKU

NIC ------. Proyecto de ley orgánica de la Universidad Nacional de
66   Nicaragua. León: Editora Los Hechos, 1953. 13 pp.
         Support for creation of a modern organic law for the National
University and a petition for its rights. KU

NIC ------. Sesquicentenario, 1812-1962. León, 1962. 171 pp.
67   Chronology from 1670 founding of a seminary in Leon through
1812 decree from Cadiz establishing a university, to 1961 reforms.
Speeches on significant occasions, press comments on sesquicentennial,
congratulatory messages. KU

NIC ------. La Universidad Nacional y sus problemas económicos.
68   León: Universidad Nacional de Nicaragua, Secretaría de
      Relaciones Públicas, 1965. 6 pp.
         The data support the contention that the University of
Nicaragua is the weakest in Central America in financial support. KU

NIC ------, Asamblea General Universitaria. Documentos de trabajo,
69   resoluciones. [León: UNAN], 1963. ca. 100 leaves.
         Annual meeting of representative body hears rector Mariano
Fiallos Gil describe UNAN as having fewer resources from government
than any other university in Central America, with increase since 1957-
58 from 919 to 1,494 students. Considerable progress despite handi-
caps; impetus given by CSUCA toward regional cooperation in establishment of General Studies and three-year development program. Resultant
resolutions. KU

NIC   ------. <u>Documentos de trabajo, resoluciones</u>. [León: UNAN],
70   1968. 25 pp.
        In 1968 Carlos Tünnermann Bernheim was elected rector of the
National University in León. Major development of the year was
physical planning for the second campus, Recinto Universitario Rubén
Darío, in Managua. NiLU

NIC   ------. <u>Memoria</u>. León: UNAN, 1968. 25 pp.
71   After 1967 meeting was postponed by "tragic events," the
representative body was convened in 1968 for deliberations which produced several recommendations related to autonomy, finance, and student
participation in university governance. KU

NIC   UNIVERSIDAD NACIONAL AUTONOMA DE NICARAGUA, Comisión de Planea-
72   miento Universitario. <u>Plan de desarrollo 1966, 1969, 1972</u>.
        León: UNAN, 1965. 223 pp.
        Projection of growth of 263 percent in student body; re-
structuring of university with departmentalization, further development
of general studies, upgrading of staff, creation of courses in basic
disciplines and applied subjects. KU

NIC   UNIVERSIDAD NACIONAL AUTONOMA DE NICARAGUA, Facultad de Ciencias
73   y Letras. <u>Escuela de Ciencias y Letras: Programa de Estudios
        Generales, 1968-1969</u>. Managua: Universidad Nacional de
        Nicaragua, [1968]. 27 leaves.
        The general studies programs in the newly established campus
in Managua. Reflects reform effort to broaden base of purely professional education. KU

        UNIVERSIDAD NACIONAL DE NICARAGUA. See Universidad Nacional
        Autónoma de Nicaragua.

NIC   "Vasto plan cultural de la Universidad de Nicaragua." <u>Repertorio
74   Centro Americano</u>, July 1965: 32.
        A three month summer school for working class and middle
class people is in its fifth year, in twelve different towns, offering
courses in such topics as humanities, mathematics, homemaking, foreign
languages. Preparatory courses for entering students, in-service
courses for secondary school teachers, and a seminar on Central
American economic integration are also offered.

Panama

PAN AMADO, MIGUEL. <u>Evolución del concepto universitario y sus mani-</u>
1   <u>festaciones en Panamá</u>. Panamá: El Panamá América, 1942. 27 pp.
    Lucid explanation of philosophies regnant during establish-
ment of European and Anglo-American universities; finds concept of
humanistic studies praiseworthy. Indicts transfer of Spain's intellectual sterility to Latin America; pleads case to change University of
Panama from "a night school for adults" to true university, with a
single, planned campus. DPU

PAN ARIZ, CARLOS MARIA. "Docencia e investigación en la Universidad
2   Santa María la Antigua." In <u>La universidad y los universitarios:</u>
    <u>Carrera docente, investigaciones, estudios postgrados</u>, edited by
    Ana Herzfeld, Barbara Ashton Waggoner, and George R. Waggoner,
    pp. 91-95. Lawrence: University of Kansas, College of Liberal
    Arts and Sciences, 1974.
    Rector of Catholic University describes new university sta-
tute setting forth new administrative and academic structure based on
departmentalization. Regulations concerning teaching career and advancement in system, educational and research policy. WKU

PAN BERNAL, JUAN BOSCO. "Estudio de educación y recursos humanos en
3   la especialidad química: El caso de la Escuela de Química de la
    Universidad de Panamá." <u>Acción y Reflexión Educativa</u>, no. 2
    (July 1978): 86-101.
    Study by ICASE for Office of Academic Planning of UP to
determine supply and demand for high-level personnel in the local
chemical industry until 1982. Methodology takes into account changes
in market for chemists employed by companies using foreign patents.
Conclusions and recommendations require significant changes in university's School of Chemistry.

PAN CASTILLERO R., ERNESTO J. <u>La Universidad Interamericana: His-</u>
4   <u>toria de sus antecedentes y fundación</u>. Panamá: República de
    Panamá, Publicaciones de la Biblioteca Nacional, 1943. 334 pp.
    Dreams of establishing an Interamerican university began in
1915 at the second Panamerican Scientific Congress, in Washington.
Revised periodically, and stimulated by President Theodore Roosevelt,
the idea was to create an institution in Panama to link hemispheres of
north and south through studies of law, language, health, science,

201

arts, archaeology. Speeches and supporting documents. University of Panama actively in favor of idea. TxLT

PAN   CASTRO, NILS. "Algunos problemas fundamentales en la orientación
5   de la Universidad de Panamá." Acción y Reflexión Educativa, no. 4 (December 1979):   69-76.
        During first thirty years UP satisfied already established demand for education, contributing to "socioeconomic deformation which still characterizes the country," by educating for service professions, not those directed toward productive sector. Director of academic planning at UP describes abrupt 1970 change in size and scope; positive aspect was vast increase in opportunity; problems of finance, personnel, failure or delay of students in graduating. Some proposals for solutions. Useful data.

PAN   CEDEÑO CENCI, DIOGENES. Informe anual del rector. Ciudad Uni-
6   versitaria Dr. Octavio Méndez Pereira: UP, 1980.   91 pp.
        In forty-fifth year university has over 36,000 students, double the number in 1970; in 1976-80 period UP has graduated over half its total production of professionals. Of eighty-eight careers offered forty-two are short, technical level; over half of students are in science and technology areas. Report on academic activities, administration, student services; statistical and financial data. WKU

PAN   ------. "Seminario sobre problemática universitaria actual y sus
7   perspectivas." Acción y Reflexión Educativa, no. 4 (December 1979):   43-48.
        Rector of UP recounts student demands for internal changes after period of preoccupation with Panama Canal Treaty. Many focus on improved organization and presentation of courses, grading, high failure rate. Problems of finance are paramount; troubles in several faculties enumerated. Role of ICASE in providing information.

PAN   ------. "Tendencias de la educación en la década del 80."
8   Acción y Reflexión Educativa, no. 4 (December 1979):   12-15.
        University of Panama rector joins tenth anniversary recognition of ICASE's work as an Organization of American States entity, noting it was UP's first postgraduate institute and has given service to UP and the rest of Central America while avoiding political involvement. Foresees more horizontal technical assistance among area universities.

PAN   COMISION COORDINADORA DE PLANIFICADORES DEL SECTOR EDUCATIVO
9   GUBERNAMENTAL. Informes de Comisión. Ciudad Universitaria "Octavio Méndez Pereira":   UP, 1981.   14 pp. plus 15 pages appendices.
        Crisis of massification in UP addressed by commission charged with developing national educational policy. In 1960s only 23 percent of secondary school age actually attended, with slow increase in enrollment in a relatively "élitist" university. Government policy to democratize educational opportunity led to quadrupled UP enrollment between 1970 and 1980. Funds not available to meet demands to expand university. Gives alternative post-secondary proposals for intermediate, technical careers. Need to decrease high failure and dropout rate in university; strengthened regional centers; improved academic

and administrative performance; greater resources for research are chief recommendations. WKU

PAN   CONSEJO NACIONAL DE LEGISLACION. Ley sobre la Universidad:
10   Texto completo de la nueva legislación para que sea detenidamente leído por la comunidad. Panamá: Consejo Nacional de Legislación, 1981. 4 pp.
      Law, still unnumbered and undated, made available in tabloid form for public information, sets forth goals; governance; administrative structure; roles and duties of professors and students; provisions for retirement, discipline, transitional period. Characterized by great detail. WKU

PAN   CRAMPTON, C. GREGORY. "Professor at Panama." Western Humanities
11   Review, vol. 26, no. 2, Spring 1956: 109-16.
      University of Utah history professor describes early efforts of U.S. toward cultural exchange, which included his 1955 course in social sciences at the University of Panama; the university, the students, the environment.

PAN   "Decreto que reorganiza la Universidad de Panamá." Lotería 14
12   (June 1969): 10-28.
      Official document, signed by colonel heading the provisional government and by cabinet members, decrees university autonomy and sets forth structure and rules for university governance.

PAN   DIAZ, JORGE. "Estructura y funcionamiento de los centros re-
13   gionales universitarios a nivel nacional: Aspectos administrativos." Acción y Reflexión Educativa, no. 4 (December 1979): 91-125.
      Problems, characteristics of regional centers described in useful detail. Begun as UP extension programs, centers now need adjustment to their actual roles, relations, and functions. Suggestions.

PAN   DOMINGUEZ CABALLERO, DIEGO. La universidad panameña: Algunos
14   aspectos de su misión. Panamá: Imprenta de la Academia, 1946. 32 pp.
      A series of newspaper comments on the university combined in a pamphlet. After the first ten years and the new autonomy, Domínguez has doubts about the university and its purposes. Lack of clear relation between the university and the people, of a coherent faculty of sufficient Panamanian professors, especially full-time professors; classes mostly at night; lack of funds. KU

PAN   DUNCAN, JEPTHA B. La Universidad Nacional de Panamá: Su
15   organización, su administración, y su financiamento, 1940-1942. Panamá: La Estrella de Panamá, 1942. 159 pp.
      Catalogue of courses, administration, physical facilities; by rector. TxU

PAN   "La educación básica general: Una respuesta de la reforma edu-
16   cativa." Comunidad-Escuela 1, nos. 2-3 (November-December 1977): 10-13.

All of education should be involved in restructuring efforts designed to serve populations hitherto underserved or unserved, by means of study and work, erasing from students' minds "medieval" beliefs about liberal education. Description of present poor conditions in rural areas, methodology for change, socioeconomic impact of proposed changes.

PAN   FABREGA, ANGELA A. DE. "Areas problemáticas de la Universidad de
17   Panamá." Acción y Reflexión Educativa, no. 4 (December 1979):
      49-62.
      At time of June 1978 crisis rector organized meetings in various faculties to study university problems of finance, student affairs, administration and co-government, and the teaching situation. Questionnaire analyzed by ICASE with ad hoc committee. Results of studies provide catalogue of problems, recommendations. Useful overview of institution.

PAN   ------. "Informe de las actividades realizadas por ICASE durante
18   10 primeros años." Acción y Reflexión Educativa, no. 4 (December
      1979): 16-34.
      Graduate courses, seminars, research, publications among activities of agency which originated with ODECA, made up of Central American ministries of education, served all countries. Emphasis has been on social context of supervision and administration of education. Details of projects carried out.

PAN   ------. "Presentación." Acción y Reflexión Educativa, no. 1
19   (January 1978): 3-4.
      Introduction to new journal by director of ICASE says University of Panama and its political and cultural bases have oriented ICASE toward deepening and strengthening Central American educational systems through the countries' ministries of education. Financial and technical help from Organization of American States.

PAN   INTER-AMERICAN DEVELOPMENT BANK (IDB). "Inter-American Bank Ap-
20   proves $90,000 in Technical Cooperation for University Decentral-
      ization Program in Panama." Washington, D.C.: IDB news release,
      14 July 1977. 1 p.
      To help University of Panama secure technical help in preparing feasibility studies to expand four regional centers. Background, projected expansion to 1980 for 43,000 students. WKU

PAN   JUNTA PROVISIONAL DE GOBIERNO. Universidad de Panamá, Decreto
21   de Gabinete No. 144 (3 de junio de 1969). Panamá: La Junta,
      1969. 21 pp.
      Decree which reorganizes UP guarantees autonomy, but requires compliance with Constitution and national laws. Academic freedom requires "scientific objectivity" but does not allow "partisan political propaganda or doctrines contrary to the republican, democratic regime." Governance by directive council made up of minister of education, rector, a dean, a student, three citizens named by government; other roles and duties spelled out. WKU

      LUCARELLI, ELISA, and DIAZ, JORGE. SICAPER: Una experiencia de
      capacitación a distancia de administradores educativos en

servicio, ponencia presentada al I Congreso Interamericano de
Administración de la Educación, Brasilia 9-14 dic. 1979. See
entry GEN 180.

PAN   MENDEZ PEREIRA, OCTAVIO. La universidad autónoma y la universi-
22   dad cultural (discursos académicos). Panamá: Editorial Universitaria, 1973. 236 pp.
Rodrigo Miró, member of the Faculty of Philosophy, Letters
and Education, introduces book, points out that Mendez, the first
rector of the National University of Panama, was vigorous leader in
planning the university, and that President Arias supported plans. The
university planned a central College of Arts and Sciences and also the
licenciaturas in Faculties of Philosophy and Letters, Political Science
and Economics, Law, Commerce. Mendez was rector from 1935 until 1940
and in the 1950s, when autonomy of the university was accepted, and a
central campus was created. KU

PAN   ------. La universidad y la crisis actual del espíritu. Panamá:
23   [Editora Panamá América], 1954. 17 pp.
Rector's speech at 1954 graduation criticizes conservatives
wanting university to preserve "caste system," and those who advocate
support of primary instead of university education. TxU

PAN   MINISTERIO DE EDUCACION. Informe nacional que presenta la Repú-
24   blica de Panamá a la XXXVII Reunión de la Conferencia Internacional, Ginebra, Suiza, julio de 1979. Panamá: El Ministerio,
1979. 201 pp.
Describes public autonomous University of Panama; and private
University Santa María la Antigua, whose norms are set by the former
institution. UkLU-IE

PAN   MORALES, FILIBERTO. "Bases, objetivos y características de la
25   planificación regional educativa en Panamá." Acción y Reflexión
Educativa, no. 5 (June 1980): 146-54.
Theory, plans and goals, characteristics of central region
affecting education. Role of ICASE.

PAN   NASSIF, RICARDO. "Aproximaciones a un modelo panameño de uni-
26   versidad." Acción y Reflexión Educativa, no. 2 (July 1978): 6-
23.
Historical and contemporary facts, values, needs produce
university in post-1968 transition period, trying to evolve role and
structure appropriate for more democratic society. Strong nationalistic current manifest in effort to develop model less rigid, more
responsive to development than traditional institution, which dates
from 1935. Author is UNESCO consultant.

PAN   NUÑEZ G., CARLOS E. Recursos humanos profesionales y técnicos a
27   1980 en la Universidad de Panamá. Panamá: UP, 1976. 153 pp.
With an average graduation productivity of 10.6 percent,
university tries to estimate needs for enrollments to satisfy expected
employment in the country. Some existing surpluses and deficits, some
reform proposals: need for science and research, a flexible curriculum, emphasis on co-government, and the need for departments.
University has studied the importance of departmentalization in the
National University of Mexico and accepts these changes. KU

PAN OFICINA DE EDUCACION IBEROAMERICANA. La Educación en Ibero-
28 américa: Sistema de indicadores socio-económicos y educativos.
    Panamá Serie Estadística, nos. 1-3. Madrid, Ciudad Universi-
    taria: OEI, 1980. ca. 150 pp. in 3 vol.
        Remarkably comprehensive, thorough, objective collection of
information, in folders, on the socioeconomic framework of education,
and education itself. OASDC

PAN OSORIO O., ALBERTO. "Una filosofía para la Universidad de
29 Panamá." Lotería 14 (June 1969): 5-9.
        A philosophy for the university "will be structured in the
historical and spiritual tradition of Latin America."

PAN PANAMA. Subcomisión Especial Educación Superior, Universitaria y
30 su Integración con las Formaciones de Nivel Medio. Reforma
    educativa, experiencia panameña: Informe. [Panamá: Impr. de la
    Universidad de Panamá, 1972]. 213 pp.
        Present University of Panama was founded in 1935 with Central
College of Arts and Sciences; autonomy achieved in 1946. Problems
persist in the relation between traditional cátedra (chair) and modern
departments; faculties are described as lacking in flexibility, uncoordinated; administration cumbersome, ineffective; conflicts between
conservatives and reformers; lack of economic and planning policies.
TxU

PAN PANAMA. "Decreto no. 233 de jun. 4, 1965, por el cual se crea en
31 el Ministerio de Educación un organismo fiscalizador de las
    universidades privadas y que se denominara 'Universidades
    Privadas'." Gaceta Oficial, 62 (15.409), 9 July 1965, p. 2.
        Government decree creates fiscal procedures agency for
private universities in Ministry of Education.

PAN ------. "Resolución no. 33 de abr. 27, 1965, por la cual se
32 autoriza el funcionamiento de una Universidad Privada." Gaceta
    Oficial, 62 (15.364), 7 May 1965, p. 2.
        Legal authorization for functioning of private, Catholic
Universidad Santa María la Antigua.

PAN PENNSYLVANIA STATE UNIVERSITY. The National Plan for Education
33 1969-1983. Panamá, 1969. 319 pp.
        Useful data concerning the general plan for and behavior of
the Ministry of Education, and cooperation among the ministry, AID, and
Pennsylvania State University. Limited data concerning the National
University and the Catholic University Santa María la Antigua are
given--only 4 1/2 pages. KU

PAN RODRIGUEZ, RAUL, and URRIOLA, ORNELL. Educación superior y
34 liberación nacional. Panamá: Huaca Editores, 1980. 67 pp.
        Concern that method of analysis of University of Panama being
undertaken by rector and others will only result in partial remodeling
of system and not lead to badly needed examination of its role in
society and the state. Transformation and democratization of university are indivisibly linked to battle for anticolonial and antiologarchic
liberation. Historical analysis of higher education, essence of
present crisis; advocacy of social and educational changes; planning
for coherent educational system. Last chapter comments on lack of

progress, due to lack of identifiable spokesman for or consensus within student or professorial groups; all related to post-canal-treaty un-certainties about future of the nation. WKU

PAN   RODRIGUEZ-ARIAS BUSTAMANTE, LINO. <u>La universidad ¡En crisis!</u>
35   Panamá: Editora Mundial, 1962. 24 pp.
     Aspiration of the masses to university degrees requires doing away with class barriers, serving student-worker category instead of bourgeoisie. Calls for "democratization" of mass media, improvement of professors and pre-university education, research linked to teaching, full-time professors augmented by part-time people with maturity. Ad-vocates student participation in university affairs. TxU

     ROGGI, LUIS OSVALDO. <u>ICASE, una filosofía en acción</u>. See entry GEN 224.

PAN   ------. "Un modelo de planificación educacional superior para la
36   Universidad de Panamá." <u>Acción y Reflexión Educativa</u>, no. 1 (January 1978): 51-56.
     Summary of methodological orientations for study of high level manpower needs ICASE is carrying out for University of Panama. Effort to plan on basis of market demand and in accord with National Development Plan. Role of university in development process and in-ternal decision-making structure of university to be studied.

PAN   ------. "La sociedad panameña y su sistema educativo, hoy."
37   <u>Acción y Reflexión Educativa</u>, no. 2 (July 1978): 24-47.
     Specialist of the Organization of American States in ICASE lists central problems of educational system, e.g., its still-selective nature, low productivity. Discusses need for and resistance to change in educational institutions. Data on educational level of populace, outline of systems from preschool through university. At university level, problems of growth and poor performance (only 9.8 percent of students graduate), reform efforts.

PAN   ------. "Universidad y sociedad en América Latina y especial-
38   mente en Panamá." <u>Acción y Reflexión Educativa</u>, no. 4 (December 1979): 63-68.
     OAS specialist with ICASE traces university evolution in post-colonial period, finding Latin American university life "impover-ished for lack of liberties considered indispensable for normal aca-demic functioning." Panama's relatively recently created university served different groups and purposes from the traditional ones, and student militancy was nationalistic, anti-Canal Zone, non-threatening to bourgeoisie holding power. Effects of 1968 takeover by General Torrijos and National Guard of political functions, increased power of popular classes, the canal treaty. Questions now to be faced: what kind of education should university provide vis-a-vis labor market, national needs; what is university role in democratizing country's institutions? Sees opportunities for useful interaction between UP and society.

PAN   SALAMIN, JUDITH DE. "Avance de interpretación de la evolución y
39   perspectivas de los centros regionales universitarios." <u>Acción y Reflexión Educativa</u>, no. 4 (December 1979): 126-64.

Research project on CRUs gives their history, objectives and functions, resources, criteria for site selection of centers, data on matriculation by center and career, their productivity, planning and curricula administration. All are dependencies of the University of Panama.

PAN SANCHEZ, CEFERINO. La nueva ley de la Universidad de Panamá.
40 Panamá: [UP?], 1981. 41 pp.
　　Bibliography recapitulates steps taken toward development of new law over previous three years of proposals, debates, counter-proposals. Provisional University Council readies compromise draft for action by National Legislative Council. Academic vice rector reflects on laws of 1946 and 1969, faults present proposed law as too similar to them, too detailed on matters better spelled out in university statutes, too rigid to accomodate needed change. Attacks the facultad as basic unit of university structure as "medieval," deplores lack of research, offers suggestions on governance. An inventory of UP's problems. WKU

PAN ------, and GUTIERREZ T., EDILMA. La Universidad de Panamá ante
41 la nación y su futuro. Panamá: UP, 1980. 30 pp.
　　Speeches by academic vice-rector and highest ranked graduate of 1979-80 class at graduation ceremony address some issues in the proposed restructuring of the university. Creation of the Office of Development Projects to fit university into national needs; replacement of 1969 Law No. 144 of the university with more democratic structure and more modern concept of autonomy; decentralization of programs and administration among goals of present administration. WKU

PAN SCHIEFELBEIN, E., and GRASSI, M. C. "Análisis de una dimensión
42 de la eficiencia escolar: El caso de Panamá." Acción y Reflexión Educativa, no. 5 (June 1980): 155-72.
　　Study for ICASE of retention in school system, with abundant data as recent as 1978, reveals acute problem of high desertion and repetition rate typical of much of Latin America. Obvious implications for higher education system.

PAN SOLER, RICAURTE. "La Reforma universitaria en Panamá." In La
43 Reforma universitaria, tomo 3: Ensayos críticos. Compilación y
Notas de Gabriel del Mazo, pp. 347-57. Lima: Universidad Nacional Mayor de San Marcos, 1968.
　　Professor's comments at 1963 forum point to extra-university aspects of the 1918 Córdoba Reform: anti-oligarchic, anti-imperialist and pro-social justice sentiments. These are strong in Panama. Lists intra-university reforms, such as co-government, which function there; others, such as free access by students to classes in which they do not seek degrees and limiting terms for professors, would carry out the ideals of the Córdoba Reforms. WKU

PAN ------. La reforma universitaria: Perfil americano y definición
44 nacional. Panamá: Ediciones de la Revista "Tareas," 1963. 19
pp.
　　Describes ancient and medieval content of Spanish university brought to Latin America, nineteenth century changes, and 1918 reform of Córdoba within its social context. Proposes philosophy for Panamanian university reform. KU

PAN   TEJEIRA, OTILIA A[ROSEMENA] DE. "La Universidad de Panamá."
45   Lotería 14 (February 1969): 5-21.
        Thirty-year-old University of Panama shares problems of all
universities at end of 1960s. An ad hoc group urges reopening of
university, closed by government, and offers proposals for its restructuring.

PAN   UNIVERSIDAD DE PANAMA (UP). Boletín informativo de la Facultad
46   de Administración Pública y Comercio. Panamá: UP, 1968. 160
        pp.
        Professors, degrees of five schools comprising faculty, plans
of study. WKU

PAN   UNIVERSIDAD DE PANAMA. Boletín informativo de la Facultad de
47   Ciencias Naturales y Farmacia (Provisional), 1960-1961. Panamá:
        Universidad de Panamá, 1960. 61 pp.
        Faculty has departments of biology, chemistry, physics,
mathematics, pharmacy, and agriculture; in each the degree licenciatura
is offered; medical preparatory course also given. Admission, courses
of study. KU

PAN   ------. Boletín informativo de la Facultad de Ingeniería.
48   Panamá: UP, 1968. 174 pp.
        Professors; plans of study for graduate level, three engi-
neering and four technical specialties; course descriptions. WKU

PAN   ------. Estadística universitaria no. 8. Año Académico 1962-
49   1963. Panamá: UP, Secretaría General, 1965. 44 pp.
        Data on enrollment with some analysis; 58 percent of students
are male; 40 percent are in Faculty of Philosophy, Letters and Education; most come from public schools. There were 289 graduates out of
5,056 students enrolled. WKU

PAN   ------. Estadística universitaria no. 7. Edición Revisada
50   (1961-1962). Panamá: UP, Secretaría General, 1964. 40 pp.
        Matriculation for entire university grew from 2,829 in 1957-
58 to 4,227 in 1961. Enrollment data for the six professional schools.
WKU

PAN   ------. Estatuto de la universidad. Panamá: UP, 1963. 67 pp.
51   Constitutional grant of autonomy and basic law; rules on
finance; governance; student voting rights, matriculation, performance;
degrees and awards. WKU

PAN   ------. Estatuto universitario Capítulo V: Reformar al Capítulo
52   V del estatuto universitario, aprobado por el Consejo Directivo
        el día 6 de mayo de 1980. Panamá: UP, 1980. 30 pp.
        An intermediate stage in developing new university law spells
out categories and duties of teaching personnel. WKU

PAN   ------. Guía académica 1978. Ciudad Universitaria: UP, 1978.
53   51 pp.
        Courses available at main campus and regional centers, in-
cluding many at technical level. WKU

PAN   ------. Guía Académica 1979. Panamá: UP.   116 pp.
54   Orientation for new students, degree requirements for
specialization in university's nine faculties, offerings in five regional centers.   Obligatory attendance for all aspirants in summer
orientation and capacitation courses, with possible elimination from
certain programs based on performance.   List of careers with limited
numbers of entrants.   Heavy emphasis throughout university on applied
subjects.   WKU

PAN   ------. Informe del rector, año académico 1961-1962.   [Panamá]:
55   UP. [n.d.]. 164 pp.
        Thirty-two points of some importance for academic year, plus
statistics, reports from various faculties, report of the library.   KU

PAN   ------. Memoria presentada por el rector de la Universidad de
56   Panamá. Ciudad Universitaria: UP, 1976.   199 pp.
        An annual account presented by Rector Eligio Salas Domínguez;
teaching activities; student, cultural, administrative activities for
1975-76.   Despite great expansion, policies of democratization continue.   Increase of over 100 percent in graduates for 1969-75 over
1962-68.   Strengthened centers, resources for research, services, details of related activities.   WKU

PAN   ------. Memoria presentada por el rector de la Universidad de
57   Panamá. Ciudad Universitaria: UP, 1977.   189 pp.
        Since 1975 University has had an increase of 16.2 percent in
enrollment to total of 25,046; an 11 percent increase in professors to
2,056; number of graduates has increased by 12 percent to 1,575; and
new programs were added on both the full and intermediate level.   Creation of new Polytechnic Institute resulted in 3,000 new students the
following year.   Important step was creation of research centers and
post-graduate activities.   Continuing problem for the university: its
deficit budget.   WKU

PAN   ------. Programa de desarrollo institucional: Documento de
58   solicitud de préstamo por el gobierno de la República de Panamá
      al Banco Interamericano de Desarrollo.   Ciudad Universitaria:
      UP, 1970.   385 pp.
        First half is description of university; second half de-
scribes plan for which IDB funds are sought.   Estimated need for 22,000
professionals with university degrees by 1980 to meet developmental
requirements for Panama.   Very specific figures on physical plant and
other needs.   WKU

PAN   ------. Simposio: Efectos del crecimiento y la concentración en
59   la Universidad, del 28 de julio al 2 de agosto.   Panamá: UP,
      [1980?].   273 pp.
        Some eighty professors, administrators and the minister of
education consider a fundamental "crisis" of UP in a time of its restructuring: coping with massification.   Replacing present Decree No.
144 with new law will not resolve problem of growth, says rector.
University-at-a-distance concept explored;   presentations by the various faculties.   Recommendations of three working commissions address
possibilities of greater decentralization, alternatives to present
career offerings.   Useful inventory of problems and attitudes.   WKU

PAN   ------. Universidad 26 (1° semestre 1947).   213 pp.
60   Rector Octavio Mendez Pereira prefaces book of essays with remarks on the social function of the university. Topics on education, geography and history, sciences, sociology, university life. Lists sixty-four graduates of five faculties. Professors in six faculties have large number of U.S. university degrees.

PAN   ------. Universidad 27 (2° semestre 1947).   208 pp.
61   Twenty-two essays on Cervantes as the 400th anniversary of his birth is celebrated.

PAN   ------. Universidad 28 (2° semestre 1949).   190 pp.
62   Essays on literature, philosophy and other topics, including one on education of negroes; university life, including founding of the English Club; various UNESCO meetings.

PAN   ------. Universidad 29 (2° semestre 1955).   216 pp.
63   Rafael E. Moscote, director of the review, summarizes the importance of Octavio Mendez Pereira as rector of the university for various periods and as founder of this journal. Recent study of reform of the faculties of Philosophy, Letters and Education--particularly Education--was important.

PAN   ------. Universidad 36 (1957).   288 pp.
64   Rector Jaime de la Guardia reflects on university and its problems. Emphasizes importance of humanistic development for graduates. Twentieth anniversary of university features homage to Ortega y Gasset, comments on John Dewey, essays on topics from Panamanian-U.S. relations vis-a-vis the canal to medicine.

PAN   ------. Universidad 39 (1964).   297 pp.
65   Rector Narciso E. Garay reflects on mission of university in the face of national necessities. Essays on literacy figures, philosophy, medicine, economics and other topics.

PAN   ------, Dirección de Planificación Universitaria. Boletín, no. 9
66   (December 1976).   25 pp.
       Enrollment data for UP and Regional Centers, chiefly for 1976, by faculties, sex, specializations, and academic units. Graduates, by career, 1960-61 to 1976; professors, budgets, use of campus space.

PAN   ------. Boletín, no. 10 (August 1977).   24 pp.
67   Enrollment data for first semester 1977, by center and school, specializations, sex. Comparative figures from 1973 and 1976; growth since 1963-64; graduates, library data, professors' degrees.

PAN   ------. Boletín, no. 11 (December 1977).   21 pp.
68   Besides second semester 1977 enrollment has data on professors at UP and Regional Centers.

PAN   ------. Estadísticas Universitarias. Año académico 1975, 14
69   (July 1977).   150 pp.
       Characteristics of student body, teaching personnel, graduates, libraries, financial information; main campus and regional centers.

PAN   UNIVERSIDAD DE PANAMA, Escuela de Temporada. La educación en
70   Panamá (mesa redonda sobre los problemas de la educación na-
      cional, celebrada del 18 al 22 de marzo de 1957 en el paraninfo
      de la Universidad). Panamá: Imprenta Nacional, 1957. 334 pp.
      plus bibliography.
            History typical of Latin American university; its conserva-
      tism from Spanish times through Independence. Cordoba revolution
      reached Panama in 1943. Comments on university and other levels of
      education. TxU

PAN   UNIVERSIDAD DE PANAMA. Instituto Centroamericano de Adminis-
71   tración y Supervisión de la Educación, Instituto de Formación y
      Aprovechamiento de los Recursos Humanos. Educación y recursos
      humanos en Panamá. 2 vols. Serie de Investigaciones, no. 2.
      Panamá: República de Panamá, 1978.
            First volume gives details of manpower needs and availability
      in the framework of present and planned economic situation. Second
      volume includes panorama of Panama's educational system and its produc-
      tivity at all levels, including legal and financial data. Abundant
      data, useful text. WKU

PAN   UNIVERSIDAD SANTA MARIA LA ANTIGUA. La Antigua 8, no. 14
72   (December 1979). 83 pp. Special Issue.
            Entire issue devoted to Regional Assembly of Catholic Uni-
      versities of Latin America of the International Federation of Catholic
      Universities, held from 28 August to 1 September 1979 in USMA. Papers
      focused on the Catholic university in the light of the Puebla Document.
      WKU

PAN   ------. Boletín informativo 1981. Panamá: USMA, 1981. 149 pp.
73   History of Catholic University founded in 1965; governance,
      faculty members, 1980 graduates and enrollments in twenty-five careers
      in three campuses. Plans of study, photos of new campus on outskirts
      of capital city. WKU

PAN   ------. Manual de legislación. Panamá: USMA, 1977. 147 pp.
74   Laws are culmination of university reform process begun in
      1968, carried out with USAID help. Begins with Panamanian law of 1963
      regulating all private universities; covers all aspects of USMA's
      functions. WKU

PAN   The University and Foreign Aid: Terminal Report of the Uni-
75   versity of Tennessee to the Agency for International Development
      Concerning Contract Operations in Panama, 1955-1964. Mimeo-
      graphed. Knoxville, Tenn.: University of Tennessee, 1965. 196
      leaves.
            Intended as a final report to AID on the University of
      Tennessee's technical assistance programs in public administration,
      engineering and agriculture with the University of Panama. Reasonable
      ten-year summary, with interesting accounts of the riots of 1964,
      problems with AID and general chaos at the University of Panama. Well
      worth reading. KyU

Puerto Rico

PRi   ALMODOVAR, ISMAEL. The University: Vital Artery of Puerto
1   Rico's Industrial Development. Río Piedras: UPR, 1977. 12 pp.
       President of the university, speaking before the Puerto Rico
Manufacturers Association, describes the problems and the opportunities
for collaboration. Hopes costs of oil, for example, may be overcome by
steam use. Increased costs of labor in Puerto Rico will also be solved
by local manpower properly educated. WKU

PRi   APONTE-HERNANDEZ, RAFAEL. "The University of Puerto Rico:
2   Foundations of the 1942 Reform." Ph.D. dissertation, University
       of Texas, 1966. 267 pp.
       Significant periods in university's development, especially
events of 1940s and policies personified by Chancellor Jaime Benítez.
Internal reorganization, general studies movement, social and
economic--but nonpolitical--role of university in society.

PRi   BAKER, JOHN HENRY. "The Relation between Student Activism at
3   the University of Puerto Rico and the Struggle for Political
       Independence in Puerto Rico: 1923-1971." Ph.D. dissertation,
       Boston College, 1973. 250 pp.
       Examines episodes of protest in UPR, majority of them related
to pro-independence movement. "House of studies" policy in 1950s
called repressive. Only 3 percent of general populace favored independence in 1969, but over 50 percent of students did.

PRi   BANGDIWALA, ISHVAR S., and MENDEZ, JUANA A. Employability of
4   University Graduates in Puerto Rico. Río Piedras: Commonwealth
       Post Secondary Education Commission, 1979. 58 pp.
       Commission includes presidents of all Puerto Rican universi-
ties. Development of human resources as a chief responsibility of
educational system requires academic preparation for future employment
of graduates, to avoid wasting limited resources of island. Data on
kind, place of employment; work histories, relative to education in a
specialty. Graduates in humanities, social and behavioral sciences
have most difficulty in finding employment. Suggestions: more emphasis on "practical" courses, general education courses not necessary for
a specialty should be eliminated. Results of questionnaire study given
in detail. WKU

213

PRi   BENITEZ, JAIME. La casa de estudios: Sobre la libertad y el
5   orden en la Universidad. Río Piedras: UPR, 1963. 88 pp.
          The long-time chancellor describes the plans for university
reform at time of legislative hearings and in a major speech on the
topic. PrU

PRi   ------. "Education and Democracy in Puerto Rico." In Pro-
6   ceedings of the Sixty-first Annual Convention of the Middle States
      Association of Colleges and Secondary Schools 1947, pp. 48-56.
      [Atlantic City, New Jersey]: Middle States Association, 1947.
          A year after its accreditation by the association, UPR's
chancellor gives optimistic address on the University of Puerto Rico
and the Commonwealth. KU

PRi   ------. Education for Democracy on a Cultural Frontier; Two
7   Addresses. The University of Puerto Rico Bulletin, series 21,
      no. 3. Río Piedras: UPR, 1955. 26 pp.
          Speeches emphasizing the plans and the successes during
recent years. TxU

PRi   ------. Junto a la torre, jornadas de un programa universitario
8   1942-1962. San Juan: UPR, 1962. 433 pp.
          When Benítez put together this volume of papers, chiefly his
formal presentations as president of the University of Puerto Rico, he
had already been chancellor and president for 24 years, a leader of the
university in its formative period and also in the Commonwealth of
Puerto Rico. KU

PRi   ------. La reforma Universitaria; discurso pronunciado el día
9   15 de febrero de 1943 por el señor rector de la universidad, don
      Jaime Benítez. Boletín de la Universidad de Puerto Rico, ser.
      13, no. 3. [Río Piedras]: UPR, 1943. 15 pp.
          In his second year as rector, Benítez gave this lecture.
Describes problems of the war, importance of democracy, new plans for
the university, including his enthusiasm for the new approach in
general studies. KU

PRi   ------. "La universidad como casa de estudios dentro de la libre
10   comunidad hispánica de Puerto Rico." La Torre, Revista General
      de la Universidad de Puerto Rico 17, no. 66, (October-December
      1969): 11-17.
          Praise of the University of Puerto Rico and public's support
of the university. The university in Río Piedras and in Mayagüez,
with medical school in San Juan, collaborate smoothly with regional
colleges. Emphasis on nonpolitical role for "house of studies."

PRi   ------. La universidad del futuro. Río Piedras: UPR, 1964.
11   90 pp.
          Description of plans of the university sent to the Higher
Educational Council (the equivalent to a board of regents), by rector.
ICIU

PRi   ------. The University of Puerto Rico. Río Piedras: UPR,
12   Office of Information, 1960. 7 pp. plus 11 tables and 1 graph.
          Written statement by chancellor of UPR to U.S. House of
Representatives Committee on Interior and Insular Affairs. Increase

since 1903 founding as a normal school with 154 students to over 18,000. Emphasis on financial support from Puerto Rican taxpayers, contribution of university to "transforming the sociological structure of the island," and statement that "there is no unemployment among our graduates." Data on programs, students, faculty, finance. ICIU

PRi   BENNER, THOMAS ELIOT. Five Years of Foundation Building: The
13   University of Puerto Rico, 1924-1929. Río Piedras: UPR, 1965.
      157 pp.
         As first chancellor of the University of Puerto Rico, Benner led the University from its 1903 beginning as a normal school to its becoming a university. In 1923 a full-time chancellor was appointed who developed both the university in Río Piedras and the campus in Mayagüez. (UPR is Land Grant institution, with agriculture and engineering at Mayagüez.) KU

PRi   BOWLES, FRANK H. "The High Cost of Low Cost Education." In
14   Higher Education in the United States, edited by Seymour Harris,
      pp. 199-202. Cambridge: Harvard University Press, 1960.
         University of Puerto Rico "appears" to be easy of access, low in cost to individual, accredited; in fact it is relatively restrictive in access, overcontrolled, underproductive. Lack of graduate programs is high-cost, detrimental to the economy. Faults lack of adequate accounting, poor library, internal rigidities. KU

PRi   BRAMELD, THEODORE B. H. The Remaking of a Culture: Life and
15   Education in Puerto Rico. New York: Harper and Brothers, 1959.
      478 pp.
         Evaluation of the problem of education in Puerto Rico, the similarities and differences in Puerto Rico and the rest of the U.S.; problems of language and related difficulties for the University of Puerto Rico. Importance of general studies and need for autonomy in experiments in Puerto Rican higher education. KU

PRi   CATHOLIC UNIVERSITY OF PUERTO RICO. Catalog 76-78. Vol. 22,
16   no. 1. Ponce: [Catholic University of Puerto Rico], 1976. 207
      pp.
         Catholic University of Puerto Rico is organized in a U.S. pattern, with the catalog in English; College Entrance Board tests given in Spanish or English; Middle States Association of Colleges and Secondary Schools accredits the university. Main campus in Ponce, and centers at Arecibo and Guayama. At its 1948 beginning, affiliated with the Catholic University of America in Washington, D.C. Original emphasis in the arts and training of teachers; now has colleges of Education, Arts and Humanities, Sciences, and Business Administration. WKU

PRi   COLEGIO UNIVERSITARIO DEL TURABO. Colegio Universitario del
17   Turabo, 1979-1982. Río Piedras: Fundación Ana G. Mendoza, 1979.
      113 pp.
         General information, academic programs, faculty, in private university serving some 5,110 students. WKU

PRi   COMISION ESTATAL DE EDUCACION POSTSECUNDARIA. Estadísticas
18   sobre las instituciones de educación postsecundaria públicas y

215

Puerto Rico

privadas acreditadas por el Consejo de Educación Superior. Año
academico 1975-76. Río Piedras: La Comisión, 1976. 139 pp.
    Study with a federal subsidy under the Higher Education Act
of 1965 as amended. Matriculation figures are given, along with
academic offerings in all institutions; degrees, certificates and diplomas; teaching personnel by type of work, sex and academic
preparation; and an inventory of physical facilities. WKU

PRi ------. Estadísticas sobre las instituciones de educación post-
19   secundaria radicadas en Puerto Rico. Año academico 1974-75. Río
     Piedras: La Comisión, 1976. 115 pp.
        Data under place names, not by individual institutions. WKU

PRi CONSEJO SUPERIOR DE ENSEÑANZA. La deserción de estudiantes en
20   la Universidad de Puerto Rico, Recinto de Río Piedras y Mayagüez.
     Publicaciones Pedagógicas, ser. 3, no. 31. Río Piedras: UPR,
     1966. 159 pp. plus tables.
        A study of the drop-out problem at the university level. NBC

PRi DEL CORRO, ALEJANDRO, comp. Puerto Rico: Reforma universitaria
21   1963-65. CIDOC dossier no. 6. Cuernavaca: CIDOC Centro Inter-
     cultural de Documentación, 1966. ca. 450 pp.
        Collection of all available documents concerning proposed
reform of University of Puerto Rico. Extensive bibliography includes
many entries from newspapers indicating heated conflicts. Copies of
various laws, commentary from press. KU

PRi DUNCAN, RONALD J. "Federal Student Assistance Policy and Higher
22   Education in Puerto Rico." Paper delivered at Caribbean Studies
     Association Conference, St. Thomas, U.S. Virgin Islands, 29 May
     1981. Mimeographed. 29 pp.
        Overloaded private universities, underserved students result
from federal subsidy of large numbers of poor people pursuing education
as alternative to unemployment. Deficits abound in infrastructure,
students come badly prepared, attrition is high and unemployment grows.
Basic Education Opportunity Grants nourish a precarious industry. WKU

PRi ESTADO LIBRE ASOCIADO DE PUERTO RICO, Consejo de Educación Su-
23   perior, Universidad de Puerto Rico. Reglamento General de la
     Universidad de Puerto Rico. Río Piedras: Consejo de Educación
     Superior, UPR, 1981. 142 pp.
        Rules for UPR system, composed of the Higher Education
Council, the central administration, the governing board responsible
for the campuses at Río Piedras, Mayagüez, the medical center; and the
Administration of the Regional Colleges. Besides these autonomous
units, the system consists of eight non-autonomous post-secondary
entities. WKU

PRi FUNDACION EDUCATIVA ANA G. MENDEZ. Información general sobre la
24   Fundación Educativa Ana G. Méndez y sus instituciones afiliadas.
     Río Piedras: La Fundación, [1980]. 6 leaves.
        Goals of nonprofit foundation which operates three private
institutions: Puerto Rico Junior College, Colegio Universitario del
Turabo and Colegio Universitario Metropolitano. Both associate and
bachelor degrees as well as noncredit programs are offered. WKU

PRi   GARCIA ESTEVE, JOEL, and CIRINO GERENA, GABRIEL.   "Los problemas
25   estudiantiles de la Universidad de Puerto Rico en 1971." Revista
      de Ciencias Sociales 16, no. 3 (September 1972): 419-30.
         Study of student views related to 1971 university strike
reveals concern about quality of teaching and guidance, among other
problems.

PRi   GONZALEZ, MIDGALIA.   "Boricua College will Graduate First Class
26   July 26." San Juan Star, 6 June 1981, pp. S 10-11.
         Accredited by Middle States Association, college has 1,000
students in its upper Manhattan building, plans another campus in
Brooklyn. Serves Puerto Rican and other Hispanic students in
nontraditional study modules.

PRi   GONZALEZ DE PIÑERO, EUROPA, ed.   Accountability and Change in
27   Education: Highlights of the Second Annual Conference on Edu-
      cation Held at the Inter American University of Puerto Rico.
      Danville, Ill.: The Interstate Printers and Publishers, 1972.
      72 pp.
         Teacher education, a major function of Inter American Uni-
versity, is focus of conference of university personnel. Problems
include low productivity of system; demand for accountability discussed
and dissented with. Educational hardware pushed by industry; cooperative education examined. Vigorous denunciation of some professors who
use academic freedom for partisan political ends, resulting in current
shut-down of three universities by secretary of instruction. MoS

PRi   GUINNESS, GERALD.   "UPR: A Good University but is it a Great
28   One?" Sunday San Juan Star Magazines, 16 April 1978, pp. 6-7.
         A professor in College of Humanities, UPR, Río Piedras
campus, speculates on the quality of university, stimulated by the
recent celebration of its seventy-fifth anniversary. Island and large
university suffer from the tendency to emphasize materialistic values
and to neglect intellectual and spiritual. Specifically, there is
tendency toward xenophobia, to urge that faculty members be Puerto
Ricans whether they be the best professors or not. "Intellectual
demoralization" he also laments, calling for more time for reading and
research.

PRi   HANSEN, MILLARD W.   Missions of a University in a Small Country.
29   Río Piedras: Social Science Research Center, Social Science
      Faculty, UPR, [1975]. 158 pp.
         Proposes three fundamental changes in the basic structure of
the University of Puerto Rico, with new dimensions needed: a center
for scientific research, a graduate faculty of public affairs, and a
graduate faculty of arts and sciences. The university in Río Piedras
is large but the emphasis is almost completely on undergraduate work.
A country like Puerto Rico needs university research (of which it does
not have much), high-level work on public affairs, and development of
Ph.D. programs. DLC

PRi   HARRIS, JOHN WILL.   Riding and Roping: The Memoirs of J. Will
30   Harris. Edited by C. Virginia Matters. San Germán: Inter
      American University of Puerto Rico, 1977. 211 pp.

Religious vision led to founding of Polytechnic Institution of Puerto Rico. Its evolution from its 1911 incorporation in San Germán to its status as Inter American University in 1956, as seen through the cultural, theological and moral lens of its founder. A cultural as well as personal history of the times and of Puerto Rico. WKU

PRi HERNANDEZ BORCH, CARMEN. "La Universidad Católica de Puerto
31 Rico: Síntesis de su historia." *Horizontes* 17, no. 33-34
    (October 1973-April 1974): 5-25.
      Founding, governance, accreditations, objectives, programs, degrees, campus, scholarships.

INTER AMERICAN UNIVERSITY OF PUERTO RICO. See Universidad Interamericana de Puerto Rico.

PRi LEWIS, GORDON K. *Puerto Rico: Freedom and Power in the Carib-*
32 *bean*. New York: Harper and Row, 1968. 470 pp.
      From the point of view of education, there are two interesting chapters: "The Growth of Education", especially on the aspect of higher education; and "The Character of Public Opinion", especially on the discussion and evaluations of the University of Puerto Rico. KU

PRi LIEBMAN, ARTHUR. *The Politics of Puerto Rican University*
33 *Students*. Austin: Institute of Latin American Studies, University of Texas, 1970. 205 pp.
      Useful history of Puerto Rican education and some comparative (but mid-fifties) data on retention in schools. Lack of effort to achieve independence from Spain in nineteenth century distinguishes Puerto Rico from other Latin American countries, with consequent lack of strong national persuasion. Most students in mid-sixties were not politically active; status of relationship with U.S., not ideology, is chief political party focus. KU

PRi MELENDEZ, WINIFRED ALBIZU. *The Universities of Puerto Rico*.
34 New York: Gordon Press, 1978. 330 pp.
      Historical and social background, statistical data on public and private universities, junior college; comparisons between University of Puerto Rico and Inter American University students in enrollment, social characteristics, educational goals and study habits. Problems include lack of coordination, social role of public and private systems, lack of educational philosophy; "politicization" on Puerto Rican status affects decision-making. Appendices list faculty members and their degrees. IU

PRi MORALES CARRION, ARTURO. *Discursos de ayer, con prólogo de hoy*.
35 San Germán: Universidad Interamericana de Puerto Rico, [1980].
    45 pp.
      Four speeches, from 1954 to 1978, by former rector; first, when institution was a polytechnical school with 622 students, last when it was a university with 12,766 students. All reflect concern with world and local conditions and universities' roles within these frameworks. WKU

PRi NIEVES-FALCON, LUIS. *Diagnóstico de Puerto Rico*. Río Piedras:
36 Editorial Edil, 1971. 260 pp.

Many aspects of education are touched on in this analysis of
Puerto Rico, with two chapters specifically on the university. View of
university from the inside, especially in social sciences, and the
problems of faculty government and participation. Emphasis on the
administrators rather than professors or students. KU

PRi   ------. Recruitment to Higher Education in Puerto Rico, 1940-
37   1960. Río Piedras: Editorial Universitaria, UPR, 1965. 304 pp.
        Characteristics of students in the University of Puerto Rico.
Conclusion is that the university is non-elitist but with shift to mass
education system is increasing social class differences rather than
reducing them. The purpose of the university is to create "a sort of
employment agency for the state, the pool from which to recruit the
executives and technical personnel required to operate an industri-
alizing society." Useful data and philosophical questioning. UkLU-IE

PRi   ------; GARCIA RODRIGUEZ, PABLO; and OJEDA REYES, FELIX. Puerto
38   Rico, grito y mordaza. Río Piedras: Ediciones Librería Inter-
        nacional, 1971. 285 pp.
        In March of 1971 there were crises at UPR's Río Piedras
campus with attacks particularly from the Partido Popular Democrático,
over U.S. problem of Viet Nam and of Puerto Rican independence.
Efforts to avoid political upheaval on campus. KU

PRi   OSUNA, JUAN JOSE. A History of Education in Puerto Rico. 2d
39   rev. ed. Río Piedras: Editorial de la Universidad de Puerto
        Rico, 1949. 657 pp.
        Dean emeritus of the College of Education, University of
Puerto Rico, writes about Spanish colonial policy on education, and the
request to establish a university; the 1898 American occupation and
imposition of U.S. pattern on education, incuding establishment of the
University of Puerto Rico in 1903. Specific information on UPR in
years 1920, 1925, 1931, 1936, 1942, and 1945-46. Comparing with other
nations of region he calls Puerto Rico's educational progress of last
fifty years "the wonder of the century." KU

PRi   PARKER, FRANKLIN. "Puerto Rican Educational Research: Annotated
40   Bibliography of 66 United States Doctoral Dissertations."
        Extracted from Latin American Education Research: Anno-
        tated Bibliography of 269 United States Doctoral Dissertations by
        Franklin Parker. Austin: University of Texas, Institute of
        Latin American Studies, 1964. 15 pp.
        About a dozen of the sixty-six items pertain to higher
education. WKU

PRi   PICO, ISABEL. "Origins of the University Student Movement under
41   U.S. Domination (1903-1930)." In Puerto Rico and the Puerto
        Ricans, edited by Adalberto López and James Petras, pp. 175-94.
        Cambridge, Mass.: Schenkman Publishing Co., 1974.
        Background for understanding link between university student
behavior and question of island's political status. Description of
imposed U.S. patterns and growing resistance. KU

PRi   PICON-SALAS, MARIANO. Apología de la pequeña nación: Discurso
42   pronunciado en la cuadragésima segunda colación de grados de la

Universidad de Puerto Rico, 31 de mayo de 1946. [Río Piedras]:
UPR, 1946. 37 pp.
A lecture in honor of the graduates of the University of
Puerto Rico in May 1946 includes history of the university.

PIÑERO, EUROPA GONZALEZ DE, and CLAUDIO, RAMON, eds. Crecimiento
del personal docente. See also Gonzalez de Piñero, Europa. See
entry GEN 211.

PRi   PLANADEBALL, MARTA JOSEFINA. "Problems in Reading English as a
43   Second Language at the University of Puerto Rico, with Sug-
      gestions for Improvement." Ed.D. dissertation, Teachers College,
      Columbia University, 1955. 188 pp.
          Inadequacies in reading and inferring in Spanish need cor-
recting at earliest levels as prelude to developing skills in English
needed for success at university levels. Survey in UPR showed lack of
motivation, problems of comprehension.

PRi   "Puerto Rico." Caribbean Monthly Bulletin, Vol. 15, no. 10
44   (October 44   1981): 39-41.
          Rector suspends UPR classes in Río Piedras after student
strike in protest over increased fees. Negotiations among student and
administrative groups focus on economic factors in access of students
to UPR. Governor says additional money is not available.

PRi   QUINTERO ALFARO, ANGEL G. "A Critical Analysis of the General
45   Studies Program of the University of Puerto Rico and a Plan for
      its Development." Ph.D. dissertation, University of Chicago,
      1949. 207 pp.
          General education program at UPR, the Puerto Rican situation,
and a theory of general education. University reforms, begun in 1942,
part of larger social reform efforts; general studies program "the
central factor of the university reform." Both descriptive and interpretive view by UPR assistant dean of program. Strong commitment to
general education for everyone in a democracy; consequent need for
faculty development, improved teacher training and coordination at all
levels, provision for exceptional students, attention to skills in
thinking as well as mastery of content. Changes in program leading to
1945 establishment of separate Faculty of General Studies. Data on
enrollments, finance, geographic, historical, economic, social background of educational system and reform efforts. Analysis of essentially liberal value systems, aimed at development of human person
in the Ortega y Gasset tradition. Operational necessities emerge.
Core course descriptions, other documents. An influential viewpoint in
Latin America.

PRi   ------. "Educación y cambio social en Puerto Rico." Mimeo-
46   graphed. [San Juan: Universidad Interamericana de Puerto Rico],
      1962. 14 pp.
          Philosophical comments by influential Puerto Rican educator
on situation confronting Puerto Rico at a time of rapid change,
presented at a seminar at Inter American University. KU

PRi   ------. Educación y cambio social en Puerto Rico: Una época
47   crítica. San Juan: Editorial Universitaria, 1972. 223 pp.

New plans in the University were important in the period from 1945 to 1960 when Quintero was working on General Studies, with point of view from the University of Chicago. Lack of articulation between secondary education and the university as unproductive for students; schools "overloaded" curriculums and teachers; teaching methods made little use of books and libraries. Drastic changes made in decreased classroom hours, increased independent study; weekly seminars designed to integrate learning in sciences and humanities during the 1960-68 period. His future-oriented educational philosophy reflects anti-authoritarian bias in learning, his awareness of Puerto Rican political and social realities, and his goal of a liberating kind of education. FU

PRi RENE-QUIÑONES, SAMUEL. "P.R. Senate Chief Proposes Campus of UPR
48 be Established in New York." San Juan Star, 6 June 1981.
     Several hundred hear proposal at New York's Puerto Rican Day
banquet speech.

PRi RICCIO, ROBERT ALBERY. "A Proposed Course in Humanities for the
49 College of Agriculture and Mechanic Arts for the University of
     Puerto Rico." Ed.D. dissertation, Teachers College, Columbia
     University, 1957. 143 pp.
     Many students are first generation in university, in a
society suffering great dislocations of traditional culture. University role in providing more than technical training; value will be
related to making humanities courses pertinent to daily life.
Suggestions.

PRi RODRIGUEZ BOU, ISMAEL. La educación en tres tiempos del quehacer
50 puertorriqueño. [Río Piedras]: UPR, 1953. 23 pp.
     Panoramic view of Puerto Rican progress, including education,
compared with other parts of Latin America. Accomplishments of university and its graduates, particularly in regional and hemispheric
responsibilities, are celebrated. MiU

PRi ------. Legislación de emergencia y competencia interuniversi-
51 taria improductiva. Río Piedras: UPR, División de Extensión,
     1969. 47 pp.
     Demands integral plan for all levels of education, including
the universities. Junior colleges particularly need to be related to
the high schools and to the universities. Need for a master plan. KU

PRi SAENZ, MERCEDES. Universidad de Puerto Rico: Historia y re-
52 cuerdos. Manati, Puerto Rico: Imprenta Rodríguez, 1978. 74 pp.
     In celebration of the seventy-fifth anniversary of the University of Puerto Rico, the director of the university library produces
illustrated history. WKU

PRi SARIOLA, SAKARI. The Puerto Rican Dilemma. Port Washington,
53 N.Y.: Kennikat Press, 1979. 200 pp.
     Differences among proponents of free associated status, independence, and statehood. University people have strong feelings for
independence and consequently there are a dozen or so comments on
higher education. The university strike of 1948 and the second strike
of 1971 were full of student unrest with sharp differences between the
university administration and the independistas. KU

PRi   "Se conmemora con gran entusiasmo el sexagésimo-sexto aniversario
54   de nuestra universidad." El Presidente Informa 8, no. 1 (March
      1978). 4 pp.
        Texas-born, Princeton-prepared missionary J. Will Harris
founded the Instituto Politécnico de San Germán which evolved into a
university with over 28,000 students in 1978. Along with a vignette of
the founder are enrollment data and other current news.

PRi   "66to Aniversario de la Universidad Interamericana de Puerto
55   Rico." El Mundo, 24 February 1978, p. SC1.
        The first private university in Puerto Rico has grown from a
polytechnic institute founded by a Presbyterian minister to its present
28,506 students. Thirty percent are part-time students and 90 percent
receive some kind of financial aid. President Ramón A. Cruz compares
UIA with the University of Puerto Rico in terms of costs, flexibility
and service.

        SHERLOCK, PHILIP. "The Role of Education in the Process of
        Development and Modernization of the Caribbean People." See
        entry GEN 246.

PRi   "Sobre la situación universitaria en el recinto de Río Piedras."
56   APPU 6, no. 2 (28 March 1978): 1-4.
        The non-academic Council of Higher Education is appointed by
the governor. There are partisan political aspects of the Council, and
traditionally also of professors' behavior. The APPU pushes now for a
faculty union.

PRi   SULSONA, HERMAN. Mensaje del Dr. Herman Sulsona, Rector de la
57   Administración de Colegios Regionales de la Universidad de Puerto
      Rico, ante el Overseas Press Club 8 de Agosto de 1974. [Río
      Piedras], 1974. 18 pp.
        Personal, social, economic and educational consequences of
severe unemployment of university graduates in Puerto Rico. Agricultural character of island in 1950 changed rapidly by industrialization. Mass education increased access to professional education,
with traditional bachelor's degree as only option, leaving many without
employment. Effort began twelve years earlier to create technical
education opportunities and subsequent growth described. Data on the
regional colleges. WKU

PRi   SUSSMANN, LEILA. "Democratization and Class Segregation in
58   Puerto Rican Schooling: The U.S. Model Transplanted." Sociology
      of Education 41, no. 4 (Fall 1968): 321-41.
        Rapid postwar expansion of high school and university en-
rollment led to decline in quality of education, proportionally more
working class students in university than in mainland U.S. Democratization of access increased social segregation by 1960, with more
advantaged in private institutions.

PRi   ------. High School to University in Puerto Rico. Río Piedras:
59   UPR, Faculty of Social Sciences, Social Science Research Center,
      1965. 183 pp.
        High priority given to universal education in Puerto Rico
aided prosperity and industrialization, but "blundering insistence" on

English as sole language of instruction impeded access to education for many. In 1960, proportion of age group in high school and university in Puerto Rico much smaller than in U.S. mainland, but recruitment pattern similar. DLC

PRi   TIESTES LOSCOS, P. CESAREO. "La enseñanza universitaria privada
60   en Puerto Rico." Horizontes 17, no. 33-34 (October 1973-April
      1974): 27-48.
         Short history; enrollment in public and private universities,
1960-73; degrees awarded; origins of students. Proposed reforms for
total educational system for more equity and for universities'
planning, coordination, development.

PRi   TIO, AURELIO. "Puerto Rico: Site of the Primordial University
61   of the Americas." Translated and adapted by Lynn Darrel Bender.
      Revista/Review Interamericana 4, no. 4 (Winter 1974-75): 484-
      92.
         Although it is usually said that the University of Santo
Domingo was the first university created in the New World, Tio argues
that the University of General Studies "St. Thomas Aquinas" of San Juan
de Puerto Rico was the first.

PRi   UNIVERSIDAD DE PUERTO RICO. Catálogo general: Descriptivo de
62   facultades, colegios y dependencias, así como de los cursos y
      programas. [Río Piedras]: UPR, 1953. 306 pp.
         Fiftieth anniversary of founding. Administration, services,
programs of study in Río Piedras, Mayagüez and School of Tropical
Medicine. Illustrations typical of mainland prototypes. KU

PRi   ------. A Decade of Research at the Office at the Superior
63   Council on Education. Río Piedras: UPR, 1956. 43 pp.
         Forty research projects on education, including university,
carried on from 1947 to 1956. PrU

PRi   ------. General Guide 1977-1978. Río Piedras: University of
64   Puerto Rico General Administration, Office of Academic Affairs,
      1977. 190 pp.
         Describes the boards of government, administration, degrees
offered, academic regulations, fees, the campuses and colleges,
academic programs and degrees. WKU

PRi   ------. General Guide to the University of Puerto Rico, 1979.
65   Río Piedras: University of Puerto Rico Central Administration,
      Office of Academic Affairs, 1979. 125 pp.
         Begins with docoument announcing adoption and description of
new coat of arms and seal for UPR. The previous seal, approved in
1903, now becomes official seal of Río Piedras Campus. The system and
its administration, map of the several campuses throughout the island,
academic calendar and programs. WKU

PRi   ------. Administración Central, Oficina de Planificación y
66   Desarrollo. Compendio de estadísticas de la Universidad de
      Puerto Rico. Año académico 1979-80, primer semestre 1980-81.
      Río Piedras: UPR, Area de Sistemas de Información, Sección de
      Estadísticas, 1981.

Some seventy-five tables and graphs on UPR system, including regional colleges. Item T-17.02-17.04 has enrollment data from all accredited university-level institutions, 1975-76 to 1979-80. UPR enrollment was held at around 50,000 students, while private institutions increased from around 50,000 to 76,149 in same period. WKU

PRi   UNIVERSIDAD DE PUERTO RICO, Administración de Colegios Region-
67   ales, Colegio Regional de Humacao. Catálogo 1975-1976--1976-
       1977. Humacao: Colegio Universitario de Humacao, [1975]. 132
       pp.
       The Regional College of Humacao offers similar programs to
the first years of the University of Puerto Rico. Humacao has 120
professors and 2,903 students, who may finish two-year programs and
receive their two-year degrees, and/or may shift to the University of
Puerto Rico in Río Piedras or elsewhere. The University Colleges are
accredited by the Middle States Association. WKU

PRi   UNIVERSIDAD DE PUERTO RICO, Colegio Universitario de Cayey. Catá
68   logo 1974-75, 1975-76, 1976-77. Cayey: UPR, Colegio Universi-
       tario de Cayey, 1974. 157 pp.
       A ten-year effort by Cayey citizens was rewarded in 1966 with
establishment of a regional college, a dependency of the University of
Puerto Rico in Río Piedras. In 1969 it became a four-year, degree-
granting college, and in 1974-75 was preparing for its first evaluation
by the Middle States Association of Colleges and Secondary Schools.
The catalog, like the school, is a U.S. model, with names and degrees
of faculty members. Growth since 1967-68 with 370 students to 2,753 in
1974-75; library had over 53,000 volumes. Offers the B.A. degree, the
B.S., and a Bachelor of Business Administration. WKU

PRi   UNIVERSIDAD DE PUERTO RICO. Consejo Superior de Educación. Aná-
69   lisis de la matrícula universitaria y sus proyecciones en el
       futuro. Trabajos de Investigación Auspiciados por el Consejo
       Superior de Enseñanza. Publicaciones Pedagógicas, ser. 2, no.
       17. Ismael Rodríguez Bou, director. Río Piedras: UPR, 1955.
       103 pp.
       Analysis of the university in terms of matriculation and
projections for the future. In 1943-44 the number of students was
4,669; in 1954-55, 9,258. DLC

PRi   ------. Estudio Socioeconómico. Vol. 1, Escala para medir el
70   nivel socioeconómico y análisis de las condiciones sociales y
       económicas de los estudiantes de primer año de las instituciones
       universitarias de Puerto Rico. Publicaciones Pedagógicas, ser.
       2, no. 33. Ismael Rodríguez Bou, director. Río Piedras: UPR,
       1966. 140 pp.
       Study of first-year students in Río Piedras and Mayagüez
campuses of University of Puerto Rico, Catholic University, Sacred
Heart College, Puerto Rican Junior College, and Inter American University shows socioeconomic profiles of students and institutions.
Some correlations with academic performance at UPR. CLU

PRi   ------. Ley de la Universidad de Puerto Rico. Río Piedras:
71   UPR, 1966. 21 pp.
       The laws of the university are very similar to those of U.S.
mainland universities. WKU

PRi ------. Facilidades Educativas del Estado Libre Asociado de
72 Puerto Rico. Trabajos de Investigación Auspiciados por el
Consejo Superior de Enseñanza. Pulicaciones Pedagógicas, ser. 2,
no. 20. Ismael Rodríguez Bou, director. Río Piedras: UPR,
1957. 390 pp.
Committee of Human Resources of Puerto Rico carried out
series of studies for development of human potential of the country.
Studies will help better planning for industrialization and the economy, and will also affect education. No datum unturned or unrecorded in
115 tables and 27 graphs. CLU

PRi UNIVERSIDAD DE PUERTO RICO, Mayagüez Campus. Bulletin of Infor-
73 mation. 1973-74, 1974-75, 1975-76. Río Piedras: UPR
(Mayagüez), 1975. 385 pp.
The 1908 extension of benefits of the Morill-Nelson Act
establishing Land Grant universities to Puerto Rico made possible the
University of Puerto Rico's rapid growth, mainly in Río Piedras. The
College of Agriculture, organized in Mayagüez in 1911, became the
College of Agriculture and Mechanic Arts; in 1942 it became the Mayagüez Campus, and in 1966 one of three autonomous campuses (the others
are in Río Piedras and San Juan). Still called El Colegio," it has
over 9,000 students in the Colleges of Agricultural Sciences, arts and
Sciences, Business Administration, and Engineering. History, governance, services, academic programs, course descriptions. WKU

PRi UNIVERSIDAD DE PUERTO RICO, Presidencia. Guía general infor-
74 mativa 1977-1978Ú. Río Piedras: UPR, Asuntos Académicos, 1978.
108 pp.
First edition of document designed for students, faculty,
administration, describes structure and function, rules of entire system, as well as the programs of the separate component entities. WKU

PRi UNIVERSIDAD DE PUERTO RICO, Río Piedras Campus. General Cata-
75 logue. 1973-1974, 1974-1975. Río Piedras: UPR, 1973. 490 pp.
History, government of the university, the Council on Higher
Education, function of the president, description of academic community, participation of faculty members and students, alumni association,
library. The library is the largest in the Caribbean. Detailed course
descriptions are given. WKU

PRi UNIVERSIDAD DEL SAGRADO CORAZON. Catálogo 1980-1982. Santurce:
76 Universidad del Sagrado Corazón, 1980. 222 pp.
Founded as Catholic elementary school for girls in 1880, it
evolved to present coeducational university status in 1976. Junior
college section offers terminal associate degrees in ten fields, associate degrees allowing transfer to bachelor's degree program in five
programs, and bachelor's degrees in five departments. WKU

PRi UNIVERSIDAD INTERAMERICANA DE PUERTO RICO. Catálogo general
77 1979-80, 1980-81. Vol. 10, no. 1. Río Piedras: Universidad
Interamericana de Puerto Rico, 1979. 147 pp.
Information for campuses in metropolitan San Juan area, San
Germán and the six regional colleges. Programs lead to certificates,
associate in arts and bachelor's degrees. History from 1912 founding
as vocational school to 1944 accreditation. (This is its first catalogue printed in Spanish instead of English.) WKU

PRi ------. <u>General Catalogue 1977-1978, 1978-1979</u>. Vol. 9, no. 1.
78   San Juan: Inter American University of Puerto Rico, 1977. 50
     pp.
         History, governance, academic programs, general services for
School of Law, main campuses in San Juan and San Germán, San Juan
subunits, and eight regional colleges. WKU

     UNIVERSITY OF PUERTO RICO. See Universidad de Puerto Rico.

PRi "University of Puerto Rico." In <u>Laws of Puerto Rico Annotated</u>,
79   pp. 231-322. Oxford, New Hampshire: Equity Publishing Co.,
     1974.
         Legal basis of UPR, finance, general provisions, medical
school, agricultural experiment stations, accrediting system, financing
of construction, educational fund. Also covers administration of
regional colleges. KU

PRi VIVO, PAQUITA, ed. "Education." In <u>The Puerto Ricans: An Anno-</u>
80   <u>tated Bibliography</u>, pp. 43-50. New York and London: R. R.
     Bowker, 1973.
         Of the fifty-nine entries, a larger percentage is devoted to
higher education than is found in most bibliographies. KU

PRi WHITLA, DEAN K., and HANLEY, JANET P. <u>Reponsiveness and Reci-</u>
81   <u>procity: The Role of the College Board in Puerto Rico</u>. Hato
     Rey: College Entrance Examination Board, 1971. 147 pp.
         Two important points: improvement of the admission test
program and plans for early identification of the talented. The
problems also of the University of Puerto Rico, the private colleges,
and the junior college. The UPR is the most prestigious university.
It appears that in Puerto Rico test scores are better predictors of
success than grades. DLC

PRi WORLD UNIVERSITY. <u>Graduate School of Business, Accounting and</u>
82   <u>Management, Catalog 1978-1980</u>. Ser. 1, no. 1. Hato Rey: World
     University, 1978. 70 pp.
         Calendar, goals of WU, graduate school, academic policies,
M.B.A. and M.S. programs, courses, governance. WKU

PRi ------. <u>World University General Catalogue, 1978-1979/1979-1980</u>.
83   Hato Rey: World University Press, 1978. 119 pp.
         History, philosophy of institution accredited by Puerto Rican
Council of Higher Education in 1972. Curriculum, degrees, enrollment
information for this nontraditional university. WKU

U.S. Virgin Islands

USV COLLEGE OF THE VIRGIN ISLANDS. The Caribbean Research Institute
1   1965-1975: A Tenth Anniversary Report. St. Thomas, 1975. 28
    pp.
        Brief history of college and founding of semi-autonomous
research entity. Description of projects. WKU

USV ------. Catalogue, 1976-1978 and Catalogue Addenda, 1977-1978.
2   St. Thomas and St. Croix, U.S. Virgin Islands: College of the
    Virgin Islands. 129 pp. and 15 pp.
        College established in 1962 is accredited by Commission on
Higher Education, Middle States Association of Colleges and Secondary
Schools. Full baccaleaureate programs in thirteen fields, cooperative
engineering and medical technology programs completed at other institutions, associate degree program, occupational training, and master's
program in teacher education. Courses offered, graduation requirements, calendar, faculty members and their degrees.

USV ------. Newsletter. Winter, 1978. 12 pp.
3   In the fall of 1977, 616 full time students were enrolled,
531 in St. Thomas, 75 in St. Croix, and 10 students in their junior
year in the University of Connecticut. Graduate students in education
numbered 58, part-time students 1,445. Part-time graduate programs in
business and administration and in public administration began in
January 1978. A fund drive for $110,000 assisted the college.

USV ------, Caribbean Research Institute (CRI). Report for the
4   Period January 1, 1975-June 10, 1977. St. Thomas: [College of
    the Virgin Islands], 1977. 16 pp.
        Brief history, changes, funding, facilities, staff, projects,
publications. WKU

USV ------. Report for the Period July 1, 1977-June 30, 1979. St.
5   Thomas: College of the Virgin Islands, CRI, 1979. 24 pp.
        CRI, established in 1966, pursues research in natural, physi-
cal, social and economic sciences for use especially in Virgin Islands
and other microstates. Information on staff, projects, publications.
WKU

USV ------. Self-Study Report of the College of the Virgin Islands.
6   St. Thomas, 1975. 148 pp.

Prepared for the Commission on Higher Education of the Middle States Association of Colleges and Secondary Schools. Institutional data summary followed by elaboration of history, academic programs and divisions, students, faculty, administration, facilities and finance. Follow-up study of graduates assesses strengths and weaknesses. On-going problem of helping students with academic deficiencies. Publications list and statistical material in appendices. WKU

USV VERLACK, PEARL. "Teacher Education in the United States: A His-
 7   torical Profile." Microstate Studies 1 (1977): 71-93.
     Difficulties in getting any education underway in U.S. Virgin Islands. Collaboration with University of Puerto Rico, and some attendant problems; program of New York University.

Venezuela

VEN ACOSTA ESPINOZA, NELSON, and SUAREZ GRILLO, LUIS. "La Investi-
1 gación en la Universidad de Carabobo." Papeles Universitarios,
no. 14 (March-April 1979): 40-55.
 Example of 1970s self-criticism for lack of policies regarding university research. Comments on paucity of people adequately
prepared and of projects related to national development needs. Data
on current research in university in Valencia.

VEN ALBORNOZ, ORLANDO. Acerca de la universidad y otros asuntos.
2 Caracas: Instituto Societas, 1970. 152 pp.
 First half consists of 22 essays written for popular press on
university topics such as politics, governance, student unrest, publications. Second half is more general social commentary. WKU

VEN ------. "Activismo político estudiantil en Venezuela." In
3 Estudiantes y política en América Latina, compiled by Aldo E.
Solari, pp. 209-72. Caracas: Monte Avila Editores, [1978].
 Students lacked traditional rights during the rule of Dictator Pérez Jiménez, whom they helped depose in 1958. Between 1958 and
1967 student numbers and their participation in national politics grew,
particularly in public universities, with strong criticism of the
government and the U.S., and considerable enthusiasm for the Cuban
Revolution. In 1963-64 there were 20,062 students in the Central
University; in Zulia (Maracaibo) 5,542; and in Oriente (Cumana) 1,801.
KU

VEN ------. "El aislamiento del científico social en contextos
4 académicos ideologizados." Paper presented at Fourth Annual
Meeting of the Caribbean Studies Association, Martinique, May
1979. Mimeo. 50 pp.
 Venezuelan sociologist calls social science research in
universities scarce, low in quality, little related to centers of
decisionmaking in Venezuela and elsewhere in region. Despite freedom,
the social scientist is either isolated--and even penalized for im-
partiality--or captive of some dogma which inhibits good research. WKU

VEN ------. La crisis de la universidad pública. Valencia: Uni-
5 versidad de Carabobo, Dirección de Cultura, 1972. 208 pp.

Essays by sociologist-as-social-critic analyze role of the public Central University vis-à-vis growing strength of private and other governmental universities. Raises questions about social values and conditions and their effects on higher education. Fervently democratic, critical of extreme rightists and leftists, author nonetheless believes in airing of political questions within university. Written during time of governmental efforts to protect university autonomy from perceived abuses. Second half of book devoted to lighter fare. IU

VEN   ------. "Educación, inmigración e identidad nacional en
6   Venezuela." Paper prepared for the meeting of the Latin American
       Studies Association, Bloomington, Indiana, October 17-19, 1980.
       Mimeo. 44 pp.
       Casts light, without heat, on concern of Venezuelans for effects of massive immigrations on national identity, and the possible results from Ayacucho scholarship program for thousands of Venezuelan university students in the U.S. Comments on persistent class divisions reflected in educational system, and various traditional Venezuelan university problems. WKU

VEN   ------. "Educación superior y futuro: el caso venezolano."
7   Text prepared for la Reunión Nacional sobre formas de educación
       superior para una sociedad en desarrollo, organized by
       CINTERPLAN, with sponsorship of the Universidad de Los Andes and
       the Consejo Nacional de Recursos Humanos. Caracas, 22-25 Febru-
       ary, 1983. Mimeo. 22 pp.
       Fifty years of "bonanza" and relative surplus are ending, leaving public higher educational institutions characterized by "growth without development," "bureaucratized and ineffective," overloaded with employees fighting to maintain privileges. Contraction of funds ought to reduce public university budgets, distribute more to basic education for minorities hitherto deprived, with private universities serving those who can pay. "Fourth revolution" will see education for employable skills, not just credentials, reduction in universities' bureaucratic overhead and professorial costs, less funds available for libraries and equipment. Research will have to pay for itself and "the era of literary contemplation" is at an end. Post graduate studies, "imposed by neo-colonial mentalities," were not linked to research on the productive apparatus, nor were they at an internationally accepta-ble level. Challenges much political rhetoric, assumptions about third world development and social value of higher education. Provocative and possibly all-too-accurate definition of problems for coming decade of debate. WKU

VEN   ------. "Evaluación de innovaciones recientes en la educación
8   superior venezolana." Papeles Universitarios 3, no. 13 (January-
       February 1979): 12-21.
       Address at seminar "Studies and Experience on Higher Edu-cation and Development in Latin America," Viña del Mar, Chile, gives Venezuelan socio-historical background for discussion of recent edu-cational developments. Goals of consumer society adversely affect relationships in education. Describes and comments on efforts in behalf of technical education, the Ayacucho Plan, the Open University, and a plan to transform the University of Carabobo.

Venezuela

VEN ------. La formación de los recursos humanos en el área
9   educación. Colección Estudios. Caracas: Monte Avila Editores,
     1979. 134 pp.
     Unites material previously scattered through other documents
on contemporary crises in education. Severely criticizes poor quality
and productivity of autonomous universities, politicians who, in the
name of reform, would shift social system from capitalist dependency to
socialist one. Efforts to develop human resources for national development, including policies of Plan Ayacucho, caught up in ideological battle. Proposed reforms in School of Humanities and Education,
UCV. Accuses colleagues of engaging in "disinformation," with their
tendency to dogmatize on a Marxist ideological base instead of relying
on empirical studies. NcU

VEN ------. "Higher Education and the Politics of Development in
10   Venezuela." Journal of Interamerican Studies and World Affairs
     19, no. 3 (August 1977): 291-314.
     Venezuelan sociologist describes largely marginal society,
especially in Caracas, dominated by private sector which is best served
by existing university systems. Calls for integrated system of higher
education to meet human resource needs for whole populace. Claims
present private universities such as Universidad Católica and such
governmental but autonomous universities as Universidad Simón Bolívar
serve an already favored few.

VEN ------. Ideología y política en la universidad latinoamericana.
11   Caracas: Instituto Societas, 1972. 359 pp.
     Five general chapters precede two on the Venezuelan universi-
ty (chiefly Universidad Central). Very size of Venezuelan student
population makes it important group, with uncertain economic future.
Traditional student fights against dictators produced present generation of democratic leaders. More recent rise of anti-government
extreme left also from universities, even with relatively elite
origins. Data on Central University enrollment 1948-67, and six faculties. Description of ideologies of students, professors. Efforts to
limit autonomy in 1970. KU

VEN ------. "La situación de la educación superior en Venezuela: La
12   operatividad de la incertidumbre en condiciones de crisis."
     Papeles Universitarios 2, nos. 7-8 (March-April 1978): 70-79.
     Paper prepared for Third Annual Meeting of Caribbean Studies
     Association, Santiago de los Caballeros, Dominican Republic.
     Philosophical examination of Venezuela's recent past and
present social values as they affect higher education, especially the
unwillingness to face future uncertainties. Excess of demand over
capacity in higher education produces crisis; quality suffers. Lack of
data, dependence on improvisation instead of planning, professional
rather than academic goals of universities. Recommendations include
higher quality, more professional professors, more intellectual rigor
for students.

VEN ------. "La universidad venezolana: Factor de estabilidad
13   social en el desarrollo político." Paper prepared for Seventh
     Annual Meeting of the Latin American Studies Association,
     Houston, Texas, November 1977. Mimeo. 33 pp.

Venezuela

Despite leftist rhetoric in university politics, professors are anything but leftist in behavior, being beneficiaries of government largesse through strength of their guilds. Describes a new-rich class of "subsidized leisure" where merit plays no role in salary and benefits, which, ultimately, the poorest in society pay for. Bitter denunciation, adducing evidence, of unproductive, costly, corrupt universities in an increasingly corrupt and wasteful society. WKU

VEN 14 ALEXANDER, ALBERTO GUILLERMO. "An Analysis of the Consequences of the University of Kansas-Universidad de Oriente Program: A Decade Later." Ph.D. dissertation, University of Kansas, 1977. 139 leaves.
The Universidad de Oriente in Cumana and the University of Kansas collaborated in a faculty development project with Ford Foundation help. Of initial twenty-five UDO faculty members receiving advanced degrees at KU 68 percent continue at UDO. Lasting positive effects on both institutions.

VEN 15 ALMEA, RUTH LERNER DE. "La Fundación 'Gran Mariscal de Ayacucho' en tránsito hacia el desarrollo nacional." Correo de Ayacucho, Boletín Informativo 1, no. 9 (March 1977): 4-6, reprinted from Universitas 2000, no. 9.
History and organization of government scholarship program for 10,500 students of non-metropolitan and working class origins. Selection process, choice of twenty-five countries for studies, emphasis on developmental needs, plans for reincorporation into society and employment of becarios.

VEN 16 ------. Innovation in the Harnessing and Transfer of Technology: The Gran Mariscal de Ayacucho Foundation. [Caracas: n.p., 1977]. 8 pp.
Some 11,000 students, mostly from the provinces and from poor or modest families, get scholarships, with 60 percent going abroad. Success of 80 percent in first three years. Data on fields of study, finance, organization. WKU

VEN 17 ARNOVE, ROBERT F. Student Alienation: A Venezuelan Study. New York: Praeger, 1972. 209 pp.
In the Venezuelan University of Oriente the problems of student alienation brought surprising data: those most successful academically were also the political leaders. It was not sociologists but engineers and medical students who were the leaders. KU

VEN 18 ASOCIACION DE INSTITUCIONES DE FORMACION DOCENTE DE VENEZUELA (AISFORDOVE). El mercado ocupacional del profesional docente egresado del nivel superior: IV conferencia general, Caripe, noviembre de 1976. Caracas: AISFORDOVE, 1976. 240 pp.
Representatives of Venezuela's Central University, Andres Bello Catholic University, Pedagogical Institute and others convene to discuss placement of graduates from their education faculties. Lament general lack of human resources studies in Venezuela, and problem of knowing supply/demand for teaching profession. Statistical information and comments on national educational planning policy by government. WKU

VEN   "The Ayacucho Scholarships." Venezuela Up-to-Date 20, no. 3
19   (Fall 1978). 10 pp.
      Over 14,000 students are in program begun in 1974, with 5,378
in Venezuela, 4,689 in the U.S., the rest in 29 other countries. Trend
away from such large numbers in petroleum engineering into more basic
disciplines; also shifting to more mature students, graduate studies.

VEN   BETANCOURT, ROMULO. "La nueva universidad y las especiali-
20   zaciones venezolanas." In La Reforma universitaria. Vol. 3:
      Ensayos Criticos, compilation and notes by Gabriel del Mazo, pp.
      176-79. Lima: Universidad Mayor de San Marcos, 1968.
      Written in 1947, during his first period as president of
Venezuela, by a member of the "Generation of '28'"; celebrates
Venezuela's university autonomy and egalitarian society but criticizes
lack of university places for secondary graduates and need to import
professionals. Cites need for vocational orientation of youth,
specialists to develop power and agriculture, less "scholastic"
teaching, less group selfishness, more dedication to national
development. WKU

VEN   BIANCO, JESUS M. Universidad avasallada, patria más sojuzgada.
21   Caracas: Universidad Central de Venezuela Rectorado, 1970. 14
      pp.
      Rector's commencement address, given twenty-four hours after
national Chamber of Deputies approved the University Reform Law,
attacks law as a "campaign of colonization" by foreign businesses.
Sees partial loss of university autonomy as step toward "imperial
domination," foresees compulsory birth control and physical liquidation
of the population. Predicts political control of university, with
rector only a functionary of Ministry of Education. Urges fight
against change. WKU

VEN   BLANCO ASCANIO, RAMON. "Solicitarán nulidad de decreto presi-
22   dencial que revocó creación de Universidad Politécnica." El
      Universal, 1 April 1979, pp. 1-12.
      With switch in political power after presidential election
from AD to COPEI, outgoing director of OPSU apparently had found a new
post as rector of a university hastily created by combining three
widely separated technical institutes. Not so, says new government,
revoking enabling act. Would-be rector will appeal to Supreme Court.
Typical imaginative use of educational bureaucratic apparatus for survival in and out of power.

VEN   BORGES, RAFAEL S. "La politiquería en universidades tradicion-
23   ales permite a sectores interesados desarrollar e incrementar sus
      intereses y su clientela." El Universal, 21 January 1980, pp. 2-
      30.
      Former Rector Mayz Vallenilla of the Universidad Simón
Bolívar denounces efforts to convert this experimental university to a
traditional one, where "cheap politics" serve ambitions of demagogues
and damage academic productivity. Cites fundamental flaws in 1958 Law
of Universities.

VEN   BORJAS SANCHEZ, JOSE ANTONIO. Imagen de Lossada. Maracaibo:
24   Universidad de Zulia, Facultad de Humanidades y Educación, 1966.
      101 pp.

A not very informative eulogy of an obviously gifted educational leader, Dr. Jesus Enrique Lossada, who was rector of the Universidad del Zulia for two years before his 1948 death. KU

VEN   BOZA, GUILLERMO, and SOZA, ANTONIO JUAN. UCAB: La crisis de
25   octubre. Valencia: Yadelle Hermanos, 1974. 208 pp.
       Examination of a 1972 crisis, with history, antecedent of conflict, later "unstable equilibrium," in Andres Bello Catholic University. Analysis of static internal structure; tensions among outside supporters, Jesuits, Venezuelan state; influences of change as result of Vatican II. Expulsions, strike, violence, response; changes considered. NmU

VEN   BURROUGHS, G. E. R. Education in Venezuela. Hamden, Conn.:
26   Archon Books, 1974. 121 pp.
       Chapter seven describes the universities, most of which, like the population, are near the Caribbean coast. Structure, political role, staffing; 1958 reform and uses of autonomy, and 1970 curbs on abuses. Characteristics of non-science-oriented education include lack of full-time professors and of research. Rapid social change in post-dictator era, rapid growth, creation of "experimental" universities; roles of National Council of Universities and minister of education in policy making. KU

VEN   BUSTAMANTE, COLOMBIA C. "Venezuelan Students in the United
27   States: Stereotypes of and Attitude Changes toward the Home and Host Countries." Ph.D. dissertation, University of Kansas, 1978. 135 pp.
       Among conclusions: attitudes of Venezuelan students toward U.S. most favorable at beginning and end of time in U.S., and less favorable to Venezuela at end of stay. Subjects were Venezuelan students at University of Kansas and University of Tulsa, U.S. students at University of Kansas, and Venezuelan students in two Venezuelan universities. Some implications for those returning from Ayacucho scholarship plan abroad to Venezuela and expectations for their role at home. KU

VEN   CALDERA RODRIGUEZ, RAFAEL. Responsabilidad de las universidades:
28   Once grandes temas de nuestro tiempo. Caracas: Fundación Eugenio Mendoza, 1967. 39 pp.
       Political leader, later president of Venezuela, on universal and particular problems in universities. In Venezuela there is lack of research, high failure rate. Comments on university autonomy, including Fidel Castro's apparent paradoxical changes in attitude. Opposes extraterritoriality as part of autonomy. WKU

VEN   CARVAJAL, LEONARDO. "La educación en el proceso histórico
29   venezolano (II)." Cuadernos de Educación 61 (January 1979). 108 pp.
       Analysis of education begins with "pre-capitalist, semi-colonial" period of 1830-48, following sections on "indigenous collectivism and pre-capitalist colonialism." An anthropological approach heavy on social class theory. CEE

VEN   CASAS-ARMENGOL, MIGUEL. "Desarrollo nacional, profesiones,
30   universidad." Universitas 2000, no. 2 ([1972?]): 23-27.

Venezuela

Challenges assumption that increased higher education per se contributes directly to national development. (Venezuelan increase, 1958-66: 332 percent.) Impact of Harbison's 1964 visit and consequent faith in "manpower" development. Raises moral and philosophical objections as well as practical ones. Unplanned growth, satisfaction of social mobility goals. Calls for research, rational plan for growth, measures of productivity.

VEN ------. "An Exploratory Study of the Interaction among Higher
31 Education, Human Resources and National Development in
Venezuela." Ph.D. dissertation, Stanford University, 1970. 295
pp.
Case study in field of architecture used to illustrate "reciprocal influences of society, professionals and the university, in relation to national development." If, during professional training, students are not confronted with national development problems and role of their profession in solving these problems, graduates will exhibit "individualistic" approaches to their work. Thus graduates will not, as professionals, contribute to national development.

VEN ------. "Prospectiva 1980-1990 de la educación superior y
32 tecnológica de la región del Zulia." Papeles Universitarios,
nos. 5-6 (January-February 1978): 49-52.
University of Zulia in serious condition, with traditional, rigid organizational structure, while facing explosive growth particularly at undergraduate level. Needs for decreased growth rate, institutional restructuring, research, graduate studies. Plans for decentralization in region near Lake Maracaibo, major petroleum center.

VEN ------. "La UNA, experiencia a considerar en la planificación de
33 un sistema de educación abierta y a distancia para el Caribe."
Caribbean Educational Bulletin 7, no. 3 (September 1980): 4-14.
Rector of Venezuela's Open University meets with UNICA executive committee; urges recognition of Caribbean community's common characteristics, need for non-elitist higher education. Describes Venezuela's current fancies regarding educational innovations, progress in developing programs. Lists difficulties, including use of professors and administrative practices from conventional universities.

VEN ------, and others. Consideraciones preliminares para la creación
34 de la Universidad Nacional Abierta de Venezuela. Caracas:
Comisión Organizadora de la Universidad Nacional Abierta, 1976.
34 pp.
Rector of new Open University (UNA) describes traditional universities as insufficient in size and character for post-petroleum society. UNA designed as complementary to others with new approaches to body of knowledge and teaching methods. Demographic, economic, educational data; rates of growth, 1971-76, in higher education. Tools and methods of instruction and evaluation, infrastructure requirement, stages of development, estimate of 1978-88 demand. WKU

VEN CHIRINOS, EDMUNDO; VIALE RIZO, SEBASTIAN; and FAILLACE, AMERICO.
35 "Proposiciones para una reforma universitaria." Papeles
Universitarios 2, nos. 7-8 (March-April 1979): 28-30.

Venezuela

Three deans of the Universidad Central propose remedies for intensely increased demand for university matriculation and anarchic process of creating new institutions of higher education. Statement of policies is followed by call for modifying functions and structure of UCV.

VEN CLAUDIO, IVAN. Radiografía presupuestaria de la UCV. Caracas:
36 Mesa de Redacción, 1970. 217 pp.
 Attacks upon the Central University of Venezuela in the period of Rector Bianco; problems especially acute in 1968. Hopes for renovation. KU

VEN COLMENAREZ, MARIA MAGDALENA. "Los servicios estudiantiles en
37 Venezuela." Universitas 2000 4, nos. 2-3 (1980): 53-63.
 With petroleum riches which retard moves to national self-sufficiency and conduce to excessive consumerism, the educational system is isolated from country's productive apparatus. Seventy percent of Venezuela's population is under twenty-five years old, with consequent pressure on educational institutions. Real professionalism in student services essentially lacking until creation in 1962 of national commission. Subsequent progress described.

VEN "La Comisión Electoral de la UCV deciderá la fecha de las elec-
38 ciones." El Nacional, 6 January 1978.
 Fourteen political groups propose postponing student elections at Universidad Central. Advantages in not having yearly elections with consequent loss of time, possible need to separate student government election from that choosing representatives to university governing bodies; estimate that 25 percent of 60,000 students voted in last elections. Most student parties are part of national political parties.

VEN CONDE, JAVIER. "La Presidenta de Fundayacucho denuncia:
39 Otorgadas en dos meses todas las becas del 79 por la anterior directiva." El Nacional, 24 April 1979, p. D-2.
 Outgoing politically-appointed officials of scholarship organization have awarded all of 1979's budgeted funds before March take-over by incoming party. Policy changes: more emphasis on graduate studies, bringing foreign professors to Venezuela, more grants for humanities and sports. Criticisms of previous administration.

VEN CONSEJO NACIONAL DE INVESTIGACION, CIENCIA Y TECNOLOGIA
40 (CONICIT). Directorio nacional de cursos de postgrado 1974.
 Caracas: CONICIT, 1974. 181 pp.
 Course descriptions; indices by institutions, disciplines, geographic locations. WKU

VEN ------, Comisión de Cursos de Postgrado. "Conclusiones
41 provisionales de cuatro estudios básicos sobre educación de post-grado." Paper presented for discussion at Fifth Meeting of the Commission on Graduate Studies, 26-27 July 1974. Mimeographed. Caracas: CONICIT. 24 pp.
 Small amount of graduate study in country concentrated in School of Medicine in UCV in Caracas. Weak or nonexistent programs elsewhere reveal lack of policy, planning, personnel, support.

Priority areas for national development are in production sector related to petroleum. WKU

VEN ------. "Documento de trabajo: Conclusiones y recomendaciones
42 de la V reunión de la Comisión de Cursos de Postgrado." Meeting 26-27 July 1974. Mimeographed. Caracas: CONICIT. 10 pp.
    Recommends national policy on graduate studies; inventory of existing programs; studies of manpower needs, scholarships, financing. A few weak generalizations about graduate studies elsewhere. WKU

    CONSEJO NACIONAL DE UNIVERSIDADES (CNU), Oficina de Planificación del Sector Universitario (OPSU). See entries under OFICINA DE PLANIFICACION DEL SECTOR UNIVERSITARIO.

VEN CONSEJO NACIONAL DE UNIVERSIDADES (CNU), Secretaría Permanente.
43 La educación superior en Venezuela: trabajo presentado en el XII Seminario de Educación Superior en las Américas, relizado en la Universidad Simón Bolívar, del 12-17 de marzo de 1972. Caracas: CNU, 1972. Ca. 160 leaves.
    Historical descriptive material on higher education with copies of original documents pertaining to functioning of universities. WKU

VEN CONTASTI, MAX. "La formación de los recursos humanos de alto
44 nivel como criterio de planificación para la educación superior." Papeles Universitarios, nos. 10-11 (August-October 1978): 41-53.
    Developmental myth spread through Latin America in the fifties is simplistic, presupposes infrastructure of mature capitalist state. Foreign investment took out raw materials; foreign aid tied to inadequate technology. Myths of the seventies of creating human resources and of reliance on transfer of technology. Concrete proposals for rational university improvement. Lists available people with fields of specialization 1975-80, relative to estimated needs.

VEN ------. "La problemática de los recursos humanos en relación a
45 los planes nacionales de desarrollo." Universitas 2000 3, no. 1 (1978): 195-200.
    Calls for short, middle and long term planning for manpower needs on national scale. Denounces international policies that keep third world countries from developing "clean" industries, relates this to university development needs.

VEN DARCY, RIBEIRO. Propuestas acerca de la renovación. Caracas:
46 Universidad Central de Venezuela, 1970. 207 pp.
    Proposals to restructure the country's chief university include departmentalization, reorganization of teaching, curricula and administration. This self-study would keep university autonomy and co-government. WKU

VEN "La descomposición de la educación venezolana." Papeles Uni-
47 versitarios 3, no. 13 (January-February 1979): 5-6.
    Editorial on chronic problems of cupo (space for matriculants) and repitencia in universities. Not only are too many students demanding admission to universities, but many fail, repeating courses, blocking access for future students. Non-university alternatives lack prestige. Call for coherent national policy.

VEN   "El decreto de nulidad refleja la lucha de AD y COPEI por el
48   control de la educación superior." El Universal, 9 April 1979.
        Movimiento al Socialismo (MAS) says through its party's uni-
versity secretary that COPEI's vilification of AD's "nervous creation"
of Universidad Experimental Politécnica, with post for outgoing OPSU
director, is example of fight between the two major parties for bureaucratic control of higher education. Other changes under way do not
benefit those needing education.

VEN   DELGADO OCANDO, J. M. "La verdadera misión de la universidad
49   actual." Revista de la Universidad del Zulia, no. 40 (January-
        March 1968), pp. 97-120.
        Upon his entering the university as rector, Delgado tried to
describe its goal. He quarrels about the behavior of some U.S. universities which include every kind of activity; "experts on beauty
shops to professors who teach how to drive a car." In the Spanish
university there can be "vicious academicismo." In Zulia there have
been problems of decentralization, and, he thinks, of politics.

VEN   DELPRETTI, EDUARDO. "Depende de exterior la seguridad del país."
50   El Nacional, 5 June 1979.
        Profesor at Simon Bolivar University complains that
Venezuelan scientists are not used by government or industry to solve
problems such as defense and development, resulting in dependence on
foreign technology. Says Ministry of Science managed by "a scientist
with political mentality" would be better than present mediocrity of
Ministry of Education.

VEN   DIXON, ROY-HERIBERTO. "The Role of the University in Human Re-
51   source Development: The Case of the University of Oriente,
        Venezuela." Ph.D. dissertation, University of Pittsburgh, 1975.
        164 pp.
        Discusses establishment of University of Oriente--"an experi-
mental institution with limited autonomy to serve the manpower development requirement in eastern and entire Venezuela"--to sidestep "feudal/
colonial" resistance to modernization represented by present-day Latin
American universities. Available quantitative data (scant) suggest
students being graduated with needed skills but in insufficient numbers
to meet "manpower development objectives." Students appear to eschew
technical fields in favor of white-collar-type occupations. Author
says this is consistent with "pervasive aristocratic value system that
teaches children to shun physical work and avoid social
responsibility."

VEN   "2,000 pre-inscritos en la Universidad de Oriente." Oriente
52   Universitario 3, no. 15 (12 April 1965): 1.
        Graduates of secondary schools in eastern Venezuela apply for
admission to the thirteen career programs offered at UDO.

VEN   DRAYER, B. ALBERTO. "Financiamiento y costo de los sistemas
53   universitarios." Caracas: República de Venezuela, Consejo
        Nacional de Universidades, 17 July 1977. Mimeographed. 43 pp.
        Permanent secretary of Venezuela's National Council of Uni-
versities addresses a meeting of his counterparts from elsewhere in
Latin America. Uses Venezuelan figures (and also those of many other

Caribbean nations) to show money distribution among different sectors
of education, and rising demand for more support at university level.
Discusses social factors in demand; crises in space, personnel, programs; lack of adequate administration, analysis, resources. Proposes
new funding sources plus reforms. WKU

VEN   ESCOTET, MARTHA DE, and JAIMES, ROSALVINA DE. "La formación de
54   recursos humanos a nivel técnico superior." Universitas 2000 3,
      no. 1 (1978): 173-93.
          Postulates some reasons students seek admission to tradition-
al university careers instead of ones sometimes better suited to their
capabilities and national needs. Proposes some strategy in Venezuelan
context.

VEN   ESCOTET, MIGUEL A. Venezuelan Student Problems. Cumaná: Uni-
55   versidad de Oriente, Escuela de Educación, 1970, 42 pp.
          Study of 1,200 fifth-year secondary school students and 340
first-year university students; information on attitudes, need for more
vocational and personal guidance in educational system.

VEN   "Estadísticas del proceso de preinscripción nacional 1977-1978
56   (segundo informe)." Papeles Universitarios 2, nos. 7-8 (March-
      April 1978): 82-92.
          Pre-enrollment petitions matched against available places for
students in national universities. Universidad Central, e.g., had
26,853 aspirants, space for 5,835, was assigned 8,886. Universities of
Zulia, Carabobo, Oriente also had much greater demand than spaces while
Universidad Nacional Abierta had 3,000 vacancies.

VEN   "Estudiantes de ingeniería levantaron toma de facultad y entre-
57   garon proposiciones al Consejo Universitario." El Universal, 16
      May 1980.
          Students in the faculty of engineering of Central University
end takeover of building, deliver ten-point petition to rector and
members of University Council. Request includes continuous evaluation
during courses rather than reliance on final exam for grades, changes
in disciplinary rules, reinstatement of expelled students.

VEN   "Estudiantes de secundaria en la huelga de hambre de los pre-
58   inscritos." El Nacional, 6 June 1979, p. C-2.
          Secondary school students support hunger strike by group in
Universidad Central demanding admission. Shortages of space in all
universities. March on Ministry of Education, "violent police
repression" on earlier occasion.

VEN   FEBRES CORDERO, FOCION. Autonomía universitaria. Caracas: UCV,
59   1959. 452 pp.
          Government annulled autonomy of Universidad Central in 1951
after student disturbances; a professor in dental school chronicled
events, began their publication after overthrow of the dictatorship.
Background and theory of autonomy; details of abuses, punishments of
professors, including jailing of many who became leaders (e.g., Luis
Manuel Pañalver); pertinent documents. Close-up view of conflict,
described with both heat and light. DPU

VEN   FERNANDEZ HERES, RAFAEL, and DRAYER, B. ALBERTO. "Pautos
60   generales sobre el sistema nacional de orientación y admisión al
      subsistema de educación superior y sobre los requisitos mínimos
      para permanecer dentro este subsistema." Working paper prepared
      for meeting 24 April 1980 of Natitonal Council of Universities
      (CNU) by Planning Office (OPSU). Mimeographed. 10 pp.
         Perennial political hot issues now being confronted by CNU-
OPSU: Rules for access to most prestigious programs in most prestigious institutions, and right to remain even after repeated failures.
Nationally centralized university admissions system since 1973 now to
be strengthened by orientation and advisory programs, nationally and
institutionally. Testing procedure developed. Eligibility to remain
requires, at minimum, passing 25 percent of courses per year, plus any
individual institional requirements. OPSU will undertake national
study of repeaters and dropouts. WKU

VEN   FLETCHER, GEORGE RICHARDS, Jr. "An Evaluation of Selection
61   Criteria for the Gran Mariscal de Ayacucho Scholarship Program."
      Ed.D. dissertation, Oklahoma State University, 1977. 84 pp.
         Twelve characteristics of seventy-seven Venezuelan students
in English Language Institute at OSU studied to learn their predictive
values in the Comprehensive English Language Test. In 1975 and 1976
groups, significant correlations were found between students' success
and higher mental ability, more years of education, higher socio-
economic status.

VEN   "La Fundación Ayacucho tiene nuevas metas y vamos a cumplirlas."
62   Variedades, 23 May 1979, pp. 22-24.
         Interview with new scholarship plan director, sociologist
María Cristina Osuña de Pérez Díaz, indicates emphasis on returnees,
problem of finding work for those with only undergraduate degree.
Increased emphasis on high and middle level technicians and postgraduate study. Sixty percent of recipients came from in and near
Caracas.

VEN   FUNDACION GRAN MARISCAL DE AYACUCHO. Boletín Estadístico 1, no.
63   5 (May 1978). 42 pp.
         This and next several issues contain charts on all aspects of
scholarships, by kind and place.

VEN   ------. La Fundación "Gran Mariscal de Ayacucho." Caracas:
64   [Fundación GMA], 1978, 237 pp.
         Commemorates third anniversary of scholarship foundation with
description of goals, activities, reports from eight country dele-
gations abroad, testimonial letters. Appendix for data on awards,
places and fields of study. WKU

VEN   ------. Memoria 1978: Exposición de motivos. Caracas:
65   Fundación GMA, 1979. 61 pp.
         Goals, plans, evaluations, accomplishments, projections of
large scholarship program begun in 1974. WKU

VEN   ------. Orgánica legal de la Fundación Gran Mariscal de
66   Ayacucho. Caracas: Consultorio Jurídico, 1976. 96 pp.

Venezuela

Decrees and regulations, from 1974 beginning through May 1977, for national scholarship program. Private corporation administers government and other funds in accord with needs established for development, chooses grantees and the universities they attend. WKU

VEN ------. "Presente en becas para el desarrollo." <u>Venezuela</u>
67 <u>Ahora</u>, no. 12 (1978). 8 leaves.
Summary of accomplishments of scholarship program from 1974 to 1978. Over 17,500 students, chosen from lower and middle socioeconomic sectors and for adequate grades, studied subjects related to Venezuela's drive for independent industrialization. Over half studied abroad.

VEN GODOY CASTRO, ROGER. <u>Educación y recursos humanos en Venezuela:</u>
68 <u>Un aporte al estudio de los recursos humanos de nivel superior</u>.
Caracas: Universidad Central de Venezuela, Facultad de Ciencias Económicas y Sociales, 1976. 242 pp.
Education not an end in itself but contributor to society it must serve. Rejects education to form man, artist, scientist in favor of need to prepare for the "social fight." Economist offers statistical evidence that Plan IV of the nation ignores needs for high level manpower, as have all other plans. Central University awarded 50 percent of all country's degrees in 1972 and 62 percent of all between 1901 and 1970; 27.1 percent are in most prestigious careers of medicine, law, engineering. Transcendental need for inventory and planning for needed human resources and concomitant higher education. WKU

GONZALEZ BAQUERO, RAFAEL. <u>Un nuevo esquema organizativo para la</u> <u>universidad</u>. See entry GEN 133.

VEN GONZALES REYES, EDUARDO. "La planificación universitaria en
69 Venezuela y la OPSU." <u>Universitas 2000</u> 2, no. 5 (June 1973): 1-2.
Director of National Planning Office (OPSU) of the National Council of Universities (CNU) describes its 1971 beginning, after 1970 university reform law. Studies planned in human resources, professional resources; development of plan for national system of university admissions; study of budgetary procedures and financial management, inventory of physical plant. Planning for regionalization of university resources.

VEN ------. "La Universidad de Oriente y sus perspectivas de desar-
70 rollo." <u>Ciencias Sociales</u> 1, no. 1 (December 1963): 5-10.
Director of one of UDO's five <u>núcleos</u> describes program of new university in eastern Venezuela and relation to this area's needs, chiefly in engineering, agriculture, education, basic sciences.

VEN HAMILTON, WILLIAM L. "Venezuela." In <u>Students and Politics in</u>
71 <u>Developing Nations</u>, edited by Donald K. Emmerson, pp. 350-89.
New York: Praeger, 1968.
Tour guide through political thickets of Central University, based on research for his Ph.D., foresees some changes with growth of newer institutions and more emphasis on technical studies. KU

VEN   HERNANDEZ M., ARIS ANTONIO.   "Forecasting of Manpower Re-
72   quirements and Educational Needs for Venezuela until 1988."
      Ph.D. dissertation, University of Pittsburgh, 1979.   124 pp.
          Use of manpower forecasting in developing countries for edu-
cational planning for economic goals; possible imbalance between needs
of economy and educational outputs.   Analysis of flow of students with
data from 1964 to 1976.   Necessary higher education data unavailable,
hence higher education output is missing.   Elementary and partial
secondary outputs will not meet anticipated needs if distribution of
labor force according to educational level, occupations, and economic
sectors is the same as that for 1975.

VEN   "Higher Education in Venezuela."   [John De Abate, comp.   Photo-
73   copy of typed document from Cultural Affairs Officer, U.S. Embas-
      sy.   Caracas: n.p., 1978].   218 pp.
          Description of various kinds of higher education, aims, legal
basis, staff, students, finance.   Summary of 1975-80 Five Year Plan,
its needs, goals, philosophy.   An indispensable handbook, accurate,
well organized, well written.   WKU

VEN   HOOVER, GARY.   Venezuela: A Study of the Educational System of
74   Venezuela and a Guide to the Academic Placement of Students from
      Venezuela in Educational Institutions of the United States.
      World Education Series.   [Washington, D.C.]:   American Associ-
      ation of Collegiate Registrars and Admissions Officers, 1978.
      129 pp.
          Useful overview with some specific data on universities.   KU

VEN   "Incertidumbre y preocupación en Oriente por amenaza de cierre de
75   la UDO."   El Nacional, 12 May 1980.
          Bishop of the diocese of Cumana, president of the Chamber of
Commerce and others deplore budget cuts made by National Council of
Rectors in requests of University of Oriente.   Threat of its closing
elicits considerable data on its significance in this once remote
region.

VEN   "Incorporados al mercado laboral 3.600 becarios Fundayacucho."
76   El Nacional, 27 June 1982.
          Fifteen percent of current 23,000 higher education graduates
were scholarship students of the Fundación Gran Mariscal de Ayacucho.
Report on graduates, in the fundacion's Memoria y Cuenta, says in basic
sciences (biology, physics, chemistry and mathematics) 65 percent were
becarios, as were some 37 percent of the engineers and 30 percent of
graduates in agriculture and marine specialties.   Data given for other
fields also, but no information on employment.

VEN   INSERNY NOYA, CARLOS.   Informe estadístico sobre el personal
77   docente y de investigación de las universidades - 1970-1973.
      Caracas: CNU/OPSU, 1975, ca.   160 leaves.
          Because national educational policy is based on commitment to
upgrading human resources for national development, quantitative and
qualitative changes are underway in higher education.   Statistics show,
in aggregate and by institution, numbers and categories of teaching and
research staff; plans for growth, diversity, creation of new specializations given.   WKU

VEN   INSTITUTE OF INTERNATIONAL EDUCATION. The Gran Mariscal de
78   Ayacucho Scholarship Program, 1974-1977. New York: Institute of
      International Education, [1978?]. 33 pp.
          Over 3,500 Venezuelan students are in U.S. universities, part
of 11,000 studying abroad twenty years after the end of dictatorship.
Data show huge growth in higher education was insufficient to meet
demands. Use of oil wealth to create scholarships, especially for
disadvantaged students. Most are in engineering fields. WKU

VEN   "Integración inmediata del subsistema de educación superior."
79   El Universal, 13 November 1979.
          All universities, university colleges and polytechnic schools
must be one system. Universidad Central, burdened by demand for entry,
has too few places and too many repeaters who fail first year. Interviews with four deans.

VEN   LAYRISSE, MIGUEL. "Declaraciones del Rector de la Universidad
80   Central de Venezuela, Dr. Miguel Layrisse." Caracas: [Universi-
      dad Central de Venezuela], 4 March 1979. Mimeographed. 4 pp.
          Strong response to "take-over" of university entities by
would-be matriculants to most prestigious university, with nearly six
times as many applicants as places available. Rejects violence, urges
acceptance of alternatives in higher education and describes remedy of
Consejo Nacional de Universidades to determine academic work transferable into universities after studies in other institutions. WKU

VEN   ------. "El desafío universitario." Caracas: [Universidad
81   Central de Venezuela], 19 October 1978. Mimeographed. 19 pp.
          Speech by scientist/rector of Universidad Central to former
and future presidents of Venezuela and other leaders of Christian
Democratic party. University challenge is to better meet needs of
students, stop 80 percent failure rate, improve teacher competence,
increase research funding--especially for applied research--from 0.3
percent of GNP to internationally recommended 1 percent. WKU

VEN   ------. "Palabras del Rector, Dr. Miguel Layrisse, con motivo
82   del día del profesor universitario." Caracas: [Universidad
      Central de Venezuela], 5 December 1978. Mimeographed. 7 pp.
          Speech to professors says 25 percent increase in university
"efficiency" produced 4,000 graduates. Describes structural changes
interrelating whole university subsystem in preparing entering
students, hoping to give better career orientation and cut high attrition rate and also avoid delays of up to a year after secondary
graduation before university entry. Praises faculty awards and prizes.
WKU

VEN   ------. "Palabras pronunciadas por el Rector de la Universidad
83   Central de Venezuela, Dr. Miguel Layrisse, en la ocasión de
      celebrar el 'Día de la Universidad Central del Venezuela.'"
      Caracas: [Universidad Central de Venezuela], 29 June 1978.
      Mimeographed. 9 pp.
          Celebration of 1721 founding of UCV, and 1827 statutes of
Simon Bolivar giving birth to the republican university with its reforms. Role of universitarios in the Independence movement. Past and
present importance of autonomy, especially after loss of lands given by
Bolivar to university for producing income. WKU

VEN   LEVINE, DANIEL H.   Conflict and Political Change in Venezuela.
84   Princeton, New Jersey: Princeton University Press, 1973.   285
      pp.
            Traditional opposition to Venezuelan dictators gave universi-
      ty students, especially in the Central University in Caracas, a special
      role in society.   Contemporary political parties, especially those of
      Left, have strong adherents in universities.   Case study of conflict
      and its resolution involves related structural and cultural factors
      emerging in post-1958 years.   KU

VEN   ------.   "Thinking about Students and Politics: Venezuela in the
85   1960s."   Paper for Seventh Annual Meeting of the Latin American
      Studies Association, Houston, Texas, November 1977.   Mimeo-
      graphed, 36 pp.
            Latin American and U.S. "myths" of Latin American student
      heroism, radicalism reexamined.   Argues that more attention should be
      paid by researchers to Latin politics before examining student behavior
      or universities as setting for activism.   National political changes
      more significant than academic relationship of students.   Political
      party affiliation in Venezuela begins at secondary school level.   Evi-
      dence in Venezuela of parties' monopoly of power, consequent decline of
      student power.   WKU

VEN   Ley de universidades.   Gaceta Oficial, no. 1,429, extraordinario,
86   de 8 de septiembre de 1970.   Caracas: Editorial La Torre, 1970.
      77 pp.
            Spells out national policies of finance, governance, rights
      and responsibilities of universities.   Provides for national council of
      rectors, private universities, establishment of experimental
      universities.   WKU

VEN   LIGA SOCIALISTA.   "Una respuesta revolucionaria al documento
87   'Proposiciones-régimen nacional de orientación y admisión a la
      educación superior y condiciones mínimas para permanecer dentro
      del mismo' del Ministerio de Educación y la OPSU."   Papeles
      Universitarios, no. 16 ([November-December 1979?]):   63-73.
            Majority political parties generally affirmed OPSU proposals
      for admission and retention standards for universities, but Socialist
      League wants expansion of system.   Data about age cohorts show high
      percentages outside all levels of education.   Denunciation of influence
      of transnational corporations, U.S. universities and foundations.   Spe-
      cific recommendations to improve system.

VEN   LOMBARDI, JOHN V.; CARRERA DAMAS, GERMAN; and ADAMS, ROBERTA E.
88   "Education: Universities, Schools, Education in General."   In
      Venezuelan History: A Comprehensive Working Bibliography, pp.
      386-400.   Boston: G. K. Hall, 1977.
            Forty or so items pertaining to universities.   KU

VEN   MALDONADO, IMELDA R. DE; FERNANDEZ, MARGARITA B. DE; and GONZALEZ
89   FLORES, MARISELA.   "V Plan de la nación: Análisis crítico del
      sector educativo."   Cuadernos de Educación 42 (February 1977).
      pp. 1-97.
            Rhetoric of "democratizing" education, as proclaimed by the
      Five Year Plan (1976-80), at odds with proposals to reduce rate of

increase in budget. Professors in University of Zulia describe plan, attack its assumptions, denounce limiting university enrollments as continuing to favor privileged classes. Batters Acción Democrática party leadership in government with its own language, berates use of foreign agencies in Gran Mariscal de Ayacucho scholarship project, and points to importation of foreign labor as evidence of inefficient educational system. Entire issue on the topic.

VEN MARTA SOSA, JOAQUIN. "El estado y la educación en Venezuela."
90 Papeles Universitarios 1, no. 1 (June 1977): 4-5.
     Analysis of Plan V of the nation. With respect to higher education, three principal objectives: determining (1) significance the state will attribute to higher education in national plans; (2) the concrete variances in functions the state has assigned to higher education; (3) key characteristics of possible plans for higher education which will function in a process of autonomy.

VEN ------. Problemas de la educación superior en Venezuela.
91 Colección: Los Libros de la Educación. Caracas: Ediciones Papeles Universitarios, 1979. 158 pp.
     Professor in Universidad Simón Bolívar's department of social sciences characterizes Venezuelan state as "sub-capitalist, populist-developmental, dominated by ideological limitations and socio-political interests," with rapidly expanding higher education system. State acts as agent of dominant classes, impeding creative and democratic educational processes. Analysis of planning, reform efforts. Presents alternative reform models for higher education requiring social and political changes in accord with a normative model. Bibliography has 115 citations. WKU

VEN MAYZ VALLENILLA, ERNESTO. Latinoamérica en la encrucijada de la
92 técnica. Valle de Sartenejas: Universidad Simón Bolívar, 1976.
13 pp.
     Spreading "technocratic colonialism" in Latin America influences peculiar ethos of countries, with loss of national character and even regional roots. Calls for authentic New World ethos in managing technology and rescuing man from dependence; asserts that technology must develop creative, not passive, man. Dependence originated in deficiencies in our education, which needs radical resolution to master region's own technology. WKU

VEN MINISTERIO DE EDUCACION. Colegios universitarios: Diseño
93 curricular. Eugenio R. Caricote, coordinator. Caracas:
Ministerio de Educación, 1972. 36 pp. plus 8 diagrams.
     Democratization, diversification, regionalization of education part of the "integral reform of Venezuelan education for social, cultural and economic transformation of our national reality." Government creating flood of new institutions as alternatives to already overflowing traditional universities, especially in Caracas; also trying to reduce high failure rate in first years. Year of basic cycle to be followed by professional cycle of appropriate duration, within university college or other institution. Programs and structure. WKU

VEN ------. Informe del Ministerio de Educación Nacional sobre el
94 desarrollo institucional de la Universidad de Oriente. Caracas:
Ministerio de Educación, 1962. 27 pp. plus 6 appendices.

Work of Organizing Commission since its 1959 beginning as it creates new university in five eastern Venezuelan states. Planning, organization of five núcleos with central administration in Cumana. Innovative aspects: full time professors and students, semesters, credit hours. Report on efforts to link university and community; financial situation. WKU

VEN ------. Universidad de Oriente: Bases, organización, proyectos
95 provisionales. Cumaná: Universidad de Oriente, 1962. 37 pp.
Basic information for students, programs of the five núcleos.
WKU

VEN MINISTERIO DE EDUCACION, Comisión Organizadora de la Universidad
96 Simón Rodríguez. Dos informes sobre la formación de profesores
de la Universidad Simón Rodríguez. Caracas: Ministerio de Educación, Comisión Organizadora de la Universidad Simón Rodríguez, 1972. 65 pp.
Provisional edition of report by study group for university in its planning stage describes hoped-for characteristics of graduates: adaptable to changing professional tasks, creative and imaginative. Professors must be prepared to replace fact-giving with flexibility in thought process, trained in problem-solving. Resultant type of education spelled out and diagrammed, along with organizational scheme for thirty-six week course. WKU

VEN MINISTERIO DE EDUCACION and CONSEJO NACIONAL DE UNIVERSIDADES.
97 Seminario sobre planeamiento y desarrollo de los servicios para
estudiantes en la educación superior. Caracas: Ministerio de Educación, 1965. 157 pp.
With joint sponsorship of the U.S. embassy and participation of some U.S. experts, representatives of Venezuelan ministry and universities ponder such topics as university environment, organization of student services, psychological characteristics of different groups within universities, orientation. Discussion groups and their recommendations. WKU

MORLES SANCHEZ, VICTOR. La educación de postgrado en el mundo.
See entry GEN 192.

VEN ------. "Notas para la educación de post-grado en Venezuela."
98 Universitas 2000 2, no. 5 (June 1973): 4-7.
Representative of National Council on Science and Technology (CONICIT) gives preliminary view of history and present state of graduate education, notes graduates study to be so new that scarcely any bibliography exists on the topic. Research began with medical school, Central University, in 1948. Calls present situation result of Venezuela's underdevelopment and dependence, contributing to increasing gulf between advanced and non-advanced countries; calls for bold initiatives. Degrees awarded 1901-69 in eleven faculties in Central University; 1971-72 graduate courses in various universities.

VEN ------, and others. La educación de postgrado en Venezuela:
99 Situación actual. Caracas: CONICIT, Departamento de Educación, 1974, 230 pp.

Descriptive study is part of strategy to achieve improved graduate study resources, but with caveats about lack of both quantitative and qualitative data. Points out lack of graduate study tradition, norms, policies, and qualified professors. Most graduate work is in medicine and engineering at UCV. Scarcely any in entire country in basic disciplines. System to be created must be pertinent to needs of Venezuelan society. Useful compendium. WKU

VEN "Naturaleza jurídica del contrato de beca de la Fundación 'Gran
100 Mariscal de Ayacucho.'" Correo de Ayacucho, Boletín Informativo
1, nos. 4-6 (October-December 1976): 12-13.
        Legal character of massive Venezuelan government scholarship plan; a description of rights and duties of donor and beneficiary in bulletin prepared for students in the program.

VEN NEMETH, EDWARD JOSEPH. "Faculty Participation in University
101 Decision-Making: A Case Study of the Universidad de Oriente,
Cumaná, Venezuela." Ph.D. dissertation, Syracuse University,
1969. 144 pp.
        Survey of UDO faculty used to support assertion that (1) there are low subjective estimates of competence by faculty members, and (2) there is belief by faculty members that key university decisions are subject to considerable partisan control, which lead to (3) low degree of faculty participation in decisions governing university goals.

VEN NERI, RAFAEL JOSE. Intervenciones sobre educación: La universi-
102 dad y el país. Caracas: Universidad Central de Venezuela
Rectorado, Información y Relaciones Públicas, 1974. 38 pp.
        Rector points to "permanent educational crisis" depriving youth of adequate education and dooming many who could contribute to society to ignominy; calls for a rational national policy for education. Calls for university's contributing to national development; points to lack of career orientation for youth. Lists several recent master's level programs and hopes for doctoral level. WKU

VEN NERY R., BERTILIO J. "Algunos aspectos relacionados con la
103 igualdad de oportunidades educativas de educación superior en la
región Zuliana." Papeles Universitarios, no. 14 (March-April
1979): 38-39.
        University of Zulia in Maracaibo described as sharing "critical situation" with other national universities outside Caracas: educational inequalities by sub-regions, by geographical and social origins, by age and kind of work sought, and by type of institution aspired to.

VEN "No hay inversión comparable al aumento de recursos humanos."
104 El Universal, 4 May 1979.
        Venezuela's incoming President Luis Herrera Campins affirms decision to maintain and reform scholarship program begun by predecessor.

VEN "No se pagarán salarios a empleados de Ingeniería mientras dura
105 la toma del decanato." El Universal, 4 May 1980.

Dean of engineering school says salaries of professors and workers cannot be paid since workers' takeover of buildings in labor dispute impedes access to offices and causes suspension of classes. Workers threaten to go to court.

VEN   NUÑEZ TENORIO, J. R.   Problemas universitarios.   Caracas:
106   Ediciones CEHE, 1965.   160 pp.
       "Study and fight" was the motto of much of Venezuela's Central University community in 1960 when this series of polemical articles appeared in various papers and magazines.   Vigorous advocacy of university and mission for social justice; denunciation of "imperialist penetration" in proposed academic reforms; call for science in the service of revolution, activist role for students inside and outside university.   A classic statement of the time.   KU

VEN   "Los objetivos culturales de la Universidad Central de Venezuela:
107   Programación concreta del trabajo universitario (1962-63)."
       Mimeographed, pp. 6-22.   Caracas: UCV, 1963.
       Portion of document calls for creation of Center for Cultural Research at UCV to investigate music, painting, folklore, theater, poetry, and other phenomena, to preserve and disseminate Venezuela's culture.   Organization proposed includes university extension's activities of a broad social nature.   WKU

VEN   OFICINA DE PLANIFICACION DEL SECTOR UNIVERSITARIO (OPSU).
108   Boletín Estadístico 1, no. 1 (1972).   28 pp.
       Matriculation; number of professors, students; study opportunities offered in higher education nationally.

VEN   ------.   Boletín Estadístico, 1973.   Ca. 100 leaves.
109   Data on students, faculty, graduates, 1960-72; programs of study available by institution.   Introduction cites some data-gathering problems.

VEN   ------.   "Matrícula estudiantil personal docente y de investi-
110   gación y egresados del sector universitario."   Boletín
       Estadístico, no. 2 (1975).   251 pp.
       Data on students, faculty, graduates of public and private universities, 1970-73, plus generalized charts and graphs of system as a whole.

VEN   ------.   "Matrícula estudiantil, personal docente y de investi-
111   gación y egresados de educación superior."   Boletín Estadístico,
       no. 5 (1978).   534 pp.
       Data for 1977-78 academic year on student, programs, graduates of all ninety-two institutions and centers of higher education, of which eighteen are universities; seven are in Caracas and five elsewhere in the coastal region.   Areas of knowledge offered nationally and by institution, enrollment by sex and age in various fields, graduate courses, budgets.   Enrollments from preschool to university 1964-65 to 1977-78, pupil-teacher ratios, numbers and percentages of matriculants in higher education.   UNESCO data (1974) on other countries' enrollments.

VEN   ------. "Matrícula estudiantil, personal docente y de investi-
112   gación y egresados de educación superior." Boletín Estadístico,
       no. 6 (1979). 580 pp.
       Institutions of higher education, geographic location with
maps; data on students, faculty, graduates, with some comparisons
between 1970-71 and 1978-79. General and particular graphs, tables.

VEN   ------. Descripción de actividades, proceso de preinscripción
113   nacional, año 1979-1980. Caracas: CNU/OPSU, 1979. 12 pp. plus
       fold-out diagrams.
       Steps required by National Council of Universities for
national pre-enrollment in universities and other higher education
institutions. Meetings for administrators to be held in various zones
of country, with students registering at their own secondary schools.
Admission procedure described for use by institutions, taking into
account grades, region of country, socioeconomic conditions of
students. WKU

VEN   ------. Educación superior y desarrollo. [Caracas]: CNU/OPSU,
114   [1972]. 23 pp.
       Booklet describes objectives and hoped-for results of new
planning office for all Venezuelan universities. Established in accord
with 1970 University Law as the technical office of the National Council of Universities, it is directed to calculate professional needs of
country, propose models of university programs to meet short and long
term needs, advise on budgetary matters. Structure and function of
OPSU described. WKU

VEN   ------. Oportunidades de estudio en las instituciones de edu-
115   cación superior de Venezuela, año 1978. Caracas: CNU/OPSU,
       1978. 147 pp.
       Reference guide for students participating in national pro-
cess of pre-inscription in institutions of higher education. Orients
them, parents, and teachers to national needs and careers available in
eight categories. Nine administrative regions, which reflect effort to
decentralize, with their courses of study by institutions. General
information and entrance requirements of all universities, university
colleges, and institutes, public and private. WKU

VEN   ------. Oportunidades de estudio en las instituciones de la
116   educación superior de Venezuela, año 1980. Caracas: CNU/OPSU,
       Unidad de Orientación, Distribución e Ingreso, 1980. 144 pp.
       Continuation of effort to "regionalize" education, reducing
pressure on the capital's seven universities, especially on the Central
University; twenty-six other post-secondary agencies are listed for
Caracas. Careers offered by institution and region; national priority
areas: development of agriculture, industry (especially metals and
petroleum), transportation, social services. In last ten years, fifty-
three new higher education institutions were created with 30.37 percent
increase in enrollment. WKU

VEN   ------. Proceso de preinscripción nacional año 1979-1980,
117   Informe no. 3. Caracas: CNU/OPSU, 1980. 18 leaves.
       Results of processing student applications for admission to
all public and private universities and other institutions of higher

education. Tables showing such data as secondary graduates and numbers applying, courses applied for by institution; largest numbers at the Central University in engineering, accounting and business, medicine, architecture, psychology, law; demand by institution 1977-79. Open University demand declines sharply. Important document. WKU

VEN ------. Proyecto de manual para uniformar el sistema financiero
118 en las universidades nacionales. Caracas: CNU/OPSU, 1972. 79 pp.
Document designed to prepare to bring order to chaotic budgetary process through which universities are financed. Calls for program budgeting, accountability, development within coherent planning. Lists some of universities' financial functions. WKU

VEN ------. Separata estadística: Información sobre algunas
119 variables importantes en educación superior. Caracas: CNU/OPSU, 1977. 75 pp.
Tables on aspects of enrollment 1964-65 to 1975-76, teaching and research personnel, graduates, budgets, results of national pre-enrollment, various indicators. WKU

VEN ------. "Tercer borrador: Sistema nacional de orientación y
120 admisión al sub-sistema de educación superior y condiciones mínimas para permanecer dentro del sub-sistema." [Caracas], June 1979. Photocopy of typescript. 12 pp.
Working paper discussed by OPSU staff and rectors of all universities. Proposals to cope with rising demands for admission to universities and high failure rate include early enrollment, aptitude tests, remedial work, standards for retention, integration of all higher education, improvement of teaching and service functions. All controversial topics. Early career choice still fundamental part of plan. WKU

VEN ------; INSTITUTO DE ESTUDIOS SUPERIORES DE ADMINISTRACION
121 (IESA); and OFICINA CENTRAL DE COORDINACION Y PLANIFICACION (CORDIPLAN). Sistema analítico sobre la educación superior en Venezuela. Caracas: OPSU, IESA, CORDIPLAN, [1972]. 106 pp.
Anticipated increase in 1970s of 103 percent in already saturated higher education system. Need for planning instead of current ad hoc response to demand especially in traditional professions. Opportunities for less advantaged are limited at secondary level, not much aided at tertiary level. Proposals to increase research and planning. WKU

VEN OFICINA DE PLANIFICATION DEL SECTOR UNIVERSITARIO, Unidad de
122 Apoyo, Centro de Información y Documentación Superior (CENIDES). Microtesauro de la Educación Superior en Venezuela. Caracas: CNU, OPSU, CENIDES, 1981. Ca. 80 leaves.
Need to bring Venezuelan indexing and information retrieval systems into coherence with ERIC and UNESCO/OIE systems led to design of microthesaurus. Difficulties not only of translating terms from English to Spanish but of adapting and standardizing key words. Description of methodology used, list of descriptives, guide for their use, suggestions for indexing and information retrieval using this microthesaurus. KU

VEN   OFICINA DE PLANIFICACION DEL SECTOR UNIVERSITARIO, Unidad de
123   Orientación, Distribución e Ingreso. <u>Instrucciones para realizar</u>
       <u>la preinscripción nacional, proceso de preinscripción 1979-1980</u>.
       Caracas: CNU/OPSU, 1979. 31 pp.
          Mandatory pre-enrollment in last year of secondary school for
all potential matriculants to all universities. Objectives include
orienting demand for higher education toward priority areas defined in
national development plans. Procedures, documents, code index for
choosing career in university or technical institution. Criteria used
for selection: grades, region of country, year of graduation, socio-
economic condition. Capacity and demand by careers in institutions of
higher education, 1978-79. WKU

VEN   OJEDA, RICARDO JULIO. "Characteristics and Opinions of Students
124   in la Universidad de Oriente (UDO) Venezuela--Freshman Class
       1970-71." Ph.D. dissertation, University of Wisconsin, 1973.
       141 pp.
          Findings of questionnaire survey of UDO freshmen lead author
to conclude new approaches to General Education needed to improve
student satisfaction; adopt independent study; encourage original work,
special investigations and reports; provide broad, flexible curriculum,
many electives and effective student counseling services.

VEN   OLAIZOLA, IVAN, and SILVA, MORAVIA. "Primera aproximación a una
125   sistematización de las admisiones." <u>Papeles Universitarios</u> 3,
       no. 16 (1979): 4-18, 23-24, 26-69.
          Efforts to reduce chaos in admissions system, especially for
the Universidad Central de Venezuela, by developing national plan.
Problems of demand for entry into careers and institutions, inadequate
academic preparation; orientation proposals to administer national
academic aptitude test for placement. Comments by coastal universities
on admissions and retention policies include need for broadening "subsystem" of higher education.

VEN   ORDOÑEZ, ROSANA. "2 centros internacionales para mejoramiento de
126   la educación establecen su sede en Venezuela." <u>El Nacional</u>, 2
       February 1977.
          UNESCO office for Regional Center for Higher Education in
Latin America and the Caribbean, and OAS office of Latin American
Center for Research for Educational Planning set up shop in Caracas.

VEN   ORTEGA, KALININA. "En República de Guelfos y Gibelinos
127   convierten la UCV cada vez que se avecinan elecciones." <u>El</u>
       <u>Nacional</u>, 3 March 1978.
          Proposed university reform suspect by some as possibly being
politically motivated on eve of elections. Law school dean avers that
problems are not structural but work of human beings in the system.
Resistance to any reform originating outside university itself.

VEN   ------. "Está aislada de la realidad nacional la comunidad
128   universitaria." <u>El Nacional</u>, 2 June, 1979, p. C-4.
          Secretary of Universidad Central, Gustavo Diaz Solis, meets
weeping mothers of students on hunger strike, demanding places in
university for their sons. Expresses his frustration that action is
directed against university when real problem is outside, in all of the

country, among workers, lawmakers, alumni, in neglect of higher education in general.

VEN ------. "No estoy de acuerdo con la autonomía universitaria."
129 El Nacional, 16 April 1979.
Resignation of Rector Mayz Vallenilla is partly protest against government policy decision to nullify creation of new experimental university. Denounces autonomy as interpreted in University Law Article 19 as "retrogression toward cordobización," a condition "worn out, sterile, and infertile." Objects to giving students and professors more power in choosing rector of experimental Universidad Simón Bolívar and others. Traditional universities have power, but more productive experimental universities should have more voice.

VEN ------. "Repitencia universitaria un freno a la democratización
130 de la educación superior." El Nacional, 17 February 1979, p. C-4.
Chronic "repeaters" and drop-outs occupy places (cupos) in national universities for new secondary school graduates. High failure rate increased with massification of education, as at Universidad de Oriente, where 70 percent failed basic courses. Universities leaving problem to government to resolve.

VEN PABON, MARIAHE. "Muchos becarios decían: 'Yo para técnico no
131 estudio, para licenciatura, sí.'" El Universal, 3 May 1979, p. 1.
Former president of scholarship corporation Fundayacucho, Ruth Lerner de Almea, answers critics: Venezuelan students want white-collar jobs, reject technical areas despite national needs. Comments on lack of national educational coordination, problem of change in political control. Describes grantees: 10 percent from homes of illiterate parents, 40 percent of parents have only primary education; policy in accord with desire to aid students from less favored classes.

VEN ------. "Sin estudios serios sobre necesidades del país se
132 enviaron al exterior miles de becarios." El Universal, 2 May 1979, p. 1.
Description and critical comments by Leopoldo Lopez Gil, first director of massive scholarship program. Disagreed with creation of Venezuelan bureaucracy, failure to heed Massachusetts Institute of Technology study on manpower needs. Fears lack of proper placement of returnees from abroad if they can be found in sagging labor market.

VEN Papeles Universitarios 2, no. 9 (June-July 1978). 168 pp.
133 Anniversary issue of magazine devoted to topics in higher education carries statements of their positions by the seven largest political parties. Higher education policies and problems have key importance for those competing for admission to insufficient classrooms; concern for political and social advantage for parties and individuals related to academic opportunity.

VEN PEÑALVER, LUIS MANUEL. Ciencia y tecnología en el desarrollo de
134 Venezuela. Caracas: Fundación Gran Mariscal de Ayacucho, 1979. 66 pp. includes text in English.

Lecture at Cambridge University in 1977 by Venezuela's former minister of education gives data on research needs and capabilities, outlines plans for increased attention to them. WKU

VEN ------. Cuando pasa el arado. Colección La Nueva Universidad
135 II. Cumaná: Universidad de Oriente, 1970. 115 pp.
Addresses to graduating classes 1965-70 mark accomplishments of university presided over by author since 1960 founding. Inaugural address describes goals and patterns of this "experimental" university. Speech in 1970 reviews its condition, its adaptation to social change, its definition of autonomy and co-government, contributions to development as a regional agency. Proposals for experimentation in university structure and function. WKU

VEN ------. 95 años después...hacia la revolución educativa.
136 Caracas: Ministerio de Educación, 1977. 40 pp.
Minister of education and former university rector recounts history of Venezuelan education on ninety-fifth anniversary of founding of ministry; goals of government to "revolutionize" education at all levels include better organization of subsystem of higher education. Anticipates higher education policies to better serve national needs, devise new financial formulas, develop infrastructure for science and technology. WKU

VEN PEREZ OLIVARES, ENRIQUE. "Universidad y estado en la década del
137 80: El caso venezolano." In La universidad latinoamericana en
la década del 80, (segunda parte), posibles estrategias de desarrollo, edited by Luis Scherz García, pp. 1-35. Ediciones CPU,
no. 38. Santiago, Chile: Corporación de Promoción Universitaria, 1976.
Professor in Venezuela's Central University and former minister of education describes first stage of university development within Napoleonic model, i.e., of "professionalist" character. University, as virtually only forum of free expression of political views, though independent juridically, depends administratively and financially on the state. Growth outside university of research and graduate studies. Tension under dictatorship. Post-1958 stage produces significant changes in size and quality, political warfare, creation of "experimental" universities. Law of 1970 gives considerable power to National Council of Universities and its planning policies. Describes proposed reforms. NIC

VEN PEREZ PEÑUELA, ELEAZAR. "Más de 100.000 bachilleres ingresan
138 este año a la educación superior." El Universal, 4 May 1980.
Director of OPSU explains aptitude test as "backbone of new methodology for entry into higher education" for aspirants in last year of secondary school, on optional basis. Hitherto, reliance was on grades. Also announces that in previous years all applicants got into institutions requested except for some of the 26,000 who applied for 7,000 places at Central University.

VEN PICON MEDINA, GILBERTO. "The Institutionalization of Scientific
139 Research in Venezuelan Universities." Ed.D. dissertation,
Stanford University, 1978. 265 pp.

Venezuela

Although several studies have been made of development of scientific research at national level, no systematic study exists on development of scientific research within Venezuelan universities. Questions: To what degree are nation's universities using professors with graduate training to develop research? To what degree is research now institutionalized and integrated with national needs? How do researchers perceive university environment for their research? How do returnees and nationally trained researchers compare in academic activities and attitudes? Progress is documented and results are generally positive. Comments on hindrances to achieving goals.

PIÑERO, EUROPA GONZALEZ DE, and CLAUDIO, RAMON, eds. Crecimiento del personal docente. See entry GEN 211.

VEN   "¿El Plan Ayacucho en crisis? Discusión completa sobre el
140   funcionamiento del Plan de Becas Gran Mariscal de Ayacucho."
      Papeles Universitarios, no. 3 (October 1977): 81-87.
      Denunciation by student political party groups MAS and COPEI, defense by AD students, congressional discussion, response by Plan's director, report by UNESCO representative on massive scholarship plan. Apparent slippage between rhetoric and reality.

VEN   "Preinscritos tomaron Escuela Básica de Medicina de la UCV."
141   El Universal, 16 May 1980.
      Group of pre-enrolled students takes over medical school building and sequesters director and members of the technical commission. Issue: admission of some secondary school graduates eager to study medicine, competing for few slots available, not chosen in national computer selection process because of their grades.

VEN   "El rector califica méritos, describe logros y admite las fallas
142   de todo inicio." Oriente Universitario, no. 14 (12 March 1965):
      6-7.
      Luis Manuel Peñalver, a founder and first rector of the University of Oriente, addresses first graduating class of five-year-old institution. Efforts to develop higher education in an underdeveloped region hitherto isolated and unserved. Unique system of governance to avoid partisan fights of traditional universities by having officials named by Ministry of Education. Role of planning emphasized.

VEN   REIZES, E.   "Carácter, funciones y estructura de la planificación
143   en la UNET: Proyecto UNESCO-UNET." Papeles Universitarios 2,
      nos. 7-8 (March-April 1978): 95-98.
      Good example of bureaucratic-pedantic bafflegab elevated to level of theological argument, and as likely to be effective in university planning. UNET undefined.

VEN   ROA, PEDRO, and TENORIO, J. R.   En torno a la renovación uni-
144   versitaria. Colección Revolución. Caracas: Editorial Nueva
      Izquierda, 1969. 69 pp.
      Need for radical reforms to escape imperialist upper class domination in Venezuelan universities. University role in nationalistic drive against colonial cultural influences is to reject foreign aid, scholarships, exchange of professors, loans. Need to take

political-social mission to the streets, to the working classes, with
science and revolution at the service of man. Internal university
reform is against humanistic, scientific, technical patterns; should be
replaced with education for national needs. Revolutionaries must
support Marxist-Leninist learning. WKU

VEN   RODRIGUEZ, ROMULO. "La Universidad Francisco de Miranda será la
145   entidad rectora de la cultura, la educación y la ciencia en
       Falcón." El Nacional, 10 October 1978.
       Minister of education swears in officials for new "experi-
mental" university in Coro, to begin with 500 students in 1979 in
paramedical, engineering, agricultural, veterinary studies.

VEN   ROJAS, ANDRES. "Elementos para el análisis del sub-sector edu-
146   cativo del V Plan de la Nación: Seminario sobre la problemática
       de la educación superior en Venezuela." Papeles Universitarios
       2, nos. 7-8 (March-April 1978): 6-23.
       Criticizes assumptions of 1976-80 National Plan conducing to
creation of nation of producers-consumers based on a foreign (U.S.)
model. Claims Venezuela must develop own structure of middle and
higher education to escape perpetual dependence on exploitative
patterns of advanced, developed countries; must recognize need for
class struggle inherent in present unjust system and unite teachers'
unions and student movements.

VEN   ROJAS, NANCY VELASQUEZ DE. "Problemática de la educación en
147   Venezuela: Bases para una investigación de sociología educacion-
       al." Ciencias Sociales 1, no. 1 (December 1963): 61-69.
       Social forces of race, religion, economic conditions as
barriers to education need study. UDO social science professor offers
two hypotheses for research: socioeconomic status of family related to
sending children to school; lack of school in community related to non-
attendance.

VEN   RUMBLE, GREVILLE. "The Cost Analysis of Distance Teaching:
148   Venezuela's Universidad Abierta." Mimeographed. [Caracas:
       OPSU?, 1980], 59 pp.
       Specialist from the Open University of the United Kingdom
examines cost structure and future system costs of Venezuela's UNA in
comparison with other distance teaching universities, to draw some
initial and general conclusions about cost implications for media
choice, size of an institution's academic program, number of students
in the system. Efforts to meet Venezuela's burgeoning social demand
for access to universities and production of people in scientific and
technical careers for national development. WKU

VEN   RUSCOE, GORDON C. "Individual Decisions and Educational
149   Planning: Occupational Choices of Venezuelan Secondary
       Students." International Development Review 10 (June 1968): 20-
       25.
       Although higher education has increased much in decade, de-
mand outruns supply; lack of planning and cooperation among universities. Over 97 percent of students aspire to professional occupations.
Familial and social pressures would tend to negate planned educational
incentives to choose careers based on national developmental needs;
hence lower socioeconomic group might respond to such incentives.

VEN SANCHEZ, GEORGE I. The Development of Education in Venezuela.
150 Washington, D.C.: U.S. Department of Health, Education, and
     Welfare, 1963. 114 pp.
        Humane, sympathetic but frank account of early history pro-
vides context for emergence of education out of political chaos and
deliberate neglect. Progress between dictatorships and after 1958
overthrow of Perez Jimenez brought reforms and growth, but demand
always exceeded available resources. Concludes with good description
of the state of secondary and higher education in 1961. WKU

VEN SANTOS AMARAL, DESIREE. "Bases para un arreglo entre gobierno y
151 rectores." Ultimas Noticias, 10 April 1979.
        Minister of education downplays charges of violating the
rights of rectors in the National Council of Universities by his nulli-
fying creation of new Universidad Experimental Politécnica Antonio José
de Sucre. Consequent resignation of rector of Universidad Simón
Bolívar is topic diplomatically dismissed.

VEN "Socioeconomic Background of the Venezuelan Student." Higher
152 Education 1, no. 3 (February-June 1980): 1.
        CRESALC, as part of regional program of UNESCO, undertakes
study to analyze relationship between students' socio-economic background and their access to university, and placement of students from
different backgrounds in university.

VEN UNION DE UNIVERSIDADES DE AMERICA LATINA. "La Universidad
153 Central de Venezuela propone la creación de una confederación de
     universidades autónomas de Venezuela." Universidades 77 (July-
     September 1979): 853-54.
        Rector of Universidad Central proposes link among the five
autonomous Venezuelan universities, which enroll 80 percent of
Venezuela's students, to solve common problems of finance, admissions,
"repeaters."

VEN UNIVERSIDAD CATOLICA ANDRES BELLO (UCAB). Información general.
154 Caracas: UCAB, 1978. 53 pp.
        In 1977-78 Catholic University had 8,165 students in its four
faculties, and had graduated 7,514 since 1958. Though school is private, UCAB matriculants must also pre-enroll in the national system of
pre-enrollment. Structure, courses, extra-curricular program. WKU

VEN ------. "Plan de cooperación económica al estudiante." Mimeo-
155 graphed. Caracas, May 1979. 8 pp.
        Scholarships and other plans to help students with less than
average resources contrast with past policy of equal fees for all. WKU

VEN ------. Prospecto 1967-1968. Caracas: UCAB. 48 pp.
156   Catalogue for faculties of law, engineering, humanities and
education, economics and social sciences; with enrollment information.
WKU

VEN "La Universidad Católica de Venezuela." Estudios Americanos 7,
157 no. 28 (January 1954): 732-33.
        Catholic universities in Venezuela no longer teach religious
principles. They have alienated themselves from the church and model

themselves on the private universities. The author feels that the lack
of religious content has lowered the quality of education.

VEN   UNIVERSIDAD CENTRAL DE VENEZUELA (UCV). Autonomía Universitaria.
158   Caracas: [UCV] Dirección de Cultura, Departamento de Publi-
      caciones, 1959. 81 pp.
           Decree No. 471 (18 December 1958) of the Venezuelan govern-
ment junta transfers ownership of land and buildings of the Institute
of University City (the campus) to the Central University. Decree No.
458 (5 December 1958), the Law of Universities, establishes extra-
territoriality, minimum income of 1.5 percent of national budget,
National Council of Universities, governance and organization of universities (with 25 percent student representation in the governing
assembly of each faculty), admissions policy, professors' categories
and responsibilities, and related matters. Speeches by members of
provisional government junta and university officials celebrate
patriotic feelings and hard-won academic, political, and economic
autonomy. History of Central University from 1771 to present. WKU

VEN   ------. Cursos de Post-grado 1968-1969. Caracas: UCV, División
159   de Planeamiento, Oficina de Planeamiento, 1968. 327 pp.
           First catalogue listing all graduate courses in elementary
faculties and Center of Development Studies. Rector hopes compiling
this information will lead to creation of a school of graduate studies
at UCV. WKU

VEN   ------. Las metas de las nuevas autoridades. Caracas: UCV,
160   1976. 95 pp.
           Incoming and outgoing rectors, among others, set forth goals
for university for 1976-80, at fifth change of authorities since UCV's
1972 grant of autonomy. Campus in 1972 called "land without law."
Academic and administrative reforms, including links with national and
international institutions. Fiscal and physical deficits, improved
teaching and research needs described for 50,000 students or 25 percent
of country's university students. Names of 112 rectors since 1725.
WKU

VEN   ------. "Subsistema de educación superior." Mimeographed.
161   Caracas: Consejo Universitario, 23 February 1978. 14 pp.
           Report of commission chosen to study problems of entry into
system of higher education. The 1961 law guarantees right to higher
education to all, but even with huge increases in capacity universities
are overburdened and underproductive. Recommends stages, system-wide,
of progressing toward degrees, in effort to reduce "repeaters," failure
rate of 80 percent compared with 80 percent success of scholarship
students (GMA) in foreign universities. Interpretation of data from
national sources. WKU

VEN   ------. CENDES, Centro Estudios del Desarrollo Universidad
162   Central de Venezuela: Prospecto 1964-1965. Caracas: UCV, 1963.
      17 pp.
           Describes organization created in 1960 to study economic,
social and administrative aspects of Venezuela and techniques of
planning for development; to prepare qualified personnel inside and
outside the university; to spread theory and practice of development

and promote integration of different approaches; to serve as technical
agency to Council on Scientific and Humanistic Development at UCV and
as public consulting agency. A two year graduate program and short
courses are described. WKU

VEN   ------, Consejo Rectoral. Presentación esquemática de una
163   reorganización universitaria inmediata y práctica. Caracas:
       UCV, 1971. 45 pp. plus 10 pages of enrollment figures.
       Proposal to reorganize Central University to cope with
mounting demands for increased matriculation, research, service; data
show poor student performance, high drop-out rate, suspension of
classes. Remedies should include creation of university colleges and
other alternatives to UCV, a pre-professional cycle. Traditional
faculty structure needs modification within UCV. Legal and budgetary
aspects of proposals, list of recommendations. WKU

VEN   ------. "Subsistema de educación superior." Papeles Universi-
164   tarios 2, nos. 7-8 (March-April 1978): 34-37.
       Commission appointed by University Council to study policy of
admission to higher education sets forth general problems of demand,
tendencies, finance. Proposes integration of all higher education into
one system and procedures to lessen delay of up to a year for students
trying to enter a university after secondary schooling.

VEN   ------, Dirección de Economía y Planeamiento. Análisis real de
165   la Universidad Central de Venezuela. Caracas: UCV, 1970. 59
       pp. plus 8 statistical leaves.
       Analysis includes general considerations, budget, physical
space, problems of pre-enrollment, student "repeaters" and productivity, degrees awarded 1901-69, socioeconomic aspects of student population; relationship among growth, degrees awarded, teaching and other
personnel and budget. Some candid comments in text on need for national policy on higher education, wretched state of secondary preparation.
Useful document. WKU

VEN   ------. Facultad de Humanidades y Educación, Escuela de Edu-
166   cación. "Guía Informativa de la U.C.V." Caracas, 1978. Mimeo-
       graphed. 31 pp.
       Short history from 1721 beginnings as Real y Pontificia
Universidad de Caracas, later social and political turmoil in
Venezuela, and change from aristocratic to democratic institution.
Guide produced by ad hoc group of professors covers governance of
university, faculties, careers available, student services and organizations, entrance procedures. WKU

VEN   "Universidad Central de Venezuela, Facultad de Humanidades y
167   Educación, Centro de Estudiantes de la Escuela de psicología,
       remitido, solidaridad activa con la huelga de hambre de los
       preinscritos en su justa lucha por el derecho al estudio." El
       Nacional, 8 June 1979. Advertisement.
       Hunger strike begun May 28 by eight would-be matriculants,
among hundreds demanding entry into Universidad Central, for whom there
is no space. Typical expression of support by their student peers.

VEN   UNIVERSIDAD DE CARABOBO. "Universidad de Carabobo Comisión
168   Organizadora de los Actos del XX Aniversario, Secretaría

Ejecutiva, Valencia, Venezuela." Papeles Universitarios, nos. 5-
6 (January-February 1978): 64-76.
Challenges semantic sleight-of-hand in term "open university," used wittingly or unwittingly to persuade potential clients that
their educational-professional hopes will be met by it. At best it can
be complement to, not substitute for, regular system. Analysis free of
rhetorical statements.

VEN   ------, Vicerrectorado Académico. "Trabajos realizados por el
169   profesorado en el semestre enero-junio de 1977." Papeles Uni-
      versitarios, no. 4 (November-December 1977): 108-9.
      Authors, titles of research published in faculties of law,
social and economic sciences, health sciences, engineering.

VEN   UNIVERSIDAD DE ORIENTE (UDO). Instituto Oceanográfico. Cumaná:
170   UDO, [1965?]. 12 leaves.
      Though now a dependency of Ministry of Education, this re-
search agency is to become part of UDO. Projects for research in
coastal area. WKU

VEN   ------. Memoria 1964. [Cumaná]: UDO, 1964. 52 pp. plus 16
171   charts.
      Activities after five years of existence; growth, budget,
regional aspects, emphasis on science and technology; School of Basic
Studies, professional schools. Policy and practice related to research, institutional cooperation, international relations. Useful
data. WKU

VEN   ------. Prospecto general 1964. Cumaná: UDO, [1964]. 36 pp.
172   Orientation for students explains governance, rules,
programs. WKU

VEN   ------, Comisión Organizadora. "Documentos universitarios." No.
173   4, June 1965. Mimeographed. 8 pp.
      Presentation by rector of University of Oriente, at meeting
of InterAmerican Development Bank in Paraguay. Sets forth rationale
for universities in underdeveloped countries; their role in development, studies tied to regional needs, democratizing opportunity. Calls
for involvement of alumni, students in university affairs and in community development. WKU

VEN   ------. Dirección de Planificación. Sistema de la educación
174   superior para el Oriente Venezolano, UDO--Desarrollo de 72-
      82, Fase III, Capítulo I. Cumaná: UDO, Consultores
CLADES/PROVEAS, April-August 1972. Ca. 150 leaves.
      Preliminary planning document has demographic material on
eastern Venezuela, chiefly on school population. Huge post-1958 growth
in secondary education now putting pressure on universities. Efforts
to steer students toward technical careers. UDO's function as a
regional system of higher education. WKU

VEN   ------, Núcleo de Nueva Esparta, Delegación de Extensión Uni-
175   versitaria. Pueblo, no. 1 (March 1978). 23 pp.
      One of UDO's núcleos presents information on student ser-
vices, programs offered.

VEN   ------, Presidencia y Secretaría General. Así nació la Uni-
176   versidad de Oriente; Creación, inauguración, bases y
         perspectivas. Caracas: Imprenta Nacional, 1961. 57 pp.
         A fundamental policy change which creates the new "experi-
mental" university in Venezuela. The emphasis is on regionalism and
also on placing limitations on autonomy. WKU

VEN   UNIVERSIDAD DEL ZULIA. "Ante-proyecto de programa para un curso
177   de post-grado en administración y economía de la energía."
         Mimeographed. Maracaibo: Facultad de Ciencias Económicas y
         Sociales, Centro de Estudios para Graduados, February 1980. 9
         pp.
         An eighteen-month program leading to the M.S. degree in
administration and energy economics. WKU

VEN   ------. Los cursos para graduados en la Facultad de Ciencias
178   Económicas y Sociales de la Universidad del Zulia. Maracaibo:
         Facultad de Ciencias Económicas y Sociales, Centro de Estudios
         para Graduados, 1980. 31 pp.
         Development plans for the master's degree, with hopes for
doctoral-level work in the future. Programs in applied fields chiefly
related to hydrocarbons. List of courses, organization of Center for
Graduate Studies, review of recent activities. WKU

VEN   ------. "Maestría en ciencias de la contabilidad: Proyecto."
179   Mimeographed. Maracaibo: Facultad de Ciencias Económicas y
         Sociales, Centro de Estudios de la Empresa, Centro de Estudios
         para Graduados, December 1979. 18 pp.
         Seminar paper presented at Universidad Central, in Caracas,
deplores lack of qualified Venezuelan public accountants; says their
academic preparation relies on imported technologies and that the
national patrimony suffers from "economic espionage" carried out by
transnational auditing firms. Proposes course of study. WKU

VEN   ------. Memoria y cuenta, año de 1972. Maracaibo: Editorial
180   Universitaria, [1974]. 209 pp.
         Report of action on 2,850 matters before the Consejo Uni-
versitario during forty-nine meetings. Enrollment by faculties,
numbers passing or failing by course. Details of activities by academic and administrative units. WKU

VEN   ------. Memoria y cuenta 1974. Maracaibo: Editorial Universi-
181   taria, 1976. 144 pp.
         Reports of administrative and academic units, including data
on professors, students, budget. WKU

VEN   ------. "Oferta y demanda de ingenieros de petróleo en
182   Venezuela." Papeles Universitarios, nos. 10-11 (August-October
         1976): 22-24.
         Massive effort to train petroleum engineers for companies
nationalized in 1972, both in Venezuela and abroad. Their current
unemployment; problems of poor quality charged against University of
Zulia. A response, and call for planning by government, universities,
professional associations.

VEN   ------. Seminario intra-universitario: Visión crítica de la
183   Universidad del Zulia, informe final. Maracaibo: [UZ] Dirección
        de Cultura, 1964. 154 pp.
        Principal themes: structure of the university, teaching and
research, creation of a department of university pedagogy to improve
teaching, problems of students in general, plans for rights of teachers
and problems of budget and non-academic staff. WKU

VEN   ------, Junta de Planificación Universitaria. Informe pre-
184   iminar: La Universidad del Zulia encara su futuro. Maracaibo:
        Universidad del Zulia, Junta de Planificación Universitaria,
        1962. 275 pp.
        A preliminary report covers several plans for the university:
physical installations, organization of teaching, and research. The
history of this university from 1839, objectives, recent data on economic aspects of the region and the university, and data from all
schools of the university. WKU

VEN   "Universidad del Zulia propone nuevo sistema de evaluación para
185   educación superior." Papeles Universitarios 2, nos. 7-8 (March-
        April 1978): 61-63.
        The university in Maracaibo has tested a grading system in
three faculties since 1976, recommends moving away from traditional
final examination which decides success or failure to national policy
of using tests as learning situations.

VEN   UNIVERSIDAD METROPOLITANA. Catálogo general. [Caracas]: Uni-
186   versidad Metropolitana, 1970. 75 pp.
        Private university, founded in 1965, has faculties of arts
and sciences, engineering, social and economic sciences. WKU

VEN   UNIVERSIDAD NACIONAL ABIERTA (UNA). Análisis de las variables
187   determinantes del perfil de demanda para la Universidad Nacional
        Abierta para el período académico 1977-78. Caracas: UNA, Insti-
        tuto de Investigaciones Educativas, 1978. 73 pp.
        Some 6,300 respondents, 78 percent employed in public sector;
highest demand in Andean and west central regions. Environmental
engineering most attractive (761), basic sciences least (100) of the
seventeen educational options listed. WKU

VEN   ------. Análisis de las variables determinantes del perfil del
188   estudiantado preinscrito en la Universidad Nacional Abierta para
        el período académico 1977-78. Caracas: UNA, Instituto de
        Investigaciones Educativas, 1978. 74 pp. plus 44 pages of
        appendices.
        Results of questionnaire include student characteristics,
academic needs, occupations, incomes of some 4,000 respondents. WKU

VEN   ------. Proyecto. [Caracas]: UNA, 1977. 137 pp.
189   Borrowing from U.S. and European models, organizing
commission prepares new sub-system in higher education. Rationale,
analysis of teaching-learning system, flow charts of processes,
organizational charts. Initial careers to be given by open university:
basic sciences, engineering, education, social sciences. Budgetary
projections. WKU

VEN ------, Programas Académicos. <u>Ciclo de Estudios Generales en la</u>
190 <u>UNA</u>. Caracas: UNA, 1977. 22 pp.
General Studies, in accord with UNA goal of offering education for students from diverse social strata, to meet much of social
demand for education and human resource needs of country, reduce cost
of producing graduates, make better use of leisure time, encourage
self-reliance for educational task. Model basic curriculum, career
options. WKU

VEN [UNIVERSIDAD NACIONAL ABIERTA (UNA)-UNIVERSIDAD NACIONAL ESTATAL
191 A DISTANCIA (UNED)]. <u>Experiencias UNA-UNED: La evaluación</u>
<u>institucional, tema C</u>. I Conferencia Latinoamericana de Edu-
cación a Distancia, IX Seminario de Teleducación Universitaria,
San José, 16-19 March 1981. San José: [UNED], 1981. 50 pp.
Highly theoretical-philosophical formulations of administrators of Venezuela's National Open University presented, with comment
that partisan political realities disturb continuity and function of
system. More down-to-earth process with Costa Rican model is underway.
Concludes with comparative study of students in open universities in
both countries. WKU

VEN ------. <u>Experiencias UNA-UNED: La visión de conjunto, entre la</u>
192 <u>práctica y la imagen objetiva, tema A</u>. I Conferencia Latinoamericana de Educación a Distancia, IX Seminario de Teleducación
Universitaria, San José, 16-19 March 1981. San José: [UNED],
1981. 38 pp.
Historical context for development of Venezuelan Open University well presented: optimism over meeting variety of challenges
and skeptical criticism, with theories conducing to creativity, flexibility. Costa Rica's University at a Distance describes its social and
professional extension programs. Among other projects, UNED plans to
offer, in cooperation with the Ministry of Public Education, a "diver-
sified cycle" at secondary level for people who lack secondary school
diploma. WKU

VEN UNIVERSIDAD NACIONAL EXPERIMENTAL SIMON RODRIGUEZ (USR).
193 <u>Documentos 1: Informe sobre la creación de la Universidad Simón</u>
<u>Rodríguez</u>. Caracas: USR, 1977. 93 pp.
Report of Organizing Commission prepared for National Council
of Universities in 1973; survey of needs in capital area for more
university educational opportunities projected to 1982. Hope of reducing first-year 40 percent mortality of other universities by new
"student-centered" learning techniques; degrees to be offered in education and administration. Tables of school enrollment, by region, in
Venezuela, 1969-70. WKU

VEN ------. <u>Documentos 2: Memoria y cuenta 1975</u>. Caracas: USR,
194 1977. 47 pp.
1975 restructuring; academic and administrative activities in
<u>núcleos universitarios</u>. Report of forty regular meetings of the
Rectoral Council. Two <u>núcleos</u>, with 443 students; plans to expand
outside careers. Statistics on enrollments, budgets. WKU

VEN ------. <u>Documentos 3: Memoria y cuenta 1976</u>. Caracas: USR,
195 1978. 118 pp.

Four additional nuclei open with 2,355 students. Nation-wide extension programs. Academic, administrative, financial data with comments on USR's educational philosphy. WKU

VEN ------. Filosofía y estructura de la Universidad Simón
196 Rodríguez. [Caracas]: Consejo Nacional de Rectores, 1976.
Report for new university with various núcleos, non-traditional emphasis on tutorial instead of magisterial learning. Research on administration, teaching; data on enrollment, projections. Emphasis on teacher training, some agriculture. WKU

VEN ------. Filosofía y estructura de la Universidad Simón
197 Rodríguez. Barinas: USR, 1979. 39 pp.
Report for National Council of Universities, with background, organization, statistics, policies; physical facilities scattered, but donation expected from National Race Track Institute to help create a campus. Official documents of its founding. WKU

VEN ------. Gaceta Universitaria 1974. [Caracas: USR, 1978]. 24
198 pp.
Official acts of Rectoral Council. WKU

VEN ------. Licenciatura en educación a distancia. Caracas: Vice-
199 Rectorado de Estudios Universitarios Supervisados, 1978. 16 pp.
Proposed plan of study from general courses to final apprentice work-study stage; several specialties; learning resources, regional centers. A typical brochure for such off-campus programs. WKU

VEN ------. Técnica y planes de estudio en la USR. Caracas: USR,
200 [1978]. 34 pp.
Background, degree programs, various centers; teaching methods include independent study, tutorials, work study; entry requirements. WKU

VEN UNIVERSIDAD SIMON BOLIVAR (USB). Catálogo. Caracas: USB, 1977.
201 255 pp.
Structure and administration of experimental university, founded in 1967, reflect links with national government lacking in traditional university. Academic offerings at intermediate through postgraduate levels in physical and biological sciences, social sciences, and humanities. WKU

VEN ------, Instituto de Investigaciones Educativas. El rendimiento
202 estudiantil universitario: Influencia de la condición socio-económica de los padres en el rendimiento de los alumnos del primer año universitario (región capital), síntesis comparativa. Caracas: Editorial Equinoccio, USB, 1978. 229 pp.
Study of achievement of first-year students in the universities in Caracas as related to their socio-economic origins and other factors is undertaken in effort to minimize non-educational factors and maximize strictly educational factors. Secondary education performance seems to play greater role than other factors in predicting success, and conditions of admission to universities are greater achievement determinants than socio-economic characteristics of students and/or their families. High rate of failure in Venezuelan universities urgently requires information and policy changes. WKU

VEN
203
UNIVERSIDAD SIMON BOLIVAR, Núcleo Universitario del Litoral. Información general. Valle de Camuri Grande: USB, [1977]. 20 leaves.
Branch of USB offers short courses at higher technical level needed for coastal region, such as work in customs, transportation, tourism. WKU

VEN
204
USLAR PIETRI, ARTURO. La universidad y el país: Una posición y una polémica. Caracas: Dirección de Cultura de la Universidad Central de Venezuela, 1962. 64 pp.
Seven essays describe problems of Venezuelan universities; author asserts that there are no great universities in Venezuela. One essay describes the autonomy coming from Cordoba and the weakness of the development of politics; another focuses on necessity for Venezuela to develop needed research. Final paper states the absolute need of a great national university: from a second-class university there cannot be a first-class country, he concludes. KU

VEN
205
VALERA, EDEN. "Tristeza y pesar siente el doctor Mayz Vallenilla al abandonar la Universidad Simón Bolívar." El Universal, 7 April 1979.
Rector since 1969 founding of USB resigned in protest over nullification by new minister of education of university authorized by rectors in CNU. Elements of conflict between power of rectors of experimental universities, such as USB, and autonomous universities, such as UCV. Reactions of student leader, and of rectors of other universities.

VEN
206
VEGAS, ARMANDO. La ciudad universitaria de Caracas: Documentos relativos a su estudio y creación. Caracas: Editorial Grafolit, 1947. 259 pp.
Reports results of study to establish need for and character of a campus for the hitherto fragmented Universidad Central. Data on growth, enumeration of problems, concrete proposals for site of campus. (Example of mid-forties movement in most of Central and South America to unify separate professional schools, improve quality, reduce dependence on part-time professors.) WKU

VEN
207
VENANZI, FRANCISCO DE. Mensaje al Claustro. Caracas: Universidad Central de Venezuela, 1963. 274 pp.
State-of-the-University message by rector recalls 1958 promulgation of law granting autonomy, after overthrow of dictatorship with its "persecutions, exile, jail and expulsions" of university people. Inventory of reality: lack of educated people, poverty, low economic growth, rapid population increase, foreign extraction of minerals. Expansion of UCV, its role in development, accomplishments. WKU

VENEZUELA, Consejo Nacional de Universidades, Oficina de Planificación del Sector Universitario. See entries under OFICINA DE PLANIFICACION DEL SECTOR UNIVERSITARIO.

VEN
208
VESSURI, HEBE M. C. "Science, University and Graduate Education in Venezuela: The Cases of Chemistry and Chemical Engineering." Paper presented at the Latin American Studies Association meeting, Washington D.C., 3-5 March 1982. Mimeographed. 26 pp.

Attributes Venezuela's relatively weak science education to role of industrialized countries and multinational corporations in fostering dependency, plus lack of coherent policy in UCV and IVIC. History of chemistry teaching from its fragmented beginnings in several faculties, and development of chemical engineering as a discipline since 1950s. Problems have included use of foreign models, policies, lack of research, relation of science to petroleum production, over-burdened undergraduate programs. Laments "denationalization" of science education. WKU

VEN   VILLALBA VILLALBA, LUIS. Reflexiones universitarias. Caracas:
209   Ediciones Universidad Central de Venezuela, 1962. 163 pp.
      His columns from newspapers in early fifties reveal arche-typal Venezuelan humanist: passionately loyal to alma mater (Central University), liberally educated and socially liberal, patriotic, senti-mental. Writings range from need for university in region of Oriente to education for women. WKU

VEN   VISO, LUIS RAFAEL. "Universidad Simón Rodríguez, ideas para una
210   institución modelo." Universitas 2000 2, no. 5 (June 1979): 20-
      21.
      Departure from traditional structure for new experimental university involves the teachers and the taught in planning, carrying out, and evaluating academic programs. Emphasis on education and business administration.

VEN   YEPES, ESTEBAN. "Fundayacucho becó en 7 años a treinta mil 17
211   estudiantes." El Nacional, 7 July 1982.
      Over 19,000 of the scholarship students studied outside Venezuela. Support for fields needed for national development, with effort to give greater access to higher education to less well-to-do students. New administrative offices to open. President of Fundayacucho refutes charges that graduates are unemployed or that Fundayacucho is designed as employment agency. Some adjustments to economic situation and performance requirements.

VEN   YEPES BOSCAN, GUILLERMO. Informe sobre la implementación del
212   ciclo general del Colegio Universitario de Maracaibo.
      [Maracaibo?]: Comisión de Educación Superior, Región Zuliana, Educación Superior para la Innovación y el Desarrollo, 1974. 93 pp. plus appendices.
      Report on the planning for the university college in Uni-versity of Zulia; carries out belief in broadly based pre-professional education. WKU

VEN   ZSCHOCK, DIETER K.; SCHULYER, GEORGE W.; FERNANDEZ, ANIBAL; and
213   DUNCAN, W. RAYMOND. "Education and Work Transition of Venezuelan
      University Students." Journal of Inter-American Studies 16, no.
      1 (February 1974): 96-118.
      Study for planning office of National Association of Uni-versities calls for reexamining factors in career choices. Finds youthful elite emerging from university; graduates of lower middle class origins expecting public sector employment; chief goal seems to be personal fulfillment. Implications for planning to meet manpower needs.

University of the West Indies

ALCALA, V. O. A Bibliography of Education in the Caribbean. See entry GEN 7.

UWI THE AMERICAN UNIVERSITY OF THE CARIBBEAN. School of Medicine.
1 Plymouth, Montserrat, 1978. Flyer.
Announcement of medical degree to be earned in two years, nine months, in school founded in 1978. First classes conducted in Ohio, prior to construction of campus in Montserrat. Academic information , tuition, admission requirements. This is a contributing territory of UWI. WKU

UWI The Antigua University Centre. St. John's: UWI Department of
2 Extra-Mural Studies. [1983?] Folder.
One of UWI's outreach centers in the non-campus territories which provide continuing education, in-service training, and first year course requirements toward several UWI degree programs. Resident tutor also oversees career counseling, library, a pre-school child development center, radio program and lectures.

UWI ASHBY, ERIC. Universities: British, Indian, African, A Study in
3 the Ecology of Higher Education. Cambridge, Mass.: Harvard University Press, 1966. 558 pp.
Enlightening account of events and viewpoints in England before and during development of higher education in the West Indies. Although overseas examples are not West Indian, the work of the Asquith Commission and the Irvine Committee are carefully treated. These bodies made the key decisions about the nature of the UWI and its links with the University of London, which is also usefully described. (See entries UWI 57 and 58.) KU

THE ASSOCIATION OF COMMONWEALTH UNIVERSITIES (ACU). Awards for Commonwealth University Staff 1978-80. See entry GUY 1.

UWI ------. Universities facing the Challenge of the Eighties: Can
4 They Survive in Their Present Form? Seminar papers presented during the ACU Council meeting held in the Caribbean 15-27 April 1982. London: ACU, 1982. 97 pp.
Meetings at three Campuses of UWI and that of UG by Council Representatives of ACU's 245 member institution focused on these

topics: relationships between universities and their governments, comparisons between university problems in developed and developing countries, global problems challenging universities, and national aspiration vis-à-vis academic integrity. UWI Vice Chancellor A. Z. Preston, ACU Chairman, notes ". . .the entire Commonwealth Caribbean has been a microcosm of the play of contradictory forces in the wider world...." Presentations by Rex Nettleford and Dennis Irvine, among others, bear him out with some unavoidable truths.

UWI ------. Commonwealth Universities and Society: The Report of
5 the Proceedings of the Eleventh Congress of the Universities of the Commonwealth, Edinburgh, August 1973. London: Association of Commonwealth Universities, 1974. 442 pp.
    One of a series of quinquennial meetings held alternately in Britain and overseas. University autonomy and academic freedom, the university in community, and the role of vice-chancellors discussed. Representatives from Guyana and the University of the West Indies. KU

------. Scholarship Guide for Commonwealth Postgraduate Students 1980-82. See entry GUY 2.

UWI BACCHUS, M. KASSIM. Education and Decolonization. Mona,
6 Jamaica: UWI, Department of Education, 1970. 35 pp.
    Education can play a role in decolonization, but if teachers are to succeed, their preparation must be more than pedagogical. Suggests need for university intellectual environment to broaden outlook rather than separate teacher training colleges. UkLU-IE

UWI ------. Education and Socio-cultural Integration in a "Plural"
7 Society. Occasional Paper Series, no. 6. Montreal: McGill University Center for Developing Area Studies, 1970. 42 pp.
    Compares changes among African and Asian ethnic groups, especially growth of East Indian school attendance in post-1945 era and their later increased upward mobility. UkLU-IE

UWI BAHAMAS. The College of the Bahamas Act, 1974. No. 23.
8 [Naussau], 1974. 9 pp.
    Property and lands of C. R. Walker Technical College, the Bahamas Teachers College, the San Salvador Teachers College, and sixth form of the government high school transferred to new College, a Ministry of Education agency. Post-secondary educational institutions in a UWI contributing territory. UkLU-IE

UWI "Barbados." Caribbean Monthly Bulletin 14, nos. 1-2 (January-
9 February 1980: 47.
    The West Indies Group of University Teachers (WIGUT) called on Barbados government to reconsider decision to withdraw work permit of Vincentian lecturer-political activist, Ralph Gonsalves.

UWI "Barbados to Sponsor Law Students." Trinidad Guardian, 2 May
10 1978.
    Government will begin paying $144 per year fee for law students at Cave Hill campus of UWI, treating them equally to other UWI students, although not giving them grant eligibility. Fees paid only for natives of Barbados, or those meeting residence requirements.

UWI   BAUGH, EDWARD. "English Studies in the University of the West
11   Indies: Retrospect and Prospect." <u>Caribbean Quarterly</u> 16, no. 4
      (December 1970): 48-60.
      Pressure for change following political independence and
independence .from University of London includes questioning need for
arts graduates and English studies in West Indies. Eschews nationalism
but affirms belief in new course in West Indian literature and one in
American literature; hopes for liberal view toward all literature, not
"intellectual fascism."

UWI   BELIZE, Independence Secretariat. <u>Belize: New Nation in Central</u>
12   <u>America</u>. Belize City: Government Printer, 1972. 72 pp.
      Elementary and secondary schools follow the British system.
"University education proper will continue to be obtained abroad for
the time being. Belize, by virtue of its partnership with the other
countries of the Caribbean in the regional University of the West
Indies, can be said to have its own University, and many of our
students attend that institution." UkLU-IE

UWI   BELL, FRANCIS. "Focus on UWI and its Student Problems." <u>Carib-</u>
13   <u>bean Contact</u>, 1 September 1978, pp. 15-16.
      Enrollments by faculty and by campus, 1963-64, 1970-71 and
1977-78 showing huge increases. High costs, Trinidad's White Paper,
problems of LDCs, government's fears of students and charges of with-
drawn support.

UWI   BENEDICT, BURTON. <u>Problems of Smaller Territories</u>. London:
14   Athlone Press, 1962. 153 pp.
      Papers from seminar, 1962-64, include those on political,
economic, and social problems. Reference to small Caribbean countries,
with British Honduras as case study. "Often a painful and politically
delicate decision has to be made as to whether to stress universal
primary education or technical or higher education for a few. The
latter course, although it may improve the economy, is apt to create an
elite which monopolizes positions of power and prestige and encourages
discontent." UkLU-IE

UWI   BENN, BERNARD W. "Metropolitan Standards and their Effects in
15   Caribbean Teaching." <u>Caribbean Studies</u> 11, no. 2 (July 1971):
      85-89.
      Examines effects of externally imposed examinations and syl-
labus for teaching English in West Indies, argues that most teachers
blame narrowness of Cambridge syllabus for authoritarian, traditional
teaching methods; teachers, without constraints of syllabus, would
engage in more discussions, debates, and public speaking. CGC exam
denigrates West Indian language patterns. Suggests University of West
Indies take over examination in English language at GCE 'O' level.

UWI   BLACKMAN, COURTNEY N. ["Self-inflicted Disaster: Roots in the
16   Social Science Faculties"] excerpt from untitled speech at
      Chancellor Hall, University of West Indies, Mona. (Title sup-
      plied by bibliographer) <u>Caribbean Monthly Bulletin</u> 14, nos. 6-7
      (June-July 1980): 45-49.
      Governor of Barbados' Central Bank chides social scientists
for bad scholarship, ideological aberration, deep cultural inferiority

complex. Dependence as cause of underdevelopment in former colonies a useful theory, but New World Group economists at UWI and elsewhere failed to develop operational models for development. Scorns Marxist, U.S., or other ideology as political tool, not model; calls for end to inferiority feelings and copying metropolitan models.

UWI   BLANSHARD, PAUL.   Democracy and Empire in the Caribbean: A
17   Contemporary Review.   New York: Macmillan, 1947.   369 pp.
     In 1938 the Moyne Commission gave a figure for education expenditures in British Caribbean colonies of eighty cents a head per year, compared with ten dollars for Scotland and England. Author saw lack of desks, books, trained teachers, seeming effort to perpetuate low status. Blasts the colonial system. UkLU

UWI   BRAITHWAITE, LLOYD E.   "The Development of Higher Education in
18   the British West Indies."   Social and Economic Studies 7, no. 1
     (March 1958):   1-64.
     History of various attempts to establish higher education within the area, and relation of failures to nature of social structure in West Indies. From Bishop Berkeley and Codrington College in eighteenth century through establishment of University College of the West Indies. Tensions between those favoring metropolitan standards vs. the need to develop local ones.

UWI   ------.   "The Role of the University of the West Indies in the
19   Developing Society of the West Indies."   Social and Economic
     Studies 14, no. 1 (March 1956):   76-87.
     Pro-vice chancellor of UWI, St. Augustine, Trinidad, on consequences of adoption of British system for West Indian education and subsequent problems of adaptation to West Indian realities. Reasons for need to "West Indianize."

UWI   ------.   Caribbean Examination Council Ordinance, 1972.   No. 6.
20   [Belize], 1972.   pp. 19-28.
     An ordinance to be "enacted by the Queen . . . by and with the advice and consent of the House of Representatives and the Senate of British Honduras . . . ." Outgrowth of 1964 Commonwealth countries' meeting in Jamaica, decision to create a new system of examinations. Participation of Antigua, Bahamas, Barbados, Belize, British Virgin Islands, Cayman Islands, Dominica, Grenada, Guyana, Jamaica, Montserrat, St. Kitts, Nevis, Anguilla, St. Lucia, St. Vincent, Trinidad, Tobago, Turks and Caicos Islands; "and any other territory in the Caribbean." Council of Vice-chancellors of the University of the West Indies and the University of Guyana with other representatives and government appointees. Each territory will have national and school examination committees. UkLU-IE

UWI   ------.   Development Plan, 1964-1970.   Belize City: Office of
21   the Premier, 1964.   155 pp.
     Estimates that "country in this stage of development requires a minimum of...three persons per thousand of its population be university trained." Far from goal; suggests scholarships, cites importance to region of Howard and Fisk universities, calls for strong centralized University of the West Indies in one place--Jamaica; criticizes external examinations system as weakening West Indian education.

Problem of need for Spanish language instruction, with high percentage
of Spanish speakers where official language is English. UkLU-IE

UWI   ------, Department of Education. <u>Annual Report of the Department</u>
22   <u>of Education for the School Year, 1968/1969</u>. [Belize City]:
       Government Printing Office, [1969?].
           Having achieved internal self-government, territory's advoca-
cy of political independence is underway. Estimate that 3 percent of
the population, or 1,000 people, should be university trained for
country in this stage of development. Scholarships planned. Two
hundred and eleven post-secondary students abroad for certain needed
specialties, with sixty-two in the U.S.; University of the West Indies
has fifty-four, United Kingdom forty-nine, and Canada thirty-three.
Numbers passing Cambridge 'A' Level exam. UkLU-IE

UWI   <u>British Virgin Islands, 1975</u>. London: Her Majesty's Stationery
23   Office, 1975. 37 pp.
           Population in 1970 was 10,030. Data on secondary school
performance and higher further education, which is mostly in clerical
skills. Twenty students attend UWI and seven the U.S. College of the
Virgin Islands. UkLU-IE

UWI   BROWN, JOHN. "The meaning of 'extra-mural' in the Leewards
24   Islands." In <u>Leewards: Writings, Past and Present, about the</u>
       <u>Leeward Islands</u>, edited by John Brown, pp. 5-11. [Bridgetown?]:
       Department of Extra-Mural Studies, Leeward Islands, University
       College of the West Indies, 1961.
           Extra-mural studies seen as essential component to give in-
habitants of smaller territories access to higher education of University College of the West Indies, particularly non-formal education
related to local needs.

UWI   BURNS, SIR ALAN. <u>History of the British West Indies</u>. Rev. 2nd
25   ed. London: George Allen and Unwin, 1965. 849 pp.
           Struggle and failure of the West Indies federation 1956-62.
More successful development of cooperation to establish University
College of the West Indies with campuses in Jamaica, Barbados, Trinidad
and Tobago described as part of region's history. UkLU-IE

UWI   CAREY, ALEX T. <u>Colonial Students: A Study of the Social Adap-</u>
26   <u>tation of Colonial Students in London</u>. London: Secker
       Warburg, 1956. 267 pp.
           Based on Ph.D. thesis at University of Edinburgh. Cultural
and especially racial hurdles to be overcome. Selected case studies
from eight regions. West Indian (five male, two female) examples.
UkLU-IE

       CARIBBEAN EXAMINATIONS COUNCIL (CXC). <u>Report for 1976</u>. See
       entry GUY 14.

       ------. <u>Report for 1978</u>. See entry GUY 15.

       ------. <u>Secondary Education Certificates Fact Sheet</u>. See entry
       GUY 16.

UWI   CARMICHAEL, OLIVER CROMWELL. Universities: Commonwealth and
27   American. New York: Harper, 1959. 390 pp.
        Elementary introduction to British system after which over-
seas institutions were being modeled. No mention of University College
of the West Indies, but some information on University of London, which
set UC's academic norms and granted degrees to its graduates. KU

UWI   CARR-SAUNDERS, A. M. New Universities Overseas. London: George
28   Allen and Unwin, 1961. 260 pp.
        Rise and development of universities in territories which are
or have been under the British Crown. Asquith Commission, 1943-45,
devised plans for British universities to aid territorial universities.
Résumé of earlier efforts in West Indies. Discussion of the attitudes
on higher education by British officials in the colonies. Role of
University of London as inspector of institutions and grantor of external degrees. Irvine Committee; site selection problem for College
of the West Indies. Office of Colonial Development and Welfare made
capital grants. Constitution embodied in a royal charter. UkLU-IE

UWI   CLARKE, AUSTIN. Growing Up Stupid under the Union Jack, a
29   Memoir. Toronto: McClelland and Stewart, 1980. 187 pp.
        Being poor, bright, and black in Barbados meant an agony of
preparation for the Cambridge University Senior Cambridge Examination
(Overseas), which determined the child's entire future. A touching,
personal account of surviving the rigidities of alien British schooling
in the Caribbean world, told by a novelist who passed the exam in 1950,
went on to study at University of Toronto. MoSW

UWI   COKE, LLOYD. "Science for the People: The Management of Science
30   and Technology in the West Indies." Caribbean Quarterly 20, no.
    2 (June 1974): 7-14.
        Problems confronting Jamaican scientists include their need
to operate in societies very different from those in which their metropolitan colleagues work and from societies in which a large number of
them received formal training. Prestige comes from publication in
metropolitan journals, not from problem solving at local level with
those of other disciplines. Some remedies suggested.

UWI   THE COMMONWEALTH FOUNDATION. Reports on Visit of a Working Party
31   to Universities in Ghana, Nigeria, and Sierra Leone, January-
    February 1973. Occasional Paper, no. 22. London, 1973. 76 pp.
        In 1973, seven administrators and professors of UWI and the
University of Guyana visited universities in Nigeria and others from
British background in Africa, an experiment all found valuable.
Aspects of cooperation planned: staff visits; exchanges of students,
staff, external examiners and information; collective research and
professional activity.

UWI   Commonwealth Universities Yearbook. London: The Association of
32   Universities of the British Commonwealth. 1958   .
        Continues coverage begun with Yearbook of the Universities of
the Commonwealth. See YEARBOOK. Proof copy, prepared for 1984, gives
short history of UWI. Developments include projected medical school
for Trinidad, challenge examination scheme which allows students in
non-campus territories to write first year exams at home with help from

Extra-Mural Department, distance teaching experiment, attendance of
government ministers of supporting territories in university council
meetings, major restructuring. Troublesome potential for undermining
regionality. ACU

UWI CRAIG, DENNIS and CARTER, SHEILA. "The Language Learning Apti-
33 tudes of Jamaican Children at the Beginning of Secondary School."
Caribbean Journal of Education 3, no. 1 (January 1976): 1-21; 3,
no. 2 (April 1976): 70-111.
Creole language keeps doors to education closed for majority
in most of Caribbean, hence this study of typical situation is useful.
Common Entrance Examination (CEE), taken between ages ten and thirteen,
determines what kind of secondary school is accessible; about 10 percent enter five-year course leading to General Certificate of Education
(GCE), which in turn makes university access possible. Difficulties in
shifting from Jamaican Creole to Standard Jamaican English in elementary schools, and the 1:60 teacher ratio (with almost half the teachers
untrained) make learning a third language, Spanish, extremely
difficult. Need for special help and research.

UWI CROSS, MALCOLM. "Education and Job Opportunities." In The
34 Stability of the Caribbean, edited by R. Moss, pp. 51-76.
London: Institute for the Study of Conflict, 1973.
Population growth and its shift from rural to urban centers
has overwhelmed educational resources for all of English-speaking
Caribbean. Failure of agriculture as employment source not remedied in
other sectors of the economy, nor is education relevant to needs. UWI
reflects these and other fundamental problems in a dual economy. Uk

CURTIS, S. J. History of Education in Great Britain. See entry
GUY 22.

UWI CUTHBERT, MARLENE. "UWI's Communication Plan for Caribbean."
35 Caribbean Contact, May 1981, p. 6.
Regional ministers of education recommend that UWI continue
five-year pilot project for use of telecommunications for Caribbean
education. Many possibilities for linking campus and non-campus territories emerge from study funded by USAID.

UWI "CXC Grows." CXC News 2, no. 1 (January 1982): 4.
36 Caribbean educators see continuing growth of participation in
their locally prepared and administered school-leaving examinations
begun in 1979. News carries other items on examining system which
substitutes for former level GCE administered from England.

UWI D'AETH, RICHARD. "The Growth of the University College of the
37 West Indies." British Journal of Education Studies 9, no. 2 (May
1961): 99-116.
Professor at University of Exeter and former professor at
UCWI gives background and context. Details of Irvine Committee study
and recommendations adopted by Asquith Commission are juxtaposed with
views of Eric Williams. (See entries UWI 58 and 59.) Early days of
the residential university in Jamaica, addition of campus in Trinidad;
financial and political problems of first twelve years being met.
Expresses hope for future.

UWI ------. "The University of the West Indies Revisited." <u>Overseas</u>
38 <u>Universities</u>, no. 16 (October 1970): 16-23.
    Observations, after twelve years, of a former professor from
the University of Exeter. Impressed with the tremendous growth in
size, numbers; lowered cost per student. Shift to a larger West Indian
staff from the 1950s, while yet importing the majority of senior and
some junior academic staff; passing through a phase as did Canada and
Australia, but with more stress, when there is only one university in
the country. Many aspirants to teaching posts with fewer opportunities
than in Canada and/or Britain, where supply and demand is more
balanced. The staff are nationalistic but also have a sense of be-
longing to the international academic community.

UWI "The Department of Extra-Mural Studies at the University of the
39 West Indies." <u>Caribbean Studies Newsletter</u> 8, no. 2 (Summer
1981): 8. Excerpted from [UWI] <u>Extra-Mural Notes</u>, 33rd Communication Seminar Issue, 9-13 (February 1981).
    Resident tutors and specialists work in non-campus terri-
tories of Antigua, Belize, Dominica, Grenada, Montserrat, St. Kitts,
St. Lucia, and St. Vincent. Programs: personal development, academic
certification, work toward university matriculation, in-service
training. Now administering "Challenge Examinations" for Social Science Part I, planning for exams also for Faculty of Arts and General
Studies. Three campuses administer program.

UWI DOMINICA, Department of Education. <u>Annual Report, 1960</u>.
40 [Roseau]: Department of Education, [1960].
    Resident tutor for St. Vincent and Dominica includes the
fifty plus students studying abroad by fields of study and universities. UkLU-IE

UWI D'OYLEY, VINCENT, and MURRAY, REGINALD, eds. <u>Development and</u>
41 <u>Disillusion in Third World Education with Emphasis on Jamaica</u>.
Symposium Series 10. Toronto: The Ontario Institute for Studies
in Education, 1979. 185 pp.
    Essays on qualitative and quantitative problems of elementary
and secondary education and teacher training reveal much about access
to higher education. Scarce resources, race, the colonial social and
economic heritage, religious denominational competition, unsuitable
syllabi, external examinations are among the problems; some comparisons
between Guyana and Jamaica and of both with Ghana. KU

UWI DRAYTON, ARTHUR D. "Caribbean Studies at the University of the
42 West Indies." Mimeographed. Mona: UWI, [1978]. 20 pp.
    Dean of the Faculty of Arts and General Studies, Mona, gives
details of programs, research and publications, resources of faculty
where most Caribbean studies are pursued. Anticipation of university-
wide certificate program in Caribbean Studies. Courses available.
Report of workshop on Caribbean, African, Asian studies; need for
citizen education on Caribbean, active role of UNICA. WKU

UWI DRAYTON, KATHLEEN. "UWI at the Crossroads." <u>Caribbean Contact</u>
43 August 1981, pp. 8-9.
    Fears over future following June meeting of UWI Council and
University Grants Committee, with differing views on financing and

function by Jamaica and Trinidad and Tobago on one side, Barbados and LDCs on other. Some historical background; issues raised by Trinidad White Paper and Demas IGC reports analyzed and commented on. The political dilemma, and the social order in which the university functions. Some cost projections. Useful perspective.

UWI "Education in the West Indies." <u>Overseas Quarterly</u> 11, no. 4
44   (December 1958): 111-12. Abridged abstract from the report on "Development and Welfare in the West Indies, 1957," (HMSO Colonial no. 337.1958) by Sir Stephen Luke.
     Major problems of the differing abilities in secondary schools and needs for "technical element" in education. "In the region as a whole, secondary education must, for some time to come, be selective. It is economically impossible at the present time to provide schools for all children of the age of twelve and over." Development of the secondary modern school with broader constituency than the school certification exams and General Certificate of Education.

UWI FERGUS, HOWARD. "Some Implications of the Caribbean Examination
45   Council for the Continuing Education of Teachers." <u>Caribbean Journal of Education</u> 7, no. 2 (1980): 87-109.
     School-leaving examinations, traditionally oriented to entry into Cambridge-London higher education patterns, are now being developed by the CXC to reflect Caribbean realities. Curriculum changes, many designed to produce social changes, must involve teachers in their planning; hence teachers need upgrading of both academic substance and pedagogical skills. Active role to be played by regional universities in this process.

UWI FIGUEROA, JOHN J. <u>Society, Schools and Progress in the West</u>
46   <u>Indies</u>. Oxford: Pergamon Press, 1971. 208 pp.
     Useful historical and social background for understanding University of the West Indies. Describes 1948 beginnings of University College, comments on issues and attitudes. Chief emphasis is on teacher preparation. KU

UWI ------. <u>Staffing and Examinations in British Caribbean Secondary</u>
47   <u>Schools: A Report of the Conference of the Caribbean Heads, July</u>
     <u>1961</u>. London: Evans, 1964. 64 pp.
     After dissolution of Federation of the West Indies, first meeting in five years of headmasters and headmistresses makes plans for staffing and examinations, with much of the responsibility falling on the University College of the West Indies. FU

UWI FIGUEROA, PETER M. E., and PERSUAD, GANGE, eds. <u>Sociology of</u>
48   <u>Education, A Caribbean Reader</u>. London: Oxford University Press, 1976. 284 pp.
     For teachers working on certificates and for others at degree level. Although the book is almost completely related to the UWI and the Commonwealth Caribbean, it is full of valuable and well chosen sociological papers. Analytical first chapter by the editors. KU

UWI FISHER, STEPHEN H. <u>The Commonwealth Caribbean: Study of the</u>
49   <u>Educational System of the Commonwealth Caribbean and Guide to the</u>
     <u>Academic Placement of Students in Educational Institutions of the</u>

United States. Washington, D.C.: American Association of Collegiate Registrars and Admissions Officers, 1979. 238 pp.
    Description of systems, academic programs, examinations,
credits. KU

UWI   FRIDAY, WELLINGTON REGINALD LINCOLN. "Restructuring Higher Edu-
50   cation in the Non-Campus Territory of the British Caribbean as a
       Strategy for Development: Problems and Prospect." Ed.D. disser-
       tation, University of Southern California, 1975. 450 pp.
    Effort to find new model different from elite system in-
herited from the British. Despite efforts to decentralize UWI, it is
"anachronistic and regarded as having largely failed to meet the demands and developmental needs of the non-campus territories." Problems
of size, demand, geographical space, nationalism. Need to restructure
university. Debate over U.S. land-grant model.

UWI   GONSALVES, RALPH. "The Rodney Affair." Caribbean Quarterly 25,
51   no. 3 (September 1979): 1-24.
    Lecturer in the Department of History, UWI, Mona, and Black
Power advocate banned by Jamaican government in 1968 from reentering
Jamaica. Guild of Undergraduates stages protest, is met by government
resistance; campus state of siege and diverse points of view among
students and administrators produce strong polarizations. An event in
the growing political and social awareness of the period by students in
the Eastern Caribbean.

UWI   GOODING, EARL NATHANIEL MERRIL. "Education in Trinidad: Past
52   and Present." Ph.D. dissertation, University of Connecticut,
       1961. 281 pp.
    Detailed, carefully referenced history of primary and
secondary public education in Trinidad, from 1830s. Major changes in
educational emphases are outgrowth of official commissions. "The resulting system was shaped and fashioned by the work of several education commissions, each revising, criticizing, and seeking to fashion
education according to its own concept of education for a colonial
territory." Commissioners invariably foreigners on two-week school
inspection tour of Trinidad.

UWI   GORDON, SHIRLEY COURTNEY, comp. A Century of West Indian Edu-
53   cation: A Source Book. London: Longmans, 1963. 312 pp.
    Lack of realistic education, e.g., its urban, classical memo-
ristic character, plus depressed economy, yielded poor quality and
small quantity of opportunity. An important work, making good use of
government and church documents and the press. Essential background
and incisive comment. UkLU-IE

UWI   ------, ed. Reports and Repercussions in West Indian Education,
54   1835-1933. London: Ginn and Company Ltd., 1968. 190 pp.
    Eight reports which influenced West Indian education from
1835 to 1933 gave some impetus to university development, but sentiment
was strong for elementary and vocational education. Strong recommendations also to give classical education equal to that of European universities. Clear dominance of British models. UkLU-IE

UWI   GOVEIA, ELSA. "The U.W.I. and the teaching of West Indian
55   History." Caribbean Quarterly 15, nos. 2-3 (January-September
       1969): 60-63.
          Gradual development of body of knowledge beyond European
history now permits requirement for all students of survey course in
West Indian history. Recruitment of Walter Rodney for African history
blocked by his exclusion from Jamaica.

UWI   GREAT BRITAIN, Board of Education. Special Reports on Education-
56   al Subjects. Vol. 4: Canada, Newfoundland, West Indies.
       London: HMSO, 1901. 834 pp.
          Jamaica chiefly. Useful for attitudes expressed in debates
on kind of education suited to local population, with heavy emphasis on
keeping students tied to agriculture and their "place in society."
Also has descriptions of education in British Guiana, with information
on Queen's College and preparation for examination for Cambridge and
the University of London. Policy makers in British Guiana seem more
liberal than those in Jamaica. UkLU-IE

UWI   GREAT BRITAIN, Central Office of Information. Britain and the
57   Developing Countries. London: HMSO, 1970. 67 pp.
          First British government grants for education made in 1832,
compulsory primary education with government aid in 1870. In Britain
and dependencies, education began as chiefly the task of churches and
charities, with government aid in the nineteenth century parcelled out
mostly in small grants to mission schools. Overseas Development Administration coordinates British aid to universities in developing
countries through Inter-University Council for Higher Education Overseas (IUC), established 1946, incorporated 1970. UWI campuses at
Jamaica, Trinidad, Barbados and extra-mural centers received "entire
cost of capital development out of Colonial Development and Welfare
funds before 1962." UkLU-IE

UWI   GREAT BRITAIN, Commission on Higher Education in the Colonies.
58   Report of the Commission on Higher Education in the Colonies.
       The Honorable Mr. Justice Cyril Asquith, Chairman. Cmd. 6647,
       IV. London: HMSO, 1945. 119 pp.
          Survey of existing facilities; place of universities and
university colleges in development of higher education; general academic, staffing, financial matters pertaining to all colonies. Chapter
21 report on West Indies committee recommends "early creation of a
university..., a unitary university...[which] rejects the alternative
of federated colleges being set up in ten different colonies to
function as constituents of a degree-granting university. This decision is emphatic. Bearing in mind the existence of a considerable
measure of inter-island rivalry...." Also proposes scheme of government, that it should be open to women, a site, courses of study; "that
it be staffed in a way which would be recognised in Great Britain as
conforming to a high standard"; that there will be emphasis on
research. Ties with the University of London discussed. UkLU-IE

UWI   ------, West Indies Committee. Report of the West Indies Com-
59   mittee on Higher Education in the Colonies. Sir James Irvine,
       Chairman. Cmd. 6654. London: HMSO, [1945]. 81 pp.

(Throughout report, West Indies includes British Guiana and British Honduras.) After study, recommends unanimously "that the university should be a single centralized institution...[and] that it should be entirely residential." Despite historically derived sense of separateness among islands, advocates single university, "development of a West Indian outlook"; hope that West Indian University would offer opportunities, lacking before, for women to be educated. Governance, facilities, finance, research, extra-mural department discussed. Data on racial composition and school enrollments in colonies Appendix 2. DLC

UWI   "Grenada." <u>Caribbean Monthly Bulletin</u> 13, nos. 1-2 (January-
60   February 1979): 7-13.
       Includes paragraph on governor general's announcing "priority to establishment of a 'State University,'" not to be competitive with University of the West Indies.

      HEARNDEN, ARTHUR. <u>Paths to University: Preparation, Assessment,</u> Selection. See entry FrA 27.

UWI   HOUGHTON, HAROLD. <u>Report on Education in the Bahamas</u>. [London]:
61   Colonial Office, 1958. 36 pp.
       Finds little enthusiasm or demand for education by parents or children. Ought to be some relationship between Bahamas and the University College of the West Indies, especially teacher training and extra-mural help. Uk

UWI   HOYOS, F. A. <u>Barbados: A History from the Amerindians to Inde-</u>
62   <u>pendence</u>. London: Macmillan Education, 1978. 293 pp.
       Beginnings of education with bequest of Christopher Codrington in 1710. Church role, British government grants, resistance of planters to black education. Codrington College affiliation in 1875 with Durham University for higher educational opportunities. Educational history interwoven with other social, economic, and political events. UkLU-IE

UWI   HUNTE, CHRISTOPHER NORMAN. "The Development of Higher Education
63   in the West Indies with Special Emphasis on Barbados." Ph.D.
      dissertation, Washington State University, 1976. 210 pp.
       Main purpose was to examine critically the major developments of higher education in the West Indies, particularly in Barbados. In general, finds higher education too limited and also ineffectual in meeting manpower needs. Recommends that U.S.-type community colleges would be economically sound. At the university level more women are needed. UWI should collaborate with teacher training colleges. Advocates more public expenditures in education--up to 5 percent of their gross national product--with emphasis on vocational-technical education.

UWI   INSTITUTE OF JAMAICA. <u>The Jamaican National Bibliography, 1964-</u>
64   <u>1974</u>. Millwood, N.Y.: Kraus International Publications, 1981.
      439 pp.
       Particularly useful list of possible sources in periodicals and newspapers. Education included in section on social sciences. Many items published <u>by</u> UWI, but few <u>about</u> UWI. KU

UWI   INTER-GOVERNMENTAL COMMITTEE ON THE UNIVERSITY OF THE WEST
65   INDIES. "Background Paper." Mimeographed. January 1976. ca.
       80 leaves.
           Heads of Government Conference requested report for use in
making recommendations on the role, character, functions and orientation of university education in the Commonwealth Caribbean, with
reference to possible changes and adaptations of offerings, decision-
making, role of non-campus territories, and finance. Plan of work for
an inter-governmental committee and its membership outlined. Text and
appendices describe UWI; brief section on University of Guyana
included. WKU

       INTER-UNIVERSITY COUNCIL FOR HIGHER EDUCATION OVERSEAS. IUC and
       Related Services, A Guide. See entry GUY 30.

UWI   ------. Report 1946-47. James C. Irvine, Chairman. Cmd. 7331.
66   London: HMSO, [1947?]. 12 pp.
           Sir James Irvine and other council members visited West
Indies in December 1946-January 1947, assisted the Principal-designate
in selection of site for the College, in arrangement between College
and the Imperial College of Tropical Agriculture, Trinidad, for degree
courses in agriculture. Report also covers visits to other colonies,
e.g., Ceylon and East Africa, noting in all cases lack of sufficient
number of qualified local educators to staff colleges. Discusses
students, scholarships, library development, Colonial University Grant
Advisory Committee. KU

       ------. Reports of the Vice-Chancellors' Conference, March 1979,
       Jamaica. See entry GUY 31.

UWI   ------. Second Report 1947-49. James C. Irvine, Chairman. Cmd.
67   7801. London: HMSO, [1949?]. 13 pp.
           Some difficulty in staffing new university colleges in West
Africa and West Indies; suggests incentives for faculty members from
home universities to teach abroad. Incipient research plans. Extra-
mural Studies, under Philip Sherlock in University College of the West
Indies, set up before any internal departments. "Embarrassing delay"
for some university colleges in setting up "regional colleges" for
technical education. KU

       ------. Vice-Chancellors' Conference, Summer 1976, Aspen,
       Colorado. See entry GUY 32.

UWI   JAMAICA, Department of Statistics. Education. Facts on Jamaica.
68   [Kingston]: Department of Statistics, Jamaica, [1973]. 61 pp.
           Brief résumé of educational systems plus current data on
institutions, enrollment, attendance, teachers, and examinations in the
public sector. Student registration and graduates at University of
West Indies and numbers coming from other territories. DLC

UWI   JAMAICA, Ministry of Education. Annual Report, 1961. Kingston:
69   The Government Printer, [1962].
           Chapter 8 has data on further and higher education. Sixty
Jamaicans attend the University College of the West Indies, while 2,690
study in Britain, 1,145 in the U.S. and 370 in Canadian universities.

UWI   ------. <u>Annual Report, 1975-1976</u>. [Kingston]: Ministry of Edu-
70   cation, Publications Branch, [1976].
       Includes data on government contribution to university and
the West Indies, Jamaican enrollment in University of the West Indies,
numbers and kind of staff, needs for Ph.D. programs. U.S. and Canadian
agencies and their contributions.

UWI   ------. <u>Annual Report, Minister of Education, 1967-1977</u>.
71   Kingston, [Ministry of Education], 1980. 109 pp.
       Fourth chapter devoted to tertiary education, including Uni-
versity of the West Indies. Enrollment statistics. UkLU-IE

UWI   ------. <u>The Education Thrust of the '70s</u>. Kingston: [Ministry
72   of Education], 1973. 37 pp.
       Half of Jamaica's people are under age seventeen. Policy
statement includes higher education expansion, especially for teachers,
engineers, architects. List of serious shortcomings shows only 8
percent of age group is admitted to high schools after passing exams;
only 50 percent of these passed school-leaving exam, to be eligible for
university entry. New development plans to remedy the identified need
explained in detail. Mention of National Service program at end of
formal education, but no details. WKU

UWI   ------, Working Party on Post 'O' Level Education. <u>Report</u>.
73   Kingston, 1973.
       Proposes increase in sixth form students, training colleges
and new programs for manpower needs.

UWI   JONES-HENDRICKSON, S. B. "Education in the Economic Transfor-
74   mation of the State of St. Kitts-Nevis-Anguilla." <u>Micro-
       state Studies</u> 2 (1979): 40-67.
       Correlation between education and economic development
indicates developing nations should invest in education. St. Kitts-
Nevis-Anguilla hampered by growing population and inadequate teaching
facilities. Territories served by University of West Indies. Problems
of brain drain, appropriateness of university education abroad.

UWI   KING, WINSTON. "The Development of an Integrated Science Program
75   for the Caribbean--Part I." <u>Bulletin of Eastern Caribbean</u>
       Affairs 4, no. 1 (March-April 1978): 1-11.
       Member of Institute of Education, University of West Indies,
Barbados, describes development of program for secondary schools, with
efforts in several territories, including Trinidad. Caribbean Examinations Council developing 'O' level exams. The various curricula
served over 40,000 students.

UWI   KUPER, ADAM. <u>Changing Jamaica</u>. Kingston: Kingston Publishers,
76   1976. 163 pp.
       Chapter entitled "The Educational System" denounces system
for poor productivity, perpetuation of class differences. Dismal performance on examinations for most, with chances for small-holder's
child estimated at 3 in 100 of getting into academic secondary school,
much less university. Parental social class, not merit, determines
educational opportunity and continuation in social class. KU

UWI LALOR, G. C. "Project Satellite Report." Mimeographed. Mona,
77   Jamaica: University of the West Indies Senate House, June 1978.
     77 leaves.
          Pro-vice-chancellor describes USAID and NASA experiment in
use of satellite communication between two campuses of the University
of the West Indies and a non-campus territory. Twenty-seven televised
programs, most in outreach projects, were produced over two month
period. Data on university history, geography (great distances sepa-
rating UWI campuses and territories), governance, per capita incomes of
support territories, degrees is useful. Need for improved communication as substitute for travel is clear for improved administration;
academic outreach offers great possibilities for unserved and underserved. Need for further cost-effectiveness research, improved
technology. WKU

UWI LATIN AMERICAN SCHOLARSHIP PROGRAM OF AMERICAN UNIVERSITIES
78   (LASPAU). "Postsecondary Faculty Training Needs in the English
     Speaking Caribbean." Mimeographed. [Cambridge, Mass.]: LASPAU,
     8 February 1977. 27 pp.
          Report of on-site visits to Trinidad and Tobago, Grenada,
Barbados, and Jamaica by LASPAU and OAS representatives. Did not
include University of West Indies, but endeavored to identify other
postsecondary needs in region. WKU

     LEMKE, DONALD A. "Education in the English Speaking Caribbean."
     See entry GUY 38.

UWI LEO-RHYNIE, ELSA. "The performance of Jamaican Sixth Form
79   Students in the Cambridge 'A' Level Examinations." Carib-
     bean Journal of Education 5, no. 3 (1978): 155-67.
          Jamaican economy relies heavily on graduate output of UWI for
needed professionals in technological, commercial, professional fields.
UWI depends on sixth forms of secondary schools to supply capable
students. In 1973, working party studied national problem of wastage
at sixth form level, but percentage of Jamaican passes remains very
low, poorer than Trinidadian scores, and both far poorer than scores in
Great Britain. Summaries of performance, deficiencies; several
explanations--but no remedies--posited.

     LEWIS, [W.] ARTHUR. "The University in Less Developed
     Countries." See entry GEN 176.

UWI LITTLE, KENNETH. Negroes in Britain: A Study of Racial Re-
80   lations in English Society. 2d. ed., rev. London: Routledge
     and Kegan Paul, 1972. 309 pp.
          Owing considerable to its 1948 first publishing, it is never-
theless a useful description of West Indians' acceptance and lack
thereof in Britain. Most significant is contrast author finds between
West Indians and Africans, saying Jamaicans and Barbadians especially
regard England as their "homeland." Education in West Indian schools
is entirely on English lines. The educated West Indian is unprepared
for the ignorance and prejudice he finds in England, where he must go
to attend a university (in 1948). UkLU-IE

     LOGAN, DOUGLAS. "The Commonwealth Scholarship and Fellowship
     Plan." See entry GUY 40.

LOPEZ YUSTOS, R. ALFONSO. "Education in the West Indies." See entry GEN 180.

UWI 81   LOWENTHAL, DAVID. West Indian Societies. London: Oxford University Press, 1972. 385 pp.
    A rich lode of anecdotal material and data showing the peculiar divisiveness of European tradition in largely black societies. Educational opportunities alienate privileged from poor in the West Indies, and skin color is a social barrier in the metropolis. Hierarchical, classical values slavishly copied are self-defeating. Passion for insular cultural uniqueness impedes cooperation. All these affect and are affected by education. UkLU-IE

UWI 82   MAINGOT, ANTHONY P. "The Future of the University of the West Indies." Caribbean Review 7, no. 3 (July-September 1978): 48-53.
    Comments on 1977 White Paper on National Institute of Higher Education of the government of Trinidad and Tobago: attempt to clarify "generalist-specialist" controversy over role of UWI reveals its vulnerable political situation. Mid 1950s hopes of West Indian Federation that University would aid regional bonding not fulfilled; failure to develop needed technical personnel or maintain sufficient growth. White Paper urges more influence of regional governments; author faults academics for radical political rhetoric and privileged status.

UWI 83   MALE, GEORGE A. The Struggle for Power: Who Controls the Schools in England and the United States. Sage Library of Social Research. London: Sage Publications, 1974. 199 pp.
    British educational policy continues to affect West Indies by virtue of establishing patterns and by educating migrants. Growth of centralization; chapter of conclusions summarizes some problems of democratizing effects in post-World War II Britain. UkLU-IE

UWI 84   MANIGAT, LESLIE F. "The Institute of International Relations and the White Paper on Science and Technology Issued by the Government of Trinidad and Tobago." Mimeographed. St. Augustine, 13 January 1978. 8 pp.
    Reply by director points out problems of institute if status is changed from being an autonomous unit within structure of University of the West Indies. Emphasizes present graduate program's practicality for regional needs. WKU

UWI 85   MANLEY, MICHAEL. The Politics of Change: A Jamaican Testament. London: Andre Deutsch, 1974. 217 pp.
    Educational needs in Third World are different from those of colonial times, especially for high-level technical skills. Proposes special attention to directing gifted students toward university after primary level. Some kind of national service should be required of all. KU

UWI 86   MARTIN, SIDNEY LANCELOT. "The History of the University of the West Indies." Mimeographed. Cave Hill: UWI, 1976. 18 pp.
    From talk given by principal, UWI, Cave Hill and pro-vice-chancellor, UWI. Identifies periods: Pre-teaching, 1945-48; University College and association with University of London, 1948-62; UWI

chartered as independent institution with support from contributing governments, 1962-69; period of reappraisal, 1969-72. Continuous patterns throughout: financial straits, internal structure and devolution of authority, academic programs and their relevance, competing needs, particularly of less rich territories. Elaborates on these times and themes. WKU

UWI   MATHURIN-MAIR, LUCILLE.   "The Student and the University's
87   Civilizing Role." <u>Caribbean Quarterly</u> 15, nos. 2-3 (June-September 1969): 8-19.
          A retrospective look at student behavior and values from beginning at Mona Campus, Jamaica, to 1968; from academic socializing to social activism.

UWI   MILLER, ERROL. "Education and Society in Jamaica." In <u>Sociology</u>
88   <u>of Education: A Caribbean Reader</u>, edited by Peter M. E. Figueroa and Ganga Persaud, pp. 47-66. London: Oxford University Press, 1976.
          Four levels of society in Jamaica: upper, traditional middle, emerging middle, and lower strata identified. Describes the total system of education and points out the same stratified characteristics in education. The University of the West Indies finds students in each of these four levels. KU

UWI   ------. "Reappraising the Sixth Form Idea." <u>Caribbean Quarterly</u>
89   18, no. 2 (September 1972): 7-22.
          Describes sixth form as functionally the first year of university though it is physically within the high school. Flawed system because of its elite clientele (some 10 percent of the cohort group), its undue impact on schools' social structure, its restrictive nature (choosing science or arts), its content answerable only to 'A' level external examinations run by University of Cambridge Overseas Examination Syndicate. Problem of high failure rate remains; with UWI accepting the 2 percent of the cohort who pass 'A' levels, space remains for more students. Reform proposals to improve costly, insufficient system.

UWI   MURRAY, REGINALD. <u>Education in a Changing West Indies</u>. Address
90   to the Catholic Teachers Association of Trinidad and Tobago, 10 February 1961. [n.p., n.d.] 8 pp. Pamphlet.
          British emphasis on empire resulted in English textbooks and sending of all the best students to universities in Britain. Oxford and Cambridge Joint Board controlled most, and, as Dr. Eric Williams said, it "creamed off" the best people.

UWI   NATHANIELS, LIZ. "Education Standards Improved, and 'Getting
91   Better.'" <u>Journal of Commerce</u>, Section 4 (18 November 1974): 19-23.
          Ministry of Education of the Bahamas is largest ministry in government with three to four times more people than any other. Cites disdain for manual work, lack of preparation for other. British style "common entrance" exams at age eleven abolished, to "bring education at junior and senior high ranges more on a level with the egalitarian American system." More and more teachers, of which 55 percent are foreigners, are from the U.S., and the majority of students studying abroad on Ministry of Education scholarships are in U.S. universities.

UWI   NILES, NORMA A., and GARDNER, TREVOR, eds. <u>Perspectives in West</u>
92   <u>Indian Education</u>. Papers from the Second Annual Conference of
the West Indian Student Association, May 1977. East Lansing:
West Indian Student Association, Michigan State University, 1978.
226 pp.
        Useful panorama of English-speaking Caribbean education di-
rectly and indirectly related to universities, especially with regard
to colonial heritage. WKU

UWI   "Now One of Those Medical Schools Comes to Kingston." <u>Caribbean</u>
93   <u>Contact</u>, February 1979, p. 16.
        Opening of an "off-shore" medical school in St. Vincent
elicits criticism based on 1978 report of CARICOM health ministers,
which said such schools "have no rational role to play in the immediate
or future health needs of the Caribbean Commonwealth." Some fifty-
seven medical schools serving mostly U.S. students unable to enter U.S.
medical schools are in Mexico and the Caribbean.

UWI   NUNES, F. E. "Management Education and Ideology: The Ex-
94   periences and Concerns at the University of the West Indies."
<u>Caribbean Journal of Education</u> 6, no. 2 (1979): 111-33.
        Concern for effects of technology transfer from metropolises
to host countries of Third World: the Jamaican experience. Change
from plantation style management to sugar cooperatives, in context of
regime which is critical of old-style capitalism and advocates social-
ism. Ideology undergirds means and ends of decision-making process;
problem of bringing techniques of rich nations to poor nations needs
examination. University students privileged in developing countries;
how to protect the poor? Schism between management program at UWI and
rest of faculties, especially in social sciences. Influence of
business community and outside donors. Calls for careful analysis of
criticism, issues, values. A lucid, rational presentation, free of
cant.

UWI   "One Year Silence on Demas Report - Then a Trinidad White Paper
95   on UWI's Future." <u>Caribbean Contact</u>, March 1978, pp. 5-6.
        Government of Trinidad and Tobago 1977 White Paper proposed
restructuring of University of West Indies, giving stronger impetus to
service and technologies in Trinidad and Tobago. Fear that other
territories' roles in UWI would be weakened; problem of role of particular governments in policy making; comments from Cave Hill campus in
Barbados. See UWI 119.

UWI   OXAAL, IVAR. <u>Black Intellectuals Come to Power: The Rise of</u>
96   <u>Creole Nationalism in Trinidad and Tobago</u>. Cambridge, Mass:
Schenkman Publishing Co., 1968. 194 pp.
        Oxford graduate Eric Williams and other leaders in education
and politics are described. Growth of nationalism in the fifties and
push for university in Jamaica. KU

UWI   PEARSE, ANDREW. "Education in the British Caribbean: Social and
97   Economic Background." <u>Vox Guyana</u> 2, no. 1 (February 1956): 9-
24.
        Plantation system had scant need or infrastructure for edu-
cation. Some elementary education provided by private bequests in

eighteenth century for whites; slow growth of "Christianizing" efforts, but fear and/or prohibition of literacy for slaves. Nineteenth century influence of churches, with little British government help. Analysis of main currents of ideas and practices in post-World War II era. Useful background.

UWI PENSON, LILLIAN M. Educational Partnership in Africa and the
98 West Indies. Glasgow University Publications. Glasgow: Jackson, 1955. 25 pp.
    University of London history professor and member of Asquith Commission for developing "principles which should guide the promotion ...of 'higher education in the colonies'" describes problems, philosophy, progress in speech at University of Glasgow. Useful perspective. UkLU-IE

UWI PRESTON, ASTON ZACHARY. "The Caribbean: Changing Needs in a
99 Changing Society." Times Higher Education Supplement, no. 352 (11 August 1978): IV.
    As Twelfth Commonwealth Universities Congress convenes, vice-chancellor of UWI writes about recent changes in Caribbean universities as function of recent socio-political changes in Caribbean countries. Using UWI and UG as examples, cites popular demand for university cooperation in providing technical training "in terms of the manpower needs of the Caribbean," and university response to that demand: establishment of regional campuses, new emphasis on engineering, medicine, business, and other applied fields; institution of various new degrees and certificates; provision for part-time and evening university registration.

UWI ------. "University Development in the Caribbean, Plans,
100 Problems and Needs." In Vice-Chancellor's Conference, Summer 1976 Aspen, Colorado, pp. 68-71. [London]: Inter-University Council for Higher Education Overseas, 1976.
    Report of UWI vice-chancellor at Conference of Vice-Chancellors of Commonwealth Universities gives background--full of difficulties--for UWI. Human and financial problems including brain drain, university plans for region. WKU

UWI RAJBANSEE, JOSEPH. "An Overview of Management Studies in Some
101 Caribbean Universities with General Observations." Caribbean Educational Bulletin 3, no. 2 (May 1976): 17-42.
    Survey of need for, status of management education in universities shows most programs weak, unrelated to Caribbean reality, and with scant cooperation among institutions.

UWI RAMCHAND, KENNETH. "The Colour Problem at the University: A
102 West Indian's Changing Attitudes." In Disappointed Guests: Essays by African, Asian, and West Indian Students, edited by Henri Tajfel and John L. Dawson, pp. 27-37. London: Oxford University Press, 1965.
    Institute of Race Relations, London, sponsored essay contest for these overseas students in British universities. Personal account of black student in white world, with social "sabotage of the West Indian personality," especially for males. KU

UWI   RAMESAR, ESMOND D. <u>The Present Organization, Operation and Needs</u>
103   <u>of the UWI Extra-Mural Studies Unit, St. Augustine Campus: A</u>
       <u>Memorandum Submitted at the Request of the Campus Planning and</u>
       <u>Estimates Committee</u>. St. Augustine: UWI, St. Augustine, 1977.
       35 pp.
           Description of extra-mural operation in Trinidad and Tobago
lists staff, program, enrollment, training projects of this off-campus
section of the University. Reminds committee of resolution of Special
Conference of Heads of Government calling for expanded efforts at
promoting national and West Indian culture, development of courses in
non-university territories. WKU

UWI   <u>Report of the Review Team from Western Carolina University to the</u>
104   <u>Minister of Education, Jamaica</u>. [Kingston: Ministry of Edu-
       cation], 1976. 62 pp.
           Given requirements for producing teachers in large numbers
and cultural realities, study recommends greatly enlarged role for
alternatives to "traditional university," UWI, with community (junior)
colleges and the College of Jamaica; last would combine work now given
in dispersed fashion among such agencies as seven teachers colleges and
a college of agriculture. WKU

UWI   ROBERTSON, AMY; BENNETT, HAZEL; and WHITE, JANETTE, comps.
105   <u>Select Bibliography of Education in the Commonwealth Caribbean,</u>
       <u>1940-1975</u>. Mona: UWI, School of Education, Documentation
       Centre, 1976. 196 pp.
           Pages 72-76 have twenty-seven entries, mostly for the three
campuses of the UWI and UG libraries. Entries by territories and
topics for all levels of education, including higher; some works on
professional education. List of theses on education in the region
accepted at universities abroad. MnU

UWI   ROBINSON, LESLIE R. B. "Report by Pro-Vice-Chancellor Robinson
106   on Discussion Held in St. Kitts in November, 1980, on the Pro-
       posed Tertiary Level College." Mimeographed. Mona: UWI, 1980.
       12 pp. plus 4 leaves appendices.
           Outgrowth of Inter-Governmental Committee discussion calling
for greater UWI involvement in non-campus LDC territories. UWI and UG
confer with St. Kitts minister of education and resident tutor over
probable number of students needing first years of arts and sciences
subjects. Teacher training and health services are high priority
fields. Discussion of student preparation with '0' level qualifications. Appendices cover accreditation, challenge examinations (with
high rate of failure probability); recommendations of IGC for transfer
and terminal programs in LDCs. WKU

UWI   RUBIN, VERA, and ZAVALLONI, MARISA. <u>We Wish to Be Looked Upon:</u>
107   <u>A Study of the Aspirations of Youth in a Developing Society</u>. New
       York: Teachers College Press, 1969. 257 pp.
           Study done in Trinidad and Tobago analyzes hopes along
racial, ethnic lines; looks at reality/unreality of them. University
education goals within and without country described. Statistics and
personal statements. KU

UWI   RUCK, S. K., ed. The West Indian Comes to England. A report
108   prepared for the Trustees of the London Parochial Charities by
        the Family Welfare Association. London: Routledge Kegan Paul,
        1960. 187 pp.
            Demographic and economic pressure impelled migration of
thousands of poor, ill-educated West Indians to Britain in post-World
War II era. Remedial education of adults needed, reflecting serious
flaws in West Indian education. Background for understanding question
of access to higher education. UkLU-IE

UWI   The St. Augustine Campus of the University of the West Indies.
109   St. Augustine: UWI, 1976. 32 pp.
            Description of Trinidad and Tobago campus of UWI includes
history, administration, student services, statistics, campus map. WKU

UWI   SHERLOCK, PHILIP M. "Education in the Federation of the West
110   Indies." School and Society 85, no. 2120 (23 November 1957):
        356-58.
            New University College of the West Indies (founded in 1948)
is important for success of the independent British islands in the
Caribbean.

UWI   ------. "The Extra-Mural Programme." Caribbean Quarterly 2, no.
111   3 (1952?): 4-13.
            The programs are taught by resident tutors in conjunction
with the University College of the West Indies. Participants, aged
twenty to forty, tend to have secondary level educations and are from
the lower professions. Adult education and special programs are particularly successful on the larger islands.

        ------. "The Role of Education in the Process of Development and
        Modernization of the Caribbean People." See entry GEN 246.

UWI   SIMMONS, GEORGE C. "West Indian Higher Education--The Story of
112   Codrington College: The Question of Continued Affiliation be-
        tween Codrington College and Durham University." Caribbean
        Quarterly 18, no. 3 (September 1972): 51-72.
            Role of Codrington College, first institution outside of
Great Britain to grant a residential degree of a British university,
called into question in 1950s with development of University College of
the West Indies. Useful insights into colonial higher education;
cultural differences, distance and communications problems.

UWI   Speeches Made at the 1974 Graduation Ceremonies of the University
113   of the West Indies on the Campuses at St. Augustine, Cave Hill,
        Mona. [Mona]: UWI, 1974. 30 leaves.
            Twenty-fifth year of UWI as fully operating institution.
Speeches by Vice-Chancellor Preston include useful facts; those of
others, such as Jamaican Prime Minister Manley, express strong emotions
about the human condition in the Caribbean. WKU

UWI   Speeches made at the 1975 Graduation Ceremonies of the University
114   of the West Indies on the Campuses at St. Augustine, Cave Hill,
        Mona. [Mona]: UWI, 1975. 26 leaves.
            Speeches by Chancellor Sir Allen Lewis and others reveal
progress, pride, problems. WKU

UWI   SPRINGER, HUGH WORRELL. "The Historical Development, Hopes, and
115   Aims of the University College of the West Indies." Journal of
        Negro Education 30, no. 1 (Winter 1962): 8-15.
            Began with "33 students reading pre-medical science with 4
professors in a hutted camp at Mona in Jamaica." By 1961 it had 980
student, 150 teachers, two campuses (Jamaica and Trinidad); with
"hundreds of extension students." UWI was conceived as "of the British
'Red Brick' kind," with norms of the University of London. Still 3,000
West Indians abroad in universities. One-third of the staff is West
Indian.

UWI   ------. "University-Government Relationships in the West
116   Indies." Relations between Governments and Universities, no. 2
        (January-May 1967): 83-93.
            Secretary general of Association of Commonwealth Universities
and West Indian educator gives geographical setting and brief history
of UWI. Pre-Federal period, 1946-56; Federal period until 1962 breakup
of West Indies Federation, and current period defined by differing
relations of university with governments. Significant strains among
Barbados, Jamaica, Trinidad governments seriously affected UCWI, but
were much lessened by appointment of W. Arthur Lewis as its first West
Indian head. Trauma of Federation's end ameliorated by Eric Williams'
leadership. Founding of university under colonial auspices gave
strength to tradition of autonomy, but independence has seen conflicts
over security and immigration. Unity of university is precarious.

UWI   "Student Statistics." Mimeographed. [Mona: UWI, 1975]. 9 pp.
117   Tables show: growth of course registration at Mona, St.
Augustine, Cave Hill campuses-1967-68 to 1973-74; enrollments by faculty 1969-70, 1971-72, 1973-74; territorial distribution of 1973-74
registrations by type of degree program and sex; faculty distribution
of 1973-74 registrations by type of course and sex; admissions, enrollments, degrees awarded in regular first degree programs 1969-70, 1971-
72, 1973-74; statistics in engineering and medicine; transfers and
dropouts from 1972-73 registrations in faculty of natural sciences,
Mona. WKU

UWI   TRINIDAD. University Education in the West Indies with Special
118   Reference to Trinidad and Tobago. Port-of-Spain: Government
        Printing Office, 1962.
            Useful information on predecessor institutions to UWI, on the
eve of its establishment, especially on the Imperial College of Tropical Agriculture at St. Augustine. Uk

UWI   TRINIDAD AND TOBAGO. Draft Plan for Educational Development,
119   Trinidad and Tobago, 1968-1983. 3d printing. [Port-of-Spain]:
        Government Printery, 1968. 98 pp.
            With UNESCO help, plans develop for major changes as local
responsibility grows and British control wanes. Increased availability
of secondary education will lead to phasing out crucial, harmful
eleven-plus examination, for example. Population projections; content,
goals and organization of schooling°°all with great significance for
higher education, especially UWI. An important document. WMUW

UWI   ------. White Paper on National Institute of Higher Education
120   (Research, Science and Technology). [Port-of-Spain]: Government
Printery, Trinidad, 1977. 39 pp.
        Conviction that "science and technology are variables on
which the whole process of human evolution has always depended and
still depends" requires radical change in government policy to coordinate and control policy and practice for national development. Recent
criticism of lack of response of UWI to "legitimate demands of States."
Trinidad and Tobago government redesigning institutional framework for
development of science and technology, in complement to which two
models for incorporating university function are presented. Advocates
creation of National Institute of Higher Education (Research, Science
and Technology) as independent national body, and a National Council
for UWI Affairs. Implementation of these policies would completely
alter UWI's relationship to governments. Appendices include "Recommendations of the Report of the Caribbean Task Force Regarding the
University of the West Indies and Proposal for Expansion." Part 2
contains proposals for restructuring UWI. Diagrams. WKU

UWI   TURNER, A. D. "Science in the 70s: Observations on Science Edu-
121   cation in Jamaica." Caribbean Quarterly 20, no. 2 (June 1974):
15-22.
        Gap between science education in metropolises and Third
World; dominance of General Certificate of Education means that science
education is for brighter students, not part of general education.
Role of Educational Broadcasting Service, Association of Science
teachers, Ministry of Education, UWI.

UWI   UNITED NATIONS, Educational, Scientific and Cultural Organization
122   (UNESCO). Report of the UNESCO Educational Planning Mission to
Trinidad and Tobago, 15 March 1964 - 5 June 1964, prepared by
C.L. Germanacos, H. J. Finkel, Avner Hovne, and S. Szrimis,
August 1964, 138 pp.
        Needs, recommendations for education, especially technical,
scientific, agricultural. Problems of loss of those graduating abroad.
Criticism of inappropriateness of British-style secondary education and
examination system. Much data on elementary and secondary education.
Favorable impact after the establishment of the Trinidad and Tobago
campus of the University of the West Indies in 1963. UkLU-IE

        UNIVERSITY COLLEGE OF THE WEST INDIES. See UNIVERSITY OF THE
        WEST INDIES.

UWI   UNIVERSITY OF THE WEST INDIES (UWI). The Bursary. St.
123   Augustine: UWI, 1975. 52 pp.
        Broad outline of university-wide service has sections on
finance, budget, cost and statistics, projects, internal audit, steno-
graphic and bursary service, the UWI financial code. WKU

UWI   ------. Calendar, Academic Year 1973-1974. Vol. 1. Mona: UWI,
124   1974. 136 pp.
        Senate committee recommended in 1970 that volume 1 be
published every three or four years, that it contain charter, statutes,
ordinances, financial code, regulations for academic boards, standing
orders for faculties, regulations for library, examinations, matriculation. Short history and description of UWI. WKU

UWI ------. Calendar, Academic Year 1978-1979. Vol. 2. [Mona]:
125 UWI, 1978. 265 pp.
     Annual volume has academic diary, officers, staff members
with their degrees, student amenities, fees and charges, regulations
for matriculation, students, faculties. Courses and syllabi to be
published in separate faculty brochures. WKU

UWI ------. The Chapel Mona. Mona: UWI, [1970?]. 12 pp.
126 Her Royal Highness, the Princess Alice, Countess of Athlone
and chancellor of University College of the West Indies, helped fund
stone-by-stone removal of 1799 building from a sugar estate to the
university for use as a chapel in 1955. Local symbols and materials
embellish this testament to empire. WKU

UWI ------. Departmental Reports 1976-1977. [Mona]: UWI, 1977.
127 483 pp.
     Eight faculties of the three campuses report on staff,
teaching, research, publications, courses, examinations. Appendices
(also available bound separately as Statistics Extracted from Departmental Reports 1976-1977) include enrollments 1948-49, 1976-77,
admissions from territories, degree data, graduates, staff. WKU

UWI ------. A Guide to Applicants. [Mona]: UWI, 1978. 5 pp. plus
128 12 leaves in 3 appendices.
     Choosing career, entry requirements, selection, financing,
facilities; degree, diploma and certificate courses offered and
campuses where available; background of UWI. WKU

UWI ------. Institute of International Relations. [Port-of-Spain],
129 [1975]. 46 pp.
     An autonomous agency, affiliated with the UWI, with studies
at postgraduate level. Began in 1966, with help of Swiss government,
became regional institution in 1972. Library, staff, admissions,
courses. WKU

UWI ------. Institute of Social and Economic Research Progress
130 Report 1955-1957. [Mona]: University College of the West Indies
     Jamaica, 1957. 33 pp.
     Founded and financed by Colonial Development and Welfare fund
to foster teaching and research in social sciences, especially on
regional topics. Collaboration with academic departments and with
universities and professors abroad. List of staff publications,
reports, studies. WKU

UWI ------. The Last of Our Beginnings: A Record of the Instal-
131 lation of the Second Chancellor of the University of the West
     Indies, Saturday, November 13, 1971. Mona: University Public
     Relations Office, UWI, 1971. 28 leaves.
     Sir High Wooding is installed as first native West Indian
chancellor. Photographs, history, officers, addresses. WKU

UWI [UNIVERSITY OF THE WEST INDIES]. "The Main Stages of University
132 Restructuring (Abridged Version)." Photocopy of typescript.
     [n.p.], 17 September 1982. 7 pp.

Background paper for presenting restructuring exercise reviews changes during previous thirty-three years. Three major stages: as University College of the West Indies under University of London tutelage until 1962, development and changes with three campuses until 1972, period after 1972 with new needs of contributing territories. An important collection of dates, events, issues, and titles of significant documents. WKU

UWI   ------. Mona Campus: An Historical Guide. Mona: UWI, [1976].
133   16 pp.
        Seventeenth century beginnings for two sugar estates, part of whose grounds form this campus of UWI. Guide to their ruins and some data on their past. WKU

UWI   ------. Principal's Report, 1949-1950. [Kingston: University
134   College of the West Indies, 1951].
        Her Royal Highness, the Princess Alice, installed as first chancellor, and foundation stone laid for library, hospital, first residence hall. Faculties of Arts, Sciences, Medicine, Extra-Mural Studies. Library with over 18,000 volumes. UkLU-IE

UWI   ------. Principal's Report, 1953-1954. [Kingston: University
135   College of the West Indies, 1954].
        Financial aid sought in region and Britain. First students graduate from the Faculty of Education; natural sciences research; Extra-Mural's Residence Teachers. Five hundred and two students. UkLU-IE

UWI   ------. Principal's Report, 1956-1957. [Kingston: University
136   College of the West Indies, 1957].
        Total students: 494; library has 64,000 volumes. UkLU-IE

UWI   ------. Principal's Report, 1961-1962. [Kingston: University
137   College of the West Indies, 1962].
        New Royal Charter for the UWI as a degree-granting university, 2 April 1962, after 1961 problems over its future with Jamaica's plan to withdraw from Federation of the West Indies. Collaboration with Trinidad and Tobago to keep UWI together. Enrollment: 1,268. UkLU-IE

UWI   ------. Report on the Development of a College of the Bahamas.
138   [Mona?]: UWI, 1968. 73 pp.
        Vice-Chancellor requests report on feasibility and need for upper-level and post-secondary programs; institution also to serve as base for UWI extra-mural program. DLC

UWI   ------. Theses Accepted for Higher Degrees, August 1963-July
139   1974. Prepared by the University of the West Indies Library.
        Mona: UWI Printery, 1976. 120 pp.
        Some 150 masters and doctorates during this period, including seventy-two doctorates in agriculture, arts and sciences, education, engineering, law, medicine, natural sciences and social sciences. UkLACU

UWI ------. <u>University of the West Indies: Graduation and Open Day,</u>
140 <u>February 3, 1968</u>. [Compiled by G. M. Sammy]. St. Augustine:
UWI, 1968. 39 pp.
    Although this pamphlet does describe the graduation and Open
Day 3 February 1968, in St. Augustine, it is essentially a description
of the important features of the University of the West Indies, St.
Augustine campus, Trinidad. Faculties of Agriculture, Engineering, and
the John F. Kennedy College of Arts and Sciences, institutes of education, international relations, and the virus laboratory. TxU

UWI ------. <u>Vice-Chancellor's Report, 1962-1963</u>. [Mona]: UWI, 1963.
141 174 pp.
    Prime Minister of Trinidad and Tobago, Eric Williams, becomes
first pro-vice-chancellor. Data on students, staff and budget.
UkLU-IE

UWI ------. <u>Vice-Chancellor's Report, 1963-1964</u>. [Mona]: UWI, 1964.
142 206 pp.
    Information about academic activities; data on enrollment,
sfaff, finance. UkLU-IE

UWI ------. <u>Vice-Chancellor's Report, 1964-1965</u>. [Mona]: UWI, 1965.
143 227 pp.
    Besides data on students and staff, describes incorporation
of the Imperial College of Tropical Agriculture into the University of
the West Indies in the St. Augustine branch in Trinidad and Tobago;
establishment of Faculty of Engineering. UkLU-IE

UWI ------. <u>Vice-Chancellor's Report, 1966-1967</u>. [Mona]: UWI, 1967.
144 225 pp.
    University has produced 2,518 graduates since 1951.
Libraries: Mona has 109,950 volumes, St. Augustine, 68,794. UkLU-IE

UWI ------. <u>Vice-Chancellor's Report, 1974</u>. [Mona]: UWI, 1974.
145 40 pp.
    Acting Vice-Chancellor Sidney Lancelot Martin reports high-
lights of activities in the various faculties on the three campuses.
Financial problems with governments unable or unwilling to pay certain
increased costs. Staff changes, activities. WKU

UWI ------. <u>Vice-Chancellor's Report, 1976</u>. [Mona]: UWI, 1976.
146 56 pp.
    New chancellor, A. Z. Preston, reports on labor problems,
need for postgraduate work, funds from University Grants Committee and
USAID, accomplishments of the nine faculties on the three campuses.
WKU

UWI ------. <u>Vice-Chancellor's Report, 1977</u>. [Mona]: UWI, 1977.
147 64 pp.
    Difficulties include a strike at St. Augustine, staff vacan-
cies caused by inadequate salaries. Accomplishments: expansion of
arrears of LDCs, new outreach center in Belize. Response by faculties
to pressure to "democratize," new "Caribbean" courses created, decentralization of examinations. WKU

UWI ------. Vice-Chancellor's Report, 1978. [Mona]: UWI, 1978.
148 26 pp.
 Among needs to be met: strength in science and technology; adequate financial support. Increase, to 8,000, short of anticipated enrollment for 1976-77; data for seven years. Faculty reports, libraries. WKU

UWI ------. Vice-Chancellor's Report, 1980. [Mona]: UWI, 1980.
149 101 pp.
 Regional and world economic woes affect university, natural disasters harm some participating territories. Enrollment growth slower than expected; increase from 695 full-time students in 1959-60 to 6,654 in 1979-80, plus 2,312 part-time students. Growth of campuses in Barbados and Trinidad. Caribbean heads of government still have not considered problems arising out of 1977 White Paper on Proposals for Restructuring the University, issued by the Government of Trinidad and Tobago. (See entry UWI 121.) Academic reports. WKU

UWI ------, Cave Hill Campus. "Caribbean Studies Registration
150 1977/78." Mimeographed. Cave Hill: UWI, [1979?]. 9 leaves.
 Ninety-four students, their topics, first tutors, department/ discipline; wide variety of interests. WKU

UWI UNIVERSITY OF THE WEST INDIES, Institute of Education. "Final
151 Annual Report, 1 August 1971-31 July 1972." Mimeographed.
[Mona: UWI, 1972?]. 49 pp.
 As of 1 October 1972 the Institute will fuse with the Department of Education, University of the West Indies. Begun to assist teacher training colleges in the territories in 1954, as the Centre for the Study of Education, with funds from the Carnegie Corporation. The Institute of Education took over and expanded work in 1964, with five years' financing jointly by West Indian governments and the Ford Foundation, later entirely by the University Grants Committee. Specialized in research, reports, testing; concern with "problems peculiar to the West Indian situation." Activities of staff, list of publications. UkLU-IE

UWI ------. Forecast of Educational Development in Antigua. [Mona:
152 UWI, 1965]. 32 pp.
 Traditional report: problems of numbers of teachers, but plenty of scholarships for study at the UWI or elsewhere. UkLU-IE

UWI ------. New Horizons in Teacher Education: Report of the
153 Conference of the Institute Board of Teacher Education, Mona,
Jamaica 6-10 September, 1971. [Mona: UWI], 1971. 79 pp.
 Problems of upgrading the teachers of teachers include dealing with English language capabilities in this Creole-speaking population; need to recruit teachers with fewer formal qualifications, and develop alternative methods of instruction. IU

UWI UNIVERSITY OF THE WEST INDIES, Development and Planning Unit.
154 "University Restructuring: Summary of Matters on which Consensus Has Been Reached." Photocopy of typescript. Mona: UWI Development and Planning Unit, 5 November 1982, revised 7 August 1983. 13 pp. plus 3 leaves.

Restructuring, under discussion for some years, was subject of talks between representatives of UWI and Trinidad and Tobago government, in University Council, and Committee of Ministers. Consensus that elements of a regional university will be retained in new structure, and that there will be more individual campus autonomy. Details of new administrative, academic and financial structure given, with suggestion for matters still to be resolved and a suggested timetable. WKU

UWI UNIVERSITY OF THE WEST INDIES, Institute of Social and Economic
155 Research. "Activities and Development 1976-1977." Mimeographed. [Mona]: UWI, 1977. 17 leaves. Draft copy.
United Kingdom funding under Colonial Development and Welfare Act at 1948 beginning; financing assumed by University Grants Committee of UWI in 1960s. Changes in work approach from use of global models to empirical research in region. List of projects underway. WKU

UWI "University of the West Indies." Caribbean Monthly Bulletin,
156 vol. 16, no. 1 (January 1982): 41
Chancellor announces major expansion at St. Augustine campus, Trinidad, including a second medical school, plus degrees in dentistry and veterinary medicine. Sees more autonomy for individual campuses ahead, while regional character of UWI will be preserved; campus territories recognize obligation to help less fortunate territories.

UWI "UWI's Role in Serving Region Must be Judged on its Record."
157 Caribbean Contact, March 1978, 6-7.
Response to Trinidad and Tobago White Paper from Mona campus in Jamaica. (See entry UWI 120.) Reviews 1960-70 manpower studies in region; lack of coordinated government action and financial support. Need to control standards and maintain a genuinely regional institution.

UWI VERNON, PHILIP E. Selection for Secondary Education in Jamaica.
158 London: University of London, Institute of Education, 1960. 106 pp.
Professor of educational psychology studies problem of admission to secondary school with tests from England, the Common Entrance Examination. Only about 17 per 100 eligible at age eleven-plus attempt it. Overcrowded or unavailable schools, lack of parental interest, unprepared teachers, language inadequacy all contribute to small pool of those ultimately eligible for university. UkLU-IE

UWI WALKER, DAVID. "V.C. Attacks Late Payers." Times Higher Edu-
159 cation Supplement, 13 June 1975: 13.
Vice-Chancellor of University of West Indies decries lack of payments from ten contributing territories, with deficit of nearly £270,000. Jamaica, Barbados, Trinidad and Tobago, and Bahamas had to float loan. Urges continued university growth and development.

UWI WALTERS, ELSA HOPKINS. A Brief History 1952-1972. The Institute
160 of Education, University of the West Indies, 1952-1972. London: Published privately by Sir Hugh Springer, 1977. 44 pp.
Chronology includes 1954-56, development of Center for Study of Education; 1957, Regional Conference for the Training of Teachers in

the British Caribbean; 1957-61, development of courses; 1961-68, Institute of Education and Faculty of Education established; 1972, latter two combined as School of Education. Leaders were Professor R. D'Aeth and Professor John Figueroa. ACUL

UWI ------. Teacher Training Colleges in the West Indies. Histori-
161 cal introduction by Shirley C. Gordon. London: Oxford University Press, 1960. 149 pp.
    Introduction gives perspective on efforts to develop education, and on problems of designing education appropriate to region. Description of colleges. KU

UWI WEST INDIA ROYAL COMMISSION. Report. Walter Edward, Baron
162 Moyne, Chairman. Cmd. 6607. London: HMSO, 1945. 454 pp.
    Royal warrant of 1938 establishes commission "to investigate social and economic conditions in Barbados, British Guiana, British Honduras, Jamaica, the Leeward Islands, Trinidad and Tobago, and the Windward Islands and matters connected therewith, and to make recommendations." Getting about in the chairman's yacht, group held hearings relating to such topics as history, geography, agriculture, racial discrimination, finance, health, housing. Chapter 7 gives overview of education, noting that previous efforts to establish higher education, despite need, "have come to nothing." Criticizes policy of dependence on religious denominations to provide education. Concrete proposals by West Indians for establishment of a university, analysis of problems, recommends "a system of faculties in different countries ...rather than a comprehensive university in some single Colony." Essential, well written document for understanding context of educational system. KU

UWI WHYTE, MILLICENT. A Short History of Education in Jamaica.
163 London: Hodder and Staughton, 1977. 128 pp.
    Written primarily for those in teacher training colleges, it covers developments since Emancipation and the frustrated attempts at creating higher education before the founding of the College of the West Indies in 1948. Pressures for meeting "real needs" of the society. DLC

UWI WILGUS, A. CURTIS. "The University College of the West Indies."
164 In The Caribbean: British, Dutch, French, United States, edited by A. C. Wilgus, pp. xi-xix. Gainesville: University of Florida Press, 1958.
    An excellent summary of efforts to create the University College of the West Indies, beginning with earliest British West Indian educational agencies, culminating in 1949 granting of UC's charter. Description of first campus buildings in Mona, financial details, ties with the University of London. KU

UWI WILLIAMS, ERIC EUSTACE. Education in the British West Indies.
165 Foreword by John Dewey. [Port-of-Spain]: The Teachers' Economic and Cultural Association, [1950]. 167 pp.
    Mostly written in 1945. Quotes Cuban Jose Marti's warning on literacy, urban-style education imposed on Latin American agricultural societies; attacks the "medieval" British residential university as

model for the West Indies. Interest in U.S. university models, criticizes Britain's examination system at secondary level. Concrete proposals for a university in Kingston, Jamaica. UkLU-IE

UWI ------. "Establishment of a University of the West Indies."
166 Journal of Negro Education 13, no. 4 (Fall 1944): 565-98.
    Why were the British West Indies so slow in creating a university? In the early colonies in New England and Virginia there were real colonizing efforts, but in the British West Indies the concern was simply with sugar plantations. The University of the West Indies was created in World War II when the region finally had an identifiable culture. Williams tried to bring together elements of British and U.S. approaches to education and also incorporate Caribbean values.

UWI ------. Inward Hunger: The Education of a Prime Minister.
167 London: Andre Deutsch, 1969. 343 pp.
    Upward mobility with educational opportunity, via Oxford, for this scholar-politician from Trinidad and Tobago. Devoted to Caribbean cooperation and development, a fighter against racism and social injustice, he served as pro-vice-chancellor of the University of the West Indies. Attention to his educational philosophy. UkLU-IE

UWI ------. The University: Symbol of Freedom. Address to the
168 Graduating Class at the University of the West Indies, Jamaica,
    February 16, 1963. [Port-of-Spain]. Government Printing Office,
    1963. 10 pp.
    Expanding university with night classes at Mona (Jamaica) or in auxiliary colleges in Barbados and Trinidad called "monument to the unity of the West Indian region." Predicts UWI will be "powerful attraction to students of Surinam...Curaçao...Martinique and Guadeloupe." Gives breakdown of graduates by countries and territories; all from British West Indies. Calls for responsibility to West Indian communities. TxU

UWI WOLFE, DAVID. Welcome to the Antigua Centre Library. St.
169 John's: UWI Department of Extra-Mural Studies (Antigua), 1983.
    28 pp.
    Library begun in 1967 has 6,000 titles, selected chiefly by librarians from Cave Hill campus, to help students at 'O' level, 'A' level, or first year of university. Dependence on donations, with no budgeted funds for purchases. This guide prepared by Peace Corps volunteer.

UWI ------, comp. Adult Education in Antigua and Barbuda: A Di-
170 rectory of Opportunities and Resources. St. John's: UWI
    Department of Extra-Mural Studies (Antigua), 1983. 60 pp.
    Example of services for non-campus territories organized by resident tutors. Shows a few paths toward university for persons not now in school.

UWI WRIGHT, LENA [pseud. Carter, J.]. "Education in Jamaica: A
171 Brief Outline 1834-1968." Compiled for Jamaica Library Service
    ...Independence Exhibition...August 1968. Mimeographed.
    Kingston: Jamaica Library Service. 39 pp.
    Draws heavily on Shirley C. Gordon's A Century of West Indian Education (Longman's, 1963). (See entry UWI 52.)

UWI   <u>Yearbook of the Universities of The Commonwealth</u>. London: The
172   Association of Universities of the British Commonwealth.   1914-
      57. (interrupted 1942-46).

    A valuable panorama of universities world-wide, among them
the University of the West Indies, founded in 1948.   The edition of
1951, describing events of 1949-50 at the University College of the
West Indies, mentioned installation of first chancellor, appointment of
contractors for construction of buildings.   There were 70 students,
"including 16 women."   Later editions give more details: history,
staff, degrees, academic programs, requirements.   Also contains information on Association of Commonwealth Universities.   After 1957
<u>Yearbook</u> becomes <u>Commonwealth Universities Yearbook</u>.

List of Foreign Periodicals

Accessions Bulletin. Formerly Select List of Accessions. Bimonthly.
St. Augustine, Trinidad. Staff Library, University of the West
Indies.
Acción y Reflexión Educativa. ICASE. University of Panama.
International Technical Assistance of OAS.
African Caribbean Newsletter. University of the West Indies Library.
Kingston, Jamaica.
América Latina. Centro Latino Americano de Pesquisas
en Ciencias Sociales.
Anales. Universidad Autónoma de Rio de Janeiro. Santo Domingo.
Dominican Republic.
Anales de la Universidad de Costa Rica. San José, Costa Rica.
Anales de la Universidad de Cuenca. Cuenca, Ecuador.
Anales de la Universidad de Santo Domingo. Ciudad Trujillo. [Santo
Domingo]
Annual Report. Publications Branch, Ministry of Education, Jamaica.
La Antigua. Universidad Santa María La Antigua, Panama.
Anuario Bibliográfico Cubano. Ediciones Anuario Bibliográfico Cubano,
1938-. Havana.
Anuario Científico. Universidad Central del Este. Dominican Republic.
Aportes. Quarterly published by El Instituto Latinoamericano de
Relaciones Internacionales (ILARI), Geneva. Administrative
Offices in Paris.
Apuntes Universitarios. Guatemala.
Bibliografía Cubana. Havana, Medellin, Gainesville, Miami.
Boletín. Panama.
Boletín APPU. Puerto Rico.
Boletín de Estudios Latinoamericanos y del Caribe. Centro de Estudios
y Documentación Latinoamericanos de la Universidad de Amsterdam.
Boletín de la Escuela de Ciencias Antropológicas de la Universidad de
Yucatán. Mexico.
Boletín Estadístico. Coordinación de Planeamiento, División de
Programación, Presupuesto y Estadística, Departamento de
Estadística. Caracas.
Boletín Oficial. Universidad Central de las Villas, Cuba.
Boletín Oficial Universitaria. Barbados.
The Caribbean. Port-of-Spain, Trinidad.
Caribbean Contact. Caribbean Council of Churches. Bridgetown,
Barbados.
Caribbean Education.

Foreign Periodicals

Caribbean Educational Bulletin. Association of Caribbean Universities
and Research Institutes. Kingston, Jamaica.
Caribbean Issues: A Journal of Caribbean Affairs. University of the
West Indies, St. Augustine, Trinidad.
Caribbean Journal of Education. School of Education, University of the
West Indies.
Caribbean Monthly Bulletin. Institute of Caribbean Studies. Río
Piedras, Puerto Rico.
Caribbean Review. Hato Rey, Puerto Rico.
Caribbean Studies. St. Augustine, Trinidad.
Caribbean Studies Newsletter. Caribbean Studies Association. Hato
Rey, Puerto Rico.
Caribbean Quarterly. University of the West Indies. Jamaica.
Carta Docente. Universidad de la Habana. Cuba.
El Caribe. Newspaper. Santo Domingo.
Ciencia. Universidad Autónoma de Santo Domingo. Dominican Republic.
Ciencia y Sociedad. Dominican Republic.
Ciencias Naturales y Matemáticas. Universidad de Oriente. Cuba.
Ciencias Sociales. Universidad de Oriente. Cumaná, Venezuela.
Ciencias Técnicas. Instituto Superior Politécnico José Antonio
Echevarría, Cuba.
Comunidad - Escuela. Universidad de Panamá.
Co-operant Educational Abstracting Service. International Association
of Universities. Paris.
Crónica Universitaria. Universidad Autónoma de Centro América. San José
Rica.
Cuadernos de Educación. Laboratorio Educativo. Caracas.
Cuadernos Universitarios. Universidad Nacional Autónoma de Nicaragua.
Digest of Education Statistics. Ministry of Education. Barbados.
Docencia, Post-secundaria. CAMESA. Guadalajara, Mexico.
Educación. Ministerio de Educación. Havana.
La Educación: Revista Interamericana de Desarrollo Educativo. Pan American
Educación Superior. UNESCO publication.
Educación Superior Contemporánea. Havana.
L'Education. Paris.
Encuentro. Revista Bisemestral. Universidad Centroamericana.
Managua.
Estadística. Universidad de la Habana.
Estadística Panameña. Departamento de Información
y Divulgación Estadística. Panama.
Este y Oeste. Caracas.
Estudios Americanos. Caracas.
The Europa Yearbook. London.
Experiments and Innovations in Education. International Bureau of
Education. Geneva.
Extra. Tegucigalpa, Honduras.
Gaceta. Mexico, D.F.
La Gaceta. Nicaragua.
Gaceta Oficial. Panama.
Gaceta UDUAL. Mexico.
Gaceta Universitaria. Caracas, Venezuela.
Granma. Newspaper. Cuba.
El Guatemalteco. Guatemala.
Higher Education. CRESALC. UNESCO. Caracas.
Higher Education and Research in the Netherlands. The Hague.

Foreign Periodicals

Higher Education in Europe. Bimonthly in England, France and U.S.S.R.
   European Center for Higher Education. UNESCO.
Horizontes: Revista de la Universidad Católica de Puerto Rico.
   Ponce, Puerto Rico.
Indice General de la Revista Universidad de la Habana.
   Universidad de la Habana.
Inter-American University of Puerto Rico. San Germán, Puerto
   Rico.
International Handbook of Universities. London.
International Institute for Educational Studies. Belgium.
Islas. Universidad Central de las Villas. Cuba.
Jamaica Here. Kingston.
Jamaican National Bibliography. Annual. Jamaica.
Journal of Commerce. The Bahamas.
Listín Diario. Newspaper. Dominican Republic.
Ley de Universidades. Editorial La Torre. Caracas.
Lotería. Panama.
Microstate Studies. Center for Latin American Studies. University of
   Florida and the University Presses of Florida for the Caribbean
   Research Institute, College of the Virgin Islands.
Minerva. London.
Le Monde de l'Education. Paris.
El Mundo. Newspaper. San Juan, Puerto Rico.
Mundo Hispánico. Madrid.
Mundo Nuevo: Revista de Estudios Latinoamericanos. Universidad Simón
   Bolívar. Instituto de Altos Estudios de América Latina.
   Venezuela.
Mundo Universitario. Colombia.
La Nación. Newspaper. Costa Rica.
El Nacional. Newspaper. Caracas.
Nobo Dialuna. Newspaper. Curaçao.
La Noticia. Dominican Republic.
Noticias del CSUCA. Costa Rica.
Nuestro Pueblo y la Universidad. El Salvador.
Nueva Frontera. Bogotá.
Oriente Universitario. Cumaná, Venezuela.
Overseas Quarterly. London.
Overseas Universities. Association of Commonwealth Universities.
   London.
Papeles Universitarios. Venezuela.
Plural Societies. Foundation for the Study of Plural Societies. The
   Hague.
La Prensa. Newspaper. Willemstad, Curaçao.
La Prensa. Newspaper. Nicaragua.
El Presidente Informa. Puerto Rico.
Presencia Universitaria. Editorial Universitaria. Tegucigalpa.
Prospects: La Revista Especializada en Educación de la UNESCO. Paris.
Pueblo. Nueva Esparta, Venezuela.
Repertorio Centroamericano. Secretaría Permanente del CSUCA. San
   José.
Reportorio Americano. Universidad Nacional de Costa Rica. Heredia.
La República. Newspaper. San José.
Revista Centroamericana de Ciencia y Tecnología. Costa Rica.
Revista de Ciencias Sociales. Universidad de Puerto Rico.
Revista de Historia. Universidad Nacional de Costa Rica. Heredia.
Revista de la Biblioteca Nacional José Martí. Havana.

Revista de la Educación Superior. Asociación Nacional de Universidades
    e Instituciones de Enseñanza Superior. Mexico City.
Revista de la Universidad. Universidad Nacional Centroamericana.
    Tegucigalpa, Honduras.
Revista de la Universidad de Yucatán. Mérida.
Revista de la Universidad de Zulia. Venezuela.
Revista del Pensamiento Centroamericano. Managua.
Revista Estudios Generales. San Juan.
Revista Internacional de Países Socialistas. Havana.
Revista Mexicana de Sociología. Mexico.
Revista Pedagógica. Universidad de Oriente. Santiago, Cuba.
Revista/Review Interamericana. Interamerican University of Puerto
    Rico. San Juan.
San Jose News. Newspaper. San Jose.
San Juan Star. Newspaper. San Juan.
Seminario Universidad. University of Costa Rica.
Serie Controversa. Centro de Investigación y Educación Popular.
    Bogota.
Serie Cuadernos Universitarios. Ciudad Universitaria Rodrigo Facio.
    Costa Rica.
Siete Días en la USAC. Universidad de San Carlos. Guatemala City.
Sobre Educación Superior. Universidad de la Habana.
Social and Economic Studies. Institute of Social and Economic
    Research. University of the West Indies.
Studies and Surveys in Comparative Education. International Bureau of
    Education. Geneva.
Studio. Revista de la Universidad del Atlántico. Barranquilla.
Thunder. Journal of Peoples Progressive Party, Guyana.
El Tiempo. Newspaper. Bogotá.
Times Higher Education Supplement. London.
Trinidad Guardian. Trinidad.
Utimas Noticias. Newspaper. Caracas.
El Universal. Newspaper. Caracas.
Universidad. Ciudad Universitaria Rodrigo Facio. Costa Rica.
Universidad. Panama.
Universidad de Honduras. Tegucigalpa.
Universidad de la Habana. Cuba.
Universidad de Panamá. Panama.
Universidad del Aire, Habana Cuadernos. Cuba.
Universidad del Atlántico. Revista. Barranquilla.
Universidad Popular. Conferencias. Ministerio de Educación. Havana.
Universidades. Unión de Universidades de América Latina. Mexico.
Universitas 2000. Caracas.
Universities Quarterly. Oxford.
Uno Más Uno. Newspaper. Mexico.
Variedades. Newspaper. Venezuela.
Venezuela Ahora. Venezuela.
Ventana. Managua.
La Verdad. Newspaper. Caracas.
Vida Universitaria. University of Havana. Cuba.
Vox Guyana. Paramaribo, Suriname.
De West Indische Gids. Amsterdam.

Author Index

Author Index

Author Index

Author Index

Author Index